The Daytime Serials of Television,
1946–1960

The Daytime Serials of Television, 1946–1960

JIM COX

McFarland & Company, Inc., Publishers
Jefferson, North Carolina, and London

Photographs provided by Photofest.

LIBRARY OF CONGRESS CATALOGUING-IN-PUBLICATION DATA

Cox, Jim, 1939–
The daytime serials of television, 1946–1960 / Jim Cox.
p.   cm.
Includes bibliographical references and index.

ISBN 0-7864-2429-X (illustrated case : 50# alkaline paper) ∞

1. Soap operas—United States—History and criticism.   I. Title.
PN1992.8.S4C69   2006   791.45'6—dc22   2006006085

British Library cataloguing data are available

On the cover: Mary Stuart, Larry Haines and Melba Rae
in *Search for Tomorrow* (Photofest)

Manufactured in the United States of America

McFarland & Company, Inc., Publishers
Box 611, Jefferson, North Carolina 28640
www.mcfarlandpub.com

For
Claire Connelly, Doug Douglass
and David Schwartz

Acknowledgments

Many authors begin their thanksgiving here hoping not to leave anyone out in a courageous attempt to name their contributors. Others start by stating that they hardly know where to begin. I try to avoid that by maintaining lists of names of helpers alongside every manuscript I write, making a conscious effort not to overlook anybody. If I've done so it is truly unintentional and I sincerely apologize to whomever I've shortchanged.

If it were not for David Schwartz, Claire Connelly and Doug Douglass, a liberal slice of this volume in your hands simply wouldn't exist. That is a fact. This trio of unpretentious, munificent and determined colleagues proved worthy investigators every time out as they responded with credible material following onerous detective searches, frequently and consistently exceeding the author's highest expectations. Their efforts resulted in a much more detailed, dependable, impartial and appealing reference guide than you might have been reading otherwise.

David Schwartz, working on the West Coast, supplied copious particulars that not only swelled the ranks of Appendix C, but also appreciably added to the flow of the text within the body of the manuscript. Just when yours truly thought we were done, again and again another batch of facts arrived from David, who toiled defiantly to the end!

Claire Connelly, operating within the shadows of the nation's capital, with a long-practiced penchant for burrowing into the details of obscure people's lives, once again offered reams of minutiae that fleshed out many a performer's biography. She also added some anecdotal tidbits that transformed a ho-hum tome into something more exciting.

Doug Douglass, entrenched on the East Coast, is a walking encyclopedia of history and knowledge about people and locales in and around New York City. He provided what seemed like volumes on CBS's Liederkrantz Hall, and a lot more logistical data that only someone with his strategic vantage point and drive could tap into.

Together, their efforts were invaluable. They are due plenty of the credit for this project — *and* my deepest appreciation.

Still others assisted with the collection, verification and correction of data, especially Danny Goodwin, John Leasure, Phillipa Lord, Gary Mercer, Gregg Oppenheimer and Ron Sayles. They, too, are entitled to take a bow for providing ample assistance. I am sincerely grateful to them all.

I'm cognizant of a vast host of hobbyists who, without fail, inspire authors like me with their ready encouragement — people who vicariously enjoy the fruits of combined labors while urging us scribes to press on. Invariably they stand ready to deliver whatever is lacking, for they are a generous lot. Among these loyal patrons who bolster nostalgic causes, and who have been especially helpful to me, are Bob Axley, Frank Bresee, Glenn Brownstein, Bob Burchett, Chris Chandler, Steve Darnall, Jack French, Eddie Ginsburg, Tom Heathwood, Jay Hickerson, Walden Hughes, Ted Kneebone, Ken Krug, Stuart Lubin, Patrick Lucanio, Ted Meland, Robert Newman, Charles Niren, Hal Sampson, Chuck Schaden, Jim Snyder, Derek Tague, Paul Urbahns, Bob Wheeler, Marilyn Wilt and Stewart Wright. I'm grateful for the continuing efforts made by each and every one of them.

To have a supportive companion, Sharon Cox, and family in these endeavors is a blessing. I'm thankful that mine relinquishes enough time for me to adequately pursue these quests in lengthy stretches, and I do recognize the sacrifices they make. I'm deeply indebted and continually blessed.

And to all of you — the readers who bought this book — I am grateful, too. My hope is that you'll find some things you did not know, delivered to you in a package that makes it a joy to peruse. I hope this will be a most pleasant stroll down memory lane.

Table of Contents

Introduction

The promising embryonic television era of the late 1940s and all of the 1950s was a powerfully magical time in American entertainment. Citizens of the globe, in fact, were treated to the transmission of pictorials that had formerly existed only in the imaginations of audiences. Those new televiewers who had never seen anything like it were simply awestruck; there were reports from everywhere that some sat and watched the little beam of light that gradually diminished after those early sets were turned off until it vanished altogether at last.

It was an incredible age in which to live! And until the countrymen got used to the newfangled invasion in their living rooms, it was the object of intense conversation, which included skepticism, scorn and ridicule alongside the fervor it more frequently generated. Mostly, the nation simply found itself engrossed by TV's beguiling charm, unable to do much with it but to watch and see. That was the system's charismatic appeal as people became accustomed to a new approach in acquiring mass-distributed in-home amusement and knowledge.

From the earliest days, most of the forms that had prevailed in radio were transported to the new medium. For the very first time listeners were able to put faces to many of the names they had heard and adored. Comedians, vocalists, instrumentalists, actors, newscasters, quizmasters, variety hosts, athletic, religious and political figures, and numerous other legends representing a myriad of genres turned up on the little black-and-white screens. So, too, did many of the breeds that were popular in aural settings. One of the leaders of the pack was the daytime drama, the continuing tale of a specific troubled family or a beleaguered heroine whose poignant soapy saga was wrung out piecemeal over protracted periods.

"Please ... I want some more," a pensive idiom that Charles Dickens included in *Oliver Twist*, precisely articulates the quest of the daytime serial buff. In the pages to follow, every attempt is made to secure the flavor of what transpired during the debuting, beckoning soap opera era of primitive television. From an occasional faux pas before live cameras committed by neophyte actors, stagehands and technicians as they tried to get it right and sometimes missed, to the occasional inspired and flawless delivery of prose, facial expressions and action performed on makeshift (but somehow believable) sets under trying circumstances, it was a stimulating time to be tuning in!

As the new medium developed, so did the narratives and the methods used to convey meaning. Simply speaking lines from the pages of a script, as radio thespians had done for decades, no longer sufficed while attempting to attract a video audience. Profound care had to be given as to *how* and *where* and to *whom* those lines were delivered. Painstaking memorization and protracted rehearsals on exceedingly tight schedules became an everyday occurrence. Despite all of the distractions and limitations, somehow those live quarter-hour serials got on and off the air every weekday with — to those vast numbers of observers at home — minimal effort. It was generally only behind the scenes that things ran amok. A considerable portion of this book details the turmoil that frequently reigned just out of public view, especially when deep-seated emotions came into play.

The early chapters set the stage for the birth of televised melodrama with an overview of the diverse forms of serialized entertainment that humanity witnessed in the decades (centuries, actually) before the tube's impact. Recitation, print, film and radio conditioned mortals to anticipate the ensuing installment of a narrative. As replacement structures emerged, it wasn't long until all of these models adapted the serialized yarn, integrating it into novel alternative forms of communication.

When television burst onto the American scene in the late 1940s, it became the ultimate mode of expressing a continuing tale over time. Not only did it corral a massive audience, it combined all of the elements of verbal, animated and visual charm that had previously existed in disparate formats. Viewers discovered an all-encompassing sensorial experience in the comfort of familiar surroundings, one heretofore unavailable. For addicts of the enduring story, it was an exciting time to be alive.

The Golden Age of Television, as a matter of practicality, has been classified as the years before 1960. This book explores the successes and failures among 40 daytime serials that were a part of this panoply. Unfortunately, there were more failures than successes as the pioneers sought some sure footing in the quagmire of unworkable suppositions surrounding them. Some reasons for the failures will be advanced; given the perspective of hindsight, it's possible to posit how a few repetitious mistakes that made a difference in the outcome might have been easily avoided. Yet those early days were practice runs that yielded important lessons. Those that studied well and implemented their conclusions sometimes profited handsomely. This is borne out by the fact that a string of soap opera conceptions premiering in the early to mid–1950s were enormously well received. The innovators behind them reached a remarkable plateau that was not to be challenged anytime soon by the competition. How they pulled it off offers an intriguing investigation in itself.

There are lots of personalities presented within these pages, including figures who used daytime television as springboards to celebrity status. There are many more who never earned widespread recognition, who literally "stayed by the stuff," performing their jobs daily to their utmost capabilities, often at high levels of quality. They are deserving of recognition, too, and many get it here. Furthermore, you'll meet a woman whose powerful command over video soaps was legendary. Her rise to the top came to a screeching halt as she, like Humpty Dumpty, suffered a great fall. Ah, but those years in the catbird seat...

Early television daytime serials were a trial period for those in the industry and for those tuning in. Nobody had been doing their jobs before — neither performing nor watching. This is the story of what came to pass between both groups.

1

Antecedents of
the Daytime Serial

Since the initiation of mass culture at the turn of the nineteenth century, inspired visionaries of fiction-by-installment have sought to tempt an audience, prompting its members to thirst for more. The stories they recounted through multiple structures left crowds of eager followers on the edge of their chairs. Had their experiences not been so engaging, none would have bothered to return. These artists, scribes and capitalists— possessing remarkably heightened imaginations— delivered precisely what the listeners, readers and viewers were craving.

Before proceeding any further, let's be sure we understand exactly what comprises a serial.

There are certain properties peculiar to serials, whether in prose, cartoon, television, or any other medium. A serial is, by definition, an ongoing narrative released in successive parts. In addition to these defining qualities, serial narratives share elements that might be termed ... "family resemblances." These include refusal of closure; intertwined subplots; large casts of characters (incorporating a diverse range of age, gender, class, and increasingly, race representation to attract a similarly diverse audience); interaction with current political, social, or cultural issues; dependence on profit; and acknowledgment of audience response (this has become increasingly explicit, even institutionalized within the form, over time).[1]

Citing a litany of dates across a couple of centuries when several types of sequential storytelling commenced and prospered, sundry authorities have recorded how those formats reached their summits. Like the yarns they told, some of those media declined and ultimately vanished. Yet the remnants of a few are still with us, although they exhibit significantly weakened substance and meaning. Our exposure to ongoing tales and fascination with them dates to the very beginning of time, one scholar allows.[2] Adam and Eve, caretakers of the Garden of Eden, told stories to their offspring. The practice caught on with successive generations who shared mythical accounts, too, spellbinding their own broods. A classic tradition resulted and became a fundamental practice of every early culture.

Eventually the verbal storyteller concentrated on action and suspense that sustained his listeners' attention while meting out bits and pieces of plot over time. Heroic poetry was the most prevalent strain. Those tales often focused on danger, adventure, monsters, shipwrecks and a myriad of similar stuff designed to thwart a hero and amuse listeners. As folklore increasingly shifted from attempts to explain global uncertainties to legends about denizens who faced seemingly insurmountable obstacles— but who demonstrated incredible resilience and strength — the third-person narrative started to predominate.

The purpose of this deliberation is to offer a succinct but intriguing overview of the multiple forms encountered in the progression of continuing stories. While storytelling may have been the chief (and, perhaps, only) option available to civilization for much of its existence, within the last 200 years the dawn of industrialization has carried Earth's inhabitants from an oral tradition to popular literature, screened exhibitions and broadcast media. The introduction of printing launched a variety of storytelling styles that no one could have fathomed previously. The motion picture serial presented exciting new routines and coerced eager audiences to return for more. Finally, with the development of the daily soap opera beamed across the ether into domiciles everywhere, the continuing saga reached its zenith.

The oral storytelling ritual offered many worthy legends, including this one:

An autocratic, high-ranking official, sultan Schahriar of the Persian Empire, attained a reputation for marrying many women — one at a time — and having them murdered on the morning following a night of matrimonial bliss.[3] Yet the monarch's routine was severely tested when he wed Scheherezade. She was a profound raconteur who introduced something utterly unanticipated into his pattern. In the nocturnal hours of the next 1,001 days, the teller of tall tales offered her husband one exciting expository gem after another, invariably ceasing her recitations just before reaching a denouement. Her spouse was so awestruck by her enduring parables that, for the moment, he couldn't possibly have her slaughtered until he extracted the rest of the story on the following night. A skillful Scheherezade — knowing her very life depended upon her inventive mind — was able to string out her narrative to so many successive chapters by initiating a new sequence as each one approached its finale.

The Arabian Nights, from which Scheherezade's tale descends, has been branded the *very first soap opera*, based solely on its format.[4] The scheme she employed is one that broadcast serial buffs have long recognized: when an episode ends, the underpinnings of another are already in place in an unremitting plot, guaranteeing an audience will be available to "tune in again tomorrow." And as for Scheherezade and Schahriar, after nearly three years together, they were parents of a couple of kids and — like some soap opera heroes and heroines— deeply devoted to one another. Surmised a connoisseur: "What might have been just another 1,001-night stand turned into a happily-ever-after love story."[5]

The advent of industrialization instituted changes in how ongoing tales were recounted. While oral storytelling would always be an option for transfixing an audience, practical methods were introduced in the 1800s and 1900s that capitalized on new technologies, widely diversifying the means for sharing a serialized story. The printing press (circa 1450), however, was the *first* such innovation. Not only did it make literature more accessible to many more people, it contributed significantly to education, beginning with the fundamentals. Before the printing press was in widespread use, only a handful of inhabitants could read and write. The oral tradition would have been the vast majority's only means to experience a continued story. Thus, for the typical individual, putting a narrative on paper would have served no useful purpose.

The cartoon — which will be examined in greater detail presently — became an outlet for expressing humor as well as for social and political satire. Swiss illustrator Rodolphe

Topffer originated "picture stories" in 1827, a string of sequential images that illuminated fables.[6] A lot more art was on the way and would be widely recognized before the turn of the century.

The serial narrative's introduction into modern popular culture, meanwhile, can be pinpointed as 1836.[7] Although yarns with ultimate conclusions offered in episodic construct were mass distributed before that, that year the first tale without a projected ending was supplied. It happened when the publishing firm of Chapman and Hall invited novice British newspaperman Charles Dickens, then 24, to supply fictional accounts in uniform installments to parallel the drawings of trendy cartoonist Robert Seymour. Dickens presented the witty deeds of some rather odd participants in an urban fraternity who traveled to Ipswich, Rochester, Bath and beyond. They called it *The Posthumous Papers of the Pickwick Club*, since commonly dubbed *The Pickwick Papers*.

The series appeared between April 1837 and November 1837.[8] Although a weekly print run of 400 copies was projected, as the episodic novel neared completion, that number increased a hundred–fold, to 40,000 reproductions, with readers on two continents devouring it. The craze became so great that, reportedly, "needy admirers flattened their noses against the booksellers' windows eager to secure a good look at the etchings and to peruse every line of the letterpress that might be exposed to view, frequently reading aloud to applauding bystanders."[9] The phenomenon wasn't limited to the British Isles. "American fans waited at seaports and train stations every week to pick up the new installment and to read how last week's episodes turned out, and to learn what was in store for the characters this week."[10] It confirmed the viability of merging text and illustration, and many (some of whom would trigger a proliferation of the form) were taking notes.

Fourteen years later (1850) *Harper's Monthly* magazine further stimulated the serialized novel's expansion. Ongoing narratives by Nathaniel Hawthorne, Henry James, Mark Twain and their ilk soon mesmerized Americans who not only connected with a story's subjects, but also engaged other subscribers to informally ponder what might transpire next.[11] Many periodicals established mediums that permitted readers to express their thoughts on story progress. "Such camaraderie has been part and parcel of the serial narrative ever since, as anyone in a soap opera chat room on the Internet can testify," noted an observer.[12]

By the final decade of the nineteenth century, printing technology had realized such giant leaps that color could be integrated into newspapers. In 1893 *The New York World* owner Joseph Pulitzer purchased a four-color press to feature faithful renderings of celebrated works of art.[13] His competitors did likewise. Color illustrations and supplements quickly became an integral part of newsjournals.

Two years later color printing and cartooning came together when Pulitzer's enterprise began publishing *Hogan's Alley*, drawn by R. F. Outcault. Though often credited as the first comic strip, *Hogan's Alley* displayed a single panel rather than a series of images.[14] Nevertheless, it maintained a permanent setting with a continuing cast headed by a bald adolescent clothed in a gold-colored shirt. His adventures appeared every Sunday. The feature was so well received by subscribers that the comic strip's place was assured, ushering in the Sunday "funnies" (as newspaper cartoons were soon called), an art form that survives to the present day. At least one authority maintains that the practice descended from the images accompanying the Dickens installments six decades earlier.[15]

Harry Conway (Bud) Fisher was responsible for one of the earliest "funnies." In 1907 his *A. Mutt* (which later evolved into *Mutt and Jeff*) began appearing not just on Sundays but every day of the week in *The San Francisco Chronicle*. "Fisher understood the power of the comics to bring readers back morning after morning," one historian observed. "Increasingly, he showed his protagonist, compulsive gambler Augustus Mutt, engaging in activities that could be resolved in future strips."[16]

Nevertheless, *The Chicago Tribune* would become the most active single entity influencing the continued story form — and would do so by instigating a trio of eccentric innovations. Though a concern that was principally in the business of publishing the news, the *Tribune* transitioned the "funnies" from gag strips to continued stories, implemented the first continued motion picture short with holdover suspense, and aired the first daily radio serial — a marvel that is little short of astonishing.

The newsjournal brought about the next advance in comic strip serials with a penetrating focus on a mythical family. *Tribune* publisher Captain Joseph Patterson and cartoonist Sidney Smith envisioned that *The Gumps* would pictorially portray the dreams intrinsic to Theodore Dreiser's social-realist novels. Smith caused "everyday things to happen" to the Gump clan, which he depicted as typical Americans anxious to identify with the opulence of the Jazz Age.[17] One source intimated that *The Gumps*, airing over *Chicago Tribune* station WGN in 1926, introduced the serial format to radio, although that can be challenged (despite the fact it was the first daytime serial based upon a comic strip).[18] Other documentarians claim *The Gumps* didn't arrive on the ether until 1931; and there is ample evidence that other serialized fare was already on radio by 1925.

In the meantime, the *Tribune* syndicate didn't rest with *The Gumps*. Before long it was also offering continued stories on the comic pages of U.S. dailies under the monikers *Gasoline Alley* and *Little Orphan Annie*. In addition, it contributed several more strips to the nation's papers, including *Dick Tracy, Dondi, Harold Teen, Moon Mullins, On Stage* and *Winnie Winkle*. A few segued into ongoing dramas on-screen or in radio, as did cartoons of other newspaper syndicates that were active in fostering the motion-picture serial.

Comic strips, it may be scrupulously noted, swayed writers, illustrators, fine artists and filmmakers during the form's halcyon days. And comic *books* originally were designed to duplicate some of the more widely acclaimed newspaper strips. Speaking of comic books, one examiner opined: "It's not the same as having a weekly or *daily* dose of storytelling brought right to your doorstep. The regular flow of gradually unfolding plot twists, characterizations and cliffhangers, presented in a seamless melding of words and images, has its own unique and valuable appeal."[19]

At about the same time, other venues of print journalism were starting to encounter samples of long-term fiction. An unnamed scribe was surely oblivious to the fact that he or she was generating the earliest chapter-play heroine when producing a "remarkable story of a remarkable girl" that appeared in *The Ladies' World* magazine in August 1912. On the cover was a striking portrayal of a stunning young woman, illustrated by eminent artist Charles Dana Gibson. The girl's name was Mary and her likeness suggested that a majestic exploit awaited readers within the pages of that issue. If her depiction didn't persuade potential buyers to open the cover and flip to page three, the inscription it bore would have surely convinced many:

ONE HUNDRED DOLLARS FOR YOU IF YOU CAN TELL
"WHAT HAPPENED TO MARY"

The narrative *What Happened to Mary* encompassed the tale of an infant abandoned on a shopkeeper's doorstep, along with $500 in cash. A note nearby promised $1,000 more if he would raise the girl until she was grown, and wed her to an eligible man. But when she turned 18, Mary refused the fellow that her adoptive father picked. Learning the details of her early existence, she fled. Having second thoughts a short time later, she turned back. What happened next? Readers were told only that something defining occurred within the next 20 minutes. Anyone who could figure it out, and state it concisely in 300 words or less, would be gifted with a $100 cash award — a considerable number of greenbacks for the time. Lucy Proctor of Armstrong, California, rightly predicted that just as the shopkeeper and Mary's "intended" were about to corner her for their evil scheme, a gay blade whizzed in with a horse-drawn buggy and ferried her to safety in the nick of time. The rescue was detailed in the magazine's September issue.

Earlier that summer *Ladies' World* editor Charles Dwyer happened to cross paths with Horace G. Plimpton, manager of Thomas A. Edison's Kinetoscope Company, one of the foremost film producers of the day. As Dwyer excitedly relayed his intent to include a yarn about Mary in every installment of the periodical, with monetary prizes for readers who could deduce what would next transpire in the girl's life, Plimpton became intrigued. The studio executive urged the editor to go one step further. He proposed that Edison film a rendering of each monthly installment and release it to cinemas across America the same week the magazine went on sale.

Dwyer bought into Plimpton's inspiration.[20] Mary Fuller, a five-year veteran of the silver screen, was signed to portray Mary in the movie version. William Wadsworth played the shopkeeper, perhaps the first serial rogue. As Mary was pursued around the globe, readers and viewers discovered with her that an inheritance was hers to claim if she met certain provisos before age 21 — and was the shopkeeper's reward if she didn't. Would she or wouldn't she collect her fortune? Many theatergoers had already read what was to happen in a given episode in the pages of the latest issue of *The Ladies' World*. It was the first example of a screen serial, a narrative with continuing characters that was broken into a series of conventional installments.

Author Raymond William Stedman offers judicious insights on multiple formats that were to appear in serials before long. *Mary* is commonly, although mistakenly, labeled a *series film* now and then due to the fact it has no high-suspense finish. Stedman thinks that's a misnomer for it neglects recognizing that every chapter play is, in theory, a sequential progression anyway. He cites Blondie, the Hardy family and Francis, the talking mule, as examples of series films wherein characters and sometimes locales persisted. When audiences went to the cinema, they never considered that what was being screened was merely a portion of a sum total; at the same time, they couldn't be sure that any subsequent films would be produced.

There were plenty of relevant examples of pithy, self-contained movies like 119 railroading films released under the *Hazards of Helen* appellation. The hero or heroine was propelled into terrifying, spine-tingling circumstances week after week. Local motion picture houses screened those installments in whatever order they chose, showing just segments of a series if they preferred. None of it was offered as components of an intact unit. What was transpiring couldn't be easily mistaken for what is commonly perceived as a chapter play, therefore. Series films were precursors of B-picture adventures of the sound era like Boston Blackie, The Falcon, Lone Wolf, Philo Vance and The Saint detective stories and the westerns of Tim Holt, Charles Starrett and more.

In 1913 *The Chicago Tribune* combined an ongoing print scenario with a biweekly screen version of *The Adventures of Kathlyn*, the first continued film with holdover suspense.

By then a cycle of recurring serials bearing themes of women in peril proliferated. More importantly, the serial form had become a part of many fans' moviegoing experience, and this was particularly true of adolescent viewers.

Mary Fuller also starred in the 1914 Edison production *The Active Life of Dolly of the Dailies*. The career-gal yarn focused on a feminine journalist with romantic designs on a male colleague. That serial was a forerunner of several early radio soap operas, while many nighttime TV shows exhibited its traits, too. A year later Reliance's *Runaway June* was another dalliance with what was to become the essence of soap opera: an irrational bride (actress Norma Phillips) is unable to cope with a trivial domestic calamity. Heroines, for certain, were the bedrock of the early movie serials. Just as they would be in the radio washboard weepers a few decades hence, masculine figures were rarely as prominent as their feminine counterparts. On the screen, men were more often limited to rescuing damsels in distress or countering circumstances fostered by melees between scoundrels and leading ladies.

Silent films also featured popular serial stars that were, more often than not, protagonists in weekly dilemmas with dire consequences. When acclaimed actress Pearl White starred in *The Perils of Pauline*, she found herself in mortal danger as each episode sped toward a climactic finish. She might be lashed to a railroad track or grasping a crumbling ledge (giving rise to the term *cliffhanger*) or facing any number of petrifying dangers. But as each new chapter began, invariably she freed herself — only to discover new threats lurking around the bend. It was the stuff that kept audiences coming back for more in the early days of moviemaking.

When the full-length motion picture rose to the forefront of theatergoers' consciousness, however, the serial — at least among fans above the teenage years — was doomed. A significant decline in viewer interest occurred before the Roaring Twenties arrived. From this point on, the cinematic chapter-play focused wholly on younger fans, legions of whom filled movie palaces for Saturday matinees over the next four decades. Thrilling adventures in the lives of Dick Tracy, Flash Gordon, Gene Autry, Hopalong Cassidy, Johnny Mack Brown, The Lone Ranger, Red Ryder, Rin Tin Tin, Roy Rogers, Tom Mix, Wild Bill Hickok and other celebrated heroes unfolded every week in gripping installments.

At the time some of this was playing out at the Bijous, Plazas, Orpheums and Rialtos across the nation, the embryonic efforts of the continued story were being transmitted through the ether into people's homes.

WJZ announcer Norman (Broke) Brokenshire of New York City credited himself years later for initiating the soap opera.[21] He based that distinction on an on-the-air miscue that he was involved in during 1923. Broke had agreed to fill a half-hour with a variety program and solicited a few artists to perform at the microphone. By a fluke, all of them were detained and arrived *after* the program went on the air. To compensate for their absence, an innovative Brokenshire launched the half-hour by reading aloud from a short story volume that he spied in the studio. He hadn't quite reached the story's conclusion when the others showed up, and he laid the book aside to focus on the appointed performing entourage.

But plenty of disappointed listeners remained in Radioland who frankly felt cheated by the unexpected turn of events. Within a few days the station received hundreds of requests for Broke to read the yarn's ending. Much later he maintained that he had found the original audience for an as-yet-unnamed performing art — drama by installment, later billed as *soap opera*. As previously witnessed via different formats, there was an audience that would habitually petition for the rest of the story.

WJZ, incidentally, aired a mystery serial that same year, 1923. *The Waddington Cipher* was one of sundry spotty, short-run projects found on local radio.

The Smith Family aired over Chicago's WENR in 1925 and was the first drama of significant proportions in the fledgling strain. It included elements that would become staples in establishing an ongoing narrative as a viable mode for amusing the masses. Vaudevillians Jim and Marian Jordan, who a decade later would become the more noteworthy and durable *Fibber McGee and Molly*, were the principals.

The series, branded "the great-granddaddy of the soap operas,"[22] set a pattern that was often repeated: establish a family drama with a heroine as the central figure — and include other continuing characters in a permanent setting — in installments that connected with past and future action. Surprisingly, the Jordans later insisted that they had never been in a soap opera or even a proto-soap, citing the jocularity of *The Smith Family* as eliminating that possibility.[23] They appeared to have forgotten that numerous radio soaps received daily inspiration from farcical fundamentals, among them *Clara, Lu 'n' Em, The Couple Next Door, Easy Aces, Ethel and Albert, The Goldbergs, Lorenzo Jones, Vic and Sade* and more. Despite that, one observer noted, "*The Smith Family* took on some rather daring story lines (which would become staples of the soaps later on) including one in which an obviously Anglo-Saxon Protestant Smith daughter dates a Jewish boy."[24]

Also in 1925, veteran theatrical and radio performer Patrick Henry (Pat) Barnes joined another Chicago station, WHT, as chief announcer and program director. With an ability to act, narrate, sing and impersonate, Barnes reportedly developed a daytime serial drama that year titled *Henry Adams and His Book.*[25] Regrettably, any further details of the program have been lost to history.

The next most important development in bringing the serial to the airwaves resulted when an Anglo-Saxon pair consisting of Charles Correll and Freeman Gosden — touring comedians and minstrel show performers — took a humorous sketch to radio as a couple of Negro gents from the South who relocated to the North. Initially naming themselves *Sam 'n' Henry*, the duo aired over Chicago's WGN for two years (1926–27) and were an instant success. When they decided to record the show and distribute it to other stations outside the immediate vicinity, however, *The Chicago Tribune*, owner of WGN, blocked them, observing that it also owned the show's title. Unhesitatingly, in 1928 an invincible Correll and Gosden responded by transferring their series to rival station WMAQ, owned by *The Chicago Daily News*. The pair altered the feature's moniker to *Amos 'n' Andy* and proceeded about their business.

On August 19, 1929, the NBC Blue chain picked up the show and beamed it to a national audience of grateful listeners who all but halted what they were doing for a quarter-hour daily to tune in to the twosome's hilarity. The country was experiencing its most devastating economic reversal in history, the Great Depression, and Americans welcomed a lift in the midst of such overpowering financial woes. "Just as Marian and Jim Jordan laid down the foundation upon which daytime serials were to be built, Correll and Gosden did the preliminary work of conditioning listeners across the nation to following a continued radio program," one pundit pontificated.[26] Indeed, *Amos 'n' Andy* offered the daily quarter-hour format, the musical signature, and the opening and closing commercial in an appealing parcel — components that would so on become standard fare in daytime broadcasting.

Amos 'n' Andy introduced an ongoing stable of characters, all of them initially played by the two originators, who appeared in a familiar setting with links to previous and future episodes, elements that would be familiar in the soap opera model that emerged. The surfeit of raw materials available to series creators signaled that it was just a matter of time until a women's narrative would be offered as a matinee feature. "The feasibility of the continued story was ... overwhelmingly shown," recalled another media critic. "A basic dilemma continuing for weeks, far from alienating listeners, enmeshed ever-widening rings of addicts.... *Amos 'n' Andy* ... built audience frenzy and became mealtime and commuting train talk across the continent. All this would bring a flood of radio serials in succeeding years."[27]

Not only was *Amos 'n' Andy* the first nationwide network presentation of a fully sponsored daily serial (for Pepsodent toothpaste), the bizarre frenzy that resulted in its wake made radio a national commercial medium.[28] Demonstrating the appeal of the serial radio form, in its heyday *Amos 'n' Andy* drew 40 million listeners per week. Its sponsor had stumbled upon a marketing phenomenon of previously unimaginable proportions, while *Amos 'n' Andy* comic strips and phonograph records were "spun off" from the network program.

Some local stations were beginning to implement serialized features, too, no doubt as a direct result of the unparalleled success of *Amos 'n' Andy*. For instance, KMBC in Kansas City launched *Happy Hollow* in 1929, a six-night-a-week "true-to-life portrayal of happenings in any small town in the United States." Also a comedy, it set Uncle Ezra, mayor, leading merchant and station agent of the hamlet of Happy Hollow, against city slicker Harry Checkervest. A twice-weekly town hall talent show added variety to the lighthearted mix. Uncle Ezra pleased the sponsors by picking up their goods from the shelves of his general store and extolling their merits to sell them to his customers. It was typical of the fare creeping onto the airwaves in cities and towns all over America — not soap opera as such, but containing some of its basic precepts.

Before finishing an analysis of the antecedents of the daytime drama, a pithy survey of multiple categories of serialized fiction on the air will possibly enlighten the reader. The author is indebted to Raymond William Stedman, whose painstaking inquiry into the distinguishing characteristics of the genre's formats affords the roots of this inspection.[29] Stedman helps readers understand what soap opera *is*— and what it *is not*— and how it differs from other continuing broadcast narrative styles.

Episodic serials, for example, a very large subset of dramas within the category, departed considerably from soaps. Although an expansive narrative framework persisted, in episodic serials the plotting of almost every installment arrived at a resolution by the close of an individual broadcast. While, for instance, the war against evil pursued by The Shadow did not end, every week he faced and won a different battle — an encounter that could be followed by the fans from beginning to end without requiring them to have heard a previous episode. Other programs in the episodic serial mold included *The Adventures of Sherlock Holmes, Big Town, The Adventures of Ellery Queen, The Falcon, Mr. Chameleon, Mr. District Attorney, Mr. and Mrs. North, Nick Carter* and scores more. Throughout radio's golden age (roughly the mid–1920s to the early 1960s) and into the epoch of television the episodic serial was the prevailing form of continued dramas in the primetime listening and viewing hours.

In the meantime, during the late weekday afternoons and early evening hours, juvenile adventure serials took over much of the network airwaves. Those dramatic action yarns featured one or more leading figures in quarter-hour snippets (in their early years, with half-hour shows dominating by the late 1940s) aimed squarely at adolescents. They could be separated from the nighttime episodic serials by their open-ended, suspenseful final act in each chapter. Only when a story with ongoing characters was brought to a conclusion was there any momentary resolution. That might occur after some weeks or months of stimulating episodes.

More often than not a new mystery was introduced in a revolving-scheme pattern during the concluding installment of the previous tale, a method of making sure those young ears would tune in to the successive storyline. *Bobby Benson, The Cisco Kid, Jack Armstrong, Little Orphan Annie, Sergeant Preston of the Yukon, Sky King, Tom Mix* and others were prominent examples of this model. Cliffhanging on radio serials had its start with one of those pubescent features, by the way. It arrived with the NBC Blue chain's rendering of *Little Orphan Annie* on April 6, 1931, a program that had begun locally over WGN in 1930.[30]

It should be noted that some daytime radio serials applied the latter formula, particularly those dispatched from the assembly line of Frank and Anne Hummert, the genre's most prolific producers. Hummert narratives were sequentially written; that is, a group of malefactors entered a storyline for a few weeks or months, and interacted with a handful of permanent cast figures until a dilemma or crisis was resolved. Then the visitors departed while another contingent came on for the following segment. Soap opera wordsmiths employed many chapters to introduce a new plot instead of a single episode as the juvenile adventure scribes did. Furthermore, seldom would the soap authors end a sequence on a climactic moment filled with suspense, a habitual trait of the kiddie features.

Returning briefly to *Amos 'n' Andy*, that series solidified Chicago as a major center for radio drama. Conversely, the variety-show format, which depended on stars for its appeal, developed in Los Angeles and New York. Proximity to movie and theatrical artists was much less a dynamic in narrative programming. Instead of personalities, drama depended on an audience's appreciation of dramatic content. The Windy City offered advertising agencies and broadcasters a sizable coterie of radio actors at much lower rates than on either coast.

In the same period, several Chicagoans who were in positions to influence the outcome of the future of daytime radio programming mused over the implications of exploiting drama as a major advertising outlet. One of those individuals was E. Frank Hummert Jr., a bespectacled, somber gentleman of towering physical proportions who — along with his aide and future bride, Anne S. Ashenhurst — would become daytime radio's most influential moguls as together they built an ethereal empire of incredible scale. In 1958 Hummert humbly reminisced about those early days in which he was searching for a means to amuse legions of stay-at-home listeners:

> As I remember it now the idea for a daytime serial was predicated upon the success of serial fiction in newspapers and magazines. It occurred to me that what people were reading might appeal to them in the form of radio drama. It was as simple as that. And results prove that my *guess* was right.
>
> I stress the word "guess" because that was all it was. Not a flash of so-called genius, but a shot in the dark. Hence I take no credit for it. Believe me, none is deserved.

The long period of acceptance that the printed serial had experienced impressed Hummert more than anything he might be hearing on the air. His search for the "right show" for homemakers was reportedly based on what had appeared in pulp form as opposed to assorted serialized features already emanating from radio sets.

If the daytime serial was to go forward, it must not only entertain the target crowd, but it had to convince them to purchase specific commodities. After all, women were the nation's principal purchasing agents, figuring extensively in making a family's brand-name buying decisions. The daytime serial must be delivered within a context that didn't unduly distract this dedicated homemaking workforce from performing its accustomed tasks, too. All of this was transpiring, of course, in an age in which not many of the creature comforts or timesaving conveniences existed with which the modern woman is familiar.

As Hummert, Ashenhurst and other visionaries contemplated possible options, their notion, once put into practice, was to modify the ethereal landscape for as long as network radio was to be a viable institution. Ultimately, some of their suppositions have impacted daytime television in the contemporary period. The long history of the continuing narrative and its many enchanting variations proffered all sorts of promises. That saga's enduring legacy certainly wasn't about to reach a finish line any time soon.

2

Bubbles in the Air

Henry Selinger was managing radio station WGN for *The Chicago Tribune* in 1930. You may recall that the *Tribune* was a pioneering influence on no fewer than three distinctive styles of the dramatic serial model: it turned printed gag strips into continuing yarns on the comic pages; it underwrote the original celluloid tale that maintained holdover anticipation; and, finally, it introduced the first daytime radio serial. Henry Selinger was in charge when the final piece of that three-pronged puzzle fell into place, and was instrumental in bringing it to completion.

That spring he contacted one of America's premier advertising agencies, Lord and Thomas, with a proposal for initiating an episodic yarn that would attract a feminine following. At the same time he figured the program would need to entice industrial makers of household or personal care goods that could be pitched to the target audience. Little could Selinger realize that his premise conceived the embryonic stages of an art form that was to outlive him by more than a lifetime.

He envisioned a storyline focused on an Irish-American mom and her daughter, with most of the narrative's action occurring in their home. A staff writer and a single actor were engaged to generate a few audition episodes. It was Selinger's hope that the Super Suds Company, a detergent manufacturer that was later purchased by Colgate, would look favorably on that venture; therefore, the drama was offered under the moniker *The Sudds*.

Potential programming underwriters were skeptical in those pre-ratings services days, however; it was obvious that there were fewer listeners for daytime features than there was during the evening hours, and a serial aimed at women had never been tried. When Super Suds wasn't impressed with WGN's proposal, the scheme was re-titled *Good Luck Margie* and pushed to the Jelke Oleomargarine Company, which also swiftly turned it down. The crux of these firms' hesitancy seemed to lie with the fact that the idea hadn't been tested— no one was really sure if daytime drama would find a receptive audience. It would be at best a calculated risk. What if it failed?

While all of this was going on, in late May 1930 a gallant young Dayton, Ohio, schoolmarm knocked on WGN's door seeking summer employment. Irna Phillips, then just 28— a native Chicagoan who would in due course influence daytime drama more profoundly (certainly in tenure) than anybody else — discovered seasonal work as an actress. Soon she was also writing conversational dialogue for the station. Finding the medium to her liking,

Phillips petitioned assistant station manager Harry Gilman to hire her permanently for acting and writing posts.

By August she lobbied Henry Selinger to put her in charge of developing the proposed women's daytime serial that had been floundering since spring. He acquiesced to a persistent Phillips (it wouldn't be the last time she got her way — more on this in Chapter Six), and she gave up her teaching career to labor full-time in radio. Selinger instructed her to pen 10 scripts that would focus on an Irish woman's family, including a mother, a daughter and a friend of the daughter. The outcome was a drama-by-installment that was to be known as *Painted Dreams*.

WGN again peddled the series to several prospective sponsors. But just as before, none rushed to sign on the dotted line. Finally, that fall Selinger decided to bite the bullet and proceed with the model anyway, hoping that once it was on the air a sponsor would sally forth to support it. On October 20, 1930, *Painted Dreams* debuted as a sustaining (unsponsored) program airing for a quarter-hour Monday through Saturday. For a salary of 50 dollars a week, Phillips was assigned to write the series and play the lead character of Mother Moynihan, as well as appear as Sue Morton, who rented a room from the Moynihans.

Not until October 1931 — a full year after the feature's premier — did a commercial outfit pick up *Painted Dreams*. Chicago-based meatpacker Mickleberry Products Company was the pioneer enterprise to underwrite a daytime drama for women. By then the series was firmly entrenched, having demonstrated its ability to draw a following.

The experiment with *Painted Dreams* quickly resulted in competition, as other programming innovators started to capitalize on its trailblazing initiative, infiltrating the daytime ether with like fare. Their collective efforts would later lead to an assessment by media critic Gilbert Seldes that "the great invention of radio, its single most notable contribution to the art of fiction, is the daytime serial."[1] That model, in his opinion, was a new theatrical form that comprised a tale meted out in fragments "that wouldn't interrupt your life." In the late 1940s a Procter & Gamble executive, William M. Ramsey, termed the radio serials "a twentieth century version of the same story-telling that has entertained mankind for several thousands of years and will undoubtedly continue to entertain as long as mankind exists."[2] Agnes Nixon (featured in Chapter 12), one of Irna Phillips' protégés in developing TV serials, defined a good tale as one that "makes 'em laugh, makes 'em cry, and makes 'em wait!"[3] To acknowledge it candidly, the compelling influence of continuous storytelling is little short of awesome!

Before the decade of the 1930s was finished, a plethora of sobriquets were derived to classify the daytime serials. Some of the more common included "dishpan dramas," "drainboard dramas," "soapy sagas" and "washboard weepers," each one reflecting an aspect of a homemaker's daily pattern. By 1939, reporters — seeking a shortened handle and disapproving of the cumbersome "daytime dramatic serials" then in widespread use — dubbed the series "soap operas." The name stuck, reflecting the fact that several large detergent manufacturers were underwriting the bulk of those narratives on the ether. To this day the label "soap opera" (or a shortened form, "soap") is applied to the daytime dramas broadcast over contemporary television screens.

On February 15, 1932, a comedic serial that had been generating laughs among nighttime audiences over the past 20 months for Super Suds detergent — the very same sponsor that had turned down *The Sudds* (a proposed appellation for *Painted Dreams*, and a series that had originated over WGN) — was transferred to a morning timeslot. *Clara, Lu 'n' Em*, a tale of three gossipy neighbors, became the foremost network daytime episodic feature, then airing over the NBC Blue chain. With that shift, people all over the country were hearing drama-by-installment. The program introduced the husband with wanderlust. "His eyes wandered and the rest of him lusted," quipped a modern pundit. "Now, we had two parts of the soap opera formula in place: sponsorship and the betraying (and, by inference, the betrayed) spouse."[4]

In the meantime, as noted in the first chapter, Frank Hummert was one of those individuals who had long harbored a faith that radio listeners at home during the daylight hours might appreciate some dramatic entertainment while tending to their chores. The same year (1931) that *Clara, Lu 'n' Em* became network radio's first daytime dramatic serial, Hummert — creative director of the Chicago-based Blackett-Sample-Hummert advertising agency — persuaded Robert Hardy Andrews to pen a new serial for women which he called *The Stolen Husband*. Andrews' promising career until then had focused on a succession of newspaper chains, most recently as author of some serialized fiction for *The Chicago Daily News* that had caught Hummert's eye.

The title of their initial foray into radio serials, *The Stolen Husband*, instantly revealed the plot, of course, and bore a theme that was to be repeated in the years ahead. While their inaugural attempt at a soap opera proved less than successful, it provided Hummert and his assistant (and soon-to-be bride) Anne S. Ashenhurst, and Andrews unparalleled experience that they would quickly apply to many subsequent ventures. Before long that intrepid trio was charming mammoth segments of the radio population.

In 1932 they offered *Just Plain Bill*, unquestionably the first serial with long-lasting appeal, which persisted all the way to late 1955. It was the story of the barber of mythical Hartville, a tonsorial artist who had time to set his clippers aside and take on the trials and tribulations of the homefolks, people who needed a little help in running their lives. Bill Davidson's warmhearted approach to humanity made him a trustworthy confidante, admired by most of the locals who carried their troubles to him and perpetually found a sympathetic ear. They knew from years of observation that he had the ability and the resolve to figure things out. His was, as a radio interlocutor claimed, "the real-life story of people just like people we all know."

In 1933 Hummert, Ashenhurst and Andrews added two more daytime features to a budding inventory that were to become staples of the new dramatic form: *The Romance of Helen Trent*, aimed at those who fantasized about midlife crises; and *Ma Perkins*, which focused on a revered "mother of the airwaves." Both series continued for the next 27 years.

Helen Trent was a widowed Hollywood fashion designer whom fate — and her exasperating indecisiveness — mercilessly kept from the altar a second time as dozens of lowlife males, including an occasional murderer, pursued her relentlessly for their own ends. Gil Whitney was different, however; as her most enduring admirer, the handsome lawyer manifest the patience of Job while hoping Helen would say "yes" to his multiple proposals. She couldn't, of course — to do so would have betrayed the theme of the series, and was a prospect the creators simply wouldn't allow. As her epigraph proclaimed, she was constantly rediscovering "that because a woman is 35, or more, romance in life need not be over; that the romance of youth can extend into middle life, and even beyond." Unfortunately, in her circumstances she couldn't do a lot with it.

Ma Perkins managed her late husband's business, the Perkins Lumberyard in imaginary Rushville Center — a misnomer for a serial hamlet if ever there was one, considering the action's creeping pace. A critic labeled her "Bill Davidson in skirts," and she demonstrated the homey approach that embodied all of serialdom's helping-hand characters. Folks in Rushville Center knew they could turn to Ma, who possessed the wisdom of Solomon, for compassionate understanding in their time of crisis, and for good-natured advice to put their lives back on track. Occasionally Ma encountered difficult situations within her own clan that required her delicate negotiation. But the stouthearted matriarch of impeccable integrity manifest a resilience that invariably saw her through the sorry times, until things turned brighter once more. The series, incidentally, debuted in a trial run over Cincinnati's WLW in the summer of 1933. It emerged before a national audience 16 weeks later when Frank Hummert was placed in charge.

With *Just Plain Bill*, *The Romance of Helen Trent* and *Ma Perkins* under their belts— each a literal success story — the futures of Frank Hummert, Anne Ashenhurst and Robert Hardy Andrews were pretty well set. Their trio of formidable soap operas set the pace for scores of others to follow, and became the standards against which many successor dramas were to be gauged. The three innovators also opened the door for a surfeit of Hummert-produced narratives over the next two decades.

The Hummerts (Frank and Anne wed in 1935) would eventually bring to the airwaves no fewer than 125 radio series in a half-dozen genres. Their most prolific format was soap opera. The couple oversaw an incredible quantity of daytime serials— at least 61 having been documented to date (almost half of their entire output), and there are indications there may have been more. While the list of their entries is too lengthy to acknowledge, some of their most noteworthy serials (in addition to those named already) are worth mentioning. Scholars and students of serialized fiction will readily recognize them, for they are among the prime examples of the genre: *Amanda of Honeymoon Hill*; *Backstage Wife*; *Betty and Bob*; *Chaplain Jim, U.S.A.*; *The Couple Next Door*; *David Harum*; *Easy Aces*; *Front Page Farrell*; *John's Other Wife*; *The Life of Mary Sothern*; *The Light of the World*; *Lora Lawton*; *Lorenzo Jones*; *Our Gal Sunday*; *Stella Dallas*; *The Strange Romance of Evelyn Winters*; *Valiant Lady*; and *Young Widder Brown*.

In addition to those sagas, the Hummerts were responsible for introducing such other aural favorites as *The American Album of Familiar Music*; *Hearthstone of the Death Squad*; *Jack Armstrong, the All-American Boy*; *Little Orphan Annie*; *Manhattan Merry-Go-Round*; *Mr. Chameleon*; *Mr. Keen, Tracer of Lost Persons*; *Waltz Time*; and many other amusing novelties.

In 1938 the Hummerts moved to New York City to relocate near the headquarters of the radio networks and many of the large national advertising agencies. Not long after that the duo decided to begin moving most of their radio features to Gotham, too, to take advantage of a glut of theater artists (actors, announcers, directors, musicians, sound technicians) that could enrich their programming in diverse genres. (From 1947 to 1949 the production of a quartet of Irna Phillips' serials transferred from Chicago to Hollywood until they, too, shifted to the East Coast.) The upheaval created by the transitions meant that some of the talent did not move with the programs on which their voices had long been familiar to listeners. Still, in many cases the performers did make the jump and continued appearing from new venues without interruption in continuity.

Eventually the Hummerts— with a dozen or more daytime dramas airing simultaneously alongside their other features— decided to break away from their longstanding association with the Blackett-Sample-Hummert agency of Chicago and form their own outfit. Air Features Incorporated, the new production shop under their aegis, capitalized on the Hummerts' business acumen and enormous capability to offer an expansive list of audio programming. They built a literal dynasty, controlling in fact, the bulk of daytime radio schedules on all four nationwide chains.

To accomplish this they employed assembly-line methods that allowed them to multiply their creative ideas, establishing many stories with mass appeal concurrently. The Hummerts personally crafted the plots of their many series, then assigned a battery of scribes to the tasks of fleshing out the individual storylines with dialogue and action while adhering closely to their skeletal outlines. In so doing they signified themselves as "creators of original plot lines" and seldom gave on-air credit to those who actually contrived the scripts.

Meanwhile, these shrewd entrepreneurs formed a subsidiary, Featured Artist Service Incorporated, which hired artists for their own radio shows and those of other producers. That allowed the Hummerts to pocket additional fees that would have otherwise been paid to outside talent agencies. The resolute duo remained characteristically aloof, detached from hundreds of minions who labored in their soap opera workshop and appeared on their numerous programs while the gurus lived opulently imperial existences. The Hummerts' personal likes and dislikes were delineated in memos and reflected in stringent policies that those who toiled in the trenches were bound to carry out or risk instant dismissal. For a comprehensive look into the lives of this shockingly beguiling couple, the reader is directed to their biography—*Frank and Anne Hummert's Radio Factory: The Programs and Personalities of Broadcasting's Most Prolific Producers*, by this author (McFarland, 2003, 224 pp).

Irna Phillips, in the meantime — the original drama mama — wasn't letting any moss grow under her feet either. As radio's second most prolific daytime serial creator, before the golden age passed she was credited with introducing numerous narratives to the aural audience. In addition to *Painted Dreams*, her inspirations included *The Brighter Day*, *The Guiding Light*, *Lonely Women*, *Masquerade*, *The Right to Happiness*, *Road of Life*, *Today's Children* and *Woman in White*. She also supervised the scripting of *Young Doctor Malone* for a while. Phillips would be even more influential in televised soap opera, as Chapter Six will bear out. At the beginning, this spinster typed her own scripts, writing as many as three serials concurrently (reportedly 60,000 words every week — the equivalent of an average novel), until it became too cumbersome. At that juncture she dictated dialogue to a secretary, or to a machine, for later transcription. Eventually, when her creative workload became more than was humanly possible for her to handle herself, Phillips hired professional writers to convert her verbal instructions to printed scripts.

A major contrast between the Phillips regime and the Hummert camp was their attitudes towards their scribes. Phillips placed a high value on her colleagues and paid them well for their services; her wordsmiths were normally compensated at rates twice those paid to Hummert writers. While the Hummerts focused on voluminous output, Phillips infused her plots with extensive character development that, she believed, was more appealing to listeners. She also focused on professional occupations such as doctors, nurses, clergymen, teachers and attorneys, believing those to be "more interesting" categories than barbers, dress designers and lumberyard owners. Her powerful influence lingers to the present day.

Another prominent instigator of daytime serials also got an early start. Elaine Sterne Carrington possessed an ostensibly inexhaustible pen, customarily contributing fiction that appeared in several leading women's magazines of the day. Her bylines sporadically turned up in such fêted slicks as *Collier's, Good Housekeeping, Harper's, Ladies' Home Journal, Pictorial Review, Redbook, Saturday Evening Post* and *Woman's Home Companion*. Encouraged by a program director at NBC, in 1932 she tried her hand at authoring a weekly episodic adventure about what she perceived to be a typical American family, based on her own.

The series was initially titled *Red Adams*. It went through several permutations (including gaining the new appellations *Red Davis* and *Forever Young*) before evolving into the warm-hearted tale of *Pepper Young's Family*, a program that (counting all the predecessors) survived for 27 years, even outliving its creator. For most of those years the show was a quarter-hour mid-afternoon feature surrounded by other soapy sagas.

Carrington eventually created several more radio serials, including *Marriage for Two, Rosemary, Trouble House* and *When a Girl Marries*. She also made a single, all-too-brief foray into television soap opera with *Follow Your Heart* (detailed in Chapter Four), based on the early storylines of *When a Girl Marries*. Most judges of her radio dramas credit her for her literary qualities, some citing her stories as "believable" and "possible" in an environment in which the majority of serials were melodramatic and unreal. Unlike the Hummerts and Irna Phillips, Carrington never employed ghostwriters to author her narratives. Instead, she dictated every word of every story she wrote. A secretary transcribed her words from a machine into scripts.

On the West Coast, at about the same time Elaine Carrington was shifting gears from printed to audio fiction, ex-newspaperman Carlton E. Morse was tinkering with his own concept of a homespun family drama. When radio beckoned in 1930 he cast aside a promising career in print journalism, severed his ties with *The San Francisco Chronicle*, and created a now seldom-recalled mystery serial for Bay Area listeners. Subsequently he scripted dramatic, action and adventure fare. Even though Morse was to initiate several radio series that would maintain large followings across his career (*Adventures by Morse, Family Skeleton, His Honor — the Barber, I Love Adventure, I Love a Mystery, The Woman in My House*), his crowning glory arrived early.

In 1932 *One Man's Family*, a story of the foibles and revelations of the fictional Barbour clan of San Francisco, premiered on local station KGO. A year later NBC beamed the tale to a nationwide audience, for whom it ran another 26 years, turning into a matinee epic in its final four years. The program was one of two soap operas to earn a coveted Peabody Award in the 1940s for distinguished radio drama. It also went to television for brief runs on two occasions, once as a daytime serial (see Chapter Four).

Weekday radio was soon brimming with ongoing narratives. Many other innovators, wanting a piece of the rapidly developing action, launched other dramatic installments.

The multi-talented Don Becker and Carl Bixby collaborated on multiple series, penning the long-running *Life Can Be Beautiful* (1938–1954) — *their* coup d'état — while actively scripting several more. Together or separately they produced, directed, acted in and conducted the music for a half-dozen daytime dramas in audio formats. Bixby also became a head writer for CBS-TV's *The Secret Storm* a few years later.

In the interim, Addy Richton and Lynn Stone, jointly writing under the pseudonym Adelaide Marston, originated the venerable *Hilltop House*, plus *This Life Is Mine*, while also penning scripts for the Hummerts' *Valiant Lady*.

There were many other typewriter keyboard artists, too numerous to mention, who were responsible for solo serials that appeared on radio in the 1930s, 1940s and 1950s. Each drama produced was distinctive, its attributes setting it apart from the pack of nearly 300 broadcast soap operas aired on the four national radio chains.

Business-wise, the daytime serials quickly became an industry of astounding proportions. When *McCall's* magazine asked 1000 housewives to name their "most essential household appliances" in 1934, the top four answers — in order of ranking — were: iron, radio, vacuum cleaner, refrigerator.[5] In 1937 soapmaker Procter & Gamble spent $4.5 million on radio advertising, more than 90 percent of which underwrote daytime serials. [6] Between 1939 and 1941, approximately $40 million annually was devoted to staging and airing daytime serials—nearly half of all network disbursements and a third of all radio financial outlays in this country.[7] By 1940 a whopping 57 serial dramas commanded 77.5 percent of commercial daytime radio.[8] During the audio soap's halcyon days, more than 20 million people were listening to daytime serials every week. CBS claimed in 1957 that a single quarter-hour serial broadcast five days weekly still reached an audience of 6.4 million at a mere 49 cents per thousand listeners. [9] Soap operas, indeed, were a phenomenal and prosperous commercial industry!

Of course, there was never any doubt about who comprised the majority of radio soap opera listeners. Perhaps nine out of 10 in its vast assemblage were women. Just as some of the form's originators had speculated well before soap opera took off, milady was looking for a little gratification to accompany her frequently colorless, monotonous and sometimes miserable circumstance, an interlude in her day that might make it all manageable.

The reality of the situation — and especially for those living through the Great Depression and post–Depression epoch — was that large numbers of their gender faced profoundly grueling surroundings. Time-saving appliances didn't appear until the middle of the century. A historian noted: "The whole morning or afternoon could be spent rubbing a big bar of soap across a washboard, lifting a heavy scalding-hot iron, cooking budget foods from scratch. There were often too many children. Divorces were neither afforded nor tolerable. Men were the undisputed masters of their homes."[10]

Into that disheartening milieu some make-believe heroines were introduced who resided in engaging venues of distraction that disconsolate housewives could only daydream of. For a brief while each weekday the *real* women were transported past their ordinary circumstances into a fantasyland that gave them at least a flicker of hope that they, too, might some day realize delivery from their lots. Helen Trent, one of those imaginary queens, and typical of a host of others, "lived, inexplicably, a spectacularly glamorous life as a Hollywood dress designer who attracted one handsome devil after another with her invisible charms. At thirty-five, Helen had romance and no husband, and no children, and no drudgery."[11] What a life!

The itinerant wordsmith Robert Hardy Andrews, who possessed the most facile pen on Frank and Anne Hummert's assembly line during soap opera's inaugural decade, composed a few lines under the heading "A Voice in the Room." In it he spoke volumes about the stay-at-home housewife who was so obviously comforted by her newfound escape.

The average woman lives by a schedule in which no element changes from one day to the next....
The accomplishments of such days may be great in their value to humanity, but the hours are — or were, in the past — long, empty, and deadly dull. But now a new thing has happened.
There is, or can be, a voice in the room. A friendly, unhurried, likable, listenable, neighborly voice that is created by the turning of a dial....
The housewife turns on her radio. She goes here and there, into her living room, upstairs to make the beds and clean the bathroom, out in the yard to hang up the washing, back to the kitchen to prepare lunch for the children....
She knows, without thinking much about it, that the voice in her room tells her what is being heard by other women like herself. Therefore, she is a member of a great group....
She is grateful, because in the world at last she has at least one neighbor, who is many voices in one, who talks to her all day long every day. And it is talking, the sound of a voice, not music or a joke that must be thought about or drama so artistic that she must sit down to listen to it, that the woman wants to hear. That is what she is grateful for: the voice in her room.[12]

Parenthetically, until finally acknowledging that he "got tired," the author of "A Voice in the Room" consistently hammered out scripts for four to seven daily radio shows, most of them soap operas. Working in a penthouse apartment on New York's Central Park West, Robert Hardy Andrews—tapping at his typewriter as he consumed 40 cups of coffee and chain-smoked 100 cigarettes daily—labored seven days a week from noon to midnight. His weekly production rate usually surpassed 100,000 words. As a sideline he penned novels and dozens of movie scripts, alone or with one or more co-authors. When he finally quit, the Hummerts were never able to replace him. No workhorse would emerge to duplicate his impressive endurance or his incomparable output.

Gilbert Seldes correctly observed that the daytime serial was founded "on the assumption of immortality: everyone is expected to live forever, nobody gets any older, time is shrunk or ignored and nothing is ever resolved."[13] A modern pundit exclaimed: "Soap operas were novels for the ear—the first audio books, really—that went on for years, decades, in a state ... called 'sustained anxiety.'"[14] Yet another deduced: "Daytime dramas of the period affirmed the belief that life was but a series of misfortunes intermingled with periods of happiness."[15]

Who populated serialdom on radio? Most denizens were "middle-class, not poverty-stricken or ... of great wealth, neither ignorant nor well educated," according to a couple of analysts exploring the topic.[16] The pair compartmentalized those fictional figures into a trio of factions—*good people*, most frequently women; *bad people*, most frequently prosperous individuals, internationals and unlawful offenders; and *weak people*, most frequently men.[17] Males in soap operas were predictably submissive to females. It was there that a woman tuning in could identify passionately with another of her gender whose grace, proficiency and common sense habitually appeared to dominate her frequently ineffectual counterpart. Sometimes there was no masculine hero of any import in a storyline—he might be absent for long periods of time, totally inferior in capability or perhaps never having been present, as in the cases of widowed heroines Ma Perkins, Helen Trent and Ellen (*Young Widder*) Brown. The producers of daytime serials clearly understood who was listening and took precautions to cultivate a tender and affable reception for their leading ladies.

The radio audience ratings weren't limited to the primetime hours when multitudes of all ages were listening across the ether. Taking the pulse of the daytime serials was just as vital as it was for every other programming category. C. E. Hooper and A. C. Nielsen were two of the largest firms tallying audience numbers then. Advertisers and networks applied the data gleaned from the surveys to determine how to spend their budgets and what to offer on the air. Once the daytime serials took hold, some of them found large followings that frequently put them head and shoulders above their competition. Rival strains on the air most frequently consisted of audience participation programs, game shows, music, interviews, and news and information features.

Any show that received a 5.0 rating during the medium's heyday (extending to the early 1950s) could virtually be assured of avoiding cancellation due to low response. Translated, that figure (5.0) meant that of 100 persons polled in a sample, five were listening to a specific radio offering. The highest rated daytime programs in a 19-year span between 1937 and 1956 are listed in the following table. The figures are based on a one-week analysis during mid-winter each year. While the table is not meant to be an absolute measurement, it reflects the listening preferences of Americans during the daytime hours at a similar point annually.[18]

Season	First Place Show/Rating	Second Place Show/Rating
1937–38	*The Story of Mary Marlin*/10.4	*Vic & Sade*/8.8 (NBC Red broadcast)
1938–39	*Ma Perkins*/11.3	*The Goldbergs*/10.0
1939–40	*Ma Perkins*/10.4	*Jack Armstrong, the All-American*
	Vic & Sade/10.4	*Boy*/9.8
1940–41	*Ma Perkins*/10.0	*The O'Neills*/9.6
1941–42	*Woman in White*/9.1	*Life Can Be Beautiful*/9.0
1942–43	*Big Sister*/8.9	*Aunt Jenny's Real Life Stories*/8.6
		Young Widder Brown/8.6
1943–44	*When a Girl Marries*/9.0	*Portia Faces Life*/8.7
1944–45	*When a Girl Marries*/9.2	*Breakfast in Hollywood*/8.7
1945–46	*Breakfast in Hollywood*/8.3	*Ma Perkins*/8.2 (CBS broadcast)
1946–47	*When a Girl Marries*/8.8	*The Right to Happiness*/8.1
1947–48	*Big Sister*/7.9	*Ma Perkins*/7.8 (CBS broadcast)
1948–49	*Ma Perkins*/9.1 (CBS broadcast)	*When a Girl Marries*/8.2
1949–50	*The Romance of Helen Trent*/11.0	*Arthur Godfrey Time*/10.5
1950–51	*Ma Perkins*/9.4	*The Romance of Helen Trent*/9.3
1951–52	*The Romance of Helen Trent*/8.4	*Our Gal Sunday*/7.6
1952–53	*The Romance of Helen Trent*/7.5	*Our Gal Sunday*/7.2
1953–54	*The Romance of Helen Trent*/6.9	*Our Gal Sunday*/6.8
		The Guiding Light/6.8
1954–55	*The Guiding Light*/5.5	*Perry Mason*/5.3
	Ma Perkins/5.5	*This Is Nora Drake*/5.3
		Young Doctor Malone/5.3
		Young Widder Brown/5.3
1955–56	*The Guiding Light*/4.7	*Ma Perkins*/4.5
	The Romance of Helen Trent/4.7	
	Young Doctor Malone/4.7	

Not surprisingly, every feature cited except three—*Arthur Godfrey Time, Breakfast in Hollywood* and *Jack Armstrong, the All-American Boy*—is a women's serial, signifying the form's utter command of the daytime airwaves.

In the late 1940s the fortunes of radio began to ebb. While the erosion was slight, almost unnoticeable at first, as the 1950s arrived the pace quickened. One by one, individual series and sometimes whole programming blocks disappeared — in primetime, on weekends and on weekdays. The most visible culprit was television, of course, then just emerging as a serious challenger to radio, vying for its audiences, artists and advertisers. By the mid–1950s the new medium had essentially captured all three. On daytime television, engaging serials were becoming firmly entrenched, giving homemakers new reasons to switch off their radios and turn on their TVs.

There was another major factor that helped bring radio's golden age to a close, one possibly even more intimidating than television. Throughout the 1950s the affiliates of the big webs were clamoring for fewer scheduled program offerings from their networks so that they, themselves, might sell time — the only commodity they possessed — to commercial enterprises. In so doing they could earn much more than the pittance they were getting from the chains for carrying network features. Soon, what had begun as a murmur became an outcry and — as the decade progressed — a hostile pressure from the local stations, who threatened to boycott network programming or, worse, fail to renew their operational agreements. That would free them up to become independents or to join other rival chains. In some markets those stations were powerhouses that delivered large audiences as well as projected high profiles for their respective webs. The prospect of losing them was a daunting one.

While the Mutual Broadcasting System withdrew its soap operas and many of its other features quite early, the American Broadcasting Company continued to air its single remaining open-ended (ongoing storyline) soap opera, *When a Girl Marries*, until August 30, 1957. At that juncture it abandoned the form forever.

To its credit, the National Broadcasting Company persisted with its handful of long-playing daytime remnants into 1959, canceling *Pepper Young's Family* on January 16. *One Man's Family* and *The Woman in My House* departed on April 24 as NBC wiped its programming slate clean of a model that had existed on its airwaves since 1931.

That left the Columbia Broadcasting System as the lone holdout still carrying daytime serials. CBS had stubbornly refused any retrenchment, and would budge only when convinced there was absolutely no alternative. It persisted with much of its daytime agenda intact for another 19 months following NBC's sweeping erasures.

In August 1960, doubtlessly accepting the inevitable and untenable position into which it had been sorrowfully shoved, CBS at last publicly set an execution date for the remaining residue of its once robust soap opera surfeit. All of the dialoguers attempted to tie the loose ends of their storylines together quite rapidly — ends that had dangled for years — before the time ran out and the familiar visitors reached a final farewell. Seven daytime serials and some other major dramatic and amusement fare disappeared from the web's programming log following the broadcast day of November 25, 1960 (surely it was the original "Black Friday"). Of its final soaps, a quartet of open-ended stories had persisted longer than a decade (and three of those — all but *Burton* — had lasted for more than *two* decades): *Ma Perkins, The Right to Happiness, The Second Mrs. Burton* and *Young Doctor Malone*.

Despite that inglorious ending which left millions of listeners dispossessed, there was never a doubt that radio's donations to episodic fiction would be acclaimed and documented for posterity. The medium had provided a worthy conduit in the natural progression of drama-by-installment. The contributions of the aural form could hardly be summarily dismissed.

3

Primitive Stages

Anybody who matured during the epoch after television was elevated to the predominant source of information and entertainment entering American households likely sustained widely different media perspectives from those born during the radio era. The baby boomers, for one thing, could have some difficulty accepting the notion that current classy, costly, complex daytime serials on TV trace their heritage to the oft-maligned radio soap operas of yesteryear. As a consequence, it might be easier for the TV generation to consider that only the *initiative* of daytime serials was successfully transported from that aural precursor, not the substance. Despite any such premise, all of the form's roots are deeply embedded in radio, nonetheless. Video merely refined and urbanized an already established, gratifying model of leisure-time amusement. "After all," rationalized one informant, "television is just radio with pictures."[1]

On the other hand, from the outset the mere intimation that one or more daytime serials could be staged on live television every single weekday seemed absolutely preposterous to anyone with a grain of sense. To attempt an undertaking of that magnitude was far too ambitious, countless insiders believed. Why, the impracticalities were positively staggering!

Faced with such a nerve-racking prospect, the human body itself could hardly be expected to perform consistently over an extended period. Endless memorization of lines and flawlessly delivering them without benefit of teleprompters while making strategic movements on specific cues; laboring under incredibly hot lights (three batteries of 48 three-thousand-watt bulbs then) in minuscule quarters on makeshift cardboard sets that sometimes toppled over on actors; devoting several laborious hours to rehearsals daily; departing from home while it was still dark and returning when it was dark again; and answering large volumes of mail while making countless photo-op appointments, interviews and public appearances to give a show high visibility simply didn't sound like a picnic in the park. "It was beyond human capacity," a pair of wags pontificated. And the actor who left his radio microphone to go before the cameras—where he previously only read his lines in a couple of pre-show rehearsals, then read them again in a live quarter-hour broadcast before continuing on with his life — would have fervently intimated that one was purely nuts!

The debilitating effect on the human condition, of course, was only one depressing argument against beaming a daily live serial to the cathode ray tube. Whereas *Ma Perkins* was produced on radio at a cost of about $1,300 a week in the mid–1940s, it would take nearly $7,000 each week to do the same thing on television at the time — more than five times the outlay for a radio serial.[2] And by 1950 a quarter-hour video serial ran up a production tab of $8,650 every week![3] TV devoured expensive sets, lights, props, costumes, cameras and technical equipment while demanding a large crew of stagehands with professional expertise to augment transmissions, plus appreciably higher salaries for performers. In addition, the production apparatus for television was highly complex and — in the early days — often unreliable.

And if that wasn't enough to stop somebody, how was anyone to know whether there would be an audience for such fare? Daytime serials on TV hadn't been tried. In fact, daytime programming — what little there was of it — hardly registered with anybody. The four TV webs, including ABC, CBS, Dumont and NBC, concentrated their earliest efforts on the early evening and primetime hours, when they knew *somebody* would be watching. Just how many viewers could be corralled for a matinee? It was anybody's guess. And equally important, could a sponsor be found to underwrite it?

Perhaps — just perhaps — they didn't know all that when a few innovators began conjecturing and experimenting with live daytime television drama in the 1940s.

Let's digress momentarily to include an overview of television's development to that point. Wesley Hyatt, who chronicled much of daytime video's history, attests that the first working TV demonstrations occurred in 1925, fostered by an American, Charles Francis Jenkins, and a Scotsman, John Baird, the latter experimenting in England.[4] While General Electric launched the first regularly operating TV station in Schenectady, New York, in 1928, and a few others followed, the stock market debacle in October 1929 that resulted in the Great Depression curtailed those tests. It was radio that took off while TV was stalled. Much of the aural medium's gargantuan earnings underwrote further TV development, in fact.

NBC opened a New York City TV station in 1930, and CBS followed suit in 1931.[5] But it was not until the New York World's Fair in 1939 that the fledgling medium gained high profile visibility before some eager potential buyers. The following year, electronics manufacturer Allen B. DuMont opened a Gotham TV station and announced plans for a chain that would embrace his own surname. NBC rallied in 1941 with a station hookup linking New York City, Philadelphia and Schenectady. Each had the capability of relaying shows from one of the outlets to the others, although no regular series was scheduled.

CBS and NBC obtained licenses for commercial programming on their New York stations on July 1, 1941. But by the end of the year the outbreak of the Second World War stunted growth and hindered innovative programming. The requirements for manufacturing sets and for advancing new technology were largely channeled into the war effort, a major setback for those with longtime screen dreams that were again put on hold. Not quite all of TV's creativity was dead, however. Some of it even emerged during the sunlit hours.

The first of the daytime dramas may have been a hazily recalled narrative on a Philadelphia station in 1942, *Last Year's Nest*.[6] Airing in the early evening once a week over the Philco Corporation's WPT (later renamed WPTZ), an outlet offering a handful of Philco set purchasers (and others) something to see, the feature was a dramatic anthology. Scenery was almost non-existent for the primitive trial (a trial, possibly, in more ways than one). Many years afterward, Leonard Valenta, who became one of the directors of *As the World Turns* down the road a spell, recalled acting opposite Louise Bolger on *Last Year's Nest*.

When he portrayed Abraham Lincoln, Valenta remembered a tinted cardboard background placed on the set. It was so slender that if the TV camera swung a foot to either side of it the audience would be looking at stagehands! Each week's performance offered a new story with newly minted characters. With the same actors featured in every episode, however, the viewers received an impression of connecting with the prior — and upcoming — shows. In that sense they were exposed to a fundamental element of serialized fiction.

Valenta had the opportunity to ply his thespian craft on a later series, *Action in the Afternoon* (broadcast over CBS for a full year in 1953–54). The actors and TV crew were as mesmerized as the viewers at home when the series moved outside for some live adventures. Shootouts in Western towns while droning airline engines crisscrossed the sky above were emblematic of those early efforts. Despite the drama's negligible funding, the project fascinated nearly everybody who encountered those never-before-witnessed exploits.

When the war ended in 1945, people within the broadcasting industry who were pushing TV — which most of the country had yet to experience — moved heaven and earth to secure a permanent foothold. As more stations went on the air, not much programming existed prior to six o'clock in the evening (when a small cadre of viewers might be available in larger markets). In August 1946 the NBC station in New York, WNBT, transmitted some of its nightly series to Schenectady for simultaneous airing. By October, WNBT and WPTZ in Philadelphia were airing each other's shows. That same month Dumont relayed some nighttime features originating over its WABD in New York City to its WTTG in Washington, D.C. The following month NBC started telecasting what may have been the first network daytime series, *NCAA Football*.[7] The stage was set for much more!

In 1946 a CBS station in Chicago became the very first to telecast one of the more popular quarter-hour radio serials of the day in a one-time test.[8] (Some authorities claim this transpired as early as 1944, even though a preponderance of historians cite 1946.[9]) There was no attempt to act out the plot of *Big Sister* on that occasion; there were no props or simplistic sets surrounding the performers. The troupe merely gathered about a microphone and read their lines from scripts, just as they were accustomed to doing in an audio-only venue. For the production, however, hot lights raised the studio temperatures to an estimated 120 degrees, and a camera was trained on the subjects, shipping their black-and-white images over the ether to tiny distant video receivers. Although the experiment — for that's what it was — was of little consequence in itself, it permitted a small corps of early viewers in the Windy City to contemplate what might lie ahead. It also gave the networks, the advertisers and the producers something to ruminate about for the future. Certainly the implications of the single-shot venture conducted that day would extend far beyond the barriers of time, substance and geography.

The year 1946 turned out to be a fairly important one in the timeline of the nascent screened soap opera. That summer the General Electric station in Schenectady, WRGB, telecast *War Bride*, a serialized tale completed in 13 installments. It concerned a newlywed GI returning home with his young wife from the Second World War. His new bride proved unwelcome to both his sorrowing mom and his ex-fiancée.

There may very well have been other daytime serials offered on local stations elsewhere, but it would take the networks to give real credence and impetus to the televised soap opera. And some fledgling seeds sown in that soil were about to sprout.

That very same year, 1946, the Dumont web (which linked outlets in New York and Washington, D.C. *only*) telecast what a pair of pundits credited as "the first example on network television of a durable and tear-stained program type — the soap opera." The effort contained many of the elements that contemporary serial fans long ago came to expect — a couple of broads chasing one guy, a dysfunctional family, a heap of envy, a pile of resentment and heartaches aplenty, all gathered together in complicated plotting. There was also an announcer urging the audience to "tune in next time," a sure holdover from radio. But this daytime drama aired once a week and at night. The half-hour *Faraway Hill* premiered at 9 p.m. Eastern Time on Wednesday, October 2, 1946. It left the small screens for the last time only a dozen weeks later on December 18.

That amorous allegory involved a widowed, affluent New York sophisticate who went to the farm to visit relatives after her spouse died, actually seeking emotional refuge. Conflict erupted with the backwater brigade when heroine Karen St. John habitually displayed noticeable fits of haughtiness. At the same time she developed a passionate affection for a lad whom the farm folks had taken in and adopted. The country clan had promised him their daughter's hand in marriage, setting up the inevitable romantic triangle.

Broadway actress Flora Campbell, who would be one of CBS-TV's major daytime heroines (*Valiant Lady*) a few years later, was featured in the lead role of Karen St. John. Campbell played in several early TV soaps, including *The Edge of Night, Love of Life, The Secret Storm* and *The Seeking Heart*. Mel Brandt was the object of her affections. He turned up in the 1950s narrating two NBC daytime serials, *From These Roots* and *Modern Romances*. There were also a lot of unknowns awaiting discovery among *Faraway Hill's* performers: Julie Christy, Barry Doig, Munroe Gabler, Bill Gale, Eve McVeagh, Melville Galliart, Jack Halloran, Vivian King, Ben Low, Frederic Meyer, Lorene Scott, Ann Stell, Hal Studer and Jacqueline Waite.

The producer-director-writer of that early primetime effort, David P. Lewis, possibly thinking his serial would eventually develop into a daytime soap opera, reportedly sought formulas that didn't demand total viewer concentration. He claimed the housewives should be able "to turn away and go on peeling potatoes or knitting."[10] Lewis concocted a stream-of-consciousness technique, an off-screen voice that probed the heroine's thoughts. He inserted still other unique devices into the drama.

> On the initial episode the various characters were introduced with their names and relationships shown on the screen, so that viewers could keep everyone straight. Each subsequent episode began with a recap of what had gone before (illustrated by slides from the shows) and a reminder of who was who, narrated in emotional tones by Karen.... Occasional film sequences were worked into the otherwise live show to depict such details as passing trains. The whole production was done on an absolutely minimal budget of $300 per week.[11]

Innovative ideas, but if you're still wondering why the series perished after just 12 weeks, read the last sentence once more for a telltale clue. One pundit observed that occasionally the show added film shot on location, "a costly endeavor that would become popular on soap operas thirty years later"[12] — but unthinkable on a show produced for 300 bucks! The take-home pay for actors and crew must have amounted to virtually nothing.

Not long afterward, Irna Phillips — who created the original soap opera in 1930 with all of its manifest trappings, and who was a prolific letter writer in addition to script plotter — expressed surprising doubts about then-current attempts to launch soap operas on TV. In a 1948 epistle to Procter & Gamble official William Ramsey, the maven of matinee melodrama allowed: "I have had very little interest in television from a daytime standpoint, and unless a technique could be evolved whereby the auditory could be followed without the constant attention to the visual as far as the home maker is concerned, I see no future for a number of years in televising the serial story."[13] (Eat your words, Irna!) Those perceptions, mind you, came from a woman who would introduce her first daytime serial to TV only four months later! And as a result of that initial project (though the solo effort itself was a complete failure) she would fall utterly in love with the new medium and ordain it as the wave of the future!

These Are My Children, a new appellation for Phillips' *Today's Children* radio narrative, appeared over NBC-TV from Chicago, Monday through Friday, at 5 p.m. between January 31 and February 25, 1949. (All times cited herewith are Eastern.) It was the very first major TV network daytime serial, and — after only four weeks — was also branded as the one with the briefest run. Its quick demise was attributed to a notice by American Telephone & Telegraph Company that the Eastward coaxial cable from Chicago wouldn't be accessible for program transmissions starting May 1, 1949, some two months after the serial was withdrawn. Even so, *Billboard* magazine revealed that the NBC brass was disenchanted with the finished product and believed series from the East Coast would achieve greater program excellence in the future. The reviews were spotty, too, with *Variety*, an industry bible, suggesting such fare faced "tough sledding" and conceding that the actors "won't win any awards." *Television World* chided: "There is no place on television for this type of program; a blank screen is preferable."

The drama's storyline concerned family life in postwar America. Its focal clan, the Henehans, consisted of a matriarch, a weak son, the son's wastrel spouse, an egotistical daughter, still another girl, plus an aunt and a caring young woman who rented a room in the Henehan domicile. Anyone familiar with the prior plotting of *Today's Children* and *Painted Dreams* will readily recognize the many parallels in this Phillips escapade.

Ironically, of the eight recurring cast members in *These Are My Children*, seven of them apparently never appeared on another TV series, daytime or primetime, sliding into oblivion after their ephemeral moment of fame. Were the grueling demands of memorization, protracted rehearsals, hot lights and low wages not worth those 15 minutes of notoriety? Or was the competition for future roles not long afterward so strenuous that these actors were simply incapable of winning any more parts? Whatever the individual cases, their fleeting encounters with destiny resulted in less-than-spectacular conclusions to a handful of budding careers that promised so much only a few weeks before.

Only one, Eloise Kummer, who played Katherine Carter, the Henehans' boarder, got another shot at video on a short-lived soap called *The Bennetts* (1953–54). Kummer was still a proficient daytime artist, having played in several earlier radio narratives: *Backstage Wife, Betty and Bob, The Guiding Light, Lone Journey* (as the heroine), *The Right to Happiness* (heroine for the first three years, 1939–42), *Road of Life* and *The Story of Mary Marlin*. Kummer also appeared in *American Women* (as narrator), *Hot Copy* (as the lead), *Dear Mom* and *Silver Eagle, Mountie*. She was the only remnant of that earliest NBC soap opera company (beyond creator-writer Irna Phillips, of course) to survive the ordeal — and then only for one additional fling before hanging up her own run forever.

Even before *These Are My Children* was rudely halted, video's second daytime drama debuted over the Dumont network. *A Woman to Remember*, created by John Haggart, who was penning the radio scripts of *The Brighter Day* at about the same time, premiered on February 21, 1949, at 3 p.m.[14] Its heroine wasn't wholly dismissed overnight — she persisted unsponsored for 10 weeks in daytime through April 29 before transferring to 7:15 p.m. each weekday starting May 2, 1949. It was the first and only time a daytime soap has moved to primetime for more than an exclusive episode. There the series languished for another two-and-a-half months until it was cancelled on July 15, 1949. A couple of wits wryly opined,

"A more appropriate title might have been *A Woman to Forget*."[15] The feature was to be Dumont's singular attempt at putting a true daytime serial on the air.

Christine Baker, the heroine, was a mythical radio soap opera lead who interacted with Steve Hammond, imaginary program director and Christine's fiancé. She mingled with colleagues Bessie Thatcher, an actress, and Charley Anderson, a sound technician, and with a nemesis, Carol Winstead, a strident social and career challenger. Of the five members of the *real* cast of actors, only one — John Raby, in the part of Steve Hammond — had established a long legacy of playing in radio dishpan dramas: *Amanda of Honeymoon Hill*, *The Brighter Day*, *House in the Country*, *Joyce Jordan, M.D.*, *Our Gal Sunday*, *Wendy Warren and the News* and *When a Girl Marries*. The others had little or no track record before *A Woman to Remember*.

Unfortunately, Dumont's television theater, which was located in the basement of Wanamaker's department store, was so small that, as one ingénue recalled, the cast stayed put in the scenes, unable to move about freely on the minuscule sets. As there were no dressing rooms, performers changed clothes in the restrooms. There was only one camera available, and one three-hour rehearsal before airtime. The show's entire budget was a paltry $1,750 weekly! The quintet of thespians each received a hundred dollars per week, a far smaller sum than they would have earned for a similar 15-minute radio serial. And on radio they wouldn't have had to memorize lines and would have spent far fewer hours perfecting their performances. They knew they were breaking new ground on behalf of a fledgling operation (Dumont) that might not survive — and perhaps considered it a golden opportunity to achieve superior visibility. But it was literally a tough way to make a few greenbacks.

One day the air conditioning system quit in the cramped Wanamaker quarters. Five stagehands, overcome by heat exhaustion, fainted. Another time, radio veteran John Raby, playing the male lead in *A Woman to Remember*, did what he had to do when a petrified actress tried to leap from the scene before it was over. Raby seized her, pressed her into a chair and restrained her. "I can *guess* what you came to tell me," he said emotionally. While she flailed frantically, he uttered her lines as well as his own. When the scene ended he proceeded to the bathroom and vomited. Such were the horrors of live television.

Parenthetically, from September 6, 1949, through January 10, 1950, the Dumont network tried reprising a weekly nighttime serial, *The O'Neills*, that radio had made popular (ultimately it had aired on all four major chains between 1934 and 1943). The yarn centered on a widowed ladies fashion designer, Peggy O'Neill (played by Vera Allen), in the little hamlet of Royalton, and her struggles with a pair of fatherless children. A cantankerous uncle, a prying friend and a couple of neighbors filled out the cast of regulars. One pundit assessed: "Actresses Janice Gilbert [as daughter Janice O'Neill] and Jane West [as inquisitive Mrs. Bailey] were veterans of the radio show, but their presence was not enough to save the video version of it, which folded after a few months." With the exception of the nighttime *One Man's/Woman's Experience* that Dumont carried for six months in the 1952–53 season (serialized adaptations of classical literature, realistically *not* soap opera), for all intents and purposes Dumont's few attempts at programming the form died when *The O'Neills* was withdrawn.

NBC-TV also sought to capitalize on its enormous radio success with its homefolks drama *One Man's Family*, originally at night and later as a daytime serial. Both tries proved less than stimulating. The narrative was introduced to viewers on November 4, 1949, and ran through June 21, 1952, as a weekly half-hour primetime feature. Because this volume is focused on daytime programming, however, a detailed description of the story of the Barbours is reserved for Chapter Four, where it appears in its proper chronological daytime sequence.

With several sunshine serial casualties already tabulated (although they imparted plenty of education and experience as they unfolded), television was about to launch another daylight effort. *The First Hundred Years*, with a weekly production budget of $11,500, arrived on CBS-TV on December 4, 1950, at 2:30 p.m. The drama persevered all the way to June 27, 1952, missing the mark projected in its title by roughly 98-and-a-half years.

CBS, meanwhile, touted the serial as a landmark breakthrough in daytime programming, which in effect it was. In a press release issued October 6, 1950, the web boasted: "The first major program sale in network daytime television, sponsorship of a daily serial by Procter & Gamble Co. on the full interconnected CBS-TV Network, has been announced by J. L. Van Volkenburg, CBS Vice President in Charge of Network Sales." The puff piece went on to cite P&G as "one of radio's biggest advertisers," spelling out 11 weekday quarter-hour series and two weekly half-hours that P&G was then underwriting on CBS Radio. The new TV venture for Tide detergent was to be merely the tip of the iceberg for daytime P&G involvement, of course, an involvement that persists to this day.

One reviewer declared that author Jean Holloway "all but doomed *The First Hundred Years* to an early death from the very beginning" because she created "a soap opera with a sense of humor."[16] The pundit scolded: "Soap audiences wanted to cry, not laugh." Yet another authority caustically proclaimed: "Holloway was writing with radio conventions in mind and with no regard for the visual possibilities of TV. Holloway also brought her radio-oriented drama to *Love of Life* almost thirty years later, contributing to that show's untimely demise in 1980."[17]

In spite of Holloway's perceived handicaps, *The First Hundred Years* demonstrated that serialized fiction could survive for more than a few weeks on the tube—all the longevity the form had shown up until then. Historians of the genre still point to it as the first televised soap opera of any consequence. Gloria Monty, in fact, who in the 1980s and 1990s was to be the executive producer of one of the premier daytime dramas, ABC-TV's *General Hospital*, cut her teeth for that assignment by producing *The First Hundred Years*.

The First Hundred Years sprang from an inconsequential 1948 ABC Radio summertime feature that was reprised in early 1950 on a Monday night dramatic anthology labeled *Silver Theater* (from October 9, 1949, to July 10, 1950, CBS-TV). Jimmy Lydon and William Frawley appeared in the video cast. Soapmaker Procter & Gamble, daytime radio's foremost commercial sponsor, subsequently resolved to blend the show into that firm's initial foray into daytime TV serials. Lydon and Frawley were expected to continue. But before the show went on the air, Frawley signed for the memorable role of Fred Mertz on CBS-TV's *I Love Lucy* that debuted on October 15, 1951. Billions of viewers across several continents and generations instantly recognize his face as a result of that career decision.

The theme (and name) of *The First Hundred Years* was inspired by a dated maxim: "The first hundred years are the most difficult in marriage." At the time, CBS claimed, "Its emphasis is on hilarious comedy, bordering on the farce, about the ludicrous aspects of young married life."

Lydon, then 27, who earlier had been cast in mostly lighter radio roles after his launch as a juvenile on *Let's Pretend*, continued in the part of Chris Thayer. A reviewer lamented that signing him as the male lead was "a crucial stumbling block" to the show's success. "Lydon's claim to fame was playing the title role in the lucrative Henry Aldrich film series," the source cautioned. A few years earlier Jimmy Lydon was grinning at the American public from dozens of magazine covers, the prototype of the typical, freckle-faced American boy. After two years of posing as a model, the native New Yorker played in multiple Broadway productions before he embarked on celluloid pursuits that led to nine Henry Aldrich motion pictures. The pundit continued, "His portrayal of the gawky, scatterbrained teenager left such a strong mark that viewers had difficulty accepting him in a romantic leading role. Critics [also] accused the fledgling series [itself] of being a talky, televised radio program."[18]

Lydon appeared opposite two virtual unknowns, Olive Stacey (to early 1952) and Anne Sargent (thereafter), who portrayed his bride, Connie Martin Thayer. Following their nuptials during the show's first week on the air, the couple moved into a crumbling three-story, seven-bedroom, bat-infested Victorian manor replete with a library, ballroom and mounds of dust, a gift from Connie's dad. The storyline revolved around contentious in-laws on both sides of the family, plus Connie's teenage sister Margy, who often empathized with the newlyweds, and ongoing struggles with the house itself, bills, work, etc. Newspaper critic John Crosby once carped that the drama featured the leisurely tempo characteristic of its type—the couple at last arrived at a country club social after being in transit for 11 days!

Footage was shot on Long Island and in Westchester County to provide bona fide backdrops of area cottages. The pioneering series introduced the teleprompter, a face-saving device that cued the actors with their lines when they had trouble recalling them before live cameras. In addition to the thespians, the show required a production crew of 27, plus an announcer, organist and product demonstrators. It started out with a weekly budget of $8,650, several times the going rate for a radio soap opera.

Organist Clarke Morgan composed a 32-bar mini-waltz that he titled "The First Hundred Years" as the show's theme song. Yet, while he played it five or six times during every installment, each time emerged as a different variation. Sometimes it was gentle and romantic in mood; on some occasions it was tinged with light humor; and at still other times it was darkly tragic. It was a curiosity, no doubt, and a motif that other serials coming along behind it would not embrace.

The series also established a rehearsal pattern that was to extend to several more daytime dramas launched during that decade. Each day the show's cast practiced for four-and-a-half hours on a stage at CBS's Deutscher Liederkranz Hall, a striking four-story turn-of-the-century brick structure situated on East Fifty-Eighth Street near Park Avenue in New York. Launched as a performing venue for German vocalists, by mid-century the formerly laid-back palace had been captured by video and all of its inherent pressures and extraordinary paraphernalia. (More detail surrounding this facility's intriguing history is included in Chapter Five.)

One of the thespians of that era, Hildy Parks of *Love of Life*, recounted her memories of Liederkranz Hall: "There was so little room there to move and work that ... you'd go right out a door and find yourself up against a studio wall."[19] The set, typically shown at angles, might include a divan, chair and table framed in front of a black velour curtain. Because they were so cramped, cameramen stewed over the prospect of shooting wildly off sets. The video soap opera was evolving in primitive stages—while literally occupying the same!

Another who regularly acted there, Jada Rowland, remembered: "We used to do shots on the back stairs of Liederkranz ... and we all thought that was very arty."[20] She observed that the adjacency of so many shows occupying the same facility meant that everybody interacted regularly. *Captain Kangaroo* was a next-door neighbor to *The Secret Storm* on which Rowland worked. An elephant ate her purse one day while a cow chased Gloria Monty, the drama's director. Meanwhile, Virginia Dwyer, who would perform on *As the World Turns* in future years, was spat on by a llama!

While a dressing room for stars didn't exist at Liederkranz Hall (each gender had its own changing room), it was an improvement over the bathroom robing facilities at Dumont. In time, when multiple daytime serials were produced at that site, rehearsal hours were deliberately scheduled separately to avoid overwhelming a single cramped make-up area.

Shortly before it left the air, *The First Hundred Years* climbed the ratings charts to join the top 10 among daytime televised features. It was still not enough to save the show from cancellation, however. Procter & Gamble suddenly yanked it from the schedule and replaced it with a soap opera that — as one reviewer theorized —"might actually last a hundred years." It was none other than the longest story ever told (as of this writing, at least), *The Guiding Light*. It will provide fodder for a couple of later chapters.

Several actors in *The First Hundred Years* went on to other roles in subsequent series. A radio veteran of hundreds of dramatic parts, Larry Haines made a few appearances in the series, and that undoubtedly projected him into a major role on CBS's *Search for Tomorrow*. He joined that show in late 1951 after it had been airing for only a few weeks. He was still playing Stu Bergman when the series came to an end more than 35 years later. Haines, an unknown in video until then, with only a bit part in the narrative, ultimately became the most celebrated thespian from *The First Hundred Years*.

NBC officials were watching all of this and saw an opportunity, perhaps an imperative, to act, and to do so promptly. They had not carried a televised daytime serial since the fateful Irna Phillips trailblazing venture *These Are My Children*, which disappeared after only four weeks in early 1949. Now that CBS was demonstrating at least a modicum of success with *The First Hundred Years*, NBC resolved to dip its toe into matinee waters for another try. On March 12, 1951, some three months following the inception of the first CBS serial, **Miss Susan** premiered at 3 p.m., with Colgate-Palmolive-Peet underwriting it. This clearly wouldn't be the end of NBC's search for a permanent daytime serial, however, as *Miss Susan* was also cancelled following a brief run, on December 28, 1951. But it had survived longer than the Peacock chain's first soap opera, offering hope for better dramas ahead.

Originating in Philadelphia, *Miss Susan* focused on a wheelchair-bound paraplegic, a feminine barrister whose love life was tempered by physical constraints. In the debut episode, the namesake heroine, Susan Martin, returned to her hometown of Martinsville, Ohio, in the company of a nurse-companion. Susan confronted Laura, the family housekeeper, who was accused of petty larceny. Concluding the episode, a narrator pondered, "Laura can't be a thief, or can she?" It sounded like radio. So did the trauma of the ever-present physical limitations that Susan and her intended, Bill Carter, encountered. He harped habitually on his desire to raise a large family, wholly unaware that she could not have children. Things between them would never be precisely the same once that bombshell dropped.

A real paralytic, rising film actress Susan Peters (paralyzed from the waist down after a 1944 hunting accident) appeared as Susan Martin. She had performed in a minor role in the 1941 release *Meet John Doe*, and was nominated the following year as Best Supporting Actress after playing in *Random Harvest* opposite Ronald Colman and Greer Garson. Following her spinal injury, Peters appeared in *The Sign of the Ram*, a 1948 motion picture release, in which she costarred alongside Alexander Knox and Phyllis Thaxter. Surmising that there wouldn't be many movie parts for a disabled actress, Peters quickly signed a contract when NBC offered her the lead in *Miss Susan*.

Later, when critics and fans complained that the show took advantage of the lead's tragic circumstances, the series was suddenly renamed *Martinsville, U.S.A.* and refocused on other figures. In September 1951— six months into the run —*Billboard* informed its readers that Peters was not well. That may have been true; she died at age 31 the following year of pneumonia and kidney failure.[21]

Shortly before Susan Peters' premature death, Colgate-Palmolive-Peet cancelled *Miss Susan/Martinsville, U.S.A.* to put its money into a daytime game show, *The Big Payoff*. It persisted through March 27, 1953, on NBC-TV and then on CBS-TV until it was withdrawn October 16, 1959, during the infamous quiz show scandals. (A syndicated version aired in 1962 after the storm quieted.) Some of its celebrated stars included Denise Lor, Randy Merriman, Bess Myerson, Robert Paige, Bert Parks and Bobby Sherwood. Regarding *Miss Susan/Martinsville, U.S.A.*'s cancellation, one observer moralized: "The press and viewers could then rest easy that they had rescued Peters from being exploited — and employed — five days a week."[22]

Actor Mark Roberts, who played Bill Carter, won roles in a trio of primetime TV series after his ephemeral experience on *Miss Susan/Martinsville, U.S.A.*: *Three Steps to Heaven* (1953–54), *The Brothers Brannagan* (1960–61) and *The Naked Truth* (1995–96, 1997–98). Most of the others in the serial's cast faded into oblivion.

Deciding to strike again while the iron was still lukewarm, NBC's executives put their next daytime serial on the air by borrowing a series that had already gained national exposure the previous year as a primetime summer replacement. ***Hawkins Falls*** (which debuted over a Chicago channel in 1946) ran at night on NBC-TV under the moniker *Hawkins Falls, Population 6,200* from June 17 to October 12, 1950. Initially it was on for an hour at 8 p.m. on Saturday, although it shifted to a half-hour at 8:30 p.m. on Thursday after August 19.

Roy Winsor created the show, a man who was to become one of daytime television's foremost figures in the not-too-distant future. (One wag dubbed him "the father of televised soap opera," a soubriquet that wears well.) Billed as a comedy-drama, the Chicago-based evening series contained an eclectic blend of situation comedy, light drama and music, although one pundit labeled it an "updated version" of radio's homespun yarn *Ma Perkins*. A real hamlet, Woodstock, Illinois, where some exterior sequences were filmed, served as a model for the village of Hawkins Falls, U.S.A. Shooting on location made *Hawkins Falls* one of television's most expensive soap productions of the time — and, according to one commentator, ultimately contributed to its demise.

Frank Dane, a veteran radio serial character actor (*Backstage Wife, The Guiding Light, Perry Mason, Road of Life*, et al.), appeared as Clate Weathers, editor of the town's journal. Each week he narrated local happenings as a sketch dramatized them. Multiple documentarians claim that Phillips H. (Phil) Lord, the creative force who brought *Gangbusters, Mr. District Attorney, David Harding — Counterspy, Treasury Agent, Seth Parker, We the People* and several other eminent radio series to the air, appeared as the serial's court judge. His daughter, Phillipa, nonetheless (while anxious to perpetuate her dad's legacy, yet convinced he never appeared on programs he didn't create, produce or direct), confirmed to this author that the actor identified as Phil Lord in *Hawkins Falls* was another thespian with that moniker.

In addition to the judge, the town of Hawkins Falls had room for a derelict, Laif Flaigle, as well as Belinda Catherwood, the local garden club ramrod. Each chapter in primetime exhibited a self-contained adventure without tying its action specifically to whatever transpired in a previous or succeeding performance.

When the show was overhauled for a daytime audience, it became a weekday drama with episodic plotting. Premiering before dusk at 5 p.m. on April 2, 1951, it continued to occupy that timeslot through July 3, 1953. The drama shifted to 11 a.m. on July 6, 1953, through January 8, 1954. On January 11, 1954, it moved to 12:15 p.m., where it ran until July 2, 1954. Its last time block was at 4 p.m. from July 5, 1954, through July 1, 1955, when it left the air forever. By then its four-year, three-month run had set a longevity record for NBC-TV daytime serials that was to remain unchallenged until *Young Doctor Malone* merely equaled it in 1963, nearly eight years later. *Hawkins Falls* was, in fact, its network's only open-end (continuing storyline) daytime serial in the 1950s to persist for more than two years until *From These Roots* arrived in 1958. With weekday production resources of just $10,250 per week two years beyond its premier, *Hawkins Falls*, though costly for a soap opera, was still one of the lowest budgeted properties on daytime television.

Despite its avowed intention to air its programming from the East Coast after the *These Are My Children* debacle, NBC reversed its policy and permitted *Hawkins Falls* to continue broadcasting from Chicago. Small town life was at the crux of the storyline; the show's musical theme chanted the familiar "Skip to My Lou, My Darling." One pundit told what took place in the opening installment and where the plot went from there.

> On the afternoon debut, ill, bedridden Knap Drewer befriended runaway Roy Bettert, and he and his wife Lona adopted Roy, stirring up much talk among local gossips, including busybody Mrs. Catherwood. Later developments included the standard soap opera story lines—divorces, murders, affairs, etc.—and the show lived up to its new subtitle, "A Television Novel." The Drewers mainly reacted to various subplots throughout the run, although Knap died when Frank Dane [who played that part] was judged too difficult to handle off the set, letting Lona wed Dr. Corey.
>
> Other characters were Toby Winfield and his wife April, who was expecting a baby; Laif Flagle, the town bum; Millie Flagle, Laif's one-time wife who received a marriage proposal from Sheriff Boylan in 1954; Mitch Fredericks, a local reporter who fended off the advances of young Jenny Karns; and Dr. Glen Bowdon, who became Dr. Corey's assistant.[23]

Or, as another reviewer succinctly put it, *Hawkins Falls* consisted of "tales of a remarried widow, her doctor husband and their gossipy small-town neighbors."

Hugh Downs, then near the start of his long television network career, was the announcer on the daytime *Hawkins Falls*. Hope Summers (as Belinda Catherwood), Win Stracke (Laif Flagle) and Phil Lord (the judge) reprised their roles from the nighttime rendering the year before. Tom Poston was among the notables in the daytime cast who went on to numerous bigger and better things: *The Steve Allen Show* (1956–59, 1961), *Split Personality* (1959–60), *To Tell the Truth* (1965–68), *On the Rocks* (1975–76), *We've Got Each Other* (1977–78), *Mork & Mindy* (1978–82), *Newhart* (1982–90), *Good Grief* (1990–91), *Bob* (1992–93) and *Grace Under Fire* (1995–98).

A trio of prolific radio thespians also made fleeting appearances in *Hawkins Falls*: Carlton KaDell, Arthur Peterson and Beverly Younger.

KaDell appeared in several action adventure series from the 1930s to the 1950s (*Tarzan, Wings of Destiny, Red Ryder, Armstrong of the SBI*). He announced some important features, like *Big Town* and *The Jack Carson Show*, and filled many character roles on daytime serials (*Backstage Wife, Masquerade, The Right to Happiness, Road of Life* and *The Romance of Helen Trent*), as well as on primetime dramatic programs.

Peterson was only 24 when he was tapped to play the cleric of Five Points, Dr. John Ruthledge, when *The Guiding Light* debuted on radio in 1937, a role he carried for nearly a decade. He supplied voices on the aural soapy sagas *Bachelor's Children, Girl Alone, The Story of Mary Marlin* and *Woman in White*. Elsewhere Peterson could be heard on *The Barton Family, The First Nighter, Silver Eagle — Mountie* and *Tom Mix*. In 1949 he starred in a weekly quarter-hour ABC-TV sitcom, *That's O'Toole*.

From 1937 to 1941 Beverly Younger played the namesake role in *Kitty Keene, Incorporated*, a daytime radio serial. She was also Mathilda Pendleton, the busybody spouse of the banker of Rushville Center in *Ma Perkins*. Younger played on the short-lived ABC-TV series *Studs' Place* in 1950, and subsequently turned up in the cast of another NBC-TV soap opera, *The Bennetts* (1953–54).

On July 5, 1954, NBC transferred *Hawkins Falls* out of a difficult spot against CBS's *Love of Life* at 12:15 p.m., a serial that had dominated its time slot since its inception three years earlier. *Hawkins Falls* was moved to what NBC hoped would be a relatively safe quarter-hour at 4 p.m. That very same day CBS shifted its minister's family narrative into the 4 p.m. slot, too. The two soap operas competed for a year; *Hawkins Falls* faltered so badly in the ratings it was removed altogether.

September 3, 1951, proved to be a defining date in the annals of soap opera telecasts. Not only was it history-making for the genre, it was also a red-letter celebration occasion for CBS. For many years that network would be able to boast that on September 3, 1951, its video serial fortunes literally took off. Two serials debuted on the same day on CBS-TV. One was predicted to become an instant winner, and it turned out to be a dud. It was cancelled before a year was over. The other hung around more than three-and-a-half decades, becoming a model for several other popular serials that followed. And just three weeks after that duo's launch, CBS added yet another important daytime drama that survived for nearly two decades. That web either got lucky or plainly had to be doing something right. Most likely, it was both.

In 1945 **The Egg and I** was a best-selling novel, exceeding a million copies in sales. City slicker Betty MacDonald detailed the amusing catastrophes she met while attempting to adjust to life on a chicken farm in Washington state. Two years later the book was turned into a hit motion picture starring Claudette Colbert and Fred MacMurray. Beginning in 1949 the producers milked the idea still further with a series of comedic films featuring the MacDonalds' neighbors, Ma and Pa Kettle. Marjorie Main and Percy Kilbride were featured as the adorable, zany Kettles who raised a large family in the country amid primitive trappings. Americans were laughing uproariously in theaters everywhere over their unpredictable, disarming performances. The film series included:

The Egg and I (1947)	*Ma and Pa Kettle on Vacation* (1953)
Ma and Pa Kettle (1949)	*Ma and Pa Kettle at Home* (1954)
Ma and Pa Kettle Go to Town (1950)	*Ma and Pa Kettle at Waikiki* (1955)
Ma and Pa Kettle Back on the Farm (1951)	*The Kettles in the Ozarks* (1956)
Ma and Pa Kettle at the Fair (1952)	*The Kettles on Old Macdonald's Farm* (1957)

By 1951 CBS purchased the rights to the title and filmed a half-hour audition with William Prince and Diana Lynn as the leads. But before it could be developed into a series, the web changed its mind and introduced it as a quarter-hour daytime serial instead. It was the first TV soap opera adapted from a motion picture, and the first altogether droll daytime serial. With a weekly production budget of $15,000, *The Egg and I* premiered

September 3, 1951, at 12 noon. CBS was utterly convinced it had a frontrunner in the property.

Parenthetically, one of the show's writers, Manya Starr, was an oft-unidentified wordsmith who earlier crossed her employer, the infamous Anne Hummert. Hummert and her husband, Frank, created more than 60 daytime radio serials, easily the most prolific producers of the breed. With a word, Anne Hummert could inspire terror in her dialoguers. Yet, undoubtedly without thinking about any potential reprisals, one day Starr challenged her superior. When Hummert instructed Starr to "include God on every page of every script," the scribe shot back: "And who will play the part?"[24] The redoubtable Ms. Hummert fired Starr on the spot, generating a tale that apparently boosted Starr to legendary status within the trade. (In 1954–55 Starr was to pen *First Love*, one of NBC-TV's more successful but all-too-brief serials.)

The Egg and I on television was faithful to the premise in Betty MacDonald's tome, which the Colbert-MacMurray celluloid version also emulated. The narrative wasn't typical of most daytime serials, of course, focusing on humor as opposed to pathos. After the MacDonalds arrived from the city on the chicken farm, the Kettles and handyman Jed Simmons routinely helped them adjust to rural life. The cast included Pat Kirkland and Betty Lynn as Betty MacDonald (Kirkland departed to have a baby in early 1952), John Craven as Bob MacDonald, Doris Rich as Ma Kettle, Frank Twedell as Pa Kettle, Grady Sutton as Jed Simmons and a few other recurring characters.

One source noted that ratings showed that, within a few months of its commencement, *The Egg and I* led all daily network shows telecast before 5 p.m. By February 1952 Procter & Gamble was underwriting the show two days a week, Tuesday and Thursday. That left the network to pick up the bulk of the production's tab, however. When P&G withdrew its support in June, no other firm stepped up to the plate. Radio serials continued to command larger audiences at that time, a convincing reason why prospective sponsors were reluctant to accept such heavy financial commitments in TV. *The Egg and I*, with no advertiser, left the air on August 1, 1952, becoming CBS's first daytime serial folly. A reviewer explained: "While certain soaps have comic elements, no comic soap has ever done well on daytime."[25]

Thirteen years later CBS turned the premise into gold. Airing at night, *Green Acres*, starring Eddie Albert and Eva Gabor, persisted for a half-dozen years (1965–71), one of several comical sitcoms in that era displaying rural life in the United States. Together those series made tens of millions of dollars in revenue for the chain that carried them. Whatever CBS paid for the rights to *The Egg and I* must have looked like chicken feed by comparison.

The chain's red-letter day, September 3, 1951, resulted from the inception of the long-running drama *Search for Tomorrow*. It was the first of several soap operas that offered real permanency among daytime narratives. In fact, it could be credited with single-handedly establishing the television soap opera. For 14 seasons that serial would never fall out of the first, second or third place ranking among all competing programs of its genre, frequently capturing the top spot. Before *Search for Tomorrow* there was little evidence that TV washboard weepers had stability or serious drawing power. That show proved otherwise, becoming the leader in a long line of popular episodic features that persuaded people to turn on their TV sets during the daylight hours. *Search for Tomorrow* is such an important daytime drama that it merits a separate chapter (see Chapter Eight).

With the inception of *Search for Tomorrow*, CBS-TV took an undeniable lead in soap opera development on the tube. Throughout the 1950s that web added several more compelling dramas to its daytime portfolio. The most popular of the type, in chronological order, were *Love of Life, The Guiding Light, The Secret Storm, As the World Turns* and *The Edge of Night.* Whatever the competition threw against them invariably paled by comparison. Together they became a formidable force on television's scene during the sunlit hours, maintaining a dominant position through an epoch that extended well into the succeeding decade. All of those imposing stories form the basis of separate chapter evaluations ahead (see Chapters 9–13).

There are plenty of opinions about when the golden age of television reached its culmination. Unlike network radio, which clearly dispersed after it was no longer a viable narrative medium, television continues. If we commonly submit that the golden age began in the late 1940s (respected academics favor varied years) with the inception of an escalating stream of live programming, when did it end? Some renowned authorities, frequently bearing prodigious credentials in analytical research, appear unable to agree on a specific date. But a few concur that it transpired about the time of the passing of live programming, when most primetime shows went to videotape, late in the 1950s. A sample of current thinking underscores the point.

Referring to 1960, one researcher allowed: "The so-called Golden Age of Television was on its way out. The term 'Golden Age' usually refers to the era of Sid Caesar and live nighttime television dramas like *Philco Playhouse, Armstrong Circle Theater,* and *Playhouse 90.*"[26] The last of several comedy-variety shows hosted by Sid Caesar ended in 1964. Published schedules indicate *Philco Playhouse* terminated in 1955, *Armstrong Circle Theater* in 1963 and *Playhouse 90* in 1960.

Another source confirmed: "In the nineteen-fifties, the so-called Golden Age of Television, before the advent of videotape recording, most TV drama was live, including the daytime serials."[27]

"The Fifties is known as the Golden Age of Television in large part because of the variety shows which dominated the early part of the decade," affirmed another.[28]

And finally: "The 'golden age' of American television generally refers to the proliferation of original and classic dramas produced for live television during America's postwar years. From 1949 to approximately 1960, these live dramas became the fitting programmatic complements to the game shows, westerns, soap operas and vaudeo shows (vaudeville and variety acts on TV) that dominated network television's prime time schedule."[29]

This author recalls sitting in a college classroom in early 1960 when a discussion about television ensued. Living in a dormitory and working every day outside the pursuits of academia while having little access to a television set, the writer was literally stunned to hear the professor state that "almost all TV programming has gone to film — there's hardly any live programming left." The preponderance of thought gleaned from multiple sources (including several beyond those already quoted) indicate that the year 1960 might be an appropriate cutoff date for this text.

Put simply, the daytime serials that debuted on television between 1946 and 1960 are highlighted in this volume; those premiering in 1960 and beyond aren't. Our concentration is on the earliest years of the new medium, characterized by black-and-white images of actors performing on low-budget sets under primitive and often trying circumstances. Stay tuned for the next exciting chapter.

4

In Need of a Fix

The coaxial cable carrying television programming was completed to the West Coast in September 1951.[1] For the very first time America could experience national TV from coast to coast. That factor doubtlessly contributed appreciably to the early success of *Search for Tomorrow*, launched by CBS-TV on September 3, 1951.

It was the beginning of an era that permitted the web to occupy the catbird seat among television daytime serial programmers for nearly two decades. It must have seemed to others that no competitor was ever let in on whatever secrets CBS acquired on how to make TV soap operas click. While NBC was winning in primetime in the early 1950s with features like *Dragnet, Kraft Television Theater, The Texaco Star Theater* and *Your Show of Shows*, not one contender arose to seriously threaten CBS's daytime supremacy. With the exception of a handful of negligible missteps, virtually everything CBS sent out over the ether resonated with the folks at home. Its triumphs were so complete and so frequent that CBS habitually kept its only legitimate rival for daytime programming, NBC, off balance and sputtering for fresh ideas. Parenthetically, by mid-decade CBS-TV had also overtaken its rival in primetime, too, with *Arthur Godfrey and His Friends, The Ed Sullivan Show, Gunsmoke, I Love Lucy, The Jack Benny Program, The Red Skelton Show, Studio One* and several others.

Figures compiled by the A. C. Nielsen Company's Nielsen Media Research confirm the web's unequivocal lead in daytime serial programming during television's golden age. Nielsen posts annual ratings that estimate the percentage of American homes tuned to various series. Witness the leaders of the breed. (Numbers indicate composite annual rankings.)

1952–53

Search for Tomorrow	CBS	16.1
Love of Life	CBS	15.1
Hawkins Falls	NBC	13.7
The Guiding Light	CBS	11.3

1953–54

Search for Tomorrow	CBS	15.8
The Guiding Light	CBS	14.4
Love of Life	CBS	14.0
Valiant Lady	CBS	10.2

1954–55

Search for Tomorrow	CBS	15.2
The Guiding Light	CBS	14.6
Love of Life	CBS	13.1
Valiant Lady	CBS	10.5
The Secret Storm	CBS	8.5
Modern Romances	NBC	8.5
The Brighter Day	CBS	8.4

1955–56

Search for Tomorrow	CBS	13.1

The Guiding Light	CBS	13.0
Love of Life	CBS	10.9
The Brighter Day	CBS	10.5
The Secret Storm	CBS	10.2
Valiant Lady	CBS	9.2

1956–57

The Guiding Light	CBS	11.4
Search for Tomorrow	CBS	11.0
The Secret Storm	CBS	10.0
The Edge of Night	CBS	9.7
The Brighter Day	CBS	9.2
Love of Life	CBS	9.1
Modern Romances	NBC	9.0
As the World Turns	CBS	8.4

1957–58

The Guiding Light	CBS	10.1
As the World Turns	CBS	9.9
The Verdict Is Yours	CBS	9.9
Search for Tomorrow	CBS	9.8
The Edge of Night	CBS	9.7

| The Secret Storm | CBS | 9.7 |
| The Brighter Day | CBS | 9.3 |

1958–59

As the World Turns	CBS	9.8
Search for Tomorrow	CBS	9.8
The Guiding Light	CBS	9.7
The Verdict Is Yours	CBS	8.7
The Edge of Night	CBS	8.6
The Secret Storm	CBS	8.6
The Brighter Day	CBS	8.2

1959–60

As the World Turns	CBS	9.9
The Guiding Light	CBS	9.6
The Edge of Night	CBS	9.5
Search for Tomorrow	CBS	9.5
The Secret Storm	CBS	8.9
The Verdict Is Yours	CBS	8.6
The Brighter Day	CBS	8.2

Total entries: 50

Tally by chain: CBS — 47, NBC — 3

ABC, for its part, avoided daytime programming for years, almost as if it was a plague. While holding operating costs of that financially struggling network down, it also denied the American viewers another choice in a day in which cable was far off in the distance. ABC-TV finally submitted a half-hour dramatic anthology, *The Road to Reality*, in late 1960, but it was gone in less than six months.

Dumont, as noted already, never attempted another daytime serial after *A Woman to Remember* collapsed in 1949. (To be inclusive, however, it must be noted that it programmed a weekly daytime quarter-hour between October 6, 1952, and April 3, 1953, that presented dramatic adaptations of serialized classics. It featured men one week and women the next under the appropriate monikers *One Man's Experience* and *One Woman's Experience*, altered later to *One Man's Story* and *One Woman's Story*. To label the series a soap opera would be stretching the definition, however.) In 1956 the Dumont network went belly-up and ceased operations altogether.

Meanwhile, with rare exceptions (and then only minimally), NBC left a surfeit of matinee serial carnage scattered all throughout the decade as one failed experiment dissolved into another. Between 1949 and 1960 the Peacock chain premiered 22 daytime dramatic series. Only four persisted beyond a couple of years (*Hawkins Falls, Modern Romances, From These Roots* and *Young Doctor Malone*).

Not until ABC became serious about daytime programming, and NBC eventually figured out its mistakes and decided to do something about them, did CBS even begin to face any serious rivalry for the serial viewer. Incredulously, it took ABC nearly 30 years (well into the 1970s) to reach parity with CBS and NBC in audience size.[2] The destiny of the rival networks didn't begin to modify until both introduced separate medical dramas on a single day. On April 1, 1963, ABC bowed with *General Hospital* while NBC premiered *The Doctors*. Viewers flocked to both within a short while. Two-and-a-half years later NBC inaugurated an enormously compelling drama, *Days of Our Lives*. It finally seemed that the network's long national *daymare* was over.

But we are getting ahead of our story.

From NBC's failed daytime soap opera attempts with *These Are My Children* in 1949 (lasting four weeks) and *Miss Susan* in 1951 (nine months), and a modicum of success experienced by *Hawkins Falls* (1951–55) and a few other features in the late 1950s, after many tries NBC had no sustained advantage in the sunshine hours of the golden age. The reader may discover some of the reasons for that outcome after venturing through the 1950s and surveying NBC's maneuvers to alter daytime's landscape.

Before continuing, it's important to introduce a topic that, for unfamiliar readers, at least, will cause confusion when it surfaces later unless there has been some modest interpretation of its distinguishing patterns. It concerns the terms "open-end" and "closed-end" dramas.

By far the predominant style among soap operas has always been the open-end narrative. It was that way in radio, and later held true in television. The "open-end" scheme is characterized by a tale that hypothetically never ends. It unfolds gradually while meandering unimpeded over lengthy periods of time (that's the premise anyway), and it may extend for years and possibly decades. (There are several contemporary examples the reader may recall.) A permanent group of figures interacts and mingles with other characters that are added to a cast from time to time; the newcomers may become enduring members of the troupe or may disappear from the plot after a while.

Conversely, a soap opera with a "closed-end" storyline predictably reaches an anticipated ending, sometimes called an "ultimate conclusion drama." When a tale is over, a new yarn with a new protagonist and support players is introduced. Often there is a continuing narrator, host or hostess to connect each episode. While no such daytime drama currently airs as of this writing, several anthology-type features were staples of television's earliest decade (*Hotel Cosmopolitan, The House on High Street, Modern Romances, The Verdict Is Yours, Way of the World*, et al.). The narratives were played out in anywhere from one performance to five weeks of installments. Several persisted for a week's duration before a new story was introduced.

The open-end soap operas, meanwhile, never ended —*except once* (when the network or advertiser pulled the plug and they were cancelled). Then there was (and still is) a rush to tidy up many of the loose ends of a dangling storyline. These two distinctive types of soap operas will be encountered many times throughout this book, so it is imperative that the reader be cognizant of their differences.

And now ... back to our story.

Following *Hawkins Falls*' premier, the next entry NBC brought to the small screen was **Fairmeadows, U.S.A.**, ostensibly the only network soap opera to be telecast on Sunday. It debuted at 3 p.m. on November 4, 1951, in a weekly half-hour format.

In the plotting, John Olcott had just moved his family — including his spouse Alice, oldest daughter Mary, son Jim and youngest daughter Evie — back to their hometown of Fairmeadows where he hoped they could start all over. John's associate in business in an unidentified metropolis had borrowed $250,000 against the company's assets, then gambled it away and ultimately committed suicide. All of this transpired before the serial's launch (in what is commonly known as the backstory). Now in their new digs, John took over the Fairmeadows general store as proprietor. The Olcotts didn't have long to make an impression on their new neighbors, however; the sponsor cancelled and the show left the airwaves on April 27, 1952, just six months into the run.

Never say die, however.

In an unusual rotation, that next autumn the narrative resumed as the third quarter-hour of *The Kate Smith Show* (4–5 p.m. on NBC-TV), a variety hodgepodge hosted by the fabled singer. The drama appeared under the new moniker *The House in the Garden*. There were also a couple of casting changes.

In the Sunday afternoon incarnation Howard St. John played protagonist John Olcott. St. John was then having a field day as third, fourth or fifth banana in a string of popular movies: *711 Ocean Drive* (1950), *David Harding, Counterspy* (1950), *The Men* (1950), *Born Yesterday* (1950), *Strangers on a Train* (1951), *Three Coins in the Fountain* (1954), *The Tender Trap* (1955), *One, Two, Three* (1961), *Sex and the Single Girl* (1964) and *Don't Drink the Water* (1969). From 1966 to 1970 St. John played various supporting figures on CBS-TV's *The Jackie Gleason Show*.

Lauren Gilbert replaced St. John as Olcott in *The House in the Garden* on weekdays. Gilbert later accepted fleeting steppingstone character parts on ill-fated TV dramas like *Three Steps to Heaven* (1953–54) and *Concerning Miss Marlowe* (1954–55) to get to the meatier role of mobster Uncle Harry Lane on *The Edge of Night* (1956–59). He also secured several recurring appearances on *Love of Life* (1958).

When the story evolved into *The House in the Garden*, most of the *Fairmeadows, U.S.A.* troupe remained intact, the only further substitution being Monica Lovett for Hazel Dawn Jr. as the elder daughter Mary. (The complete cast lineup is included in Appendix C for this serial and others shown during TV's golden age.)

None of the rejuvenation efforts were enough to create long-term success, however, and the yarn disappeared before Kate Smith's season was over. The following season Smith offered her viewers a sketch that was titled *The World of Mr. Sweeney* (to be encountered again elsewhere in this chapter). Sweeney was also a general store proprietor. *World* departed from Smith's show to become a humorous soap opera in a separate daily quarter-hour timeslot, persisting on its own for 15 months.

In the summer of 1953 NBC introduced a trio of daytime serials, pitching them in the hour *before* CBS's winning soap opera lineup placed the homemakers under its spell. **The Bennetts** was the first of the triumvirate and broadcast live from Chicago, a city that NBC-TV executives had indicated was unsatisfactory as an origination point just four years earlier. (That group was to contradict itself on this matter several times in the days ahead.) The new series premiered on July 6, 1953, at 11:15 a.m. It was to last but six months, to January 8, 1954.

In the imaginary hamlet of Kingsport, attorney Wayne Bennett and his wife Nancy were perpetually mired in the complicated calamities of a few friends, some of those jams requiring legal aid. At the storyline's zenith was the theme of childless neighbors Blaney and Meg Cobb being duped by an illicit adoption bureau. At one point Wayne vindicated his pal Bert Wells of thievery charges only to later discover Bert was guilty. Bert further revealed plans to marry his secretary, Helen Meade, by divorcing his bride of 15 months. In only a half-year the series managed to wallow in a profusion of pure melodramatic goo.

That said, the serial showcased a trio of actresses who demonstrated skilled and experienced artisanship.

Eloise Kummer, who portrayed Nancy Bennett in the soap's latter days, was the most practiced. Her radio repertoire included *Backstage Wife, Betty and Bob, Lone Journey, The Guiding Light, Road of Life, The Story of Mary Marlin* and *The Right to Happiness* (1939–42, as the original Carolyn Allen, the show's heroine), before that drama left Chicago for New York. She also played in NBC-TV's first short-lived soap opera, *These Are My Children* (1949).

Beverly Younger, portraying Meg Cobb in *The Bennetts*, was a heroine on radio's *Kitty Keene Incorporated*, and appeared in the casts of *Ma Perkins* and NBC-TV's *Hawkins Falls* (1952–53).

Viola Berwick, who was Speedy Winters in *The Bennetts*, was on radio's *Road of Life* and *Scattergood Baines*. When *The Bennetts* departed she turned up that same year (1954) on NBC-TV's *A Time to Live*.

A month following *The Bennetts*' debut, NBC brought two new serials to the small screen on a single day, August 3, 1953: *Follow Your Heart* at 11:45 a.m., which vanished after five months (along with *The Bennetts*) on January 8, 1954; and *Three Steps to Heaven*, initially at 11:30 a.m., departing on December 25, 1953, only to be brought back on March 1, 1954, at 10:45 a.m., and fading until biting the dust at last on December 31, 1954. At least one performance of *Three Steps to Heaven*, on March 23, 1954, was shown in color, undoubtedly as a test of equipment, operating systems and technical staff.

The first of the new duo, **Follow Your Heart**, recounted the tale of a Philadelphia debutante, Julie Fielding, who turned against the affluent, well-connected young man (Harry Phillips) her mother had picked for her. Instead she falls for an FBI envoy, Peter Davis, who was rejected by her mom for not being listed in the Social Register. The narrative took off from there and focused on the up-sides and down-sides of their budding courtship.

Shunning the idea of developing a new premise, author Elaine Sterne Carrington simply borrowed the 1939 storyline that she had employed on her debuting radio soap opera *When a Girl Marries*. (Over a long career Carrington also penned the popular radio serials *Pepper Young's Family* and *Rosemary*, plus a couple of lesser-known drainboard dramas.) She also drew on the names of her radio characters as she assigned monikers to the TV figures. Radio heroine Joan Field became Julie Fielding in the video reenactment. The man Joan married after six months on radio was Harry Davis; the man TV's Julie was set to marry was Harry Phillips before she dropped him for Peter Davis. When Carrington found appellations she liked, she stuck with them. And in both the radio and television versions, it was a case of mistaken identity that brought the lovers together—each time the family thought the young man had arrived to tune the piano. By 1953 Carrington must have reasoned that surely nobody would remember all of those little details from 14 years ago! (Given the eventual outcome, either they did remember, or they never liked the thesis in the first place.)

When the reworked scripts didn't draw an appreciable audience to TV, the plot was radically revamped. Julie and Peter's romance was toned down, and Peter's career of chasing thugs became the theme of paramount importance, leaving *Follow Your Heart* as an awkward title for a spy thriller filled with shady figures and nefarious dealings. Still, almost nobody tuned in and the series was hastily withdrawn—three weeks before the planned nuptials of Julie and Peter, divesting the drama of any gratifying finish for the few fans that had stuck with it. Viewers missed a mobster-managed kidnapping of the heroine and her last-minute rescue by the dashing young hero that had been scheduled just prior to their wedding. It wasn't a smooth finish from any vantage point.

"Perhaps it was *Follow Your Heart*'s efforts to move with the times, to grapple with what were felt to be more serious and adult themes, that proved its undoing," one critic postulated. "If it had concentrated more on the emotional struggles of its characters with each other, and less on rickety plotting based on world doom ... it might have developed and held a place for itself on television. It might even be with us still."

Follow Your Heart was Mrs. Carrington's first and final attempt to write a televised serial; she died four years later. While enormously prosperous in radio, she was unable to replicate her aural triumphs in video, never experiencing the accomplishments that Irna Phillips enjoyed in dual mediums, the only individual to have done it all — *twice*. There was a contributing factor, too: CBS was beating the socks off NBC at the same hour with *Strike It Rich*. Emcee Warren Hull, eyes frequently brimming, visibly empathized with his contestants who had encountered sad life circumstances. On this real-life human interest saga, tears of anguish and joy flowed down their faces. Who could turn *that* off?

In a bit part as Mrs. MacDonald in *Follow Your Heart* was radio thespian Anne Seymour. She had acted on *Buck Private and His Girl*, *Our Gal Sunday*, *The Story of Mary Marlin* (where she was the heroine between 1937 and 1943), *Whispering Streets* (as hostess), *A Woman of America* (as heroine), and had filled in for several months while the actress playing the heroine on *Portia Faces Life* recuperated from an accident (in 1948). Seymour later appeared in a few TV sitcoms.

Irving Vendig created and wrote **Three Steps to Heaven**, the other NBC daytime serial that premiered alongside *Follow Your Heart*. The enormously prolific writer was at the same juncture scripting CBS Radio's *Perry Mason* and CBS-TV's *Search for Tomorrow*. Just ahead, in 1956, his greatest challenge (and triumph) awaited — creating and penning *The Edge of Night* (with a close resemblance to *Perry Mason* on radio). Because he loved to fill storylines with mobsters and other reprehensible types, Vendig could be expected to provide some tense moments in every drama he touched. *Three Steps to Heaven* was no exception; one of the underworld figures residing there, Vince Bannister, attempted to entice the heroine's sibling, Barry Thurmond, into organized crime.

The title was derived from the philosophical notion of one of the show's prominent figures, Uncle Frank, who reared an orphaned trio of youngsters. Frank advocated that three steps were required to produce a happy and useful life: courage, love and faith.

Mary Jane (Poco) Thurmond, the leading lady, who hailed from a tiny burg in the hinterlands where Uncle Frank raised her, left for Gotham to chase her dream of becoming a model. She might have been more infatuated with Bill Morgan than her ambitious career plans, however. Both lived under the same brownstone roof. A trio of stair steps to the gallery of Poco's run-down dwelling was a constant reminder to her of Uncle Frank's beliefs (and thus the show's title). There she could flee the refuse beneath her flat and eye the firmament above, offering some temporary distraction from her humble digs. Bill was a writer affected by his Second World War experiences, although he was kind, which made him especially attractive to her. Thankfully, *this* program's handful of fans got to witness their wedding before the show's cancellation was announced.

Regrettably, the leads were recast so often in the limited time the show was on the air that it was difficult for viewers to truly connect with them as a pair. Poco was played by Phyllis Hill, followed by Diana Douglas, followed by Kathleen Maguire. The role of Bill featured Walter Brooke, then Gene Blakely, then Mark Roberts. Six individuals portraying two parts in just over 13 months of air life? I don't think so! They either couldn't get it right or somebody couldn't be satisfied; either way, that's too many modifications. It must have seemed to the faithful that strangers had arrived to exchange their vows at the altar that triumphant day.

Announcer Don Pardo's voice is familiar to viewers today as the interlocutor on *Saturday Night Live* (1975–2005). Earlier he introduced contestants and game show hosts Bill Cullen on *The Price Is Right* (1956–63) and Art Fleming on *Jeopardy!* (1964–75, 1978–79). He was narrating *Follow Your Heart*, that other ill-fated serial, during the same era.

The year 1954 was to witness the premier of eight new daytime dramas on NBC-TV. One would be gone before the year was out; and all the rest but one would disappear before 1955 ended, with most of them vanishing a whole lot sooner. A quartet of those dramas premiered on the same day — July 5, 1954.

One Man's Family re-debuted on NBC Television in 1954. It had been offered earlier as a weekly primetime half-hour (November 4, 1949, to June 21, 1952). That incarnation concluded because nobody was watching — at least, not in sufficient numbers to satisfy a sponsor and the network. Regrettably, the same thing was about to transpire a second time (you've heard that the murderer returns to the scene of the crime?). The weekday serialized quarter-hour yarn opened at 10:30 a.m. on March 1, 1954, and persisted through July 2, 1954. On July 5, 1954, it was shifted to 3 p.m. and continued through August 27, 1954. On August 30, 1954, it moved to 3:30 p.m., the timeslot the series would occupy until its cancellation on April 1, 1955, just 13 months since its reemergence.

The long-winded tale of the Barbour clan of San Francisco was familiar to most viewers. It originally appeared on a local station in 1932 and by 1933 was carried to the whole country by NBC. It became one of radio's most genuinely beloved family dramas and, due to the literary talent of its creator and primary author, Carlton E. Morse, won virtually every prestigious honor given for radio theater, including a coveted Peabody Award. It persisted on radio into the spring of 1959.

Many fans of the series would characterize father Henry Barbour, a banker, as a fuddy-duddy, pure and simple. He was conservative to a fault, extremely autocratic, and unbending in most situations. He could not easily be persuaded to accept new lines of thinking, and that set up an ongoing dialogue and conflict with his "bewildering offspring." His mate, mother Fanny Barbour, nevertheless struggled to foster the children's natural independence. A quintet of progeny included Paul, the eldest, a wounded, single war vet who returned to the Barbour domicile and to whom the others regularly turned for prudent counsel; Hazel, the oldest daughter, courted by Bill Herbert and ultimately marrying him, although their union was one of stormy unrest; fraternal college twins Claudia and Cliff, who attended Stanford University and gave their daddy fits by railing incessantly against his traditional ideology; and Jack, the youngest, who amused everybody with his congeniality and unexpected exploits.

The family resided in an upper-middle-class dwelling in the Sea Cliff sector of San Francisco overlooking the bay. While several of the characters were involved in romantic pursuits during the video serial, the underlying theme was unquestionably the ongoing intergenerational hullabaloo.

A scant 13-month TV run for an extremely popular radio drama that lasted 27 years seems curious until one considers a grievous error committed by the producers — not once but twice. "Rather than air the same episodes on both radio and TV as *The Guiding Light* was doing," one pundit pointed out, "the decision was made to begin the TV version of *One Man's Family* from where the radio show debuted while the radio show continued moving forward. To further confuse fans, the TV version set its seventeen-year-old plotlines in the present day."[3] And those comments pertained to the primetime series in 1949 that departed in 1952. "It turned up two years later a daytime soap, where it began the saga of [the] Barbour family from the very beginning all over again, with plots that were now more than twenty years old."[4]

Contemporary viewers weren't particularly concerned about a family in 1955 living with concepts that might have prevailed in 1932! While the radio version continued to draw

Principals in a second tele-version of the venerable radio serial *One Man's Family*, this one on NBC daytime in 1954–55, were Theodor von Eltz (Henry Barbour) and Mary Adams (Fanny Barbour), and — looking on from the staircase, from left — Martin Dean (Jack), Linda Leighton (Hazel), Anne Whitfield (Claudia) and Russell Thorson (Paul). Not shown is James Lee (Clifford). Thorson and Lee reprised their roles from a 1949–52 primetime TV edition, while the other figures were recast for the weekday entry.

millions of faithful listeners every evening to its storyline set in the present, the outmoded TV embodiment was a turn-off to the majority. It was a discovery that nobody would have to make a third time, although it actually came close. General Foods was ready to return *One Man's Family* to the small screen for yet another spree in 1965. But NBC officials nixed that notion before it could be launched, substituting a premiering daytime serial called *Days of Our Lives* in its place. That new entry is still running four decades afterward, obviously a more astute choice.

The evening run of *One Man's Family*, which preceded the daytime rendering, produced at least a trio of talented artists who in due time were to see their names go up in lights: Mercedes McCambridge (who played Beth Holly), Tony Randall (Mac) and Eva Marie Saint (Claudia Barbour). No one of that stature emerged from the show's daytime adaptation. In fact, there is no evidence that a dozen of the 13 major players in the sunlight rendition ever appeared on any other televised series. Oh, but acting was the lifeblood of Les Tremayne, the 13th thespian (in the role of Bill Herbert)—who had already spent a professional lifetime as a radio dramatist before reaching TV!

On radio Tremayne turned up repeatedly in the casts of daytimers *Betty and Bob, The Dreft Star Playhouse, Joyce Jordan, M.D., Lonely Women, Ma Perkins, One Man's Family, Real Stories from Real Life, The Romance of Helen Trent, The Second Mrs. Burton, Wendy Warren and the News, The Woman in My House* and *Woman in White*, occasionally in leading roles. At other times he could be heard on *The Abbott Mysteries, The Adventures of the Falcon, The Adventures of the Thin Man, Author's Playhouse, The Bob Crosby Show, The Chicago Theater of the Air, Cloak and Dagger, Cousin Willie, The Edward Everett Horton Show, The First Nighter, The Fog Lifts, Ford Theater, Grand Hotel, Heartbeat Theater, Hildegarde's Radio Room, I Love a Mystery, Jack Armstrong—the All-American Boy, The Jackie Gleason–Les Tremayne Show, The MGM Theater of the Air, Movietown Radio Theater, Night Court, The Old Gold Show, Radio Reader's Digest, Romance in Rhythm, The Shadow of Fu Manchu, The Six Shooter* and *That's Rich.*

In addition to both televised runs of *One Man's Family*, Tremayne performed regularly on the tube in *Ellery Queen* (1958–59), *Shazam!* (1974–80), *One Life to Live* (1987), and *General Hospital* (1988–91), and as a guest on *Mission Impossible, Perry Mason* and *Peter Gunn*. Tremayne also provided voiceovers for two animated cartoon series, ABC-TV's *Curiosity Show* (1971–73) and *The Pirates of Dark Water* (1991–92). While still in radio Tremayne performed in an 18-month Broadway run of *Detective Story*. He played in no fewer than 33 motion pictures—*The Blue Veil* (1951), *Francis Goes to West Point* (1952), *The War of the Worlds* (1953), *Susan Slept Here* (1954), *A Man Called Peter* (1955), *The Lieutenant Wore Skirts* (1956), *North by Northwest* (1959), *Goldfinger* (1964), *The Fortune Cookie* (1966), *Starchaser: The Legend of Orin* (1985), *Attack of the B-Movie Monster* (2002) and many more.

Married to a prolific radio actress, Alice Reinheart (*The Adventures of the Abbotts, Gangbusters, One Man's Family, Casey—Crime Photographer, John's Other Wife, Life Can Be Beautiful, Her Honor—Nancy James*, et al.), he and she presided over a six-day-a-week breakfast talk show, *The Tremaynes*, on New York's WOR Radio for several years. In the 1970s he returned to the microphone to play on *The CBS Radio Mystery Theater*. With more than 50 regularly scheduled broadcast series under his belt, Les Tremayne stands among the upper echelon of prolific actors on the air.

The first new drama premiering in 1954 to be caught in NBC-TV's revolving door, coming and going quickly, was **A Time to Live** (not to be confused with ABC-TV's *A Time* *for Us*, a daytime serial that ran from December 28, 1964, to December 16, 1966). It occupied the quarter-hour at 10:30 a.m. starting July 5, 1954; but, faced with the incomparable *Arthur Godfrey Time* as competition on CBS, *A Time to Live* died a comparatively unheralded death on December 31, 1954.

This Adrian Samish creation originating in Chicago "played out," according to one critic, "like a movie from the 1940s." Julie Byron and Don Riker were both print media journalists. At the story's start she was a modest proofreader, anxious to gain some experience as a feature correspondent. In due course, at age 28 her ambition was realized with her promotion to an investigative reporter. There she and Don pursued scandals involving Greta Powers and the slaying of Lenore Eustice. On the sidelines Julie had a torrid love affair going — at least by 1954 standards— with Chick Buchanan. He was soon framed for murder, naturally, and was ultimately vindicated before their romance reached the altar. It did so in the serial's final performance on New Year's Eve, a seemingly propitious beginning/ending for a soap opera.

Ingeniously, when the scripts called for a hospital corridor setting over a protracted timeframe, an inventive set designer, Curt Nations, transformed an NBC studio hallway into a convincing medical passage. Every morning — while the talent was made up for that day's live telecast — Nations camouflaged the windows with wrapping paper to mask the Chicago skyline. He added cards reading "Laboratory," "Doctor's Lounge," and "Waiting Room," concealing normal signage reading "Entrance," a studio number or "On the Air." An eyewitness reported, "On-camera, the hall looks so much like a hospital corridor that one actor said you can almost smell the ether."

Having just completed a brief run on *The Bennetts* six months before the debut of *A Time to Live*, Viola Berwick (in the support role of Madge Byron) was possibly the only thespian among a rather large company of virtual unknowns who had previous TV daytime network exposure. Others were being introduced to home viewers. Some would go on to better things. Len Wayland, for instance, who portrayed Julie's intended, Chick Buchanan, turned up in recurring parts in *From These Roots* (1958–61) and *Love of Life* (1967).

A Time to Live showed signs of trouble even before it arrived on the air. An NBC publicity release distributed a fortnight prior to the soap opera's launch hyped actress Jeanne Jerrems in the role of the heroine. Pat Sully, another untried thespian, replaced Jerrems before opening day, a revealing occurrence noted by watchful pundits. In its first month on the air, an equally unknown John Himes replaced the serial's leading man, initially played by Larry Kerr. Meanwhile, Jeanne Jerrens, the gal who had originally been tapped for the lead, later substituted for actress Zohra Alton in the prominent role of Greta Powers. It goes without saying that casting for this show was provisional and possibly figured profoundly in its demise after only a brief stint on the ether.

A word should be said about Adrian Samish, the show's creator, as his name became widely recognized among insiders for his considerable impact on the genre. He will reappear several times in this volume, in fact. Earlier he was director of the daytime program department at NBC Television. Samish was responsible for bringing three soap operas to the small screen in one summer (just as Roy Winsor did, whose prime efforts went to CBS projects, a man who will be presented in some detail in Chapter Eight). In addition to *A Time to Live*, there was *First Love* debuting five hours later on the very same day, and *The Greatest Gift*, launched eight weeks after that duo surfaced. Samish had also produced *Follow Your Heart* and *Three Steps to Heaven* earlier.

Regrettably, all three of his creations suffered the indignities that resulted from short run programming, a pattern that NBC officials applied to most of their daytime dramatic fare in this decade. Shows were given little chance to find an audience and develop over extended periods of time, although *First Love* persisted for 18 months, a drastic departure from the median. Perhaps Samish possessed an inferior creative mind when he plotted those soaps. Maybe he didn't have enough resources to secure decent talent (writing and acting), skilled crews and imposing sets, even if they were cut out of cardboard. Maybe his narratives and others were scheduled at the wrong times (when there wasn't much of an audience for soap operas) or against unbeatable odds. Maybe NBC didn't know what it was doing or maybe it didn't care. The possible explanations for the lousy results run on and on. NBC was stuck in a rut and was destined to repeat its inability to get it right many more times. Meanwhile, the reader is encouraged to note the blueprint that was entrenched here, and try to think of a possible rationale for why this happened so frequently, so repeatedly. There will be much more on this subject for reflection later.

Golden Windows, at 3:15 p.m., persisted from July 5, 1954, to April 8, 1955, about nine months—or three months beyond the lifespan of most NBC-TV daytime serials to this point. (Surely the cast celebrated somewhat anxiously and prematurely when they reached six months without news of cancellation!) The drama's title, incidentally, was derived from an ancient fable that told of a boy who saw golden windows on a nearby mountainside. Traveling there, when the sun was setting, he found from that vantage point that the windows of his own home were golden, too, as they reflected the solar ball. The television narrative, according to an NBC publicist, was "the love story of two young people who are frustrated in their feeling for each other because of her desire for a singing career, and his wish to escape a world which has dealt harshly with him."

In this yarn about a perseverant (some might say headstrong) young lady, viewers found a quite youthful heroine (at the drama's start the actress-vocalist playing her was only 21) whom no man could satisfy. During the serial's brief tenure she was actually head over heels over a trio of gents. One might speculate—if her tale had only lasted—how many more flings might she have had?

This serial about a career in entertainment presaged two impending show business daytime dramas, *From These Roots* and *The Young and the Restless*. At the start of *Golden Windows*, Juliet Goodwin, an at-times-impetuous young woman, lived on Capstan Island, Maine. Dissatisfied with what she perceived as a dead-end street for a girl with ambition, she chucked it all. Chasing her dream as a professional vocalist to New York City, she left her fiancé, John Brandon, in the dust. Her bewildered foster father, Charles Goodwin, was also ditched, yet was never so far away that he couldn't be summoned when the plot needed his help. Her pursuits as a singer allowed the show to include an occasional pop tune in the storyline, a practice that wouldn't become commonplace in soap opera until the 1970s.

In Gotham Juliet's career advanced under the tutelage of vocal instructor Joseph Kindler. She also speedily found a new suitor, Tom Anderson, a chap with an intriguing past. Alas, he was in trouble with the law, and Juliet and her dad were drawn into it as possible accessories to his errant behavior. Tom was accused and found guilty. Juliet subsequently linked with conspirator Carl Grant to finger another potential culprit, thereby freeing Tom. Released, ex-con Tom was hired by an oil refinery that carried him far from New York City and Juliet. He, too, apparently never looked back.

In Capstan Island, in the meantime, Juliet's ex, John Brandon, dropped her like a hot potato, picked up Ann Summers as his new babe and married her in a shindig at Gray

Gables, his mom Ruth's palatial estate. As the convoluted plot wound further, Charles became ill while in New York on a visit, requiring Juliet's close observation. Adding to the churning tide was her mounting notion that an older European gent, an admirer who went backstage to see her after a performance, might really be her natural father. (The girl had good vibes: he was.)

Paul Anderson, a medic, became Juliet's newest beau. By then the roguish Carl Grant resurfaced with a co-conspirator, Otto (anybody without a surname is either famous or up to no good), and the pair kidnapped Juliet for purposes undisclosed. Viewers had the feeling it wasn't healthy. The series ended with her rescue and the assurance that she would love Dr. Paul until ... the next charming fellow came along.

As the show faded from the screens on its final day, an announcer offered the kind of melancholy, hackneyed conclusion that radio audiences had come to expect across two decades as their favorite daytime serials departed: "This is the final broadcast in the current series of *The Golden Windows* over this network. We would like to thank all our listeners for their interest in our story. We know you join us in wishing Juliet Goodwin a pleasant life with her newfound father and happiness in her love for Paul." Note the mention of "the current series," leaving the door open for any possible extension that might occur. While this did happen occasionally in radio, it almost never did in TV, as plenty of new series awaited tryouts. Also observe that the announcer thanked the "listeners" instead of the "viewers."

This narrative was John M. Young's only attempt at writing for television. One of the show's dual wordsmiths, Young was a veteran when it came to penning drama-by-installment for the ear. Over a lengthy career he churned out scripts for radio's *Bright Horizon, Gunsmoke, Road of Life, The Right to Happiness, The Second Mrs. Burton* and *Yours Truly—Johnny Dollar*. It was probably quite difficult for him to adapt to a new and unfamiliar medium.

Brooklyn-born Leila Martin was the talented heroine who could both act and sing. Having harmonized in 200 USO shows during World War II, she debuted in a bit part in Broadway's *Two on the Aisle* in 1950. She later appeared there in *Wish You Were Here*. Following *Golden Windows*, Martin resurfaced in a prominent role on CBS-TV's *Valiant Lady* (1956–57).

Eric Dressler, a veteran radio soap opera actor (*Big Sister, Central City, Easy Aces, The Light of the World, Miss Hattie, Young Widder Brown*) and prominent in other aural dramatic series, appeared as Charles Goodwin. Prompted by a reversal of his family's fortunes, Dressler entered the professional theater by way of vaudeville at age 18. The native New Yorker was on Broadway by 1924, appearing in several prominent productions opposite leading ladies like Helen Hayes, Miriam Hopkins and Katherine Cornell. For a long while Dressler and his wife, former actress Patricia Calvert, resided on a farm at Delaware Water Gap, Pennsylvania, where they raised goats and sold goat milk. Late in his career, in the 1970s and 1980s, he was a sporadic guest in plays aired on *The CBS Radio Mystery Theater*.

Joe De Santis—another prolific radio drama supporting thespian (*The Brighter Day, The FBI in Peace & War, Gangbusters, Official Detective, Space Patrol, Time for Love, True Detective Mysteries, Under Arrest*)—appeared in the role of Carl Grant in the daytime serial.

Ethel Remey, as Miss Bigelow in *Golden Windows*, was also the grousing Victoria Loring, sibling of heroine Ellen's longtime suitor Dr. Anthony Loring during a portion of the radio run of *Young Widder Brown*. She was in the recurring cast of radio's *The Adventures of Leonidas Witherall*, too.

Over its brief run the cast of *Golden Windows* practiced in dual facilities, customary in that epoch due to a shortage of rehearsal and production halls. Following each afternoon's live quarter-hour presentation ending at 3:30 p.m., players scheduled for the following day's episode removed their makeup and reassembled at 4 p.m. at the nearby Dauphin Hotel. There they participated in a one-hour run-through of the succeeding day's script. They would reassemble at the Dauphin at 11:15 the following morning for another hour-long practice. Transferring to the NBC studios at 101 West 67th Street at 12:15, they'd be in makeup until 1 o'clock when a half-hour was set aside for a dry run on the set. An hour lunch break at 1:30 was followed by a dress rehearsal at 2:30 with airtime at 3:15. The procedure was typical of the schedules pursued by other daytime serials in TV's earliest years.

Unlike it did with most of its predecessors, NBC granted another serial that debuted on July 5, 1954, **Concerning Miss Marlowe**, enough of a reprieve to allow it to telecast for a full year. The 3:45 p.m. drama continued to July 1, 1955. Its premise was a thinly veiled imitation of *All About Eve*, a 1950 motion picture that starred Bette Davis, Anne Baxter and George Sanders. Both the celluloid and small screen versions centered on a maturing leading lady of the stage whose future was increasingly jeopardized by a youthful challenger. Bette Davis appeared as Margo Channing on the silver screen, while the tube heroine's moniker was Margo (nicknamed Maggie) Marlowe. The similarities were obvious to anyone who'd seen the movie.

While Maggie Marlowe, then 40, had long been a star of the footlights, she fancied retirement, intending to settle into being a housewife. As the serial premiered, she was returning to New York from a performing engagement in Great Britain and about to be married a second time. She was met with the heartrending news, however, that her fiancé had just died. That unexpected turn of events helped soap opera to maintain a perception that the loss of a mate or one's intended was altogether customary in launching daytime dramas (e.g., *Faraway Hill, Portia Faces Life, Search for Tomorrow, The Secret Storm*, et al.).

A critic who listed several NBC-TV daytime heroines with brief life spans, including Maggie Marlowe, observed that none of them threatened radio's unforgettable leading ladies, blaming NBC's erratic policy. A quartet of those women were still single when their dramas bit the dust, he noted, and denoted another weakness of NBC serials: "Housewives could not identify with the heroines as they could with those of ... CBS Television's *Valiant Lady*, who acquired the necessary scars of connubiality."[5]

Adjusting to the realities that had struck so swiftly, Maggie returned to the theater for emotional and financial security. There she accepted a part in an ill-fated production in which a determined young ingénue, Kit Christy, upstaged her, damaging her reputation as an end result. In typical soap opera fashion, Maggie discovered that Kit was the daughter she had "lost" in Europe 14 years earlier, after hiring private eyes to locate her! (A ditzy grandma had "misplaced" the youngster in France it seems.) Kit also now had a boyfriend, Ralph. To stoke the storyline after that big revelation, the scriptwriter introduced Jim Gavin, a dashing, married barrister with whom Maggie launched a scorching dalliance. Strangely enough, Jim's spouse, Barbara, appeared less miffed by her husband's unprincipled liaison than did his mother, Belle Mere Gavin, who was utterly infuriated by these shenanigans.

Later, believing her career would benefit, Kit welcomed the overtures made by an unscrupulous director known simply as Bojalian (another single-named character obviously up to no good!). Maggie and Jim's fling was put on hold while she sought a movie contract.

In that period, Barbara, Jim's wife, died rather mysteriously, the result of an overdose of barbiturates. Naturally, Jim was suspected at once of causing her demise. But Mike Donovan, Barbara's lover on the side (and apparently an honorable man!), confessed to the crime just in time for the serial to leave the air.

Louise Allbritton won the lead in *Concerning Miss Marlowe* but left the role three months before the drama was pulled. Allbritton, the wife of CBS broadcast newsjournalist Charles Collingwood, appeared in the 1947 motion picture *The Egg and I* starring Claudette Colbert and Fred MacMurray, which evolved into a 1950 soap opera on CBS-TV (detailed in Chapter Three). After she left *Marlowe*, actress Helen Shields, who had been appearing in the story as Dot Clayton, was promoted to the heroine's role. That had to have been a perplexing change for the viewers and may have figured into the show's departure a few weeks later.

Strangely, actress Sarah Burton also played two characters in the serial's short life, appearing as both Barbara Gavin and Linda Cabot. Were there simply not enough actresses to go around, or were these women that good? Shortly before Allbritton left the heroine's role, the storyline had Maggie Marlowe fighting to prevent Kit Christy from stealing her part as the show's leading lady. In real life, somebody else onstage did. And at what cost to viewership?

The narrative's cast included Efrem Zimbalist Jr. as Jim Gavin in that actor's initial TV role, the start of an impressive array of video assignments. Zimbalist starred in ABC's *77 Sunset Strip* (1958–64); he played recurring parts on ABC's *Hotel* (1986) and Family Channel's *Zorro* (1990); and he provided voiceovers for Fox's *Batman: The Animated Series* (1992–93). Without a doubt, however, Zimbalist's most celebrated role was as Inspector Lewis Erskine in ABC-TV's long-running detective series *The FBI* (1965–74).

Confusion Alert! A thespian named John Gibson portrayed Harry Clayton in *Concerning Miss Marlowe*. Actually, there were *two* John Gibsons acting in television daytime serials. This one appeared on *The Edge of Night* and *The Guiding Light* later on. He was *not* the John Gibson who showed up on *The Young and the Restless* and *One Life to Live*. And the Jane Seymour who played Harriet the Hat in this serial was not the same one who later starred as TV's *Dr. Quinn, Medicine Woman*.

Concerning Miss Marlowe is also recalled for one of the most comical gaffes in live television history. In a scene in which Maggie (then played by Louise Allbritton) was dialoguing with her French maid, the telephone rang at a time it should not have. Perturbed by it, the heroine picked up the receiver, spoke a few words into it and promptly handed it to the maid. "It's for you," she confirmed, exiting the stage and leaving the distraught domestic to fend for herself. The poor woman, standing in front of live cameras, had to fill the time until the next commercial with ad-libs! Accidents like that were common in the early era of daytime drama, and sometimes provided innocent and refreshing reminders of what *authentic* reality TV was all about.

The last of the quartet of serials debuting on NBC on July 5, 1954, was to continue longer than any since *Hawkins Falls*. It was called **First Love** and it stuck around until December 30, 1955, a run of 18 months. It premiered at 3:30 p.m. but was moved a few weeks later (a reporter observed that it was initially "sandwiched between two losers, *Golden Windows* and *Concerning Miss Marlowe*"). On August 30, 1954, *First Love* aired at 4:15 p.m., pitted against CBS's recent entry, *The Secret Storm*, which soon became a raging, deadly typhoon to all its early rivals.

Adrian Samish—the ex-mogul of daytime programming at NBC-TV—created *First*

Love. Manya Starr, the woman whom radio matinee impresario Anne Hummert got into a tiff with over Deity-inspired scripting, penned the show. It was a tale that was intentionally focused on the hero instead of the heroine, breaking the pattern that characterized the predominate thought in launching a successful soap. Could that possibly be why it lasted a bit longer?

A jet engineer, Zach James, and his bride, Laurie, were the focal figures. Recognizing for a long while that he had been an unwanted child, Zach was fixated on his professional quests. To her credit, his young wife stood by him through his recurrent and frequent mood swings. Sporadically, Laurie's parents, Paul and Doris Kennedy, entered the storyline. Zach and Laurie became friends with Chris and Amy, a couple about their age that, strangely enough, seemed to have no surname either. The wheels came off soon enough for Zach, who labored alongside a vengeful, deceitful Wallace Grant. Grant continually plotted against Zach. Learning that Zach was having an adulterous affair with Priscilla (Petey) Cummings, Grant broadcast the news. When Laurie heard it she split. A reporter picks up the complex story:

> Laurie moved from the fictional town of Harrison when she accepted a job offer from Washington, D.C.... Laurie began seeing David, an attorney, in the nation's capital, but circumstances ... brought her back to Harrison and her husband. Tony Morgan, a newcomer, had a fling with Petey ... until she turned up murdered. Zach, who collapsed in her apartment, became ... [the] prime suspect. Laurie was sure of her husband's innocence, and with the help of David they ... found proof that exonerated him.... Tragedy struck Amy ... when her pilot husband Chris died in a test flight, leaving [Wallace] Grant to make a move on the widow. She ... moved out of town briefly, then returned and married Bruce McKee..., even though he had to cope with the possibility that a ... girl ... named Jenny might be his biological daughter.
>
> As for the newly reunited Laurie and Zach, she went to work at a dress shop, and he came back to the jet engine plant.... Zach's father Matthew ... started working at the plant too.... Jack Doyle broke into the plant and wounded him fatally. Zach survived..., and on the show's last episode could ... be hopeful that he and Laurie might be heading for a less eventful new year.[6]

Whew! What an incredibly complicated scenario!

"One of *First Love*'s tragic Friday fade-outs turned into high comedy when [Val] Dufour [as Zach James], after witnessing a plane crash [in which Chris died], was to tell [the actress playing his own wife Patricia] Barry and [the wife of the deceased, played by Rosemary] Prinz, 'Chris cracked up the plane'— Chris being Prinz's husband. Instead, Dufour rushed up to the women and said, 'Chris crapped.' Horrified, he stopped for a moment, then, desperate, added, 'on the plane.' Barry giggled at the news, and when the camera panned to the supposedly bereft wife, Prinz was shaking uproariously with laughter. Viewers wrote in to say they loved the spontaneity of the obvious blooper, thus saving the stars from receiving pink slips."[7]

It was the same Val Dufour, incidentally, who would win an Emmy in 1976–77 as Outstanding Actor in a Daytime Drama Series for his portrayal of John Wyatt on *Search for Tomorrow*, a part he played from 1973 to 1979. Earlier Dufour played recurring roles on *The Edge of Night* (1965–66) and *Another World* (1967–72). He appeared on *First Love* through April 8, 1955, and was followed by Tod Andrews in the leading role. Andrews turned up later in the cast of NBC-TV's *Bright Promise* (1969–72).

Some others in the *First Love* cast also used it as a springboard to further opportunities.

Patricia Barry, who portrayed Zach James' young spouse, Laurie, was seen later in episodes of *Days of Our Lives* (1971–74), *For Richer, For Poorer* (1977–78), *All My Children* (1980–81), *Guiding Light* (1984–87) and *Loving* (1992).

Peggy Allenby, who was Doris Kennedy (Laurie's mom) on *First Love*, went on to display her acting skills for a full decade (1956–66) on the debuting *The Edge of Night*. A veteran of radio serials, she had prior experience on *Aunt Jenny's Real Life Stories, David Harum, Life Can Be Beautiful, The Light of the World, Road of Life* and more.

The résumé of Rosemary Prinz (Amy on *First Love*) was to include *As the World Turns* (1956–68, 1985, 1986–87, 1993), *All My Children* (1970), *How to Survive a Marriage* (1974) and *Ryan's Hope* (1988–89).

Paul McGrath, who appeared as Matthew James (the hero's father in *First Love*), was immortalized as the incomparable voice of Raymond, chilling radio host of *Inner Sanctum Mysteries* (1945–circa 1952). He also appeared in aural serials, including *The Affairs of Dr. Gentry, Big Sister, Lora Lawton, This Life Is Mine, When a Girl Marries* and *Young Doctor Malone*. McGrath concluded a lengthy broadcast career with a fleeting part on CBS-TV's *The Guiding Light* (1967).

After a quartet of premiers at mid-year 1954, NBC-TV introduced **The Greatest Gift** to viewers on August 30, 1954, at 3 p.m., shifted it to 3:30 p.m. on April 4, 1955, and removed it from the schedule entirely on July 1, 1955. Offered live from Philadelphia, and also created by Adrian Samish, the serial was one of the first to focus on the medical profession.

Dr. Eve Allen, played by nasal-voiced Anne Burr, may have been the genuine groundbreaking article among feminine physicians in television soap opera; if not the first, she was surely among the earliest in a long line that extends to the modern era. An Army veteran, the widowed Eve was returning to her hometown of Ridgeton, Connecticut, following the Korean conflict as the show began. She had been discharged from the Army Medical Corps. In Ridgeton she intended to run her late uncle's medical practice, which was situated in a decaying part of town. She was met with a coarse reception. Because she was a woman and therefore a pioneer in her profession, she was greeted with substantial mistrust. A pundit remarked that the prejudice against women doctors was "obviously shared by the TV audience, which refused to watch," referring to the series' lack of staying power.

Eve's own emotions could range from passionate to chaotic while she scrutinized the private lives of the ill and acquaintances, too. At the same time, she carried on an amorous, though often stormy relationship with a fellow physician, Dr. Phil Stone, played by Phillip Foster. "Luckily for her patients, her bad choices were in men, not medicine," wrote another critic. The black baby market received a lot of emphasis in the narrative's declining months; in fact, Eve and her disturbed sibling Fran Allen were spared in a potentially deadly hotel fire through the efforts of a member of that underworld activity's purported ringleaders, Ned Blackman. He consistently raised the antenna of Phil Stone. The show left the air without resolving much of anything, and with Eve and Phil still unattached.

Anne Burr, the actress who played possibly TV's first feminine physician, possessed a lengthy list of credits in radio. She was usually cast in heavy-handed supporting roles on daytime dramas like *Backstage Wife, Big Sister, Wendy Warren and the News* and *When a Girl Marries*. A 1940s Broadway thespian (*Detective Story, The Hasty Heart*), Burr was featured as nurse Kate Morrow in the weekly CBS Radio drama *City Hospital* (1951–58), a part she reprised on the ABC-TV show of the same name (1952–53). In 1947–48 she played numerous leading roles on Fletcher Markle's dramatic radio anthology *Studio One*. She also appeared in the casts of radio's *Mr. Keen, Tracer of Lost Persons* and *Scotland Yard*. After

The Greatest Gift departed, Burr portrayed the original Claire Lowell on the debuting *As the World Turns* on CBS-TV (1956–59).

Martin Balsam left *The Greatest Gift*, where he played Harold (Hal) Matthews, to join CBS-TV's *Valiant Lady*, in which he had another minor role in 1955. Those shows were launching pads to one of the more prolific careers among television actors. Balsam routinely turned up in premium dramas like *Hallmark Hall of Fame* and *Philco Television Playhouse*. Near the close of a distinguished run he appeared as a regular in the cast of *All in the Family* (1979–81).

Jack Klugman (as Jim Hanson) and Anne Meara (Harriet) were introduced to television audiences by way of *The Greatest Gift*. Klugman would go on to a long string of prime-time TV credits, starring in four series, two of them quite memorable: *Harris Against the World* (1964–65), *The Odd Couple* (1970–75), *Quincy, M. E.* (1976–83) and *You Again?* (1986–87). Anne Meara also enjoyed a lengthy career in primetime, turning up in character parts on *The Corner Bar* (1972), *Rhoda* (1976–78) and *All in the Family* (1979–82), while starring in the short-lived *Kate McShane* (1975). Meara returned to her acting roots in 1992, accepting an ongoing role in daytime's *All My Children*.

Before considering the next matinee drama premiering on NBC-TV, recall first that *Fairmeadows, U.S.A.*, a Sunday afternoon feature in 1951–52, made a comeback in 1952–53 under the appellation *The House in the Garden* during *The Kate Smith Show* on weekdays. The following season, on October 14, 1953, Smith introduced yet another tale, **The World of Mr. Sweeney**, starring Charles Ruggles, for a weekly 10-minute spot on her 3–4 p.m. weekday hour. Ruggles had played in several comedy films in the 1930s, including *The Smiling Lieutenant* (1931), *If I Had a Million* (1932), *Love Me Tonight* (1932), *Trouble in Paradise* (1932), *Ruggles of Red Gap* (1935) and *Bringing Up Baby* (1938). He also starred in the 1949–52 ABC-TV sitcom *The Ruggles*, in which he played himself.

Cicero P. Sweeney, like his predecessor in the earlier Kate Smith season, operated a general store, his in the little municipality of Mapleton. While he had never been out of Mapleton, he acquired "an uncanny knowledge of the world and life, and his wisdom and kindness make him a sought-after 'cracker-barrel psychiatrist,'" an NBC publicity blitz ballyhooed. Some of the better exchanges in the scripts were dialogue between Sweeney, his daughter Marge and grandson Kippie. Sweeney habitually listened to the troubles of his clientele; from him they could expect gab and guidance to go with their groceries. Each program was a complete vignette in itself.

After the Smith series folded on June 18, 1954, NBC-TV continued *The World of Mr. Sweeney* as a Tuesday/Wednesday/Friday quarter-hour at 7:30 p.m. between June 30 and August 20, 1954. The same lighthearted fare persisted, with Cicero, Marge and Kippie as the character focus. NBC was so impressed with the filler in its early evening schedule that it gave the green light for it to return as a daytime serial beginning October 4, 1954, at 4 p.m. The narrative was characterized by plenty of small-town chitchat as the locals bantered back and forth, plus rumors from some small-minded citizens and tall tales from the store's owner. It was an easygoing respite from the rest of the heavier dialogue that was appearing on sunlit television screens. *TV Guide* characterized it as "genuine solid TV fare that the medium has been neglecting in the past few years in favor of more hoopla, more noise and a good deal of more pretense."

Low ratings ostensibly killed another good show on December 31, 1955. Some of that could well be attributed to a shift in origination from New York to Hollywood on November 7, 1955. In so doing, two of the three most identified characters, Marge and a charming

Cicero P. Sweeney, played by Charles Ruggles, was the proprietor of a mercantile emporium in Mapleton who passed along advice based on his intellect and intuition to townsfolk and especially his grandson Kippie Franklin (Glenn Walken). Introduced to viewers via the popular *Kate Smith Show* weekday afternoons, the feature soon transitioned into its own quarter hour in the evenings. From 1954 to 1955 it played as a matinee serial. The lighthearted exchanges between grandpa and grandson were compelling fan favorites.

Kippie — whom audiences had connected with over the previous two years — were dismissed. At that juncture Cicero's daughter Liz, and her dual offspring, Timmy and Sue, were integrated into the plots. But it was never quite the same.

In spite of its brevity, three decades after *The World of Mr. Sweeney* departed it received a noteworthy honor. The program was recognized for telecasting 345 installments, most of them in daytime, and thereby setting a record for the greatest number of episodes of a comedy series on NBC.

Helen Wagner, the longtime daughter Marge in *The World of Mr. Sweeney*, had already appeared in *The Guiding Light* on both radio and television in 1952. But she was merely launching a professional career that would keep her face before the TV cameras for decades. She began playing Nancy Hughes, heroine of *As the World Turns*, on the day that soap premiered in 1956. While she left it for three years in 1981, she returned and has played the part (now Nancy Hughes McClosky) in every decade since the drama's inception. As of this writing, she is closing in on the half-century mark, an unsurpassed milestone in soap opera.

Glenn Walken appeared in a couple of TV roles beyond the imposing grandson on *The World of Mr. Sweeney*. He was on CBS-TV's *Exploring God's World* (1954), and was the first of several to play Mike Bauer in *The Guiding Light* (1954–56).

With a string of radio credits already on her résumé, Betty Garde (who played Abigail Milikan on *Sweeney*) burst onto the stage as Aunt Eller in Rodgers and Hammerstein's original Broadway musical *Oklahoma!* in the 1940s. She was in the 1948 motion picture *Call Northside 777* (1948). Garde played recurring roles in daytime radio's *Front Page Farrell*, *Lorenzo Jones*, *Mrs. Wiggs of the Cabbage Patch*, *My Son and I*, *Perry Mason* and others. She was also on numerous nighttime radio shows (*The Aldrich Family*, *The Big Story*, *Cavalcade of America*, *The Columbia Workshop*, *The Fat Man*, *Gangbusters*, *Inner Sanctum Mysteries*, *Mr. and Mrs. North*, *The Thin Man*, *Studio One*, *We the Abbotts*, et al.). After *Sweeney*, she acted fleetingly on *The Edge of Night* (1956).

Bob Hastings, who portrayed Ed in *Sweeney*, was also a radio veteran, best remembered for the lead in *Archie Andrews* during most of its long aural run (1943–53). On television he played in *McHale's Navy* (1962–66) at night, and in the daytime on *Kitty Foyle* (1958) and *General Hospital* (1979–86). Hastings supplied the voice of Superboy on the animated CBS-TV series *Superman* (1966–69).

At that juncture NBC Television took a new approach to its daytime dramatic serials. Its next three debuting narratives were all anthologies—stories that could be told in a few chapters, often in five episodes of a given week. In chronological order of premier, they were *Modern Romances, Way of the World* and *A Date with Life*.

Modern Romances, offering fiction from the magazine of the same name, aired on radio in several disjointed runs that extended from 1936 to 1955, with a dozen-year disruption between 1937 and 1949. A pundit assessed the aural adaptations as "confession stories in a third-person style which exchanged secret sharing for keyhole peeping." Gertrude Warner was the principal radio voice narrating those quixotic tales, while the casts changed with every new story. Warner, in fact, was identified to listeners as Helen Gregory, purportedly the editor of the slick confessional publication *Modern Romances*.

When NBC decided to capitalize on the familiar radio title and those same yarns for a daytime television anthology, actress Martha Scott was hired to introduce the stories, presented in five-part quarter-hour installments, with a new story every week. While the casts changed, Ann Flood (who later played Nancy Karr on *The Edge of Night*) and Georgann Johnson (Ellen Grant *on Somerset*) turned up often in those tales. Other familiar faces included Don Hastings (Bob Hughes on *As the World Turns*) and Robert Mandan (Sam Reynolds on *Search for Tomorrow*).

On November 29, 1957, actor Mel Brandt replaced Martha Scott as *Modern Romances* host when she departed to appear in a motion picture. Brandt remained through March 28, 1958, after which the show summoned an eclectic collection of celebrities to preside for a week at a time (e.g., Jayne Meadows, Kathryn Murray, Buffalo Bob Smith, Margaret Truman and more). In a November 1955 episode, pop vocalist Connie Francis showed up to sing a new tune especially commissioned for the serial's current storyline about an ambitious would-be lyricist.

The program debuted on October 4, 1954, at 4:45 p.m. It worked so well in that timeslot that NBC officials kept their hands off it through December 30, 1955. Effective January 2, 1956, it aired at 4:15 p.m., but reverted back to 4:45 p.m. on July 2, 1956, remaining in that slot until it left the air on September 19, 1958, marking the end of daytime quarter-hour shows on NBC-TV. *Modern Romances*, with its closed-end storylines, persisted for 47.5 continuous months as a television property. It came very close to matching the longevity record set by the open-end soap opera *Hawkins Falls* (51 consecutive months on the Peacock network). Given the innumerable soap opera casualties that fell before it, the series surely was worthy of celebration throughout the chimes chain.

Martha Scott appeared in several major cinematic productions, including *Our Town* (1940), *The Desperate Hours* (1955), *The Ten Commandments* (1956), *Sayonara* (1957), *Ben-Hur* (1959), *Charlotte's Web* (1973) and *The Turning Point* (1977). She had a fling with radio, too, dating back to an obscure 1936 CBS series, *Terror by Night*. From 1951 to 1952 Scott was a regular in the performing company on *The Somerset Maugham Theater* (CBS, NBC). In 1955–56 she was a co-host of NBC Radio's experimental, yet disastrous magazine venture *Weekday*. In 1976 she was in the supporting cast of ABC-TV's *The Bionic Woman*.

Mel Brandt was the object of the heroine's affections in the fleeting Dumont TV series *Faraway Hill* in 1946, the earliest of a new breed. He later announced *Saturday Night Live* (1981–82).

NBC's next collection of stories, **Way of the World**, premiered at 10:30 a.m. on January 3, 1955, for a quarter-hour, continuing in that timeslot for a half-year through July 1, 1955. On July 4, 1955, it shifted to 4 p.m., where it persisted for another three months through October 7, 1955, then vanished altogether.

An unknown actress, Gloria Louis, who appeared as "Linda Porter," was hostess-narrator of the show. *Unknown* is the operative word: Louis had no identifiable radio, television or film credits before or after this series. On the premier outing she informed viewers that they could expect "a variety of plays reflecting the emotions and reactions of the world in which we live." One pundit, nevertheless, characterized the series as "an anthology of short-run soap opera dramas featuring stories (and stars) of the second rank at best." Despite that flippant dismissal, several of the actors were practiced radio veterans, including Anne Burr, Claudia Morgan (the durable heroine of *The Right to Happiness*) and Ethel Remey.

The stories were adaptations of fiction drawn from a myriad of women's periodicals. Constance Ford, William Prince, Gena Rowlands and Thomas Tryon were also among those figures in the various plays that left noteworthy imprints on the profession before or following their efforts here.

Way of the World differed from the other anthology running alongside it, *Modern Romances* (whose yarns were unraveled in a week), by adopting a varied timeline strategy. Viewers didn't know whether a story would be wrapped up in a single day (some were) or perhaps be drawn out as long as two weeks or more.

The flexibility, while welcomed by some in the audience who weren't tied to a job, school or other time-conscious obligation (there were no video tape recorders then), might have held a greater downside than the predictability offered by *Modern Romances*. There, fans who couldn't make a long-term commitment to a soap opera with a never-ending storyline got what they expected: a week's tale — no more, no less — a bite-sized portion of narrative fantasy that one could digest over the short haul, knowing the terminus date at the start. *Way of the World* didn't offer that, and it was off the air in nine months; *Modern Romances* persisted for four years. While that wouldn't have been *World's* only handicap, it might have factored into the dwindling ratings numbers.

When *Way of the World* aired at 10:30 a.m., following the telecast actors would remove their makeup, change into street clothes and reassemble in the Terrace Room of the nearby Capitol Hotel at 11:15 a.m. for a 90-minute rehearsal. The next morning, or the morning of production (such as Mondays), an hour-long dry rehearsal would take place at daybreak — 6:45 a.m. Monday, Wednesday and Friday, and 7 a.m. Tuesday and Thursday — at NBC's Studio 3E at 30 Rockefeller Plaza. Following makeup, blocking with cameras, a dress rehearsal and a short break, the show would be broadcast live at 10:30, airing from Studio 8G at 30 Rock. When the serial subsequently transitioned to a 4 p.m. transmission, the routine shifted to later in the day.

The successor to *Way of the World* was yet another anthology on NBC, **A Date with Life**. It inherited *World's* 4 p.m. timeslot and enjoyed a briefer existence than *World's* nine-month lifespan: October 10, 1955–June 29, 1956. Go figure.

The telltale differences between these two story mosaics were in the hosts and the fact that *A Date with Life* linked its material to the mythical hamlet of Bay City, U.S.A., with a few connecting figures overlapping between tales. (Incidentally, in 1964 Bay City was adapted by NBC-TV as the venue for its debuting serial *Another World*.) A few characters in one story on *A Date with Life* might play in a subsequent one. Each yarn persisted for no less than a week, with an average run of about five weeks.

Editor Jim Bradley of *The Bay City News*, portrayed by Logan Field, introduced the narratives in 1955; his brother, Tom Bradley, with Mark Roberts in the role, succeeded him in 1956. They not only narrated but also provided some editorial commentary along the way. Logan Field has no known credits elsewhere, but Mark Roberts appeared in two earlier short-run NBC-TV serials, *Miss Susan* (1951) and *Three Steps to Heaven* (1954).

Most of the actors were drawn from other soap operas and were otherwise undistinguished. Their numbers could be generous, however. In the show's final installment, the talent included 18 actors for a quarter-hour drama. Among the recurring company were future notables like Georgeann Johnson (*Somerset*, 1970–76; *As the World Turns*, 1977–79), and earlier figures like Pat Sully, the heroine of the fleeting *A Time to Live* in 1954.

Barbara Britton, who had already played Pamela North in the primetime TV mystery *Mr. and Mrs. North* from 1952 to 1954, appeared in the initial and final storylines. She would resurface in *One Life to Live* in 1979, too.

Don Hastings would go on to *The Edge of Night* from 1956–60, and become Dr. Bob Hughes on *As the World Turns* in 1960, a part he continues playing as of this writing (2005).

Recurring actor William Redfield was a radio veteran, turning up often on all of these series: *The Brighter Day, David Harum, Have Gun — Will Travel, Mr. Keen — Tracer of Lost Persons, Now Hear This, The Right to Happiness, Tales of Willie Piper, Young Doctor Malone* and *Yours Truly — Johnny Dollar.*

A Date with Life drew small audiences, and was crushed by the competition at CBS, *The Brighter Day*, which had been running more than 15 months prior to *Life's* debut. One source termed the upstart soap "more like 'A Date with Disaster,'" claiming it "paid for its short attention span with a run just as short."[8] When *Life* departed, its slot was handed to Jack Bailey, host of the rags-to-riches human-interest feature *Queen for a Day*, which expanded to 45 minutes.

NBC would not introduce any more soap operas until 1958, when it brought four new-comers to the small screen. Two were gone before the year was out, while the others remained into the early 1960s. They included *Kitty Foyle, Today Is Ours, From These Roots* and *Young Doctor Malone.*

Kitty Foyle, "the living drama of a modern American girl," which premiered first, ran as a half-hour tale at 2:30 p.m. from January 13, 1958, through June 27, 1958. Packaged by Henry Jaffee Enterprises, it was adapted from a best-selling novel by Christopher Morley. The story was the basis for an award-winning 1940 movie starring Ginger Rogers and a CBS Radio daytime serial (1942–44) featuring Julie Stevens. (Stevens was subsequently tapped to be one of radio's long-suffering heroines, Helen Trent, for 16 years.) Meanwhile, NBC ballyhooed its new soap opera as "the first-person chronicle of the daughter of a Lon-donderry Irishman who falls in love with the scion of a socially prominent Philadelphia family, ... given a modern adaptation for TV."

TV's Kitty was the daughter of a working class family whose love affair with an affluent Wyn Strafford of the Philadelphia elite went nowhere. To set the mood, the show opened with panoramic location shots of Philly's central business district. Strafford's mom pro-fessed nothing short of contempt for Kitty and did all she could to discourage her son's infatuation with the girl. On the other hand, possessing a strong work ethic, Kitty rejected the elitist trappings surrounding the Straffords, preferring her occupation and liberty to a suffocating liaison with anybody. It was a great theme in which a poor Irish waif was roman-tically linked to wealth and society. That simple concept had already occurred many times in various radio serials (*Amanda of Honeymoon Hill, Backstage Wife, Lora Lawton, Our Gal Sunday, Stella Dallas,* and more).

On television the heroine did not surface until the series had been airing for four weeks, a departure from every other soap opera's modus operandi. In fact, the name of the actress who was to play the lead, Kathleen Murray, was not announced publicly until the show was already airing. Murray was selected from a group of 11 finalists that had been culled from more than 190 candidates considered for the part in a nationwide search for "just the right girl."

"By all accounts the show had a lousy debut that it never rose above," one pundit explained. "By the time the character ... made her entrance, the audience had lost interest," wrote another. *Billboard* assessed: "Judgment as to acting is very difficult when writing is so poor.... This show needs sharp improvement quickly." *Variety* found "the banality of the scripts" culpable for the show's abbreviated run. The evaluations seem incongruous con-sidering that such an esteemed, widely venerated, award-winning literary giant as Carlton E. Morse (of *One Man's Family* fame) oversaw the scripting. Despite that, the plotting was overtly representative of the melodramatic form that was prevalent in that era.

> Kitty first popped up on February 10, by which time viewers had become accustomed to her simple yet troubled family, which lived in Philadelphia. She arrived from college ready to go to her freshman dance with Flip Martin, but found her beloved Pop ill and her brothers Ed and Mack acting like strangers. Ed, who was jailed at one point, discovered some peace with his marriage to Sophie before the end of the run. Unfortunately, Mack borrowed cash from a loan shark. Kitty had her own problems, mostly in the romantic field. Deciding not to go back to school, she ditched Flip for Wyn Strafford, who naturally did his soap opera best by falling for Stacylea, a society hound. Then when Nick Amsted revealed his interest in Kitty — surprise! — Wyn decided he wanted her too.[9]

There were darker themes in the storyline, including calculated conniving and cold-blooded corpses.

A petite five-foot-five honey blonde, 29-year-old Kathleen Murray — who won the starring role in the colossal talent search — had already honed her skills in legitimate theater and television. She graced the stage of New York's Circle-in-the-Square many times (in *La Ronde, Summer in Smoke* and *Yerma*), and turned up on early TV dramatic features like *Kraft Television Theater, Modern Romances* and *NBC Matinee Theater*. For six months before the wide-ranging Kitty Foyle auditions, she performed in *Purple Dust* at New York's Cherry Lane Theatre. A soft-spoken Murray "wanted to be an actress since the day she played a flower — a marigold, she recalled — in kindergarten class." She once dragged herself out of a sick bed so as not to miss the namesake part in *Alice in Wonderland* that she performed at New Utrecht High School in Brooklyn. Lamentably, Murray was awarded no further continuing roles in video series after her four-month stint as Kitty Foyle ended. However, she continued with stage work, both on and off Broadway. Murray died at age 41 on August 24, 1969.

William Redfield, as Wyn Strafford, was a radio veteran whose professional career began in the late 1920s or early 1930s as a child prodigy on NBC Blue's *Coast-to-Coast on a Bus*. He later played on daytime radio serials: *The Brighter Day, David Harum, The Right to Happiness, Young Doctor Malone*. He acquired roles in several other series in that medium (e.g., *Mr. Keen — Tracer of Lost Persons, Now It Can Be Told, Tales of Willie Piper, Yours Truly — Johnny Dollar*), and made sporadic appearances on *The CBS Radio Mystery Theater* (1974–82). On television Redfield was the lead in Dumont's brief drama *Jimmy Hughes, Rookie Cop* (1953), and a supporting actor on NBC's sitcom *The Marriage* (1954). Toward the end of a long career, Redfield performed in several notable films: *The Connection* (1962), *Fantastic Voyage* (1966), *A New Leaf* (1971) and *One Flew Over the Cuckoo's Nest* (1975).

Les Damon, as Rosie Rittenhouse in *Kitty Foyle*, also earned substantial credits in radio, where he played on multiple soap operas: *The Bartons, Girl Alone, Lone Journey, Portia Faces Life, The Right to Happiness, This Is Nora Drake, Young Doctor Malone*. Elsewhere on radio he showed up in *The Abbott Mysteries, The Adventures of Christopher Wells, The Adventures of the Thin Man, Dimension X, The Falcon, Ford Theater, Words at War* and other series, often as the lead.

For a brief while an 11-year-old Patty Duke appeared as Kitty Foyle during her younger years. That experience jumpstarted a lifelong career, one that included TV guest shots and several continuing roles. When Duke was given her own primetime ABC-TV series at age 17 — *The Patty Duke Show* (1963–66) — she was the youngest individual at that time to have a network program with her name on it.

Kitty Foyle's dismal showing could partially be blamed on Art Linkletter. Addicts of his *House Party* on CBS, which had been running in that timeslot for more than five years, missed *Kitty* altogether. They were enchanted instead by Linkletter's repartee with precocious youngsters who disclosed family secrets from home in a genuine tell-all marathon. They were mesmerized as the affable host introduced a lady from the studio audience and plucked the contents of her handbag piece by piece, holding those articles high for all to witness ("Why on earth would you have one of *these*?" he'd sheepishly ask). And they were intrigued as Linkletter played "What's in the House?" with contestants for fabulous prizes. None of those potential viewers saw *Kitty Foyle*, and she quickly vanished from the tube.

Between 3 o'clock and 4 o'clock on June 30, 1958, NBC debuted two new daytime dramas — *Today Is Ours* at 3 p.m. and *From These Roots* at 3:30 p.m. The first one lasted a half-year (to December 26, 1958) while the other stuck around for three-and-a-half years. There were reasons why.

Today Is Ours was created by two of radio's most gifted wordsmiths, Julian Funt and David Lesan. Their forte was in scripting medical dramas—Funt penned *Big Sister*, *City Hospital*, *Joyce Jordan, M.D.*, *This Is Nora Drake* and *Young Doctor Malone*, while Lesan also authored *Malone* and produced *The Brighter Day*. Their joint serial here was TV's first soap opera to feature a heroine who had split from her spouse.

Instead of being a widow as on other daytime dramas, leading lady Laura Manning of Bolton, Connecticut (60 miles from New York City), was the divorced mom of a 12-year-old son, Nicky. Furthermore, she wasn't wallowing in depravity; she had earned a very responsible position as assistant principal of Central High School. Observed one reporter: "In an era when jobs for soap heroines were limited to mainly nurse and secretary, a safer, more typical route would have been to make Laura a teacher. Funt and Lesan clearly were not interested in playing it safe."

Quite early in the run the narrative explored the effect of divorce on offspring. At first it seemed that Laura's ex, Karl Manning, preferred her to any other options he might have had. When she turned him down, he went looking elsewhere and found a New York society lass, Leslie Williams. Nicky was obviously troubled by his father's remarriage and temporarily split from whatever security his home offered. He obsessed over the perplexing question, "Did dad actually love me any longer?"

While Laura had to deal with the problems of her job as well as those that came naturally as a custodial parent, they didn't overshadow the main thesis of the storyline. Soap operas almost habitually take refuge in flirtation and romance, and this tale was no exception. Laura sparred defiantly with an architect, Glenn Turner, who was sketching blueprints for an addition to the school's physical plant. As the narrative evolved, their perceptions shifted regarding the project and one another. Not surprisingly, the two found themselves hopelessly in love. As the series left the air it appeared that a stepfather might be in Nicky's future.

"The idea of a divorced mother was a progressive step for daytime but, as it turned out, not a very popular one," wrote a critic. "Maybe because radio and TV soaps had already conditioned the audience to think of divorcees as villainesses, the viewers did not cotton to Laura or her romance with Glenn."[10]

Patricia Benoit, who appeared as Laura Manning and who earlier had been in a supporting role on NBC-TV's primetime *Mr. Peepers* (1952–55), made a comeback on CBS-TV's *As the World Turns* (1960–62). Some of the others in *Today Is Ours* won bit parts in other television productions, while a few remained virtual unknowns. When the show left the air a handful of its characters were incorporated into the opening plotline of the succeeding *Young Doctor Malone*, also authored by Julian Funt.

The rehearsal schedule for the half-hour feature included a two-hour read-through of the next day's script beginning at four o'clock every afternoon. The live telecast ended at 3:30, giving the actors time to remove their makeup and change into street clothes before rehearsing the successive installment. On the morning of broadcast, at 8:30 a.m., a two-hour dry run ensued. Lunch at 10:30 was followed by makeup at 11:30. A two-hour rehearsal involving blocking scenes for the cameras was set for noon. Dress rehearsal was scheduled for two p.m. There was a half-hour break at 2:30, with airtime at three o'clock. Then the arrangement started all over again.

Even as the show ended, in an unusual twist, six of the principal characters were transitioned into the show's successor series—*Young Doctor Malone*—during its first month on the air. Both serials occupied the same timeslot and had common authors, making the transition fairly simple to accomplish. As one narrative played out, the other began during that overlapping phase.

From These Roots, NBC's next sequential entry, was only the second (after *Hawkins Falls*) of that net's daytime soap operas featuring open-end storylines to persist for more than a couple of years. It ran in a single time period, a half-hour at 3:30 p.m., from June 30, 1958, through December 29, 1961—a full three-and-a-half years, yielding 915 episodes! Was NBC finally putting into practice some of the lessons it repetitiously learned from so many failed attempts? Notwithstanding that possibility, one reporter opined: "*From These Roots* stayed on the air more because of the faith its sponsor Procter & Gamble had in the show than because of high ratings (it never fared well against *The Verdict Is Yours* on CBS and *Who Do You Trust?* on ABC)."

From its inception Procter & Gamble owned the show and naturally retained a keen interest in every aspect of the production. Later in the run, shortly after the manufacturing firm sold the property to NBC, the show was canceled. Had NBC's corporate mindset actually profited from its earlier experiences? It might be too early to tell.

From These Roots was created and written by John Pickard and Frank Provo, the same scribes who teamed together to produce reams of inspired dialogue for CBS Radio's *Wendy Warren and the News* (1947–58).[11] So good was their material there, in fact, that in an exclusive interview with this author 40 years later, actress Florence Freeman, who played the heroine, recalled "how marvelous those lines were we were given to say." Playwright Tennessee Williams, an avowed fan of Pickard and Provo's *From These Roots*, once wondered if his agent was selling them his unpublished scripts! Yet a modern observer noted that, despite the fact *From These Roots* was lauded for both acting and writing, it still endured a bias that daytime audiences sustained against show business serials and career women, a detail that may have diminished the program's audience (and ratings).

Like most of its radio antecedents, but not many of its television successors, this soap opera utilized an opening epigraph:

> *From these roots grow branch, leaf and flower, children of the sheltering earth, ripening into the tumult of the seasons — generation unto generation.*

In addition, 15 years before *The Young and the Restless* exploded into melody, *From These Roots* incorporated music into its plots, anticipating serials not yet conceived.

As the story commenced, 26-year-old fiction author Liz Fraser, a prodigal daughter, returned to Stratfield, her New England hometown, from Washington, D.C.[12] She intended to run *The Stratfield Record*, the newspaper owned, published and edited by her 65-year-old dad, Ben, who had suffered a heart attack. Ben's immediate family was composed of a large and dissonant lot that included two daughters and a son, a son-in-law, a daughter-in-law and five grandchildren.

Ben's daughter Emily and her spouse Jim, straw boss at a mill, divorced in 1959 following an illicit liaison he pursued with a relative by marriage. Soap opera writers seldom rewarded such behavior, and in 1960 poor Jim was murdered. As the story progressed, Emily remarried, choosing district attorney Frank Teton. Ben Jr., the newspaper publisher's son, and wife Rose struggled to operate the family farm but ultimately seemed to have a less complicated life. Eventually he was elected mayor of the town and cleaned up its less desirable elements.

Liz, on the other hand — engaged at the story's start to Bruce Crawford, who remained in the nation's capital —found herself single and looking again after their relationship fell apart. She had little trouble finding suitors, and even rekindled a fire with old flame Buck Weaver, now a physician, before tying the knot on February 18, 1960, with unpredictable playwright David Allen. The year before, Allen had married and divorced a woman, Enid Chambers, who pursued Bruce Crawford while Liz was betrothed to him!

In continuing soap saga style, a triangle emerged after Liz's wedding when oft-inebriated actress Lynn Franklin dallied with David. She was, at the time, also having a sexual affair with director Tom Jennings. As purely a diversion, no doubt, Liz and David also encountered the inevitable tribulations inherent in intensely focused dual-career households, seemingly just like everybody else who might be normal.

On one occasion, *From These Roots* offered a production of *Madame Bovary*, starring Lynn Franklin, and directed by Jennings, as a kind of show-within-a-show. The milieu of backstage life (costume changes, makeup, control booth instructions, etc.) added a curious dynamic to the performance. Viewers witnessed the play and offstage scenarios simultaneously. It was one of the more sophisticated endeavors of any soap opera to that date.

The drama was subject to the same common pitfalls of any show performed live, of course. A few minutes before the show went on the air on June 3, 1960, actress Julie Bovasso—who played Rose Corelli Fraser from the series' start—disagreed so strongly with producer-director Paul Lammers' ultimatum about saying some lines that she exited the studio and didn't come back. Associate director Barbara Searles was pressed into service, substituting for her that day and reading from a script unseen by the fans at home. Bovasso was terminated and soon replaced by Tresa Hughes. While Bovasso's TV comeback in 1991 amounted to a seven-week stint on ABC's *The Man in the Family*, she was a character actress and playwright on Broadway in between, appearing in both *Saturday Night Fever* and *Staying Alive*. Still, it was a long time between drinks of water in TV land.

It was probably no accident that the thespian playing Ben Fraser Sr., Rod Hendrickson, was a holdover from radio's *Wendy Warren and the News*. The fellows who originated that show developed this one, too. On *Warren*, Hendrickson was the heroine's aging compass, her dad Sam Warren, who had been an editor there also, of *The Clarion*. Wendy escaped life in New York's print and electronic journalism trenches—a career likely stimulated by her pop — by visiting Sam and her Aunt Dorrie on many weekends in nearby Elmdale, Connecticut.

Another radio veteran in *From These Roots*, Leon Janney, who appeared as Stanley Kreiser, was also a familiar voice all over the dial. Not only was he a regular on daytime serials (*Hilltop House, The Life of Mary Sothern, Pepper Young's Family, The Romance of Helen Trent, This Is Nora Drake*), he played supporting roles on many other series, among them: *Charlie Chan, The Chase, Cloak and Dagger, Crime and Peter Chambers, Dimension X, The Ethel Merman Show, Gangbusters, Now Hear This, The Parker Family, The Private Files of Rex Saunders* and *X-Minus One*. On TV Janney hosted the short-lived NBC game show *Stop Me if You've Heard This One* (1948–49), was Jim Matthews in *Another World* (1964–65) and appeared in the cast of the fleeting ABC crime series *Hawk* (1966). He returned to the microphone between 1974 and 1982 for an occasional part on *The CBS Radio Mystery Theater*.

From These Roots was loaded with promising talent and spawned careers of several artists who reached stardom before quitting time. They included Ann Flood (Liz Fraser Allen), Henderson Forsythe (Jim Benson), Robert Mandan (David Allen), Barbara Berjer (Lynn Franklin), Charlotte Rae (Hilda Furman) and Richard Thomas (Richard).

For Ann Flood, *From These Roots* was a prelude to still greater achievements in daytime drama. Her most celebrated role was as heroine Nancy Karr on *The Edge of Night*, from 1962 until the serial departed in late 1984. Afterward it seemed Flood methodically appeared on all the serials beginning with the letter "A." She won supporting roles on *Another World* (1986–87), *All My Children* (1988–89) and *As the World Turns* (1992–93), finally bringing to a close an illustrious career before the cameras.

Henderson Forsythe left *From These Roots* for a 30-year fling as Dr. David Stewart in *As the World Turns* (1960–90), one of the few males to achieve that mark in a single TV soap opera. Earlier he had played in *The Edge of Night* (1957) and on CBS's daytime dramatic anthology *Hotel Cosmopolitan* (1957–58).

From 1965 to 1970 Robert Mandan appeared as Sam Reynolds on *Search for Tomorrow*, the third intended spouse of leading lady Joanne Gardner Barron Tate. (Jo had a penchant for losing husbands and fiancés by death. When Sam passed away before they could wed, she married Tony Vincente, who was superseded after *his* death by Martin Tourneur, the only hubby she divorced.) Mandan added several more television credits to his resume, including bit parts in three short runs—*Caribe* (1975), *Private Benjamin* (1982–83) and *Three's a Crowd* (1984–85). His most memorable role was that of Chester Tate, a principal in the primetime series spoofing drama-by-installment, ABC-TV's *Soap* (1977–81).

Barbara Berjer played Barbara Norris Thorpe from 1971 to 1981 on *Guiding Light*, then came back and reprised the same role beginning in 1995. In between and overlapping (1985–97), she was Bridget Connell on *Another World*.

From These Roots launched Charlotte Rae into numerous primetime sitcoms, among them *Car 54, Where Are You?* (1961–63) and *Diff'rent Strokes* (1978–79). A spin-off from the latter series was developed especially for her and became her most notable role — housemother Edna Garrett at a girls' boarding school on *The Facts of Life* (1979–86). Rae was on *Sesame Street* in 1971–72 and provided voiceovers for the animated TV cartoon *101 Dalmatians: The Series* (1997, 1998). Still going strong in the 21st century, in November 2004 she performed in radio show re-creations during the convention of The Society to Preserve and Encourage Radio Drama, Variety and Comedy in Los Angeles.

Richard Thomas will always be remembered for a single part, that of John-Boy Walton, which he played on CBS's *The Waltons* from 1972 to 1977. Earlier he was in the cast of the ABC daytime serial *A Time for Us* (1964–66). Thomas' other TV series, all in primetime, included *Roots: The Next Generations* (1979), *Adventures of the Swiss Family Robinson* (1998), *It's a Miracle* (1998–2003) and *Just Cause* (2002–2003). He appeared in the motion picture *Wonder Boys* (2000).

The title of **Young Doctor Malone** was borrowed from an audio daytime drama that had survived since 1939 and was still airing as the tele-version arrived. The aural antecedent featuring Sandy Becker (since 1947) would be among a quartet of open-end serials to make history by reaching the end of the era. *The Right to Happiness, Ma Perkins, Young Doctor Malone* and *The Second Mrs. Burton* left the ether together on November 25, 1960, when CBS Radio pulled the plug on the "final four" of its daytime serials still airing, a day some media writers have since dubbed "Black Friday." The matter ended 30 consecutive years of soap opera over the nation's radio hookups. (Other chains had abandoned their serials some years earlier.) On CBS Radio, *Young Doctor Malone* centered on the medic of mythical Three Oaks and his skirmishes and triumphs with patients, the hospital's board, two wives (at different times!) and a daughter.

The transition to TV would in no way reprise the radio storyline, however, as did some video serials with origins in radio. Nor would any of the radio actors be hired for the small screen manifestation. In an unusual move, NBC transferred a half-dozen leading figures from the departing drama *Today Is Ours* to the new banner of *Young Doctor Malone.*

Included in the new drama were Laura Manning (played by Patricia Benoit), Karl Manning (Patrick O'Neal), Leslie Williams Manning (Joyce Lear), Glenn Turner (Ernest Graves), Nicky Manning (Peter Lazar) and Lester Williams (Barry Thomson). Both dramas were under the auspices of writers Julian Funt and David Lesan, facilitating the transitional phase in the storyline. As the denouement of the previous tale played out, the web simply dropped the *Today Is Ours* extension at the end of January. The setting of the action gradually shifted from Central High School in Bolton to Valley Hospital in Denison, Maryland, a more cosmopolitan venue than the one encountered in the previous yarn.

The succeeding series officially premiered at 3 p.m. on December 29, 1958, in a 30-minute format that initially was telecast in black and white, although color was added later. The drama persisted in its original timeslot through September 28, 1962, shifting to 3:30 p.m. on October 1, 1962. It remained there until it left the air on March 29, 1963.

Dr. Jerry Malone was the chief of staff at Valley Hospital, and eventually experienced one downside of metropolitan medical treatment: he was charged with malpractice, a concept that would probably have been foreign in Three Oaks during that epoch. Just as he did in radio, Jerry had two spouses, though the first marriage ended in divorce (unthinkable in radio; his first wife died in the aural-only venue, a neater way of eliminating her), which left him free to remarry. In both mediums he wed Tracey Bannister. He still had an adult daughter named Jill, product of his first marriage and a carryover from radio, but also an adopted grown son, David, in video. David followed in his father's footsteps and literally became the program's *real* young Dr. Malone.

The junior Malone, as might be expected of a melodramatic soap opera protagonist, had a complicated love life. A trio of women became seriously involved with him over the serial's four-year run: Dorothy Ferris, Eve Dunbar and Gig Houseman. Acting against his parents' best judgment, David wed Gig. He was later accused of the suspicious death of his mother-in-law, Lillian Houseman, and went through an unnerving ordeal to prove his innocence. Following that, of course, he had to overcome his tarnished image as a trusted medical practitioner. In 1962 Gig, too, died unexpectedly.

Another relative in the plot drew still more attention by becoming the personification of the proverbial wicked stepmother. Clare Bannister married Tracey's father, Emory, one of the wealthiest men in town, "strictly for his money." She soon began disparaging Faye Bannister, Tracey's then unmarried sibling, while attempting to destroy Jerry and Tracey's wedded bliss. She cheated on Emory with Lionel Steele, who was even more malevolent than Clare, if possible, though one pundit labeled him "soap opera's first 'ambivalent' villain." He came to realize too late that he possessed some principles that the vile, conscienceless Clare — with whom he had aligned himself — would never acknowledge.

Steele was after Denison Foundry, Emory Bannister's business, and connived to use Clare to acquire it. When Emory had had enough of her outrageous tomfoolery, he frightened his wife; as a result, Clare and Lionel retaliated, dragging Emory through spiteful litigation. Emory's sudden demise in January 1961 left the dastardly duo to each other's devices. Their often-stormy connection resulted in a marital union tinged with trickery, envy and mistrust. Clare eventually experienced a few misfortunes that were normally reserved for leading ladies, including the loss of a baby and a loss of sight. Before it was over she would be declared insane and committed to a sanitarium, although — not surprisingly—she employed deceptive means to get out. Lionel surely must have realized his missteps, too; his marriage to Clare was punishment far beyond anything he could have ever imagined.

Jill Malone married gambler Larry Renfrew, who was Lionel Steele's nephew. The thoughtful viewer must have wondered if there really was no other family in Three Oaks from which a Malone could select. Renfrew underwent surgery that was supposed to let him walk naturally, but he wound up in a wheelchair for life instead. When he, too, died mysteriously, Jill was accused and experienced a prolonged court trial before her exoneration. (Another thought worth pondering: Did it ever occur to anybody how many people were dying in a soap opera that fixated on a profession dedicated to saving lives?) With Jill and her brother David free to walk the streets again following their trials for different murders, the Malone story—long since off the radio, too—came to an everlasting end.

Several of the cast members of television's *Young Doctor Malone* were a little more familiar with one another than was usual.

William Prince, who appeared as Jerry Malone, later married actress Augusta Dabney, who played his TV wife Tracey beginning in 1959. As a duo in real life the pair influenced nine daytime serials, possibly a record. Together they performed as a married couple on *Another World* (1964–65, as Ken and Laura Baxter), *As the World Turns* (1966–67, as Bill and Ann Holmes) and *A World Apart* (1970–71, as Russell and Betty Barry). Prince made a pilot film for a half-hour version of *The Egg and I* in 1951, but it netted a quarter-hour soap opera without him. In 1968–69 he joined the cast of *The Edge of Night*. Dabney added several more credits to her portfolio as well: *The Guiding Light* (1970), *General Hospital* (1975–76), *The Doctors* (1980–81) and *Loving* (1983–87, 1995).

Emily McLaughlin, then married in real life to Robert Lansing, played Dr. Eileen Seaton on the staff of Valley Hospital, while Lansing appeared as Peter Brooks, a character with evil intent. The medical profession agreed with McLaughlin so well that she made a career of it as nurse Jessie Brewer on *General Hospital* (1963–91). Lansing, meanwhile, refocused on primetime TV, appearing in several transitory series: *87th Precinct* (1961–62), *Twelve O'Clock High* (1964–65), *The Man Who Never Was* (1966–67), *Automan* (1983–84), *The Equalizer* (1985–89) and *Kung Fu: The Legend Continues* (1993–94).

At least members of the very large performing company on *Young Doctor Malone* made it to the big time: Lesley Woods (who appeared as Clare Bannister Steele), Dick Van Patten (Larry Renfrew) and Joyce Van Patten (Clara Kershaw).

Lesley Woods also turned up on *The Edge of Night* (1964), *Search for Tomorrow* (1967), *Bright Promise* (1971–72), *Return to Peyton Place* (1972–73) and *The Bold and the Beautiful* (1987–89).

Dick Van Patten appeared in several also-rans in primetime: *The Partners* (1971–72), *The New Dick Van Dyke Show* (1973–74), *When Things Were Rotten* (1975) and *WIOU* (1990–91). But his career included two sterling roles for which he will long be remembered—as patriarch Tom Bradford on ABC's *Eight Is Enough* (1977–81) and, to an earlier generation, as son Nels in CBS's beloved *Mama* (1949–57).

Joyce Van Patten, who had already been in the cast of *As the World Turns* (1956–57), appeared in a brief stint on *All My Children*, but concentrated her efforts on nighttime programming. Aside from *The Danny Kaye Show* (1963–67), she performed on several series that bombed: *The Good Guys* (1968–70), *The Don Rickles Show* (1972) and *Unhappily Ever After* (1995–96).

The House on High Street is the final NBC-TV daytime serial to debut during television's golden age. (That web premiered no more serials until *Our Five Daughters* on January 6, 1962, which ran less than nine months.) *The House on High Street* was also one of the first of the breed to be videotaped, a distinct shift in the way soap operas had been fashioned previously — and denoting how most would be produced in the future.

The half-hour dramatic anthology persisted just over four months, between September 28, 1959, and February 5 1960, at 4 p.m. The network thought so highly of the series before it premiered that it ordered 13 weeks of videotapes even before it was sold to a sponsor or a timeslot was found for it. Launched against ABC's *American Bandstand* and CBS's *The Brighter Day* and *The Secret Storm* at the same hour, however, the NBC series soon fell on its face and was swiftly withdrawn.

The narratives, often surrounding juvenile delinquency and divorce, were dramatized over several days, usually three to five, but with a unique dynamic not present in earlier story collections: various figures surfaced repeatedly. One was court probation caseworker John Collier (played by Philip Abbott), who dialogued with all the parties in a given situation. As he explored various social ills, Collier obtained the perspectives of two real-life authorities — psychiatrist Harris B. Peck, a former director of the New York City domestic relations court mental health clinic; and an ex-director of that court, justice James Gehrig. The show recruited talented stage actors for guest appearances, including Alan Alda, Martin Balsam, Lynn Loring, Jan Miner and others.

An NBC press release ballyhooed the feature shortly before its debut:

> Television, stage and screen actor Philip Abbott will star in the series as John Collier, a court probation officer assigned to investigate the cases. These investigations will form the framework within which the dramas of "people in crisis" will be enacted. Abbott will be joined by a roster of distinguished performers as well as by real-life specialists ... whose daily work brings them in contact with Domestic Relations Court activities.
>
> All the stories will be true. Their treatment, however, will be unique in that the length of the stories will vary. Each will be allotted the time needed for thorough, effective presentation.
>
> To heighten the realism of the series, the court scenes and psychiatric examinations will be spontaneous, with the judge and court psychiatrist interviewing the people involved as they would in real life. Also, the final decision in each case will not be known in advance but will be given by the presiding judge, based on the facts presented.

It was a provocative concept. But the teen viewers and homemakers obviously preferred something else.

By now the thoughtful reader may have formed some impressions about the utter chaos that engulfed NBC Television's daytime landscape throughout the 1950s and for much of the 1960s. One observer characterized NBC's dilemma as inaugurating "one flop after another in an industrious but ineffective attempt to make a dent in the CBS monopoly."[13] Did competitor CBS have greater intuitive perception than the Peacock chain? Was better talent (actors, writers, directors) available to CBS? Did CBS have an unfair advantage due to more solid experience with the soap opera model? Had CBS simply encountered a stroke of good luck? No, no, no and a qualified no. While CBS was clearly blessed, there were things it did — and didn't do — that thrust it into that propitious spot.

At mid-twentieth century, the spirits that moved those two giant networks regarding daytime programming were decidedly different. Robert LaGuardia, a longtime soap opera savant in both mediums, offers some inkling of the deliberations that went on behind those cloistered walls at each web.

CBS-TV was absolutely enthusiastic about the potential of daytime TV serials.... In the beginning it was mostly CBS's pioneering spirit and indefatigable belief that what housewives wanted — and would always want — was soap operas, that gave television daytime dramas their initial boost.

NBC did not share the same faith, much to the disadvantage of its new daytime programming. So lukewarm and undecided was this network about what it wanted women to watch in the daytime that it followed a self-defeating pattern of scheduling and canceling serials on its TV network....

CBS, the broadcasting "guiding light" of the soaps, gave the go-ahead to ... *Search for Tomorrow* [on September 3, 1951].... That show, along with the ones that followed shortly afterward, proved how absolutely right was CBS's faith in the soaps in those days.

While CBS-TV was doing all the right things in establishing popular, long-lived daytime serials, NBC-TV was doing all the wrong things. The network officials simply had no concept of what viewers wanted, and whenever they did hit upon a good serial — like *First Love*— they were too insecure to keep it going. All their efforts, unlike CBS's entries, appeared and disappeared rapidly, usually within a year.[14]

Another pundit arrived at a similar conclusion: "NBC pulled the plug on *These Are My Children* [its first TV daytime serial, in 1949] before it had been on the air a full month, setting a precedent for network policy. Through the years NBC would become notorious for quick cancellations. [Series creator Irna] Phillips did learn a lesson from the experience. When the success of *The Guiding Light* gave her clout with CBS, she demanded that the next soap she created from scratch, *As the World Turns*, be given a full year on the air to build an audience."[15]

The same correspondent referred to NBC as "a network notorious for canceling soaps after only a few months."[16]

Serials scholar Raymond W. Stedman observed: "CBS kept *Search for Tomorrow* and *Love of Life* on the air and steadily added new serials.... [Meanwhile,] NBC Television made a series of sweeping changes." NBC's small morning block of daytime serials was replaced with other programming in 1953 while a two-hour block of afternoon soaps launched in 1954 was cut by 50 percent the next year. By 1956 the network had only a single daytime serial still airing.[17]

Years later, Val Dufour, an actor who played in some of those early daytime dramas on the tube, admonished: "NBC was so erratic in those days. They just didn't know what they wanted. They would confuse audiences by starting and canceling shows too quickly. Now, you know that for one show to catch on in the daytime, there should be good ones before it, and after it. NBC's policies at that time prevented this."[18]

While CBS also suffered some casualties in the 1950s (*Woman with a Past, The Seeking Heart, Hotel Cosmopolitan* and a handful of short-lived radio reincarnations, all set for scrutiny in a later chapter), CBS had to have been doing something right to sustain such an impressive string of extraordinary success stories (literally!). A key point intimated by all of the critics above indicates that leaving a show alone — giving it substantial time to build a loyal following — was consistently a prime factor that determined its ultimate fate. Compare, for instance, the air lives of the 10 longest-running daytime serials that debuted in the 1950s on the two webs:

CBS

The Guiding Light (since June 30, 1952)*
As the World Turns (since April 2, 1956)*
Search for Tomorrow— 35 years, 4 months

NBC

Young Doctor Malone— 4 years, 3 months
Hawkins Falls (daytime)— 4 years, 3 months
Modern Romances— 4 years

CBS

The Edge of Night— 28 years, 9 months
Love of Life— 28 years, 4 months
The Secret Storm— 20 years
The Brighter Day— 8 years, 9 months
The Verdict Is Yours— 5 years, 1 month
Valiant Lady— 3 years, 10 months
The First Hundred Years—1 year, 7 months
Still airing as of this writing.

NBC

From These Roots— 3 years, 6 months
The World of Mr. Sweeney— 2 years, 2 months
First Love—1 year, 6 months
Three Steps to Heaven—1 year, 5 months
Concerning Miss Marlowe—1 year
Fairmeadows, U.S.A.—1 year (estimate)
The Greatest Gift—10 months

It seems clear that CBS daytime programming executives of the 1950s were committed first and foremost to the concept that stay-at-home women *wanted to watch daytime serials.* As a result of that fundamental interpretation they put into practice several precepts that visibly demonstrated their allegiance to helping the soap opera take root and thrive. Inspired writing for a new narrative was absolutely critical, including deriving a compelling premise and setting, offering character development and long-term plotlines that would attract and hold viewers, and delivering dialogue that would grip the fans every single day. Accomplished actors, skilled and creative technical support, and ample budget resources were absolute indispensables. Beyond those, the placement of programs within the daytime schedule was a strategic decision, in addition to giving a new drama sufficient time to build a generous audience to sustain it.

For their part, NBC officials seemed to have missed some of those lessons, and in so doing were subject to frequently retracing their familiar missteps. Were those programmers ever really sure just what the housewife wanted to see on her home screen — and if they were, how determined were they to supply it in sufficient quality and quantity at a time in her daily schedule that she could take advantage of it? And, just as importantly, how long would they give her to be wholly entranced by any given drama?

In pointing out the differences in approaches between these two competing networks, our intention has never been to favor one while downplaying the other for their policy-making decisions. Instead, it has been to recount —from the benefit of a half-century of intervening time, and as objectively as possible — what appears to have been basic differences in the philosophies and practices of the two webs.

In succeeding decades NBC-TV rose to equal CBS-TV, and on occasion to surpass it, with several new daytime dramas. In the period under active study, however, CBS-TV was the overwhelming victor in establishing and cultivating a significant harvest in the newly planted garden of daytime soap operas. While CBS didn't do everything right, it did so enough times, and with enough properties, that the daytime serial prospered. As a result, any who love or hate televised soap opera in the contemporary epoch might well thank or disparage CBS for that outcome.

5

Alpha and Omega

During the 16 years that Stefan Schnabel portrayed Dr. Stephen Jackson on TV's *The Guiding Light* (1965–81), he approached his task "like an under-rehearsed opening night every day."[1] Indeed, a soap actor's workday culminates with the first and only recital of an unmistakably complex show, and does so five times a week. It's a simultaneous opening and closing in one performance, and there's little room for error. And during television's golden age, there was no margin at all. If anybody messed up, what transpired was what the viewers saw. Gaffes in dialogue, sound effects, movement, microphone placement, lighting and technical systems went out over the air just as they occurred in the studio. While live television's spontaneity might have branded it as the best of times, the unyielding pressures and potential screw-ups tagged it as the most terrifying of experiences for nearly everybody connected with a soap opera. Some examples of those perplexing dilemmas have been mentioned already; others will find their way into this narrative in due course.

It's enlightening (and fun) to delineate some of the procedures used to get a soap opera on the ether every day. The initial focus will be on the daytime serials that were broadcast during the epoch of the 1950s, when nearly all such dramas were presented live. Beyond that, the changes that came with the inception of videotape will be detailed. There will also be a quick overview of the executive producer's duties, and those of the dramatic writers, too.

Earlier the reader was exposed to the cramped conditions that Dumont actors, stagehands and technical crews dealt with during every performance in the rented confines of the basement of Wanamaker's department store. In the late 1940s and early 1950s a handful of short-lived shows originated in that poorly ventilated theater.

Then there was Liederkranz Hall, an old opera house.[2] It was the site of some primitive CBS-TV studios at which a diverse array of programming ventures were produced. While it, too, cramped the style of the individuals toiling there, its thespians enjoyed a designated eight-by-eleven-foot "changing room" for each gender, an improvement over the fused bathroom/robing facilities at Wanamaker's.

The Deutscher Liederkranz was an imposing four-story turn-of-the-century German Renaissance brownstone situated at 111 East Fifty-Eighth Street in New York on the street's north side between Park and Lexington avenues. Originally an operatic venue for German vocalists, it witnessed some of the better works of German composers through concerts, cantatas and academic courses. A formal organization was founded in 1847 and incorporated in 1860 that staged marvelous performances of Mozart's *Requiem*, Liszt's *Prometheus*, Mendelssohn's *Walpurgisnacht* and other major compositions. Membership in the sponsoring body included Anglo-Saxon musicians and students of the club's School of Vocal Music. By the 1930s Liederkranz also housed the German-American bund, a pro–Nazi alliance of local denizens.

Purchased some time afterward by the Columbia Broadcasting System, the Liederkranz structure was then converted into recording studios. With the looming demands fostered by television's arrival in the late 1940s—and with few options available to accommodate the new medium's spatial needs—CBS president William S. Paley renovated Liederkranz Hall. He subdivided it into a quartet of TV studios expressly geared to daytime programming, which, for the most part, could be performed without studio audiences. From that facility millions of viewers were to gain their first glimpses of the future of mass electronic entertainment. When the building was subsequently razed in the late 1950s and an office tower erected on the site, a primary portion of television's humble beginnings vanished with it.

Let us interrupt our progress for a moment to take a brief, illuminating look into Paleyana.

For years the young CBS owner-mogul William S. Paley was wary of the new medium of television and vigorously obstructed its development. "He was like a horse-and-buggy driver who couldn't fathom the Model T," explained a biographer. "Television appeared as a relentless expense that would end by draining attention and resources from radio, his first love."[3] Had it not been for the fact that Paley turned to Adolph Zukor, head of Paramount-Famous-Lasky Corporation, for financial rescue during Columbia's fledgling era (Zukor was intensely interested in the potential of TV and how it might affect filmdom), CBS might not have pursued TV at all.

But Paley knew that his most formidable rival, David Sarnoff, the recently named president of the Radio Corporation of America (RCA), parent of the National Broadcasting Company and its dual radio networks (NBC Red and Blue), had taken an aggressive stance towards television's development. As early as 1923 Sarnoff predicted that television would be "the ultimate and greatest step in mass communications."[4] At Sarnoff's insistence, in 1928 (less than two years after NBC Radio went on the air) RCA acquired a federal sanction allowing it to launch a first New York City–based experimental TV outlet. That station, with call letters W2XBS, went on the air in July 1930. It would take CBS a full year beyond that date to do the same.

A Sarnoff biographer reasoned, "David Sarnoff nurtured the development [of television] from unpromising beginnings to operational maturity, despite obstruction by segments of his own industry and small support from any source."[5] In 1941 Lee DeForest, who had been instrumental in sending sound across the ether as early as 1906, praised Sarnoff's resolve, claiming that without his "far-sighted vision, financial courage, faith, and persistence, television ... would still be a vague dream."[6] Three years later the Television Broadcasters Association cited Sarnoff as the "Father of American Television."[7] The return on a $50 million investment — one of the few occasions that a single company had put that much cash into a solo venture — didn't begin to appear before 1949, more than two decades after Sarnoff instigated his mission.

And what of Paley? "Television wasn't on Bill's plate," allowed CBS executive Frank Stanton, who ran much of CBS's internal affairs after 1946 and supervised TV operations in the early period. Paley's biographer explained, "His concern about the high cost of shifting from audio to video gave CBS a curiously schizophrenic character in the late forties and early fifties. Mighty radio and infant television inhabited different worlds at the company. In those days CBS advertising salesmen carried calling cards engraved 'Sales—CBS Radio' with 'Television' typed underneath as an afterthought."[8] Paley and Sarnoff had both returned from World War II to pursue opposing dreams—Paley to master his chain's fate by controlling radio programming; Sarnoff, after years of imagination and experimentation, to turn TV into reality.[9]

Yet it was this same Paley who ordered the remodeling of Liederkranz Hall into television studios, obviously with daytime programming in mind. Why had he done so? Not purely for the company's interests, although that was of paramount importance, of course. Anyone who peruses the biographies of Paley and Sarnoff will realize that both men possessed a keen, stubborn, near-bloodthirsty desire to outmaneuver the other. A spirit of one-upmanship characterized their relationship over their lengthy professional careers.[10] Paley's intents were for the body corporate, and partly personal, too. To avoid being left behind, he was taking a proactive step in renovating the structure. In doing so, years later he would be recognized as "the first man to bet several million dollars on daytime television."[11]

From the outside, the weathered red brick façade of Liederkranz Hall continued to look like an opera house, with its soaring second-story arched windows and wide marble steps pointing to the doors. Yet everything beyond that point was now changed. The doors themselves indicated warehouse purchasing in an effort to hold costs to a minimum. While ornate moldings flanked the ceilings, and the windows were shuttered in mahogany wood, the peeling plaster of yellowed walls revealed that the glory days had long passed. Thick red carpeting had been replaced by serviceable gray linoleum. Despite grime and moldy odors, a recurring daytime performer enthused, "It was a real theater, a place where dreams were born."

More marble steps and carved banisters swept beyond the front doors to a former foyer. A balcony could be reached by way of magnificent oak staircases perched on opposite sides of the vestibule. Two floors included two studios each, along with a pair of rudimentary offices and separate dressing compartments and restrooms on each floor. The upper level housed a narrow prop room.

More than a dozen live shows crowded into those tiny facilities during television's earliest years, although not all of them simultaneously. Included were the soap operas *The Brighter Day, The First Hundred Years, The Guiding Light, Love of Life, Portia Faces Life, Search for Tomorrow* and *The Secret Storm*. Mike Wallace and his wife Buff Cobb hosted a daytime talk show; *Bride and Groom* married engaged couples; Margaret Arlen yakked for a half-hour; and *Mr. I. Magination* conducted a feature for juveniles. By mid-decade *Captain Kangaroo* arrived, complete with diverse pets and disguised characters. Commercials for live productions like *The Ed Sullivan Show* and *Studio One* originated in Liederkranz during TV's primetime hours; later at night there was *The Continental*, a series in which suave bachelor Renzo Cesana wooed the ladies. On weekends such fare as *Bob Dixon's Chuck Wagon, Chromoscope, Lamp Unto My Feet* and *Rod Brown of the Rocket Rangers* emanated from that overtaxed site.

A standard-sized bowling alley situated in the basement of Liederkranz Hall was utilized as scenery and equipment storage space for all of the building's program series. Every afternoon a cluster of contestants destined for *Beat the Clock* gathered there to prepare themselves for their upcoming competitions.

In those days, to free up the four studios for live productions, soap opera rehearsals began elsewhere. *Search for Tomorrow*'s cast met each morning at 8 a.m. in a rented office on Madison Avenue, practicing for their 12:30 p.m. performance. Reflecting CBS's zealous emphasis on austerity, the cast sat in dilapidated chairs that series director Charles Irving purchased at the Salvation Army for a dollar each. They consumed bagels and cream cheese and coffee that a staff member brought each day. A floor plan and script dominated Irving's desk. He plotted camera angles with a triangle, verifying his decisions with a small viewfinder.

The first order of the day, nevertheless, was to amend the script. It was paramount that the action and dialogue run no longer or shorter than the allotted time. Occasionally scenes and conversations were cut or padded to end the action on a split second. By 10:30 the assemblage had walked the three blocks over to Liederkranz Hall and were ready to continue rehearsing, this time on the set. There they would adjust to props, cameras, lights, physical movements, etc. Actress Mary Stuart (heroine Joanne Barron) described those rudimentary operations in her memoir:

> There were three scenes and a little short teaser, and as we went through the lines and the moves for the crew, the stagehands began to build the set around us. They weren't sets the way you think of sets today, just pieces of sets. Doors and window frames were hung on piano wire from the grid to indicate walls. Then, the furniture was grouped in the imaginary space. A black velour cyclorama was hung around the walls of the studio, serving, we hoped, to hide the clutter, absorb light, and give the illusion of enclosed areas. What this actually did was give every room we used, the offices, the living rooms, even the kitchens, black walls....
>
> We had three playing areas, at least one commercial setup, three cameras, two booms, and a lot of people who wouldn't stand still. A stagehand was forever walking by outside a window that was supposed to be eighteen stories above the street, or just hanging around smoking a cigarette inside the closet of my bedroom when I opened the door. The only thing to do was stay so close on the faces you couldn't see anything else.[12]

Those piano-wire sets persisted for the first 18 months or so of the serial's life. After the show took a promising turn, and the budget increased in commensurate proportion, real props were brought in to replace the wires. By then there was even the proverbial kitchen sink. Although its pipes were connected to nothing, the sink's drain could be used when a prop man joined a hidden hose to a bucket. In a concluding scene to a somber storyline, Jo and her best friend Marge Bergman toted a five-gallon vessel of soup to the sink that another character had poisoned, and poured it into the drain. (See Chapter Eight for specifics of the escapade.) The soup itself wasn't available during rehearsal so the ladies only went through the motions there. But on the actual show the soup began to drip, drip, drip steadily and deafeningly into the pail below, never subsiding during the four minutes that scene persisted. The actresses delivered their dialogue as if nothing disconcerting was happening, although the sounds were a constant reminder that something was terribly amiss!

There were other effects that were much worse, of course. Sometimes sets toppled down on actors, cameras went dead and mike booms landed in the picture. With surprising frequency the generator stopped and everything on the network went black. On those unpredictable occasions the cameramen lost contact with the control room, and the producer and the director sitting in the control room couldn't see a thing. While attempting to remain calm under near-panic conditions, the performers tried to stay the same distance from the camera that they had been when the little red light faded. They continued talking. They never knew, of course, when they would be unexpectedly on the air again.

Even routine days were distressing. Mary Stuart recalled, "It is hard enough to remember lines that have been very lightly etched on your memory the night before and rearranged that morning.... It is next to impossible ... while a set is being built around you, a lighting man is working, three cameramen and two boommen are moving constantly and talking to the director over their headsets.... In one hour every day we built and lit the set and got all the rehearsal we were going to get."[13]

During that epoch the CBS serials depended upon iconoscope picture tube cameras supplied by the Radio Corporation of America, CBS's old nemesis. Complete with four turret lenses that were manually rotated and focused, the aging RCA cameras were patently unreliable, and subject to breakdowns at any moment — often while a show was airing. Technicians who could instantly service them were rare, adding to the complexities of keeping a live show moving. At the time it must have seemed like those RCA cast-offs were part of a subversive plot to keep CBS from making any headway as it covered new territory; but if so, that never seemed to faze anybody.

The turret lenses were advantageous in one respect, however: when a performer glanced at the camera he would know exactly what angle was being transmitted at that moment. If the lens on top was long, jutting far out from the device, it was a tight shot calling for the actors to remain in place or to move about gradually. In contrast, the other lenses were flatter and wider, allowing greater physical range of motion.

Cameramen, incidentally, were hired from the Signal Corps and Hollywood, although they were accustomed to cameras operating on tracks during film sequences. During those experimental days, sound effects personnel signed on from radio, offering a wide range of audio effects to accompany the action onstage.

Despite all the inconsistencies, the CBS troupe was a perseverant company that appeared determined to excel and exceed whatever expectations anyone might have had under those grueling conditions. "The only thing that made it possible was the people," one leading lady remembered. "Everybody tried so hard, everybody cared, and we were together from the first day, the cast and crew."[14]

Most of the daytime serials during television's golden age aired live every weekday, with a few exceptions: when they were preempted (not shown), either by a special event (such as the bowl games on New Year's Day), the delivery of an important address, or an incident that took precedence (like quadrennial inaugurations of the U.S. president); or when the show was filmed in advance of its air date so the cast and crew could be off on special occasions (like Thanksgiving, Christmas Eve and Christmas Day). Only in the latter instances did actors have an opportunity to see themselves perform. Kinescoping, an early method of filming (which lacked the quality offered by videotape when it later became the industry standard in the late 1950s), was expensive and therefore seldom employed.

Once videotape was introduced, sweeping changes occurred — not least of which was the relief that those associated with live dramatic programming must have felt knowing that if an absolutely unpardonable slip-up occurred during a taping session, it could ultimately be corrected, albeit at a price. Then as now, in staging soap operas (because every person before and behind the cameras is expected to give his or her best every day), only in exceedingly rare cases is a videotape halted. It *is* costly to do so, considering the high salaries paid to the actors, technicians and stagehands, as well as the studio time. It also interrupts spontaneity, the flow of doing a "live tape" performance.

One thespian on a long-running serial of vintage origin explained it in this manner: "Each and every actor on *The Edge of Night* is nervously aware that he is rehearsing to perform on 'live' tape — that is, the director is not going to order the tape stopped for a retake if a line is flubbed; if he did, the show would never get off the ground. It's just too expensive to stop tape, so an actor knows that his lousy performance, or his mistake, will be heard and seen by an audience larger than any stage actor could dream of.... No wonder daytime-serial casting directors try to hire only actors and directors skilled in this kind of rough-house work."[15] The professionals approach their tasks every workday as if there is no turning back. For what they are paid, they can't afford to do otherwise.

Depending on the soap opera, the normal starting time for actors on most contemporary dramas is 7:30 or 8:00 a.m., although some begin as early as 6 a.m. Today's rehearsal and performance studios are a far cry from Liederkranz Hall and Wanamaker's basement. The spacious, climate-controlled warehouses boast state-of-the-art cameras and technical systems, including lighting and sound, and physical properties on a grand scale. Sets are magnificent and are populated with actors who are attired and coiffured for a public that will judge them in multiple ways every day.[16]

The first stop for the performers is the rehearsal hall, where there is a read-through of the day's script.[17] Chairs, tables and substitute props are arranged to symbolize the sets for the day. While it's the director's job to inform the actors about when and where to speak, those thespians often interject their own notions into the mix, too. The rest of the day is composed of a run-through in the studio, with the technical crew and director on hand to block movements and select camera angles. Special attention is given to timing. There may, or may not, be another practice session before the dress rehearsal. At the end there is the live taping. Interspersed between rehearsals are visits to makeup, hairdressing and wardrobe, plus the actors get to study the script in their own dressing rooms. There's also a lunch break shortly before the dress rehearsal, when everything should be just as it will appear in the taping session.

After the show is filmed everyone pauses briefly while the tapes are examined. Once they are verified as acceptable the actors depart — unless they are summoned to a pre-rehearsal read-through of the next day's script. At home, of course, they have several hours of memorization ahead of them. Hour shows tape about 90 pages of script a day; half-hour shows consume half that, although a performer commits to memory only those scenes in which he or she is to appear. Performing in a serial means acting in "the roughest of all media," claimed one scholar. Expounding on the blocking process during the show's run-through practice session, he explained:

> Not only are the actors required to commit to memory pages of dialogue in one day, but they must also immediately learn on which line, and often which word, they are to make specific movements — such as crossing a room, picking up a cup, or walking around a sofa. On these particular words or lines, the cameramen are cued to come in for a closeup or move back for a long shot, or perhaps another camera will pick up the scene from a different angle. It can ruin a scene if an actor forgets a cue line, or faces the wrong way when he says it. Should that happen, the camera might be forced to shoot out into the studio.[18]

So what does the "executive producer" do on a soap opera? Is that a fancy title for a flunky? Hardly. He represents the sponsor and makes the ultimate decisions about how the program will look when it appears on the air. While the cast is rehearsing during the early morning with the director, the executive producer is struggling over budgets, negotiating actors' contracts, talking with officials at the sponsor's headquarters and at the advertising agency that directly employs him, discussing future script ideas with the show's head writer, and handling a myriad of little details that require his attention. The first time he hears and sees the day's program is during the run-through before the cameras. He frequently confers with the director. If the executive producer desires any changes, his colleague implements them.

Finally, a few words about scripting a soap opera: "Soap opera writers are a species unto themselves. They create life in mythical towns and for mythical families. They establish justice, mete out punishment, and arrange that everyone gets his just desserts."[19] Paul Mayer devoted some of his professional career to penning multiple daytime serials for television (*Where the Heart Is, Love of Life, Ryan's Hope*). "Sometimes, if you think of a show as a long-running novel," he explained, "then you think of stories with lots of steps in them. If you have stories with many steps, then you're golden."[20]

Since its inception, soap writing has invariably demanded a rare temperament and talent. Deadlines arrive daily and must be met without fail. Whatever a writer's current mood or inclination, he must produce compelling narrative consistently, or he will be replaced at once. "On some shows, particularly the ones with weak ratings, writers come and go so fast that the actor [playing a particular role] usually knows much more about his character — its history, motivations, involvements — than the writer does," one wag noted. "Sometimes soap opera actors become very protective of their characters. Conflicts between actors and writers develop, and it's up to the producer to mediate."[21] On the other hand, a competent and creative writer can continue at the keyboard for many years.

A big difference in soap writing today and during the televised serial's initial decade is that now the writer(s) is/are much more involved with the producer(s) and director(s). While there were only one or two scribes per show in the beginning, every current soap opera has a head writer and a staff of subordinate scribes. When there is a vacancy, these minions may ultimately be promoted to head writing duties on the serial on which they work or on another show. Occasionally some of those wordsmiths have gone on to create other durable dramas. Two of Irna Phillips' protégés, Agnes Nixon and William J. Bell, were so successful that collectively their legacies continue to impact audiences on seven of the nine daytime dramas currently airing: *All My Children, As the World Turns, The Guiding Light, The Bold and the Beautiful, Days of Our Lives, One Life to Live* and *The Young and the Restless*. Of course, their triumphs pay homage to Phillips, the original inspiration. (See the succeeding chapter.)

> The day-to-day writing of a show is a taxing process. First, a long-term story projection must be drawn up [usually referred to as a series' "bible," which includes a "back story" or what happened in the characters' lives before the serial began]. This document usually covers about one year of generalized story. After this is approved, the writers work out a more detailed outline, usually covering from six to eight weeks. Finally, each week is broken down, day by day, in an outline form from which the actual scripts are written.[22]

At scheduled intervals, annually or possibly every six months, the head writer dialogues at face-to-face working conferences with the serial's executive producer, director and representatives of the ad agency, sponsor and network. Projected plotlines are hammered out and refined in sessions that can extend for several days. When those meetings conclude, the head writer carries the freshly approved ideas back to the subordinate dialoguers to implement in the storylines, sometimes projecting actions that will occur over protracted periods of time.

There's a whole lot more that a soap opera head writer tracks. Serials often boast 35 or 40 ongoing performers, and each one has a contract stipulating the number of days he or she is guaranteed work every year. (If an actor isn't needed in the plotting for the full amount of time specified, he or she is paid for it anyway, and will be compensated additionally for any days needed beyond the contractual provision.) It's one of the head writer's chores to adjust the storylines to conform to those stipulations. If an actor is granted a vacation or extended time off to pursue other opportunities (like summer stock or theatrical appearances), the head writer has to be mindful of it and taper the action to accommodate that situation. Therefore, there is a constant juggling of thespians in the background while the narrative moves forward.

Everything was so much simpler in the 1950s, naturally, when daytime dramas aired for a quarter-hour daily (unlike today's half-hour and hour-long features). In the golden age of television, production was absolutely the alpha and the omega — the beginning and the end of a play, never to be repeated. What you saw was what you got. And despite the perilous hazards that existed and the potential for failure, an indomitable pioneering spirit among many people resulted in some pretty fair entertainment. We had never witnessed anything like it before — and never would again.

6

The Maven of Matinee

She was "the single most important influence on television soaps."[1] No one has equaled the impact Irna Phillips made on serialized radio and television drama. It's doubtful that her foresight or her accomplishments will ever be surpassed. While others have contributed greatly to the form, no one has done so as pervasively or for as long — or in dual branches of broadcasting. Her contributions are unparalleled.

Sources labeled the Queen of Soap Opera "irascible," "obstreperous," "overbearing" and "indomitable." At times she was all of those. While breaking new ground and implementing her theories, she was similarly removing stereotypical images of her gender, proving to herself and to others that she had what it took to play ball in an atmosphere dominated by males. In doing so, she challenged the established system, sometimes bucking long odds. And with zeal and perseverance, this one-woman show won many — and probably most — of her battles.

More than anybody else, Irna Phillips is recognized as the individual who left fingerprints on practically every facet of soap opera. No other comes close to providing so many innovations— advancements that have outlived her by more than three decades. While two of her radio rivals, Frank and Anne Hummert, created many more stories than she (no fewer than 61 daytime serials for radio alone), Phillips' enveloping influence also permeated video, something the Hummerts never tried. On the tube, in fact, Phillips became the dominant player, singularly robed in that propitious mantle for two decades.

She was also instrumental in placing Chicago on the national broadcasting map. The plethora of dramatic programming that sprang from her inventive mind generated scores of shows that originated within the confines of the Windy City's famed Loop. Her extensive influence, geographically reaching around the globe, is as timeless as the narratives she developed that still affect millions across multiple generations.

Born on July 1, 1901, of German-Jewish heritage to William and Betty Phillips, the owners of a small Chicago retail grocery concern, Irna Phillips was to lose her dad when she was only eight. Her widowed mom was left with a brood of 10 children to raise. Irna experienced a dull, lonely childhood mired in poverty. She obsessed that she wore "hand-me-down-clothes and [had] no friends." She spent much of her time reading and pretending, fabricating intricate stories of the experiences of her homemade dolls. She also fantasized about becoming an actress some day.

Imagine, if you can, overcoming those formidable odds to earn a bachelor's degree in education in 1923 from the University of Illinois, and a master's degree in public speaking in 1924 from the University of Wisconsin. That was no small feat for a woman in the 1920s who hailed from such a large family of minimal means. Phillips exhibited a spirited tenacity that was to characterize her attitude about life in general. Realizing that her physical features were undistinguished, plain and simple, she abandoned her dream of a career on the stage or in film. Instead, for a brief tenure she coached classes in speech and drama at William Woods Junior College in Fulton, Missouri. She left that post to accept a teaching challenge at a Dayton, Ohio, school. For the next five years she instructed students in dramatics and storytelling.

In the early summer of 1930, then 28, Phillips found seasonal work as an actress at Chicago's radio station WGN. (The fascinating tale of her early days on the air, including giving birth to soap opera, is recounted in Chapter Two.) Before long she was also writing conversational dialogue. Giving up teaching, on October 20, 1930, Phillips introduced listeners in the Windy City to the first matinee serial, *Painted Dreams*.[2] More than a decade later she would lose a court battle over possession of that drama. As creator of the storyline, she believed that the material was *hers* (she wanted to carry it to a network), but WGN successfully argued that because the drama was *their* idea and *they* aired it, it belonged to *them*.

Following that imbroglio, Phillips immediately established ownership rights to everything she wrote. That included the dialogue penned by other ghostwriting scribes whose work appeared under her name. She became a shrewd and wealthy businesswoman, eventually taking no less than a quarter-of-a-million dollars out of radio every year during her peak years. In 1948 she received $52,000 for contributing five quarter-hour radio scripts a week to *The Guiding Light* alone! Not a shabby haul for a few hours of work in postwar America (several dialoguers assisted in penning the narrative, including William J. Bell and Agnes Eckhardt).[3] In television, of course, Phillips was to earn millions more, making her one of the wealthiest people (of *either* gender) in broadcasting.

Beyond *Painted Dreams*, Phillips' serialized radio creations included *Today's Children* (which was a virtual copy of *Painted Dreams* that aired on NBC Blue and Red while her legal wrangle dragged on), *The Guiding Light, The Road of Life, Woman in White, The Right to Happiness, Lonely Women, Masquerade* and *The Brighter Day*. For a while she was also a story consultant for radio's *Young Doctor Malone*. A half-dozen of the 10 radio series would make their way onto TV, some more successfully than others. The laggards were *These Are My Children* (a fleeting 1949 experiment on NBC that worked off of the premise, setting and people found in both *Painted Dreams* and *Today's Children*) and *The Road of Life* (a six-month 1954–55 venture on CBS). The achievers included *The Guiding Light* (since 1952 on CBS), *The Brighter Day* (1954–62 on CBS) and *Young Doctor Malone* (1958–63 on NBC, which Phillips created but did not write).

In the beginning, Phillips typed all of her scripts alone, eventually keeping three serials going in tandem by herself. So fresh was some of her verbiage that, legend has it, on occasion she was making corrections and altering dialogue only moments before some of her lines were spoken on the air. In those days before mimeographing and ditto machines came into vogue, Phillips produced her scripts on a manual typewriter. She used onion-skin and carbon paper to make enough for the director and cast members to each have their own copy. Of course, those receiving the sixth and seventh duplications sometimes struggled to read them.

Although Phillips possessed a gift for storytelling, by no means could she have been considered an extraordinary dialoguer. Her actors rewrote as many of their lines as they believed they could get away with. Once, on returning to *As the World Turns* after an extended absence, the Doyenne of Daytime engendered this assessment: "Phillips' day-to-day scripting was not her best and her dialogue was atrocious."[4] This was true in the earliest radio days, and her conversations didn't improve with age. "The writing, direction and plot are in the most intense terms," said a critic shortly before Phillips went into television. "The tone is lugubrious and the pace is torpid. There is never the slightest suggestion of lightness or enjoyment, but the emphasis is constantly on emotional contortion, and mental anguish," he concluded.[5]

"Over the last few years, Miss Phillips' stories have contained a variety of brutal physical situations, divorces, illegitimate births, suggestions of incest and even murders," observed a journalist.[6] Another related how some classified her serials as "vehicles of evil."[7] It was apparent that Phillips was challenging reality head-on, demonstrably running ahead of her peers by facing some prime human concerns. All of it indicated that she would determine the pace rather than merely follow others. Despite her perceived deficiencies in dialoguing, she was quite adept at the art of plot origination. It was a talent that kept her in solid demand with advertisers, agencies and the networks carrying her programs.

By the 1940s Phillips was dictating her scripts every day, reportedly in six-to-eight-hour chunks of time. She edited her material on the spot and seldom rewrote any of it. When dictating to a stenographer, her technique was to observe that individual's (the clerical staffer's) facial expressions to determine how an audience might receive her plays. As a result of this gauge she'd sometimes make changes in what she had said only moments before. It has been estimated that by dictating she could write as many as two million words annually, the equivalent of 30 or 40 fair-sized novels. "My working process arises," she said, "from four themes that drive my daytime serials: appealing to the instinct of a woman's self-preservation, to sexual drive, to the family instinct, and some combination of the three."

Later, when even dictation became too cumbersome, Phillips modified the process by secretly adding a small staff of assistant writers (or dialoguers, in Hummert parlance). At her bidding, those uncredited wordsmiths took her plot sketches and fleshed them out into full-fledged scripts. It relieved Phillips from being tied to the grind of producing every word of several daily dramas, freeing her to pursue other projects (like creating new soap operas) and allowing her to keep her hands in every detail of every drama she had on the air. Relying on a cadre of scribes to produce her dialogue was a pattern that Phillips followed in scripting future TV daytime serials. A well-organized administrator — who operated at times in backwater style — she mapped out her serial installments on cardboard with a grid for every day's episode, projected up to six weeks ahead. She jotted down only a word or two in each square, a reminder of the storyline's future itinerary.

Incidentally, in comparison to radio's most prolific soap opera producers, Frank and Anne Hummert, who possessed a well-documented penchant for stinginess, Phillips espoused a different philosophy in conducting her business. While the Hummerts were proudly paying the dialoguers toiling in their trenches $25 per 15-minute script, Phillips reportedly compensated her scribes at $50 to $100. Although she was demanding, that spoke volumes about Phillips' natural tendency toward generosity, suggesting she valued highly the contributions of those loyal to her.

The pundits credit (or criticize) Phillips for introducing the amnesiac to soap opera's storylines. It is a ploy that was repeated frequently on the aural serials (her own and those of other scribes), especially when a show's ratings required some juicing up. So popular was the malady among radio serial authors that figures on four or five daytime dramas could experience amnesia concurrently. According to wordsmith Les White, Phillips also put daytime drama's first kidnapping on the air, as well as its first storyline about illegitimacy and its initial courtroom trial, too. She invented the tease ending, enticing listeners to tune in for the following day's chapter. She was the first to add organ music to transition from one scene to another.[8] And she crafted an ingenious device for her departing radio serials in which characters to be featured on a succeeding series (which she wrote) were introduced into the final storylines of the exiting show. Indeed, a lot of innovations that are commonplace today originated on her keyboard.

More than any other scribe in serialdom, Phillips was known for emphasizing characterization. "The important factor," she insisted, "is that the story grow out of characters rather than [the] story [being] superimposed upon characters. This I have found to be most successful, realistic and believable. We do what we do because we are what we are." Over lengthy periods of time, little by little Phillips revealed innate details about the people in her yarns, allowing the fans to be drawn to those denizens. "The success of Irna Phillips' serials came from her devotion to reality and from her careful understanding of the women who comprised her audience," a researcher suggested.[9]

She was well aware of what was important to those tuning in at home. A couple of her subjects might spend a full quarter-hour on radio dialoguing with each other. The primary craving of women, she postulated, was to create a warm and protected family—"to build securely for herself a haven, which means a husband, a family, friends, and a mode of living all wrapped up neatly and compactly into a tight little ball with the woman as the busy center of the complete, secure little world."[10] In fact, she asserted, "The foundations of all dreams of all the men and women in the world are love, family, home."

From soap opera's beginning, most of its inhabitants were plain individuals with modest higher education to their credit. Some were incessantly involved in romantic pursuits, while others were wed to people of affluence or importance, yet they lingered as simple folk whose trade or private accomplishments were the result of natural skills rather than unusual advantage. While at times lawyers and medics were included in the plots, those careers were incidental to the home-centered storylines. This began to change in 1937 when Irna Phillips introduced a new type of protagonist—the professional individual—with the launch of two new radio serials, *The Guiding Light* and *Road of Life*.

Phillips once again altered the landscape of daytime drama. Dr. John Ruthledge was a well-seasoned nonsectarian clergyman whose vestibule was often the principal venue of *The Guiding Light*. (Though Phillips was Jewish, during her youth she was impressed by a Christian minister who inspired not only this drama but *The Brighter Day*.) The diverse facets of physical, mental and emotional distress were a daily focus of Dr. Jim Brent's hospital quests on *Road of Life*. (Infirmary venues and tales of ailments and disease were vintage Phillips. A hypochondriac who routinely frequented physicians' clinics, she transferred an absorption with medicine to her work.)

Other producers quickly picked up on Phillips' innovations. Within four years another dozen daytime serials had surfaced in which blue-collar workers were passé while the white-collar crowd, including physicians, nurses, pastors, barristers, social workers and educators, were the prime movers and shakers. More would follow.

Phillips insisted that her characters led more interesting lives than the common folk populating the majority of radio narratives. The dramatic fare of prolific serial-makers

Frank and Anne Hummert, and Elaine Sterne Carrington, invariably centered on plain individuals with little to distinguish them. The professional character, on the other hand, added a dimension of believability to soap opera. After all, such heroes and heroines could easily and naturally become embroiled in the compelling circumstances of others' lives. Simultaneously, nothing kept them from encountering similar issues that weighed upon the nonprofessional figures of other serials. Phillips correctly reasoned that she could have it both ways. Those highly trained people would actively reside in — and even predominate — most of the serials she created for two mediums during the remainder of her life.

Phillips constantly relied on a host of professional specialists to help her stay on track while she penned her serials. At times she kept medical and legal experts on retainer to check her facts for her dramas. One historiographer intimated that she paid lawyers for synopses of their trial cases, filling in fictitious names when she integrated them into her plotlines. As early as 1944 Phillips informed an academic body that her tales emerged after consulting with (in alphabetical order) the American Legion, American Medical Association, Association for Family Living, Federal Council of Churches of Christ in America, National Education Association, Red Cross, U.S. Office of War Information, U.S. Navy Department, U.S. Veterans Administration and the U.S. War Department. Quite an impressive reference directory!

Ever the pacesetter, Phillips was able to place three of her highly touted radio serials (*The Guiding Light, Today's Children, Woman in White*) in adjacent time slots on NBC in 1943 and thereby instigate a "crossover effect." The characters on one drama leaped over the station breaks and appeared in the storylines of the other two dramas. A single sponsor underwrote the trio of serials, and the experiment was promoted as "The General Mills Hour." While the idea clicked for Phillips, when — on a few occasions— others attempted to implement similar measures, they never worked quite as well.

In the late 1930s and early 1940s radio soap operas began to move out of Chicago to New York City. In 1946, nevertheless, the General Mills–backed series that Irna Phillips was writing detoured briefly; they were transferred from Chicago to new NBC studios in Hollywood for a brief respite (1947–49) before shifting to New York. Subsequently, while some of the earliest TV serials originated in the Windy City and Philadelphia, new productions a few years later were concentrated in New York City or Los Angeles. Meanwhile, as a diversionary tactic, in 1945 Phillips took a sideline job instructing students in writing radio serials at Chicago's Northwestern University, one of her alma maters. (As an undergraduate, she attended Northwestern for a year.)

Phillips' supremacy in the genre allowed her to remain firmly entrenched in her beloved Chicago throughout her professional career, despite the serial moves. In an age long before the inception of fax, email, cell phones and other modern communication methods, Phillips mailed her scripts and voluminous notes to producers in New York. Beyond that, she kept her fingers in every pie through incessant telephone calls and sporadic trips to Gotham to check the progress first-hand. Actress Eileen Fulton of *As the World Turns* confirmed, "She had a special television line set up so she could watch our dress rehearsals and then provide notes.... Irna had final say on everything to do with the show."

As the closing credits rolled at the end of each day's program, the telephone was ringing in the New York production center. Irna was anxious to inform the producers and directors about what had displeased her with that day's performance. Procter & Gamble vested enough power in her that she could act unilaterally in most situations. "By this time she had earned a reputation for being nearly dictatorial in her commandments about characters and actors. When she met the actors, she would almost always address them by their character names [a holdover practice she carried from the early radio days], and those who did not please her, for any of a number of reasons, found themselves out of work," an informant validated.[11] So difficult was Phillips to work with that several acknowledged that her relentless criticism drove some of her actors, including Rosemary Prinz, to nervous breakdowns.[12] After a dozen years playing on *As the World Turns* (1956–68), Prinz vowed she would never return to daytime serials. She did, four times, but never on one in which Phillips was still actively involved.

> The irascible writer ruled her kingdom with an iron hand, frequently terrorizing producers, writers, and directors with long telephone calls that left no doubt how she felt about the execution of her ideas. It was generally agreed that even her bosses, executives with Procter & Gamble, lived in mortal fear of her. (When actress Eileen Fulton accidentally dropped her script, a shocked P & G official retrieved it with the admonition, "An Irna Phillips script is like the flag; it never touches the floor.") Actors were fired on a whim, or even if Phillips did not like their looks.... Phillips expected everyone to share her all-consuming passion for her stories.[13]

As detailed earlier (in Chapter Three), Irna Phillips was the first to introduce a daytime serial to a major television network, just as she had done on radio. While *These Are My Children* lasted on NBC-TV only four weeks, from January 31, 1949, to February 25, 1949, it couldn't be branded as a complete washout; its pithy fling exposed Phillips to the potential (and attraction) of televised serials. From that occasion forward — even though that initial effort was a disaster by most assessments — Phillips' eyes were opened, her horizons broadened.

Before that she was unconvinced of daytime drama's worth on television. But three years later she introduced her long-playing aural narrative *The Guiding Light* to a visual audience, on June 30, 1952. After it caught on she literally never, ever looked back.[14] *Guiding Light* (as it is now called) is the longest running narrative in the history of broadcasting, having begun on radio on January 25, 1937.

In the mid–1950s CBS informed Phillips that it intended to experiment with a new color system and planned to air a live episode of *The Guiding Light* in color. This pleased many connected with the serial, but Phillips, invariably disgruntled by anything she couldn't manipulate, was not. Spitefully, she wrote an installment for that day to be staged altogether in a glaring white operating room. In that way most of the color camera techniques were useless, stymied by the sterile set. After that experience, CBS avoided Phillips' show for similar auditions of new equipment. *Search for Tomorrow*, in the meantime, whose staff worked *with* the chain rather than as if it were the enemy, helped itself to quite a few color chapters telecast during the 1950s and early 1960s. In some respects it became the prototype of what was in the works.

Irna Phillips developed her own philosophy, and insisted it be followed. "I have never had a serial canceled, and every serial I created has a family at the center," she mused.[15] Citing *As the World Turns* as "the archetypical Irna Phillips creation," one critic concluded, "Drama and action are almost superfluous; it's people — their foibles, interests, habits, and worries — that make the world turn."[16]

One wag drew a number of parallels between the characters of "her greatest triumph," *As the World Turns*, and Phillips herself.[17] "In her own life," he pointed out, "Phillips, a former schoolteacher, had fallen in love with a married man who refused to marry her when he realized that she could not have children; she later [at age 42] adopted a son, Thomas [Dirk Phillips], and [at 43] a daughter, Katherine [Louise Phillips]."[18] On *As the*

World Turns, Nancy Hughes was an ex-teacher, Edith Hughes was a sympathetic mistress to a married man, Penny Hughes was infertile and Ellen Lowell was a single mom.

Ironically, another chronicle noted that while the lifelong spinster had no biological children of her own, "She gave birth to more characters and kept more actors thriving and at work than perhaps anyone else since Shakespeare."[19] Furthermore, she created a dramatic form, set a tradition in motion, labored for more than four decades at her trade, and — when she was done — had authored the equivalent of 2,500 novels over her lifetime. Not a bad legacy for someone so undistinguished in her earliest years.

> Irna saw daytime drama in terms of time and character, rather than story. She understood something that only loyal soap fans truly know: that people want to become involved with the lives of other people; that viewers follow soaps not just to see what happens next, but to experience — drink in, as it were — the characters, almost as if they lived in viewers' homes. Story to Irna was simply a vehicle; it was from the moment-to-moment emotions of her characters, expressed to each other in quiet scenes, that viewers derived true vicarious pleasure. Understanding this essential truth about the viewer, Irna needed more television time — a full half-hour — for the camera to eavesdrop on long "coffee cup" conversations, showing every facial reaction in utmost detail. Obviously, such probing scenes required the most exquisite sort of cameo acting, so Irna and partner Ted Corday — one of the great directorial talents in serials, from the days when they were all broadcast from Chicago radio studios — chose their actors with painstaking care. Each performer had to be capable of totally absorbing the viewer with his or her personality, and of handling Corday's extreme emphasis on close-ups.[20]

Despite her many contributions, sometimes Phillips' ideas could be unsettling, even to veterans of the industry. In her memoir, Mary Stuart recalled a conversation she had with Phillips one day at Liederkranz Hall. Stuart was the heroine of *Search for Tomorrow*, the quarter-hour serial that immediately preceded Phillips' *The Guiding Light* on CBS. Some time before, Phillips had publicly announced that she would no longer work on quarter-hour programs (both *Search* and *Light* were 15-minute features). Instead, she planned to devote her efforts to developing half-hour serials. (*As the World Turns* was her first, in 1956.) With the well understood influence the granddame of drama possessed with Procter & Gamble (which sponsored both shows), it seemed apparent to Stuart that one obvious option for Phillips was to combine the two quarter-hour shows into one, perhaps at *Search's* expense. "The ploy seemed obvious to me," said Stuart, "but nobody else noticed."

Only a short time before, Phillips lobbied Procter & Gamble to hire a trio of individuals for *Search* who — in Stuart's opinion — proved incredibly injurious to the serial and, maybe as importantly, to interpersonal relationships between the show's cast and crew. The threesome consisted of director Dan Levin, with whom Stuart frequently sparred in a simmering battle that persisted throughout Levin's protracted tenure, and a pair of contentious scribes, Frank and Doris Hursley. The fact that they joined *Search's* staff in the first place underscored what a formidably powerful influence (or threat) Phillips could be in pursuing her own agenda. (All of this is carried further in Chapter Eight.)

Both quarter-hour shows were eventually extended to half-hours. Although Phillips ultimately never gained control of *Search* to bring that about, in late 1996 — a full decade after *Search* left the air forever — Stuart returned to daytime television. Oddly enough, she appeared as Meta Bauer, a major character who had been absent from the plotline of *Guiding Light* for 22 years. In an incongruous twist of fate, 23 years after Phillips' demise, Stuart's mid–1950s assumption seemed to have come true: Stuart was working on the one surviving drama — four decades after Phillips hinted there was no room for two!

Phillips' intention to transform quarter-hour soap operas into half-hour daytime dramas didn't occur automatically, however; and for a while it looked as if she might fail. After she transitioned *Light* to television in 1952 (with a concurrent radio extension of four years), she began to badger P&G officials and the brass at CBS, attempting to win them over to her point of view: that housewives *would* be receptive to half-hour daytime dramas—*and they had the time* to take coffee breaks between vacuuming, washing dishes and clothes, drying the laundry on a clothesline, making beds, ironing and changing diapers. Half-hour serials would give Phillips more opportunity for slower-paced, character-driven stories, which would be of immense value to the viewer, she insisted. And, she correctly interjected, a 30-minute program was cheaper to produce than two 15-minute features.

It's unclear whether Phillips finally convinced those skeptics that it would be a good deal for them, or whether they simply grew weary of her persistent bellyaching (perhaps a little of both). But after two years of her whining, they capitulated and allowed her to create *As the World Turns*. One source allowed that P&G "only gave in to Phillips when they realized that this irascible woman was not going to abandon her pet project."[21] Not only that, Phillips collected an unprecedented proviso that the serial would not be canceled for 12 full months, no matter how grim its ratings might turn out to be. Originally she wanted to extend *The Guiding Light* for another 15 minutes (as she had strongly implied to Mary Stuart), but P&G put its foot down on that one.

Yet in finally signing on to the half-hour notion, CBS and P&G apparently became instant converts, adding a second 30-minute drama on the same day. *As the World Turns* and *The Edge of Night*, a crime melodrama, both premiered on April 2, 1956, another propitious date in the annals of soap opera and especially for CBS.[22] (Chapters 12 and 13 include more exhaustive scrutiny.) With these two debuting serials the future of daytime drama was etched. Other producers began to copy the new method. Irna Phillips, who had launched the quarter-hour soap opera more than a quarter of a century before — and who seemingly was always on the cutting edge — drove the first nail in the quarter-hour format's coffin.[23]

Irna's new show wasn't just an expanded fifteen-minute serial, but a fresh approach to a twenty-six-year-old invention — a totally visual approach. She slowed time down to a near halt, and had the cameras peer at length into the faces of actors whom she and director Ted Corday had picked with assiduous care. The Lowells and the Hugheses simply pondered family problems, and gradually, ever so gradually, increasing numbers of viewers were drawn to the show, fascinated by its realism. Never before had a soap probed its characters so deeply and so thoroughly. There were no murders, no amnesiacs, no mysterious people popping up from desert [*sic*] islands, no villains. There weren't even flawless heroines, such as Vanessa on *Love of Life* and Joanne on *Search for Tomorrow*. The situations were as real and as slowly observed as in life. *As the World Turns* was not only the most visual but also the most adult drama yet televised in the afternoon.[24]

Terming it "an approach perfectly suited to television," one reporter labeled innovative chats over ubiquitous cups of coffee, pregnant pauses and long close-ups that precipitated fadeouts "strikingly original" when Phillips introduced them. "The cameras caught the subtleties, ironies, and domestic wit," and the show was "a certified hit."[25]

Thirteen weeks into the new venture a contract dispute caused Phillips to terminate the actress who portrayed heroine Nancy Hughes, Helen Wagner. (Recall that on her shows Phillips wielded the authority of a god.) An unfazed Wagner was busily performing in a play a short time afterwards, giving Phillips the opportunity to rethink a somewhat hasty decision. When she offered Wagner her old job back, Wagner accepted — but held Phillips at bay until her current commitment to the play ended. "Irna loved being at my mercy and wanted me back on the show all the more," Wagner cooed. Today Wagner remains *As the World Turns*' only original cast member — on a serial that had now surpassed its half-century mark (in 2006), an astonishing feat both for the show *and* the thespian Phillips nearly let get away!

Despite Phillips' comprehensive grasp of the soap opera genre, and the big stick that she incessantly waved over it, at times there were tiny signals that even the insuperable prima donna of daytime possessed feet of clay. One such crack in the concrete occurred during the weeks immediately after *As the World Turns* debuted.

It must have stung something awful.

To substantially nurture something for a lengthy period of time and then suddenly have it yanked from one's clutches with little chance of influencing its future must have been disheartening at best and, quite likely, devastating to the caregiver.

The mother of soap opera, Irna Phillips, experienced it in the spring of 1956 when her ties with a previously malnourished daytime radio serial were abruptly severed.

"It doesn't seem possible that last week my association with *Young Doctor Malone* and the Columbia Broadcasting System was terminated," she launched into a typewritten invective ... to *Malone* scriptwriter David Lesan.... While her memo didn't reveal the circumstances of her separation, she acknowledged to Lesan: "Knowing Procter and Gamble, you should realize by this time they never do the obvious."

Irna Phillips' departure from a potent storyline-consulting role for *Young Doctor Malone* was particularly painful to her. Just 20 months earlier the quarter-hour narrative she had affectionately inspired [as story consultant] catapulted into first place in the Nielsen ratings among nearly three-dozen daytime [radio] dramas. That dynamic encouraged her toward even loftier heights....

For a long while it had been her intent to take the popular aural medical feature to weekday television....

Regrettably, time for her to influence the outcome ran out before the idea could be implemented. While the program ultimately arrived ... on December 29, 1958, a pundit observed: "This TV adaptation of the long-running radio serial of the same name ... transferred only the principal characters' names and the credits of Irna Phillips as creator and Julian Funt as writer."[26]

Phillips' pervasive influence, possibly for the very first time, was being challenged and actually held in check. It wouldn't be the last time. The storyline of *Young Doctor Malone* on television, incidentally, did not parallel that of its radio forebear, maybe to at least some degree because of Phillips' permanent separation from the aural series. The radio version persisted through November 25, 1960, and was one of the final four open-end daytime serials to depart the aural ether. The drama ran on NBC-TV to March 29, 1963, though Phillips' assistance with the narrative after its launch appeared minimal, if there at all.

Not long afterward, NBC premiered its first durable daytime serial winner, *Another World*, created by Irna Phillips and William J. Bell. It aired from May 4, 1964, through June 25, 1999. Surprisingly, instead of characterization, the narrative stressed melodrama. Yet all the other familiar Phillips trademarks were there, including those behind the cameras. For no apparent reason she fired an actor playing a major figure after the first performance, and another at the close of the first week. One pundit observed, "These were the initial indications of what was to be a pattern during the show's first two decades."

Phillips transferred the character of Michael Bauer on CBS's *The Guiding Light* to the storyline of NBC's *Another World* for a while, a pretty visible indication of how much stock she carried with Procter & Gamble, which owned both properties. Phillips was head writer on *Another World* for its first 10 months. One examiner exclaimed, "Phillips, more at home with the domestic drama and homey philosophy of *As the World Turns*, was clearly out of her element in the exotic melodrama she had created."[27]

The drama mama aided one of her successors in that capacity (Harding Lemay, 1971–79) by revealing some of her serial-writing techniques. "Irna Phillips was brought in to teach him the tricks of the trade. She showed him her 'three-burner method' for writing soap opera based on a metaphor about cooking: the story reaching its climax was on the front burner, on the middle burner was the story building up to a peak, and on the back burner was the story just beginning. You just moved the stories around like pots; when the front burner was all done, you took it off, moved the other pots up, and got something new cooking on the back."[28]

In the meantime, a couple of Phillips apprentices, Agnes Eckhardt Nixon and William J. Bell, were showing marked promise as inheritors of the Phillips legacy. Both contributed immeasurably to the genre. Nixon co-wrote *Search for Tomorrow* with Roy Winsor for a few weeks; co-wrote *The Guiding Light* and *As the World Turns* with Phillips; was head writer for *Another World*; created, produced and was head writer of *All My Children*; co-created *Loving* with Douglas Marland; and created and was head writer for *One Life to Live*. Bell co-wrote *The Guiding Light* and *As the World Turns* with Phillips; co-created and co-wrote *Another World* with Phillips; was head writer for *Days of Our Lives*; and, with his wife, Lee Phillip, co-created *The Young and the Restless* and *The Bold and the Beautiful*, serials for which he was also head writer. Assessing Phillips years later, Bell recalled: "She was one of the most talented, complex, fascinating persons I ever met. Brilliant. A tough lady! Very tough! A lonely lady!"[29]

In the mid–1960s, ABC added what one critic termed a "memorable serial event" to its primetime lineup. *Peyton Place* (September 15, 1964, to June 2, 1969) was based on a once-scandalous novel and a couple of feature-length movies. The network tapped none other than Irna Phillips as a special story consultant. Before the debut, a major character's career was altered from school principal to doctor, reflecting a predilection long held by Phillips, who favored medics and lawyers. The original plotline also evinced Phillips' hand: it concerned an unmarried waif who preserved her dignity by wedding the prosperous biological dad of her unborn; after a miscarriage and annulment, the story focused on the romantic pursuits of those two by other admirers and suitors. Between them the pair would have five marriages in less than five years!

With that experience on her side, suddenly...

> For once, Irna Phillips made a false step ... with a serial drama....
> She would take a central character from her *As the World Turns*, ... and build a twice-a-week evening serial around her ... a girl housewives loved to hate.... Lisa ... (Eileen Fulton) left behind ... husband and little boy ... and soon was encountering attractive males.... Ratings of *Our Private World*, ... were not ... impressive.... Lisa's new romance, therefore, was a May-to-September affair.[30]

Was Irna Phillips starting to lose her heretofore-invincible grip? Her gaffe in judgment—for that's what it was—hinted that there might be other miscalculations ahead. As her ability to persuade, which had for so long characterized her as a force to be reckoned with, gradually diminished, Phillips lapsed into a prolonged, depressing pattern of ineffectiveness. Spiraling toward an ignoble end, the legendary maven of matinee eventually lost her reputation as the robust, fearsome, outspoken, unshakable dominatrix most had always perceived her to be.

Allan Chase, Ted Corday and Irna Phillips created *Days of Our Lives*, but it was Phillips who contributed the serial's unforgettable opening line: "Like sands through the hourglass, so are the *Days of Our Lives.*" The feature began on NBC on November 8, 1965, and — as this is written — is still airing, one of the most enduring tales proffered on the airwaves.

Having long ago left *The Guiding Light* to others to pen, Phillips returned to the serial in 1967. She took a popular character, Robin Lang Holden, stepdaughter of Kathy Roberts Holden (another fan favorite whom Phillips killed off in 1958), and had her jump in front of a car (similar to the accident claiming Kathy's life a decade before). The show's faithful fumed loudly and were unforgiving, forcing Phillips' hasty departure a second time.

Phillips went on to create *Love Is a Many Splendored Thing*, which ran on CBS from September 18, 1967, to March 23, 1973. When that yarn about an interracial romance and bigotry angered enough viewers, CBS executive Fred Silverman ordered Phillips to kill the storyline by removing one of the key characters. In a fit of rage the matriarch of melodrama abruptly stormed off the show, never to return. It was left to successor wordsmiths Ira and Jane Avery to implement the edict that had led to her hasty retreat.

Citing health issues, in 1970 Phillips ended her contract with Procter & Gamble, resigning as head writer of *As the World Turns*. But she wasn't finished yet. A short time later she was hired as story editor for *A World Apart*, a daytime serial created by her adopted daughter, Katherine Phillips. Some authorities speculated that helping to secure Katherine's place in the industry was Irna's true reason for leaving *As the World Turns* after 14 years. *A World Apart* aired from March 30, 1970, through June 25, 1971, over ABC-TV. The tale focused on an unmarried Jewish soap opera author in Chicago with a couple of adopted progeny. Could anyone possibly imagine what thinly veiled individual's career the narrative embodied?

Not long after *A World Apart* folded, Procter & Gamble enticed Irna Phillips back as head writer for *As the World Turns*, which by then was in big, big trouble, having suffered a significant ratings dip during Phillips' two-year absence. She began making drastic changes in the plot, adding an incestuous relationship (that the fans protested vigorously), killing off several popular characters, and moving others out of the storyline. "I'm trying to get back to the fundamentals," she informed a pair of reporters. "For example, the way in which a death in the family or serious illness brings members of the family closer together, gives them a real sense of how much they're dependent on each other."[31]

Behind the scenes, meanwhile, Phillips obsessed over the fact that Jane House, the actress playing Elizabeth (Liz) Talbot, was appearing sans clothes in a Broadway stage production of *Lenny*. She intended to kill Liz with pneumonia, but the fans rose up in protest and CBS ordered Phillips to make her well again. House soon quit the serial, but Phillips, by then agitated over any reference to Liz Talbot, transferred her revulsion to the actress succeeding House in the role, Judith McGilligan. That thespian was in the cast only briefly before her character died of a ruptured spleen after she fell "up" the stairs!

Phillips' nearly unblemished track record soon took another hit. When she had leading man Dr. Bob Hughes (once perceived as the epitome of faithfulness by his spouse and legions of viewers) become sexually involved with his sister-in-law, Kim Reynolds, viewers were absolutely enraged. The physician's integrity was irrevocably compromised. With the ratings plummeting to the basement, in 1973 P&G fired Phillips from the show she created 17 years earlier. The long years of doing almost everything right — and of having it all her own way — had finally come to an end.

With no more projects on the horizon, Phillips used her newly acquired freedom to begin writing a long-planned autobiography. She initially titled it *The Lady in the Mirror* but finally settled on *All My Worlds*. But it was never finished. On the night of Saturday, December 22, 1973, she was lying in bed working on the chronicle in her room. The following morning her secretary, Alice Shea, went in to check on her after she failed to respond to a summons. The great author had died during the night. Had the shock of being cut from her dream series only six months earlier been more than her heart could stand?

Not wanting anyone to know of her death, she had left orders that there be no public mention of her passing when it occurred. Agnes Nixon was stunned when, calling her mentor to wish her good tidings on Christmas day, she learned that Phillips was deceased. Although they had often sparred, head writer Harding Lemay of *Another World*—upon learning that no mention had been made in the press of Phillips' passing, and thinking she deserved better—wrote an obituary and paid to have it appear in *The New York Times*. It was published on Sunday, December 30, 1973, a week after Phillips' death. On another front, neither William S. Paley, chairman of the Columbia Broadcasting System, nor David Sarnoff, chairman of Radio Corporation of America, parent of the National Broadcasting Company, made any reference to Irna Phillips in their autobiographies, nor did their principal biographers. Yet for over four decades she had been a virtual gold mine to the dual organizations they represented.

Ironically, the paradoxical entrepreneur who emphasized fulfillment of women through marriage and producing a family never wed. While condemning the preoccupation of her contemporaries who spiked their dramas with illicit liaisons and sensationalism, in her own features a free-spirited Phillips experimented with incest, illegitimacy and interracial affairs. Although she imbued her leading characters with gentleness and an affinity for those close by, Phillips remained distant, arrogant and unrelenting when her notions were challenged, her intents ridiculed or her sensibilities offended.

Nonetheless, the soap opera form never possessed a more powerful champion. She founded an industry based on her techniques, beliefs and the interlocking stories that she invented. The legacy of "the single most successful writer the soap world has ever known"[32] continues to outlive her; her presence can clearly be felt in the enduring genre she so indelibly and so passionately touched. Legions still revere her for the dynamic, unswerving allegiance she unabashedly pledged to her craft.

In a 1965 magazine article, Phillips opined that every woman's life was a soap opera.

> Troubles occupy many of our days, and moments of real happiness are rare. Show me a life full of happy endings, with no bits of unresolved plot left hanging in midair, where the meek always inherit the earth, and the devil gets his comeuppance, and I'll show you the late show. Only Doris Day movies end when the boy gets the girl. In soap opera, as in real life, that is just the beginning of the story.
> None of us is different, except in degree. None of us is a stranger to success and failure, life and death, the need to be loved, the struggle to communicate with another human being, a corroding sense of loneliness. My life is completely different from the average woman's; yet because we share the same essential hopes and fears, what is true of her is true of me.[33]

The little girl who made up stories for her dolls ultimately spent a lifetime entertaining millions with her fantasies. Perhaps her own lonely existence and the disappointments she bumped into along her journey were eclipsed by the matchless achievements of her life—which established her grasp light years beyond anything she might have dreamed.

7

Reincarnations

It probably came as no surprise to anyone that when television programming was introduced as a staple of American home entertainment, it turned to its ancestor, radio, for much of its early talent. Radio had, after all, depended on vaudeville before it. With such a precedent established, it seemed quite natural for the comedians, musicians, sleuths, cowboys, quizmasters and newscasters of one broadcasting medium to supply another. While this wasn't true consistently — because so many personalities were needed to supply the requirements of live video's voracious appetite — it happened enough times that early watchers were soon accustomed to seeing people whose voices they had only heard in the past. The pioneering visual features were in many cases adaptations of — or at least patterned after — major radio series. Only seldom were the newer medium's primitive offerings, at least at their start, unfamiliar to those who enjoyed radio's fare.

The earliest example of the phenomenal impact of television that anybody could recall was the spectacular rise of comic Milton Berle. He was the embodiment of an archetypical vaudeville stand-up slapstick comedian, generally perceived as better when he burst onto the small screens in 1948 than he was in an aural-only form. "The early history of television and the story of Berle's show were close to being one and the same thing," one eyewitness of the epoch affirmed. "The very success of Berle's show accelerated the sale of television sets; those Americans who did not yet own sets would return home after watching him at their neighbors' houses and decide that, yes, it was finally time to take the plunge."[1]

An important offshoot of Berle's overnight rise in the public's consciousness was that his extraordinary popularity prompted other comedians to consider the new medium, too — including stars who had held back from making the jump from their familiar, comfortable radio digs. Berle proved to be as much a catalyst in drawing his peers as he was adept at attracting fans and selling TV sets. As several of his contemporaries observed his dazzling rise to fame, they sought a greater share of public adulation for themselves. One by one, many of radio's most celebrated stars — who had been skeptical and reluctant to test the waters until they could see some visible evidence of the tube's magnitude — began making the transition to television. George Burns and Gracie Allen, Jack Benny, Red Skelton and a myriad of other funny people were among those leaping onto minuscule black-and-white screens.

It has been astutely argued that TV began to develop a large following after several of the biggest names in radio started appearing on it. Aiding and abetting that notion was the fact that several of the largest advertisers in broadcasting reallocated their capital funding, appropriating large chunks of marketing dollars for television. In the 1940s and 1950s a few of TV's top-rated shows had crossed the ether from radio. In addition to the comedians already named, some examples of the legions of pioneering features include *Art Linkletter's House Party, Arthur Godfrey Time, The Bell Telephone Hour, Break the Bank, The Cisco Kid, Douglas Edwards and the News, Dragnet, Gunsmoke, Kate Smith, The Lone Ranger, Lux Video/Radio Theater, Meet the Press, Mr. and Mrs. North, Mr. District Attorney, Perry Como, Roy Rogers, See/Hear It Now, Sky King, Stop the Music!, Strike It Rich, Superman, Talent Scouts, The Voice of Firestone, Your Hit Parade* and more.

With about 300 soap operas having originated on radio, it's probably not a surprising revelation that the producers of daytime serials looked intently at the opportunity they, too, provided. Were there candidates among them for conversion to the visual medium? Most of those narratives centered on the trials and tribulations of a beleaguered heroine and the lives of those she loved (e.g., *Backstage Wife, Big Sister, Joyce Jordan, M.D., Lora Lawton, Ma Perkins, Our Gal Sunday, The Romance of Helen Trent, Stella Dallas, This Is Nora Drake, When a Girl Marries, Woman in White, Young Widder Brown*, et al., ad infinitum). Such tales simply could not sustain a viewing audience for long, they deduced. That eliminated virtually all of the copious fabrications of the form's two most inexhaustible creatives, Frank and Anne Hummert, plus the dramas of numerous other producers.

Yet there were a handful of audio tales that the video powers decided could be transposed to the fledgling medium. While one (*These Are My Children*) loosely followed a formula that had worked in radio's earliest days, two (*One Man's Family* and *Follow Your Heart*) literally rehashed the storylines of their aural ancestors. A fourth (*The Edge of Night*) provided a thinly disguised tale closely resembling a popular sleuth's exploits as it offered an ever-so-slight variation on the original theme.

These Are My Children actually borrowed not just from one but from *two* radio washboard weepers—*Painted Dreams* and *Today's Children* (the latter had earlier copied the premise of the former). Lasting only four weeks, from January 31 to February 25, 1949, the serial was analyzed in Chapter Three. It was the first daytime drama carried by a major network. The plot chronicled the life of the Henehans, a family unit composed of mother, offspring and a few hangers-on. It explored their coping with life in postwar America and with one another.

Though its run was fleeting, the series seemingly contributed to soap opera by opening creator Irna Phillips' eyes to the possibilities of television as a vehicle for storytelling. Before that she was unconvinced of its enormous potential, at least in the immediate future. Afterward, she was thinking almost totally in terms of visual elements. It was a definite watershed experience for her personally, as well as for the genre, given the profusion of changes she would introduce.

One Man's Family, presented in Chapter Four, actually aired on NBC-TV twice — initially as a half-hour primetime series (November 4, 1949–June 21, 1952), then returning as a weekday quarter-hour soap opera (March 1, 1954–April 1, 1955). It centered on the Henry Barbour tribe of the San Francisco Bay area and their intergenerational foibles as five grown children (most with strong temperaments) interacted with their parents, including an unyielding though lovable patriarch.

The award-winning radio drama was an aural feature from 1932 to 1959, and it probably should have been left in that form. Creator Carlton E. Morse went back to the program's start for both its video incarnations, attempting to reprise storylines that were then two decades old. It worked better in primetime, when the narrative had little competition (in 1949) and TV was a novel thrill for its watchers. Five years later folks had adjusted to TV. Unless a tale was awfully gripping, many viewers passed (particularly given the many daytime dramas to select from). By that time most in the audience also had at least one other choice in channels, and several choices in the major metropolitan markets. The serial, therefore, may have done well to persist for 13 months on TV while the radio play continued drawing millions every weeknight. The audio plotting, set in the present, was altogether different from the archaic video drama, which contributed to the wide disparity in the numbers.

Follow Your Heart, also encountered in Chapter Four, was an unfortunate blunder by another of radio's premier authors. It was soap opera scribe Elaine Sterne Carrington's solo foray into TV serials. Unfortunately, the most literate of audio's wordsmiths fell on her face when she created this one.

Rather than developing a new premise, characters and storyline, Carrington reached back to one of her audio masterpieces, *When a Girl Marries*, and reprised its 14-year-old storyline. The video concept debuted on August 3, 1953, and instantly bombed; it was gone in five months (exiting January 8, 1954). When nobody was looking the narrative abruptly transformed in mid-plot, shifting from a yarn about a boy and girl in love to a theme of gangster chases. In that context the label *Follow Your Heart* seemed a complete misnomer, resulting in a colossal fiasco.

The Edge of Night would have been titled *Perry Mason* if the creator of the aural series about the fabled attorney-superhero had allowed it. At the time, however, Erle Stanley Gardner held out. Backer Procter & Gamble at last engaged laudable *Mason* scriptwriter Irving Vendig to create a strong imitation for television, complete with a dark theme. The web even hired the actor playing Mason on radio, John Larkin, as its star.

Edge, one of television's first two 30-minute daytime serials, debuted on April 2, 1956, and ran all the way to December 28, 1984, nearly 29 years. It featured Larkin as assistant district attorney Mike Karr. He pursued a "gung-ho, unorthodox approach to catching crooks in ways that sometimes skirted illegality [and] mirrored the manner of Mason," according to one pundit. The series' expansive dimensions are examined in some depth in Chapter 13.

In addition to those four radio reprisals, there were nine more televised daytime dramas that appeared under the identical monikers of radio serials. Sometimes they followed the aural storylines while in other cases they engaged in alternative scenarios. The nine were, in chronological order of their TV debuts: *The O'Neills, The Guiding Light, Valiant Lady, The Brighter Day, Portia Faces Life, Modern Romances, Road of Life, Kitty Foyle* and *Young Doctor Malone*.

Of these TV soaps with antecedents in radio serials, *The O'Neills* can be summarily dismissed here as it was exclusively a primetime entry. Appearing on Dumont television between September 6, 1949, and January 20, 1950, it had been offered during the years 1934 to 1943 on all four major radio networks at diverse hours. On Dumont TV it ran on Tuesday nights for a half-hour. Similar characters and actors were featured in both mediums.

The Guiding Light has become the longest-running narrative in broadcast history, of course. Irna Phillips introduced it to radio listeners on January 25, 1937. In those days it revolved around a nondenominational minister in the rural setting of Five Points. As mid-century approached, the storyline was expanded to include the Bauer clan of Selby Flats, situated outside of Los Angeles, leading to many more developmental opportunities.

Phillips sold the series to Procter & Gamble in 1946 but remained its writer (at least in name and in plotting direction). Persuading P&G to try it out on CBS-TV starting June 30, 1952, she supervised a drama that for four years accommodated both daily radio and television incarnations. The show was finally withdrawn from the aural airwaves on June 29, 1956. By then the tele-version was so well established that P&G decided it could put all of its eggs into one basket. Its decision proved prudent; as of this writing the serial is still running there, now more than a half-century after its debut on the small screen. Chapter 10 is devoted to an in-depth study of this important drama.

If the prolific radio producers Frank and Anne Hummert were to transfer their legacy to TV, it was up to **Valiant Lady** (plucked from a treasure trove that embraced no fewer than 125 features) to lead the way. But alas, that property — having enjoyed a few years on two different radio networks between 1938 and 1946, and a five-month reprise on a third chain in 1951–52 — could hardly be termed a *legacy* for such a vast empire. In practice, nothing beyond the appellation of that aural soap opera shifted to the small screen, suggesting that the Hummerts' aural wares failed to translate well to the visual medium.

The radio manifestation of that series witnessed heroine Joan Barrett's eternal struggle to keep the feet of her "brilliant but unstable" husband planted firmly on the "pathway to success," soon recognized as a losing battle. The television embodiment, on the other hand (aired at noon over CBS-TV from October 12, 1953, to August 16, 1957), followed the exploits of protagonist Helen Emerson. Her spouse Frank, an inventor, died within a few months of the drama's premier, changing everything for those he left behind. His death transformed Helen into a lonely but brave individual who was thrust into coping with a plethora of heart-rending and trying realities.

At the drama's inception, Helen was surrounded by daughter Kim, age nine; son Mickey, 19, in love with an already wedded lady, Bonnie Withers; and daughter Diane, 17, who eloped with a divorced man but returned still single to ask Helen's blessing before hitching up. In addition to her offspring's disquieting dilemmas, Helen, a practical woman, wrestled incessantly with her family's suddenly lowered standard of living, plus many other adversities. It was all far removed from the Hummert storyline in which the leading lady had little more to contend with than a lazy bum, and a few other idiosyncrasies that impinged upon their stagnated lives.

Far more interesting, in theory at least, was the tale of the resolute widow who struggled against insurmountable odds alone. And it added credence to the drama's label of *Valiant Lady*. For a while she tried to marry airline pilot Chris Kendall, but his messy divorce and the resulting custody battle over Chris' son ended in despair for her. The premise may have begun to drag when it appeared that Helen would again find contentment with the personage of Governor Lawrence Walker, whom she wed on February 14, 1957. That was six months before the serial was canceled. Maybe she was simply too happy to be desperately courageous any longer.[2]

For 14 months Nancy Coleman played the role of the superwoman at the narrative's start. Her previous acting experiences included appearances in movies like *King's Row, Edge of Darkness* and *Mourning Becomes Electra*. The pacing, memorization and the quietus put on her social life left Coleman reeling, however. She quit in December 1954, handing over the lead to Flora Campbell, by then a seasoned actress who had performed frequently on the Broadway stage.

Campbell had already been exposed to radio and TV audiences in several earlier expositions: *Brave Tomorrow* (1944, NBC Radio), *The Strange Romance of Evelyn Winters*

(1944–48, CBS Radio), *Faraway Hill* (1946, Dumont TV), *Highway to the Stars* (1947, Dumont TV), *A Date with Judy* (1952–53, ABC-TV) and *The Seeking Heart* (1954, CBS-TV). Three days after the latter series departed the teleplay skies on Friday, December 10, 1954, its heroine appeared in the lead role on *Valiant Lady*, a rapid transition for both her and the viewers who may have seen her elsewhere. Subsequently, Campbell gained recurring roles on two other CBS-TV daytime serials, *Love of Life* and *Love Is a Many Splendored Thing.*

Twenty years beyond *Valiant Lady*, James Kirkwood Jr., who played Mickey Emerson, the heroine's son (Kirkwood's only documented TV role), won a Pulitzer Prize for penning the Broadway musical *A Chorus Line.*

Meanwhile, unknowns Anne Pearson, Delores Sutton, Sue Randall and Leila Martin all appeared as older daughter Diane Emerson Soames, the most frequently recast part in the narrative. When Randall competed for it she beat 60 challengers for the role.

Lydia Reed, the first of two youngsters to play Kim Emerson, went on to become Hassie, Little Luke's older sister, on TV's *The Real McCoys* (1957–63).

Despite the trials and tribulations of widowhood, with one child still at home and older kids asserting themselves in the real world, *Valiant Lady* Helen Emerson (played for most of the run by Flora Campbell, shown) grinned even when life hurt. A single parent faced with raising nine-year-old Kim (Bonnie Sawyer), and pressured with econmic uncertainties and troublesome teens, a determined Helen faced her challenges with resolute strength, eventually marrying once more to offer some stability to her brood.

Terry O'Sullivan briefly interrupted his long-running role as Arthur Tate (1952–68), one of stressed heroine Joanne Gardner Barron Tate Vincente Tourneur's many spouses on *Search for Tomorrow*, to appear in the fleeting role of *Valiant Lady*'s Elliott Norris in 1955.

Valiant Lady marked the first time that creator Allan Chase and Ted Corday, one of the show's several directors, were paired. In the mid–1960s that duo, along with Irna Phillips, created one of TV's most successful daytime ventures, *Days of Our Lives.*

The Brighter Day, another Phillips creation that enjoyed a fairly lengthy radio run on two networks (October 11, 1948, to June 29, 1956), also showed up on CBS-TV on January 4, 1954, at 1 p.m. The narrative persisted through May 14, when it went off the air for seven weeks, returning on July 5 at 4 p.m. It remained a quarter-hour drama through June 15, 1962. At that juncture the serial was extended to 25 minutes, effective June 18, 1962, when it shifted to 11:30 a.m. When its ratings steadily declined, however, the program was removed from the air, effective September 28, 1962.

After selling *The Guiding Light* to Procter & Gamble in 1946 — a popular radio tale about a nonsectarian minister that had been running since 1937 — Irna Phillips reportedly found herself missing the day-to-day control she exerted over a serial involving a protagonist of faith. She had been impressed many years before by such an individual, and had created the show specifically with the clergyman in mind. Phillips decided to fill that void by instituting a second, similar program, *The Brighter Day*, which centered on Reverend Richard Dennis, shepherd of a humble parish in the rural community of Three Rivers. Unlike *The Guiding Light*, however, which had transitioned by then into a different setting with an altogether new cast and focus, Dennis remained at the core of the new serial's storyline in dual mediums. When Three Rivers was washed away in a flood, conveniently at the start of the tele-version, the parson shifted his sermons to a parish in New Hope, Pennsylvania — certainly an auspicious name for a fresh beginning! By the late 1950s he would fill a pulpit in the collegiate hamlet of Columbus.

The widowed reverend still had five children, along with all of their attendant problems and those of his parishioners. The kids, most of them grown, included happily wedded Liz, who was the feminine lead in radio but appeared only fleetingly in TV land; Althea, a neurotic young lady; Grayling, an alcoholic; Patsy, a typical teen; and Barbara (Babby), the baby of the brood. Aunt Emily played the traditional mother figure for the Dennis offspring (Liz had done so on radio); and she served a similar function for the community at large through an advice column she penned for *The New Hope Herald*. This milieu provided some unique dilemmas for a parson whose family lived in a fish bowl, with the community steadfastly looking on.

The Brighter Day initially followed the same route as Phillips' other concurrent serial, *The Guiding Light*, as both pursued double daily broadcasts. Yet when *The Brighter Day* climbed into first place in the TV ratings in the spring of 1956 — the only time that happened in the yarn's history — the radio edition was promptly canceled.

Over the course of the TV soap's run, Grayling had an illicit relationship with an older woman before settling down with Sandra Talbot. He wed her even after learning that she, too, came with a sordid past. After his long-barren spouse conceived at last, Grayling took the opportunity to pursue an extramarital affair with his wife's nurse. It was a precipitous incident that began a gradual erosion of the show's viewership.

In the early 1960s, after CBS purchased the property from Procter & Gamble, the web made radical changes in the storyline, some of which met with little audience approval. On July 3, 1961, production was shifted from New York City to CBS's new Television City studios in Hollywood. Suddenly, without warning, no fewer than seven of the important ongoing characters, including key figure Babby Dennis, vanished from the storyline, some without any explanation or mention again. It was as if they had never existed. Several permanent roles also had to be recast when those actors wouldn't move to the West Coast, leading to confusion until the new corps could become entrenched in the viewers' minds.

The show was obviously suffering from multiple contradictions in writing and staffing, and it lacked a permanent timeslot, too. (In 1962 it was moved to a morning niche — a universally unpopular period with most long-term soap addicts — and it was also lengthened by 10 minutes.) Not many viewers were around to care by then, and the program was swiftly axed, giving the writers, producers and actors just two weeks' notice to clean up their act.

On the final installment, Uncle Walter Dennis, who had only recently joined the troupe, faced the camera and explained how each character's predicaments would be resolved. Finally he expressed his own farewell. Other members of the Dennis family quietly receded into the background: "Soon the picture will fade. If on occasion you think of us, we hope your memory will be a pleasant one." It was a bizarre departure for a serial that had extended such uplifting promise at its inception nearly nine years earlier, and a half-dozen years before that as a daytime radio property.

Emblematic of soap operas during their first decade on television, at the conclusion of some episodes of *The Brighter Day* in the mid–1950s, a card flashed on the screen plugging another serial on a competing network as an announcer gently reminded viewers: "Be sure to see *Concerning Miss Marlowe* Monday through Friday on another network." The pitch was a remnant from radio, but publicizing shows on rival chains—even when the same commercial concern underwrote both programs—was adamantly forbidden before many years elapsed.

William Smith, who had played Reverend Richard Dennis when the drama began on radio in 1948, continued in the part on both the radio and television incarnations. He was the only radio thespian to move to the TV adaptation, in fact. Yet Smith relinquished the TV role after less than eight months, on August 24, 1954. Blair Davies, who succeeded him, carried it the rest of the way. Smith subsequently won recurring roles in several primetime series: *Laredo* (1965–67), *Rich Man, Poor Man Book II* (1976–77), *Hawaii Five-O* (1979–80) and *Wildside* (1985).

Davies was a Pittsburgh native but was reared in Portland, Oregon. He got his acting start with the Portland Civic Theatre and Henry Duffy Players. He managed commercial shows during the 1939 New York World's Fair and joined a local advertising agency. Later he understudied Fredric March in *The Skin of Our Teeth*, performing 24 times on Broadway opposite Tallulah Bankhead and Florence Eldridge. Davies' additional TV credits included guest shots in *The Adventures of Ellery Queen, Colgate Theatre, Lights Out* and *Philco Television Playhouse.*

Hal Holbrook, who portrayed Grayling for five years, used one of that figure's drunken episodes as a successful audition for the Actor's Studio. Holbrook went on to perform in four TV miniseries—*Celebrity* (1984), *George Washington* (1984), *North and South* (1985) and *North and South Book II* (1986)—as well as a trio of primetime shows: *The Bold Ones* (1969–73), *Designing Women* (1986–89, in which he was paired with real-life wife and former soap player Dixie Carter), and *Evening Shade* (1990–94). Holbrook's career embraced several major films: *The Great White Hope* (1970), *All the President's Men* (1976), *Julia* (1977), *Creepshow* (1982), *Wall Street* (1987), *The Firm* (1993) and *The Majestic* (2001). As of 2005, he and Dixie Carter were appearing sporadically in the ABC sitcom *Hope and Faith*, his TV career by then extending into its sixth decade.

Holbrook was succeeded in the part of Grayling by two other television notables. James Noble, who appeared from 1959 to 1960, is best recalled as the bumbling governor on ABC's *Benson* (1979–86). And Forrest Compton, who was Grayling from 1961 to 1962, won a recurring part in CBS's *Gomer Pyle* (1964–69) before landing the memorable role of Mike Karr on *The Edge of Night* (1971–84).

Mona Bruns, appearing as Aunt Emily Potter, had earlier played in two NBC-TV serials—the nighttime version of *One Man's Family* (1950–51) and daytime's *Three Steps to*

Heaven (1953–54). *The Brighter Day* was her swan song as a regular on a tube series, although she showed up for many single-shot acting assignments on *Armstrong Circle Theatre*, *Hallmark Hall of Fame* and *Lights Out*. Bruns was a stage veteran, having debuted there at age seven, appeared on Broadway at 14, and been part of a national touring company of *Captain Kidd, Jr.* at 16. She appeared on Broadway in *Chicken Every Sunday* and *Born Yesterday*. Acting was a family affair in her household: Bruns performed with her husband Frank Thomas and son Frank Thomas Jr. in numerous stock productions.

Patty Duke, the first of two actresses to play the part of Ellen Williams Dennis (in 1958–59), not only became a movie star (*The Miracle Worker*, 1962; *Valley of the Dolls*, 1967), but also a TV mainstay. In addition to her own headlined ABC program *The Patty Duke Show* (1963–66), there were a pair of miniseries (1979's *Women in White* and 1984's *George Washington*) and a string of short-lived features in which she starred: *Mom, the Wolfman and Me* (1980), *Hail to the Chief* (1985), *Karen's Song* (1987) and *Amazing Grace* (1995).

Portia Faces Life was one of CBS-TV's briefer radio adaptations. It surfaced on the small screen at 1 p.m. between April 5, 1954, and July 1, 1955, lasting about 15 months. Had it been on NBC, it well might have evaporated sooner. The radio series, incidentally, was heard on both CBS and NBC at varying times between October 7, 1940, and June 29, 1951.[3] But its departure there — as it wasn't continuing in dual mediums as some other soap operas had — freed the TV incarnation's creators to select a new premise if they preferred. Ultimately they persisted in the same general direction as the original play, possibly because Mona Kent — who had written much of it for radio — created the subsequent series and penned those scripts, too. None of the actors transferred from radio to TV, however.

One pundit opined: "Like the radio soap, the TV version was ahead of its time, featuring a woman who worked not because she was a widow like *Search for Tomorrow*'s Jo Gardner and had to, but a married woman and mother who worked because she chose to."[4] Named for the feminine lawyer in playwright William Shakespeare's *The Merchant of Venice*, Portia Blake Manning relished the practice of law.[5]

"Her career became a source of tension at home. Although her [second] husband Walter [Manning] had a successful career of his own — he owned the town newspaper — he was jealous of his wife's success," the pundit observed. Going with the flow of popular thinking then, Manning believed his wife's place was at home and not at the hall of justice. Actually, it may have been that he saw his role as the traditional family breadwinner being threatened by her dazzling performances in the courtroom. His annoyance over that left him, not surprisingly, susceptible to Dorie Blake. That vixen tempted him relentlessly, applying her wily tactics to exploit his growing malcontent.

The storyline became still more complex when Walter's newspaper, *The Parkerstown Herald*, fell on rough economic times, and — near the end of the run — he was brought to trial for a murder he didn't commit. Portia defended him at least twice on radio, so this was hardly anything new (or particularly gripping, either). Meanwhile, the TV serial was steadily losing its audience. In an attempt to reverse the trend, the show's focus on the wife-as-professional was appreciably diminished. On March 14, 1955, a title change was implemented. From then on the drama was known as *The Inner Flame*. No matter. That didn't stop the sagging numbers, and the series was canceled.

Frances Reid, the original Portia Manning, went on to play a brief role on *The Edge of Night* (1964). Since the premier of *Days of Our Lives* in November 1965, she has portrayed Alice Horton, and is still playing the part as of 2005. An accomplished Shakespearean actress, she performed on Broadway in *Cyrano de Bergerac*, *Hamlet* and *Twelfth Night*.

The succeeding Portia Manning, actress Fran Carlon, later appeared as Julia Burke in *As the World Turns* (1968–75) and was in the ABC-TV 1983 summertime drama *The Hamptons*. Carlon brought a long history in radio serials to TV, including recurring roles on *Attorney at Law, Girl Alone, Kitty Keene Incorporated, Lora Lawton, Ma Perkins, The Story of Mary Marlin, Today's Children* and *A Woman of America*. She played Lorelei Kilbourne on radio's *Big Town* (a newspaper crime drama), and turned up in the audio medium's *Blackstone— the Magic Detective, Joan and Kermit* and *The Chicago Theater of the Air*.

Karl Swenson portrayed Walter Manning for most of *Portia Faces Life*'s run. His three most notable roles were on Frank and Anne Hummert radio creations— as Lord Henry Brinthrope, the husband of *Our Gal Sunday*; *Lorenzo Jones*; and *Mr. Chameleon*, "the man of many disguises." A versatile dialectician, Swenson also performed on radio's *Aunt Jenny's Real Life Stories, The Cavalcade of America, The Court of Missing Heirs, Father Brown, The Ford Theater, Grand Central Station, Inner Sanctum Mysteries, Joe Palooka, Lawyer Q, Linda's First Love, The March of Time, The Mighty Show, Mrs. Miniver, Portia Faces Life, Rich Man's Darling, Spy Secrets, There Was a Woman, This Is Your FBI, The Whisper Men* and *World's Greatest Novels*.

The busy actor broke into summer stock in 1930 with the Berkshire Players, later appearing on Broadway in Leonard Stillman's musical revues and in Arthur Miller's first stage play, *The Man Who Had All the Luck*. Swenson appeared on the big screen in 29 films, mostly in bit parts, including *The Hanging Tree* (1959), *North to Alaska* (1960), *Judgment at Nuremberg* (1961), *Walk on the Wild Side* (1962), *Lonely Are the Brave* (1962), *How the West Was Won* (1962), *Seconds* (1966) and *Ulzana's Raid* (1972). He was Lars Hanson on the NBC-TV primetime series *Little House on the Prairie* (1974–78), and played in a quartet of made-for-TV movies.

Modern Romances was a closed-end narrative that survived longer than any similar omnibus feature during TV's golden age. Its four years on the air (October 4, 1954–September 19, 1958) rivaled some of the longest running open-end daytime serials on its chain, NBC. The program played to a weekday radio audience from 1936 to 1955, although not continuously. It is covered in greater detail in Chapter Four.

A radio historiographer characterized *Road of Life* as "a most important soap opera." By the time its name had been lengthened to include the definite article for showcasing on TV, that same critic might have dubbed **The Road of Life** "not much of a soap opera." Indeed, the video manifestation of the triumphant audio serial that ran for more than 21 years (1937–59) on multiple webs (sometimes with the same script broadcast *twice* every weekday on competing chains!) fell on its face on CBS-TV. It debuted there on December 13, 1954 — complete with virtually all the still-performing radio cast intact — and was withdrawn little more than a half-year later on July 1, 1955. It proved that as brilliant as she was at her game plan, creator Irna Phillips couldn't deliver a winner — even an awesome retread (e.g., *The Guiding Light, The Brighter Day*) — every single time. It should be noted further that an unusually large number of affiliates failed to make the quarter-hour time period (and the one preceding it) available to the network, soundly contributing to the show's diminished returns.

The tale revolved around one of Ms. Phillips' favorite themes— medicine. The protagonist, Dr. Jim Brent, was a physician in the little village of Merrimac. A reviewer summarized the narrative's brief fling with the cathode ray tube.

Surgeon Dr. Brent, his third wife Jocelyn, and adopted son John were nice guys surrounded by losers from Jocelyn's well-to-do family. Her foster father Malcolm Overton bickered constantly with his relative Conrad over how to raise grandson John. Meanwhile, Conrad's daughter Sybil, who harbored the hots for Jim, tried to keep Jocelyn from becoming Jim's wife. She also belittled her mother Ada; attempted to get her husband Mr. Fuller, missing in a plane crash for more than a year, declared dead so that she could claim sole custody of her daughter Constance; and generally was a bitch even when confined to a wheelchair. None of this bothered Conrad, who called his daughter "Bunny" and generally egged her on.[6]

As this was a medical drama, Jocelyn was afflicted with every dreaded disorder imaginable, as well as some unimaginable (like "rubimortis" and "Meniere's syndrome"). She was arrested for "technically" kidnapping Constance. As Jocelyn was coming home from Samoa, where she had traveled to obtain specialized treatment for one of her ailments, Sybil saw to it that Jocelyn was declared "an undesirable alien" and temporarily thwarted in her attempts to return to America.

The live tele-version appeared immediately after the CBS Radio incarnation signed off each day at 1:15 p.m. (Recall that the model for doing this was *The Guiding Light*, which aired the same episode in two mediums on the same day; *The Brighter Day* followed the same pattern as well.)

Actor Jack Lemmon appeared briefly in *The Road of Life* as a nerves-of-steel surgeon. Once, during a tense operating room scene, he turned to a nurse and growled, "Give me the hypodermic *nerdle!*" While Lemmon appeared in several short-lived early TV series — *That Wonderful Guy* (1949–50), *The Ad-Libbers* (1951), *The Frances Langford–Don Ameche Show* (1951–52), *Heaven for Betsy* (1952) and *Alcoa Theatre* (1957–58) — it was on the silver screen that he left a permanent mark. Among his cinematic triumphs: *It Should Happen to You* (1954), *Mister Roberts* (1955), *Some Like It Hot* (1959), *Days of Wine and Roses* (1962), *Irma la Douce* (1963), *How to Murder Your Wife* (1965), *The Odd Couple* (1968) and many, many more.

There were several figures of distinction behind the cameras of *The Road of Life,* too. For instance, Walter Gorman, the real-life spouse of actress Virginia Dwyer (who portrayed Jocelyn McLeod Brent), directed both the radio and television renditions.

Meanwhile, Charles J. Gussman, a major radio medical serial author (*David Harum, The Road of Life, Young Doctor Malone*), penned the scripts.

And Nelson Case, who for years introduced Philip Morris' trademark diplomat ("And now, here comes Johnny, stepping out of thousands of store windows to greet you"), was selected in the 1950s by Procter & Gamble as its chief spokesman for the firm's flagship commodity, Ivory soap. Ivory was *The Road of Life*'s sponsor, and Case narrated the show in both mediums. He possessed "the most soothing voice on the air," one critic opined.

Don MacLaughlin, featured in both broadcast versions as Dr. Jim Brent, was radio's wartime *Chaplain Jim U.S.A.*, as well as *David Harding, Counterspy*. Over a long career in daytime dramas, he is best remembered for his sterling portrayal as the patriarch Chris Hughes in *As the World Turns* (1956–86), examined in detail in Chapter 12.

His opposite, meanwhile, Virginia Dwyer (Jocelyn McLeod Brent), also brought to her role years of experience in radio soap operas: *Aunt Jenny's Real Life Stories, Backstage Wife, Front Page Farrell, Houseboat Hannah, Joyce Jordan — Girl Interne, Road of Life* and *Second Husband*. After the tele-version of *The Road of Life* left the air, she continued turning up in front of daytime serial cameras: *The Secret Storm* (1955–56), *Young Doctor Malone* (1958–59), *The Guiding Light* (1959–60), and her most memorable part, as Mary Matthews, initial heroine of *Another World* (1964–75).

Bill Lipton, who played Jim Brent's adopted son John (Butch), left a legacy in radio drama, too, including *The Right to Happiness, Road of Life* and *Young Doctor Malone*, as well as numerous non-serial features.

Kitty Foyle, a yarn about love dismissed (the heroine decided she preferred work to nuptials, at least for a while), was examined in Chapter Four. The serial aired only briefly over NBC-TV, from January 13 to June 27, 1958. The narrative was on CBS Radio from 1942 to 1944.

Young Doctor Malone, also scrutinized in Chapter Four, was another medical story introduced to television by creator Irna Phillips. NBC watchers saw it from December 29, 1958, to March 29, 1963. But if they anticipated a parallel to the radio tale that had captivated audiences since 1939 (persisting through November 25, 1960), they were in for a rude awakening. Surprise! It was almost an entirely different show.

While this concludes the summary of 13 serials that were adapted from radio incarnations, there remains a handful of short-run daytime dramas from this early period that have yet to be explored. The remainder of this chapter is devoted to *Woman with a Past, The Seeking Heart, Hotel Cosmopolitan, The Verdict Is Yours* and *For Better or Worse*. These dramas are offered in chronological order according to their premier dates.

Woman with a Past didn't have much of a present or future, considering it existed only from February 1 to July 2, 1954, at 4 o'clock, in contrast to most of its peer CBS daytime dramas. Interestingly, it debuted just 15 minutes before *The Secret Storm*—the two narratives premiering back-to-back on the same day. Yet, *Storm* persisted 60 times longer than *Past*, enduring to February 8, 1974. *Past*'s protagonist was a New York dress designer whose amorous pursuits were at the crux of the storyline. It offered a similar theme that had resulted in one of radio's most popular and resilient serials, *The Romance of Helen Trent*, in which the love life of a Hollywood dress designer was exploited for 27 consecutive years. That scenario failed to resonate with TV audiences, however, and the woman with a past was history.

Heroine Lynn Sherwood's mysterious earlier life contained dark secrets that she didn't care to have revealed: she had been, and still was, married to a convicted felon, now an ex-con; and her seven-year-old daughter Diane was born out of wedlock. Of course, those morsels were just too juicy to hide forever, and the producers found a way to reveal them at an inopportune moment for Lynn.

At long last she was about to create some permanent happiness for herself, albeit with another wedded gent. A torrid romance with Steve Rockwell, who had put up capital for her ladies' garment emporium, transpired. Sylvia Rockwell, wife of the financier, was cast in the role of a scoundrel (perhaps with the notion of adding a dash of respectability to the carrying-on of the business partners behind her back). But the fans wouldn't have it at any price and tuned away in droves. The creator of this melee, Mona Kent, was also the inventive mind behind the tele-version of *Portia Faces Life* that aired concurrently at 1 p.m. on CBS. It persisted for 15 months in that form (Kent had also written it during much of its 11-year radio run).

Ironically, even for a soap opera that typically witnessed abundant casting shifts as the plot advanced, the turnover among regulars during this program's five-month run was excessive. Of seven contract performers, two were replaced, while nearly another dozen thespians, all unknowns, floated into and out of the storyline at erratic intervals. Most were on hand for such brief flings that the names of their characters have been lost to history.

The key player, Constance Ford, as heroine Lynn Sherwood, built a solid career as an actress, nonetheless. Following her exposure on *Woman with a Past*, she turned up for stints on *Search for Tomorrow* (1955–56) and *The Edge of Night* (1964–65) before landing the unforgettable part of Ada Hobson, a part she played for a quarter-of-a-century on *Another*

World (1967–92). Ford also performed in many primetime dramatic series, including *Alfred Hitchcock Presents, Dr. Kildare, East Side — West Side, Kraft Theater, Naked City, Perry Mason, The Twilight Zone* and *The Untouchables*. She is also credited with critically acclaimed motion picture roles in *All Fall Down, The Caretakers* and *A Summer Place.*

Jean Stapleton, who portrayed one of the leading lady's close confidantes (identified in *Woman with a Past* only as Gwen), used the series as a springboard to many other parts, too. Her most celebrated, of course, was as Edith Bunker in *All in the Family* (1971–83). Later she appeared in *Bagdad Café* (1990) and *Beakman's World* (1992–97). Stapleton appeared on the silver screen in films like *Damn Yankees* (1958), *Bells Are Ringing* (1960), *Klute* (1971), *Michael* (1996) and *You've Got Mail* (1998).

The Seeking Heart was another of those rare CBS disasters. It lasted from July 5 to December 10, 1954, at 1:15 p.m. Procter & Gamble was waging "an uphill battle" with that daytime drama, one reviewer opined. The soap manufacturer attempted "to get housewives in the audience to sympathize with a husband's workplace romance." That was something that ran against the grain of most people's common sense.

Things weren't exactly right in the home of medical criminologist Dr. John Adam and his spouse Grace, Adam's subordinate — the female Dr. Robinson McKay — figured out. (Just as *The Greatest Gift* was demonstrating on NBC at the same time, feminine medics didn't make well-liked daytime heroines.) Relationships were quite strained in the Adam family; she was an unfulfilled wife and he didn't seem to care. As a result, McKay and her superior let go of their pent-up emotions and gave in to their previously unrequited desire for one another.

That set up an interesting romantic triangle — oft repeated since soap opera's earliest days — that, unfortunately for the handful of fans still in existence, CBS elected never to resolve. The show was abruptly canceled five months after its launch. What a letdown! (The viewers must have thought they were watching NBC.) "This was the first of several shows which died in CBS's 1–1:30 p.m. daily slot in the 1950s," observed one critic. Others included *The Road of Life, Portia Faces Life* and some audience participation features.

Of the small number of players in the ongoing cast, only Flora Campbell, who has been previously introduced, made a significant acting impact elsewhere. She portrayed the role of Dr. Robinson McKay. Three days after this serial left the airwaves she returned as the heroine of another CBS soap opera, *Valiant Lady.*

Hotel Cosmopolitan was a futile CBS try at programming anthology dramas, those closed-end stories that rival chain NBC inserted into its daytime schedule at frequent points throughout the 1950s. This venture aired at noon from August 19, 1957, to April 11, 1958, and was set at a New York inn known as the Cosmopolitan. Modeled on the cinematic *Grand Hotel, Hotel Cosmopolitan* focused on the lodging establishment's intriguing patrons.

Narrating the comings and goings was longtime film actor Donald Woods, who had hosted ABC's *Afternoon Film Festival* in 1956 (as himself). Among Woods' movie credits were *Fog Over Frisco* (1934), *A Tale of Two Cities* (1935), *The Story of Louis Pasteur* (1936), *Watch on the Rhine* (1943) and *Wonder Man* (1945).

Henderson Forsythe, featured as the only other continuing character (a house detective), played Dr. David Stewart on *As the World Turns* (1960–90). He was also in the casts of *The Edge of Night* (1957) and *From These Roots* (1958–60).

When *Hotel Cosmopolitan* departed the airwaves in the spring of 1958, CBS fixed its perennial noon quarter-hour difficulty by starting the exceedingly popular *Love of Life* a quarter of an hour earlier, extending its length to a half-hour. *Love of Life* had been running at 12:15 since September 1951, although by 1958 several serials had moved to the half-hour format after *As the World Turns* and *The Edge of Night* inaugurated the new model in 1956. *Love of Life* occupied its newly expanded timeslot until September 1969 before transitioning elsewhere in the schedule.

The Verdict Is Yours became the next-to-last new dramatic entry CBS introduced to daytime viewers during the golden age of television. The series had antecedents in *Cross Question* and *They Stand Accused*, a live hour-long primetime feature under two monikers originating in Chicago, and airing over Dumont between September 11, 1949, and October 5, 1952, and September 9, 1954, to December 30, 1954. A collection of tales for daytime audiences *The Verdict Is Yours* appeared in a trio of time slots: September 2, 1957, to October 9, 1961, from 3:30 to 4 p.m.; October 12, 1961, to June 15, 1962, from 3:30 to 3:55 p.m.; and June 18, 1962, to September 28, 1962, from 11:00 to 11:30 a.m.

A biographer of the unique show described what happened:

> This unscripted, anthology-style courtroom drama aired for five successful seasons on CBS. Each case was featured for nine episodes before reaching a conclusion. Actors were presented a brief outline stating the situation and then they improvised when cross-examined by real lawyers. Members of the studio audience were chosen to play the jurors, who ruled on the case's outcome, giving new meaning to the phrase, "audience participation." Actresses were encouraged to go full blast with their emotions and occasionally the real lawyers became dupes of their own histrionics. In one memorable episode, a lawyer became so frustrated with how his case was evolving he stormed off the set. He left the stunned courtroom reporter, played by Jim McKay [subsequently of ABC's *Wide World of Sports*], with the thankless task of ad-libbing until the show's conclusion.[7]

Also appearing as the court reporter at other times were Bill Stout and Jake Whittaker, with Mandel Kramer as the court bailiff. Kramer turned up on *The Edge of Night* as police inspector Bill Marceau (1959–70). Among the guest players were film star Ellen Burstyn — *The Last Picture Show* (1971), *The Exorcist* (1973), *Alice Doesn't Live Here Any More* (1974), *Harry and Tonto* (1974), *Requiem for a Dream* (2000) and others — who was known during the TV series by her original name, Ellen McRae; Forrest Compton, who was later attorney and pursuer of nefarious types Mike Karr on *The Edge of Night* (1971–84); Audrey Peters, who portrayed Vanessa Dale Sterling, the good sibling on *Love of Life* (1959–80); and Esther Ralston, the heroine Helen Lee of *Our Five Daughters* (1962).

There was a brief rehearsal before each performance of *The Verdict Is Yours* for timing purposes, but the dialogue was strictly up to the actors and attorneys and other principals. Legal troupes praised the program's realistic effect, while *TV Guide* dubbed it "contrived" yet "fascinating."

The last of the new CBS-TV series in the 1950s was **For Better or Worse**, a videotaped, Hollywood-produced anthology drama that ran from June 29, 1959, to June 24, 1960, for a half-hour at 2 o'clock. Before beginning each day's chapter of a narrative dealing with romantic crises, host-announcer Jim Bannon dialogued with Dr. James A. Peterson, the show's "resident expert." Peterson was associate professor of psychology at the University of Southern California, and the pair considered the predicament that the characters were about to encounter.

The plays themselves persisted for three weeks (if they had tied up the loose ends in one session they could hardly have been designated soap opera). Even though the series boasted some future stars in its acting company (Dyan Cannon, Peggy McCay and others), and it enjoyed a powerhouse lead-in in the form of *As the World Turns*, which ran immediately before it took to the air, *For Better or Worse* failed to hold an audience and was dismissed in just under a year. Regrettably, in selecting a replacement—*Full Circle* (an open-end soap opera)—CBS fared still worse. That one lasted little more than eight months.

Dyan Cannon, incidentally, appeared on the big screen in *Bob & Carol & Ted & Alice* (1969), *The Anderson Tapes* (1971), *The Last of Sheila* (1973), *Heaven Can Wait* (1978) and *Kangaroo Jack* (2003). On the small screen she was in the 1984 CBS miniseries *Master of the Game* and the NBC sitcom *Three Sisters* (2001–02).

Peggy McCay was the first to play Vanessa Dale, the leading lady of the debuting *Love of Life* (1951–55). Beginning in 1965 she also appeared as Caroline Brady on the debuting *Days of Our Lives*.

For all of CBS's savvy in making sensible choices for daytime television programming that enhanced the web's image and bottom line in the 1950s (see Chapters 8–13), the chain also fell on its face occasionally. No network has escaped the frustration and humiliation of getting it all decidedly wrong a few times. Yet it can be unequivocally stated that CBS understood what daytime audiences wanted most of the time and delivered the goods to supply it. It must have surely chagrined intense competitor David Sarnoff while putting an extra bounce in the steps of William S. Paley, the avowed radio man. Unable to halt the encroachment of television, Paley delighted in whipping his old nemesis in the video architect's own province.

8

Search for Tomorrow

For many a longtime viewer of televised soap opera, the genre genuinely commenced in 1951 as Procter & Gamble and producer Roy Winsor unveiled Mary Stuart in *Search for Tomorrow*, a drama originating in New York. From that watershed moment the soap opera would never be the same. With a few minor exceptions, the era of experimentation was over, as with *Search*'s inception, the few years of bona fide exploratory apprenticeship subsided. The form's basic direction coalesced around a specific story type. *Search for Tomorrow* was the instant hit that daytime had been waiting for. Overnight it captured first place in the soap opera ratings and held that coveted spot for four years. This defining show set the parameters of serialized melodrama for the next five years and affected a great deal of what daytime viewers were to be offered across the next couple of decades.

The origins of those constants can be traced in large measure to the Milton H. Biow Company, a New York–based advertising agency responsible for much of the amusement that Americans heard emanating from their radios. In the 1940s, for instance, an entrepreneurial Biow created the $64 question that became a legendary catchphrase overnight, habitually spilling from the lips of the countrymen tuning in to the quiz show *Take It or Leave It* (1940–52).[1] In 1955, when Biow divested one-half of its interest in that intellectual feature to producer Louis G. Cowan, Cowan expanded Biow's unadorned concept. That year Cowan brought *The $64,000 Question* (1955–58) and *The $64,000 Challenge* (1956–58) to television. Ultimately, the infamous quiz show scandals of the late 1950s blew all those shows—and several peer contests—off the air.[2] But Biow had quit the industry before that occurred.[3]

Milton Biow himself engaged the services of a young $15-a-week bellhop at the Hotel New Yorker and turned him into a multimillion-dollar marketing icon. At a guaranteed $20,000 annually for life, Johnny Roventini became a living trademark for the Philip Morris Company as he shouted, "Calllll for Philip Morrr-raisss!" on multiple radio series that the tobacco manufacturer sponsored. It was a stroke of genius for Biow, whose agency handled all of the Morris broadcast business.

Joining forces at mid-century with this highly successful team was a young man to whom Biow imparted weighty responsibilities. Roy Winsor, born April 13, 1912, in Chicago, the cradle of broadcast drama, was added to the Biow Company in 1950 as vice president of television and radio. The magna cum laude Harvard graduate and ex-freelance writer soon became Biow's executive producer of commercials on prominent TV series like *I Love*

Lucy (sponsored by Philip Morris) and *My Little Margie.* When Winsor later formed Roy Winsor Productions (1955–69), he oversaw commercial productions for heady projects like *Have Gun, Will Travel* (1957–63).

Long before that, however, the Chicago habitué was deeply involved in radio in the Windy City. At 26 Winsor directed *Vic and Sade.* In the 1940s he scripted and directed *Sky King.* That same decade Procter & Gamble entrusted him with the supervision of several of its renowned soap operas, among them *The Goldbergs, Houseboat Hannah, Kitty Keene Incorporated, Lone Journey* and especially Oxydol's own *Ma Perkins,* arguably featuring radio's most beloved daytime heroine. While Winsor was actually employed by the Dancer-Fitzgerald-Sample ad agency, his efforts were almost exclusively executed on behalf of P&G. In that capacity, many challenging assignments fell to him. Possibly the most delicate occurred when he was working on *Ma Perkins.*

During World War II Ma's only son John Perkins was slaughtered on a European battlefield and buried in an unmarked German grave. John was the lone major soap opera figure to become a fatality during that four-year global conflict, in fact. His loss prompted an instant, unbelievable storm of protests from the show's fans, the gravity and intensity of which could hardly be anticipated. So enraged were legions of the show's faithful listeners that many threatened to permanently boycott the network and the sponsor and anyone else they could fault for making that "atrocious decision" resulting in such a grievous act. Ma Perkins was held high in their esteem, and she didn't "deserve" that kind of heartrending sorrow! Copious callers and letter-writers further contended that mothers and wives of service personnel needed no eloquent reminders that their loved ones confronted similar perils every day.

Amid that tempest it became Winsor's lot to answer the critics. He approached his duty calmly but resolutely. If radio was to be realistic, he responded, it could not ignore the possibility of human casualty. Ma Perkins, he allowed, dealt with the same difficulty that thousands of American mothers, wives and sweethearts were coming to terms with. Winsor cited Ma's inner strength and suggested that she could be a comfort and encouragement to those facing genuine experiences in real life.

Winsor stated categorically that the author of *Ma Perkins* wouldn't bring John Perkins back, as many fans had requested. Possibly to soften the blow of the loss, nonetheless, a young man about John's age named Joseph — who looked and acted enough like John to be his twin (thereby continually confusing the denizens of Rushville Center) — showed up in the plotline. Joseph rented a room (John's old room) at Ma's home and drove a milk wagon, a job John once held. Coincidence? Conciliation? You decide. It seemed an awful lot like the serial was trying to reach out to its critics by extending an olive branch.

Maybe it also showed that Roy Winsor understood what was essential to the listeners. The episode undoubtedly broadened his perception of the audiences of serialized melodrama. Comprehending what was of paramount importance to them — and, insofar as possible, giving it to them — was vital to the success of a daytime drama. Surely this was one of the insightful lessons he gained in radio that he carried with him when he joined the Biow firm in 1950, taking charge of its broadcast machinations. It was to stand him in good stead in the years just ahead. Such comprehension prepared Winsor for the well-earned accolade he was awarded by several media historiographers that separately but collectively dubbed him the "Father of the Television Serial." Indeed, there simply was no other male whose qualifications came close.

Winsor's initial foray into the realm of video soap opera occurred in his first few months at Biow as he created the rural comedy-drama *Hawkins Falls*. Originally screened in the nighttime hours on NBC beginning June 17, 1950, it moved to weekday afternoons the following year and immediately took a melodramatic turn. It was actually the first serial of the chimes chain with staying power. It persisted for four years in daytime, all the way to July 1, 1955, in fact. While it didn't set the woods on fire, *Hawkins Falls* gave Winsor the education he needed to create other daytime narratives. His next one set the pace for much of what was to follow in the strain.

It's crucial that Mary Houchins be introduced before this background overview proceeds any further. Her influence on the early success of televised soap opera was little short of incredible. Many of the triumphs of those early days could be attributed to her. The pundits supplied an apropos nickname for her, too: "Mary, Queen of Soaps." There were copious reasons to support such an appellation.

Mary Houchins was born in Miami, Florida, on Independence Day, July 4, 1926. Talk about an all–American girl! Her family moved to Tulsa, Oklahoma, shortly afterward where Mary grew up in the midst of the Great Depression. Living in a rental house with homemade clothes on her back, it didn't take her long to realize that her family had even less than those around her.

From an early age — just like Irna Phillips in Chicago a few years earlier — Mary began to fantasize about her future. Her overriding concern was to get as far away from Tulsa as she possibly could after finishing high school. She wanted to break free of the poverty that kept her from possessing life's extras. Her ambitions took shape when she read in a radio fan magazine that leading ladies in soap operas worked two hours a day and earned $500 a week. That way they could have a home and a family, too! That inspiration persisted throughout her adolescence.

In childhood Mary developed a growing interest in music, both as a vocalist and an instrumentalist as she learned to play guitar. At about 12 years of age she went on road tours on weekends with Bob Wills and His Texas Playboys. At 17 she was performing with the USO at sundry military bases. It appeared she was destined for some type of entertainment career. Following high school graduation, Mary worked long enough as a photojournalist to cover the expense of implementing her lifelong escape strategy: soon she was in New York seeking a career on the stage.

Her first job was as a nightclub photographer and hatcheck attendant at the Roosevelt Grill. On occasion she would also sing with the hotel band — songs she had composed. One night Hollywood producer Joe Pasternak, who discovered many stars for Metro-Goldwyn-Mayer, was in the audience. She told what happened next:

> After I had finished he came over to me and asked if I wanted to be in the movies. I laughed at what I thought was a joke and walked away. Then one of the girls at the lounge told me that he certainly wasn't kidding. When I returned he told me to come to the Waldorf [Astoria Hotel] the next day for a screen test. I was awful. After it was over, Joe Pasternak walked over to me and said, "You can't sing and you can't dance. You're funny-looking and I have no idea if you can act. But you've got something." So I got a contract and went to Hollywood at the age of eighteen.[4]

Before checking out of Gotham, however, almost on impulse Mary Houchins married a local artist, a man who was never happy on the West Coast. They divorced two years afterward and he returned East. Meanwhile, Mary Stuart (her mother's maiden name, which she adopted professionally) appeared in 20 films in four years, mostly in bit parts. Frequently she stood in for Bette Davis while producers auditioned leading men to play opposite the celebrated actress. Stuart gained a few leading roles, too, costarring with Errol Flynn in *The Adventures of Don Juan* and *Colt 45*, with Ronald Reagan in *The Girl from Jones Beach*, and with Preston Foster in *Thunderhoof*.

But Hollywood didn't satisfy her. The pace was grueling; she acquired few friends there; and, most importantly, none of it fulfilled her ambition of performing on the stage. In 1950 Stuart asked someone to sell her house, her horses and car, and ship her things to New York. She walked out of her contract, boarded a plane and headed back East, never to relocate anywhere else again.

In Gotham she joined a television acting class and was soon rubbing elbows with the likes of Jack Lemmon and Cliff Robertson, future entertainment legends but then just students like her. She also renewed a friendship with advertising executive Richard Krolik. They had met in California before her divorce. In New York City their friendship turned into courtship and engagement. One day he told her that an old advertising pal from Chicago, Roy Winsor, was coming to town and the three of them would have dinner together at a restaurant. In what began as an awkward evening but ended on a buoyant note, Stuart and Winsor showed up but Krolik didn't. After an hour's wait over cocktails, the duo finally ordered dinner.

Winsor was in New York to develop new shows for daytime television. Stuart was cognizant of the possibilities this important man represented. By pure luck she had read an article a couple of days earlier in *The New York Times* about women, what they wanted and needed. The content lingered in her mind. Winsor observed that Procter & Gamble hoped to transfer some of its radio serials to TV but CBS hadn't bought into that idea yet. Women had listened to the radio as they performed their household chores, but in October 1950 it still hadn't been proven that very many were ready to sit down to view a television show during their workday.

"They will if it's important to them," Stuart matter-of-factly responded to Winsor's comment.

He asked her what she meant by that. Drawing upon the newspaper article, and fortified by their time at the bar ("an hour of cocktails can help a person rise to an occasion," said she), Stuart replied: "Women are too perfect on radio and television shows.... Their needs aren't satisfied. Why can't television do something real for them?"

With that, and a whole lot more, she evidently provided Winsor with food for thought. When he dropped her off at her hotel later he told her he would like to talk to her about playing the lead in a show he was planning called *Search for Happiness*. Winsor didn't call, nor did she think he would. She went on about her life until one night at the close of her weekly acting class, radio director Charles Irving — who attended those gatherings principally as an observer rather than a participant — approached her. "Roy Winsor has hired me to produce a show called 'Search for Happiness,'" he confided. "He said he wanted you to play the lead, and I think he's right. Let's have lunch tomorrow and talk about money." Stuart had auditioned without even realizing it!

"We did have lunch the next day and when he asked me how much I wanted, I knew exactly, $500 a week," she recalled. The following week she signed a contract for that figure for seven years. She had moved off Poverty Row, never to return. Writing in 1977, one critic noted: "Mary has appeared on more hours of television than any performer in the world!"

In January 1951 a kinescope audition was shot. Procter & Gamble was well pleased. The show's title was altered to *Search for Tomorrow*, but everything else was to stay the same. The decision was settled to take to the airwaves on May 1, 1951. Yet, for unexplained reasons, the debut was pushed back to September 3, 1951. It must have been providential. Before that Stuart required a major operation. In July she and Krolik decided to wed on August 1. It was reminiscent of her previous hastily arranged marriage before embarking on a Hollywood career. This union, however, would survive for 15 years.

Roy Winsor had not only come up through the ranks of daytime serials with countless years of practice to his credit, he also exhibited a willingness to get in touch with what audiences *wanted*—and to deliver it to them. He performed a master stroke in creating *Search for Tomorrow.*

> *Search for Tomorrow* was an immediate ratings hit despite production values only marginally more sophisticated than those on radio. The reason was simple: Winsor was the first serial creator to recognize that both the audience and the medium had changed profoundly. In an America freed from the depression and world war, soap audiences no longer wanted or needed the palliative of romantic fantasy. Instead, they craved a fictional world that reflected their own struggles and concerns. Television was tailor-made for the intimacy and realism such storytelling required. In fact, the new medium demanded it. Winsor took advantage of this fact. Borrowing elements familiar to radio audiences—the single heroine and simple theme—he created a naturalistic style of domestic drama that was as resonant with fifties audiences as the depression-era romantic fantasies had been earlier.[5]

For its first 13 weeks on the air, *Search for Tomorrow* was written by an Irna Phillips protégé, Agnes Eckhardt Nixon, who is more fully introduced in Chapter 12. But the long-haul reins were entrusted to a man whose work had been captivating radio audiences for a long while, Irving Vendig. Ironically, he resided in Sarasota, Florida, a city where the local TV station didn't carry *Search for Tomorrow*, precluding his seeing the very show he was writing! Concurrently, Vendig was penning the imaginative crime pursuit-and-capture fables that enraptured millions of listeners each weekday afternoon, CBS Radio's *Perry Mason.* He departed *Search* after five years to create the gripping, suspenseful daytime yarn *The Edge of Night.* Vendig's dossier is detailed in Chapter 13.

Meanwhile, an early network press release portrayed the premiering serial like this:

> CBS-TV's "Search for Tomorrow" is the compelling story of the Barron family—father, mother, daughter-in-law, and grandchild. It is the story of an American family dominated by the "old fashioned" elders, successful and secure. It is the story of a young widow and her child, and their pathetic struggle to voice the ideas of the young. It is the story of the folks next door, and the misunderstandings and heartbreaks that mar their lives.
>
> Son, Keith Barron, a year out of the Navy, and his wife, Joanne, come into conflict with the elder Barrons when they balk at following in the old man's footsteps. Keith's sister, Louise, is a sympathetic ally, as is young Dr. Ned Hilton. Keith's sudden death embitters his parents, who then turn their unhappiness upon their son's widow.

One pundit went further, remarking: "*Search for Tomorrow* features rather mundane and likeable Middle American families, but it has spiced up their lives with murders, mafia dealings, attacks of hysterical blindness, illegitimate children, and financial wheelings and dealings among rich in-laws that would turn any Getty or Rockefeller pale."[6]

To be perfectly honest, some reviewers took a less-than-favorable view towards the series (and possibly towards soap opera itself), as did this journalist in *TV Guide* nearly three years after *Search for Tomorrow*'s premier:

> Frankly, "tomorrow" had better come soon for the characters on this show, before they all lose their minds....
>
> The people ... are never very happy. They keep searching for happiness ... but they keep winding up in a hospital or a lawyer's office....

The plot? Well, there's this widow who is in love with this man who either has a wife or hasn't, he isn't sure, and there is this other woman, in a hospital, who keeps saying she is so his wife. Whether she will ever walk again has not yet been disclosed. One thing, though — she can still see. Most times they go blind.

The commercials were also new. Procter & Gamble was just rolling out two brand new commodities (Joy dishwashing liquid and Spic and Span cleanser for walls, woodwork and linoleum) that *Search for Tomorrow* helped introduce to milady. In the early years many of the ads were presented live, often employing a model to demonstrate a product while an announcer extolled its virtues. Veteran radio serial narrators Ron Rawson and Don Hancock were two of the most familiar spokesmen pushing not only Joy and Spic and Span, but also Cheer detergent, Gleem toothpaste and an extensive line of P&G shampoos— Shasta, Pamper and White Rain — in a handful of recurring sales pitches. As time passed, more and more of these commercials were shown on film. Their messages were simple and direct and were usually delivered in slice-of-life scenarios familiar to most homemakers.

Winsor, meanwhile, summoned the dominant heroine archetype from his predecessors' tradition to build the first viable TV soap around a single female character. He insisted on a bare-stage technique for this series. He also emphasized the camera close-up to connect his characters to the viewers.[7] There was little need for sophisticated sets or long shots; most of the action occurred in the living room or kitchen, key venues in the geography of an early soap. "The critical importance of *Search for Tomorrow*," noted one scholar, "is that it found an audience that was emotionally invested enough to make a daily commitment, which proved that the serial had a future on daytime television."[8]

Opined another: "*Search for Tomorrow* might not have been the success it was without actress Mary Stuart and the character she so completely inhabited.... She was ... a direct descendant of the serial heroines of radio. She cared about other people's problems, providing wise counsel to neighbors and friends, while facing her own heartaches with quiet dignity and resolve. But she was also the first of a long line of heroines unique to television soap opera, struggling more with issues of marriage, children, and family than those of romantic fulfillment."[9]

The quarter-hour serial was set in mythical Henderson, a little hamlet somewhere near Chicago in the rural heartland of America. At the beginning, Keith (Johnny Sylvester) and Joanne Barron (Stuart) and their little daughter Patti (Lynn Loring) were at the nucleus of the storyline. Roy Winsor (who, you may recall, supervised *Ma Perkins* in the 1940s) branded Jo— as she was affectionately known by friends— as "a kind of young Ma Perkins, the sort of woman who cared about her neighbors' problems, who could offer help to others, and who could face her own personal troubles with dignity." In those early days, Victor (Cliff Hall) and Irene (Bess Johnson) Barron, Keith's parents, dominated much of the storyline. Their idiosyncrasies, foisted upon the younger Barrons, were about the only disruptions that consistently intruded upon the genteel existence that Keith and Jo attempted to sustain.

Mary Stuart recalled that first day:

If the studio looked like a nice place for a nightmare, it was right in keeping with the way we felt. There are many sensations connected with live television....

When you are that nervous and excited you don't notice the clock till suddenly it's time. The hands have moved relentlessly in those little one-second jumps. You think your heart is going to stop, and maybe it does, but you have stepped outside yourself and into the show.

"But, Mommy, where is Daddy? Where is Daddy? Where is Daddy?"

Patti repeated the phrase in the singsongy voice of a five-year-old as Joanne tucked the covers around her and kissed her good night. Then the young mother moved to the window, being careful not to touch the frame. She looked soulfully out at the black velvet drapes, and the child began to repeat the words. This time a filter effect had been added and the child was not seen, so the plaintive question seemed to ring in Joanne's ears. The Hammond organ swelled, the scene faded.[10]

Two of the three cameras lumbered to the other side of the studio to watch a young model dip a mop into a pail of Spic & Span! ...

That first episode included a couple of very clear, sharply focused pictures of the boom mike, but aside from that there were no major mishaps, and we'd gotten off the air on time.[11]

The poignant question "Where is Daddy?" seemed like an omen, given the storyline's direction not long afterward. A few months into the drama Keith was the victim of a fatal automobile accident. (Observed one scholar: "Widowhood, almost *de rigueur* in radio heroines, was not long in becoming required of the heroines of television."[12]) Roy Winsor had considered launching the narrative at that explicit juncture but decided against it, believing viewer interest could be cultivated by the preliminaries. In that time the audience had gained empathy for Joanne and Patti, and was drawn into the yarn even more deeply than if Keith had never been introduced. Once again Winsor was right. By the close of 1951, five million households were tuning in every day. Continuing the meteoric rise, the numbers swelled to 50 million by 1960. Calling the project "box office from day one," Winsor knew he had his viewers right where he wanted them.

At about the same time, some new characters were added to the cast. They weren't expected to be there long — only a few days or a few weeks at most. Stu (Larry Haines) and Marge (Melba Rae) Bergman, and their daughter Janet (first played by Ellen Spencer, then by Sandy Robinson), moved in next door. These quick wits added charm, zest and zany banter to the melodramatic storyline. Comic relief hadn't been done in suspenseful daytime soap opera before, at least not on TV, and it was a welcome relief. The viewers expressed favorable sentiments, and Haines' particular flair for jesting was rewarded when Winsor informed him, "You've got a job for life!"

The Bergmans and the Barrons became life-long friends. Haines and Stuart would persist in their roles until the serial was canceled more than 35 years hence, the only thespians to last for the show's duration, making their contributions fundamental to the series' enduring achievements. "All the delicious bits of business he had worked out in high school with his friend Art Carney slid into the character [of Stu Bergman] ever so subtly and Larry's own inventiveness added more each day," Stuart professed in *Both of Me.* She dubbed him "genuine and wonderful." Unfortunately, at the close of 1971 actress Melba Rae died suddenly of a cerebral hemorrhage. Her character was never recast, and Stu Bergman stayed a widower for several years until he wed his longtime secretary, Ellie Harper.

Haines (nee Lawrence Hecht) was a resilient commodity in dramatic radio, working some 15,000 episodes on various crime features and daytime serials. Born on August 3, 1917, of Russian parentage at Mount Vernon, New York, he trained at the Westchester branch of City College of New York. Offered a drama grant to continue his scholarship, he rejected it to launch his professional vocation without further delay at New York's WWRL. Haines was soon auditioning for "everything," which led him to win bit parts, recurring roles and leads in a myriad of aural series: *Big Town, The CBS Radio Mystery Theater, David Harding — Counterspy, David Harum, Dimension X, The Falcon, The FBI in Peace and War, Gangbusters, Joyce Jordan — Girl Interne* (sic)*, The Man Behind the Gun, Manhunt, Mr. District Attorney, Now Hear This, Pepper Young's Family, Rosemary, The Second Mrs. Burton, That*

With the arrival of Stu and Marge Bergman, Search for Tomorrow's widowed heroine Joanne Barron had friends to lift her spirits and offer their perspectives on Jo's many troubles. The mirthful Bergmans, intended as transitory additions, were so well received by viewers they remained permanently as Jo's closest chums and neighbors. Shown, left to right: Jo (Mary Stuart), Stu (Larry Haines) and Marge (Melba Rae). While Rae died 20 years into the story, Jo and Stu remained soul mates for 35 years.

Hammer Guy and *Young Doctor Malone.* He made 80 guest shots on *The CBS Radio Mystery Theater* in the 1970s and 1980s alone!

Haines applied his talent to the Broadway stage, where he appeared in *A Thousand Clowns, Generations* and *Promises, Promises,* earning Tony nominations for the latter two. He won supporting roles in a trio of motion pictures: *The Odd Couple* (1968), *The Seven-Ups* (1973) and *Tank* (1984). He played in the 1973 TV movie *The Country Girl,* and that same decade gained a bit part in the CBS sitcom *Maude.* In 1980 he had a recurring role on the short-lived sitcom *Phyl and Mikhy.* After *Search for Tomorrow* left the air, in 1995 he turned up as alleged serial killer Neal Warren in the daytime drama *Loving*, a part — reminiscent of his radio days — that seemed deliciously tailored for him. For his performance as Stu Bergman, Haines was awarded three Emmys: Outstanding Actor in a Daytime Drama Series (1976), Outstanding Actor in a Supporting Role for a Daytime Drama Series (1981) and a Special Recognition Award (1985), an honor he shared with Charita Bauer of *The Guiding Light* and Mary Stuart of *Search for Tomorrow*.

So integral, reliable and vital were both Haines and Stuart to *Search* that — when a performance ran short in the era of live television — to fill time the director instructed whichever one was on camera to telephone the other in a "pretend" call, making up one-sided dialogue until the scene faded.

Parenthetically, let it be noted that the arriving Bergmans actually had not one child but *two*. In addition to Janet, who would be called upon at certain points throughout the serial's existence, there was also a son, her younger brother Jimmy. He ascended the stairs to take a nap one day shortly after they moved to Henderson and was totally forgotten, at least by the writer and producer! A decade later the juvenile Rip Van Winkle reappeared, courtesy of new writers. He was no longer a son, however, but Stu's nephew! It's funny how awkwardly things were sometimes handled in soap opera.

Another curious thing, which Mary Stuart recalled years later, was an unusual policy in effect during the serial's earliest years. The only time her character could sit on a bed with a male adult, she remembered, was if she was fully dressed and that individual was either her husband or a man who was perceptibly ill!

Stuart commented on some of the complexities of those early days in live TV:

> It was a marvelous time! I think one of the big reasons is because we had so little to work with. It brought out the best in everybody....
>
> We had to create a reality, out of almost nothing. The stories moved so slowly that to fill the time, to fill the reality, to make the relationships real required so much from all of the actors. All we had was each other so it was all in the listening, in the faces.
>
> It was partly because the writers came from radio and they didn't know how to write television.... You couldn't, as they used to do in radio, have somebody knock on the door on Monday and it was Wednesday before anybody answered it. It's so obvious now, but in the early days, the writers were just learning.[13]

Though overcome by her own grief following her husband's sudden demise, Jo Barron exhibited a resolute strength and faith in the days following his death that would reveal to the viewers the kind of woman she would be for the next 35 years. She was now solely responsible not only for herself but for her young daughter Patti. For the first time in her life Jo was destitute and forced into seeking employment. She landed a job as a secretary at Henderson Hospital. But that didn't erase all of her dilemmas by any means. Mounting troubles were coming in the form of Keith's mother, Irene. Grandma didn't approve of Jo's methods of raising Patti, and — truth be told — she had never liked Jo anyway. Before long the meddling mama-in-law persuaded her spouse Victor to join her in taking Jo to court to seek permanent custody of the child. The Barrons were reputedly the wealthiest, and among the most prominent, denizens of Henderson. Victor was a construction magnate and wielded a lot of political influence due to his powerful connections.

When her legal machinations failed, Irene Barron simply kidnapped her granddaughter. After a time the child was returned to her mother, and Irene settled down, although she interjected herself into Jo and Patti's affairs with disconcerting regularity.

Some time later Jo fell in love with her boss at the hospital, business manager Arthur

Tate (Terry O'Sullivan). Allowing for a brief time-out in 1955–56 for a stint on *Valiant Lady*, O'Sullivan persisted as Tate until his character succumbed to a fatal heart attack in 1968 — a lengthy run for a serial actor. Concurrently he appeared in *Days of Our Lives* (1966–68), and afterward on *The Secret Storm* (1968–69). Due to vicious rumors spread by Irene Barron in the meantime, Jo was forced to quit her job at Henderson Hospital. With some help, she opened the Motor Haven, a roadside motel for overnight guests that was later expanded to include a diner. At about the same time, she accepted Arthur Tate's proposal of marriage.

A gangster with no scruples, Mortimer Higbee (Ian Martin), was soon giving Jo fits as he attempted a myriad of underhanded methods to acquire the Motor Haven. He represented a syndicate that planned to use the property as a front for trafficking drugs. In one of his schemes, Higbee combined forces with an unperturbed, conniving Irene Barron to accomplish his selfish ends. Nonetheless, though he became a terrifying nightmare for Jo, he appeared to be thwarted at every turn. In the midst of such angst, a beleaguered Joanne was still able to deliver insightful homilies, such as: "In our search for tomorrow, we are often disappointed in what we find, for we have built today on the quicksand of trouble." Meditations like that one permitted the viewer to reflect on the enormous wisdom, perceptions and strength of this remarkably resilient woman, once again underscoring her credentials for wearing the time-honored mantle of heroine.

As luck would have it, on the day of Jo and Arthur's planned nuptials, a woman claiming to be Arthur's supposedly late spouse, Hazel (Mary Patton), showed up in Henderson. Actually she was the deceased Hazel's identical twin sibling, Sue, hired by the mob to stop the wedding in a chilling contrivance to gain ownership of the Motor Haven. The real Hazel had died in a fire many years before.

Arthur's attorney, Nathan Walsh (George Petrie, a recurring thespian in "The Honeymooners" skits on *The Jackie Gleason Show*) — who initially exhibited amorous feelings for Jo until he realized her emotions for Arthur ran deeper — uncovered the ruse. Nathan, Arthur and Jo set a trap to get Sue, who imbibed freely, to reveal the conspiracy. Hiring an actress to impersonate her late twin, they staged a phony fire. Convinced Hazel was alive, an inebriated Sue raced into the nearby forest, bent on communicating with Hazel. Unfortunately, the mob intervened and murdered her in the woods before she could spill the beans.

As was the custom in soap opera under correspondingly contrived circumstances, Jo was accused of the crime. Luckily, a perseverant Nathan and Arthur were able to furnish substantial proof of a mobster's guilt, and Jo was exonerated. Regrettably, Arthur was shot while trying to clear Jo, leaving him paralyzed. A despondent groom-in-waiting postponed their wedding due to his physical limitations.

The gangsters didn't give up. By early 1953 they had hired an unscrupulous Rose Peterson and her mute brother Wilbur, newcomers to Henderson, to ingratiate themselves to Jo and Arthur. Actress Lee Grant originated the part of Rose, followed by Nita Talbot and Constance Ford. None other than Don Knotts, who was Andy Griffith's memorable sidekick Barney Fife from 1960 to 1968, portrayed Wilbur. Soon the siblings were living at the Motor Haven, a business they had vowed to destroy. Attempting to humiliate Jo, Rose plotted to poison some soup at the Motor Haven restaurant. But before it could be served, in an awkward moment she revealed to Jo and Marge what she had done. That pair poured the soup down the drain. Not long afterward, Rose and Wilbur hightailed it out of town, their mission unaccomplished.

Despite Arthur's paralysis, Jo finally convinced him to marry her anyway. Their wedding occurred on May 18, 1955. At the time, Mary Stuart was pregnant with her firstborn, Cynthia, and could be shown only above the bust. Fourteen months later Mary's second child, Jeffrey, was born. To avoid similar protracted above-the-bust camera shots, and to add novelty to the script, the decision was made to have Jo become pregnant as well, resulting in the birth of Duncan Eric Tate on the show. This occurred not long after comedienne Lucille Ball had given birth to Little Ricky on *I Love Lucy*, but it was the first time it occurred on a soap opera. When Jeffrey Krolik was born, the show even went to the hospital to tape a mother-son bonding scene.

There were two provisos that Stuart made regarding the pregnancy-birth plotline: first, she was to have the last month off from work; and second, nothing was to interfere with a healthy pregnancy or the baby afterward. It didn't quite work out that way. The real birth due date was October 20, 1955. A week before that, Stuart was still in the plotline, and learned she was to appear in three installments the following week. She threw a wall-eyed fit on director Charles Irving, informing him she wouldn't show up the next week. Jeffrey debuted on October 17, earlier than expected. Yet that was nothing compared to what happened later.

In the most traumatic development during her 35-year *Search* career, Stuart was confronted with the news that the sponsor, a new producer, director and pair of writers had all agreed to sacrifice Duncan Eric to beef up the show's sagging ratings. He was going to be hit by a car, have surgery and linger in a coma for a week, then die. Stuart flew into a rage, arguing vehemently against it, to no avail. She debated quitting the show. She had always visualized Duncan Eric as her own son — and what mother wouldn't, given the conditions of his birth? The die was cast, nevertheless, and the sequence proceeded to its ultimate conclusion. Despite many off-camera trials that she was to experience in standing up for her character Joanne during countless tension-filled moments over the years, Stuart allowed that none cut so deeply or more personally as this one.

In the meantime, the Motor Haven was facing grave financial peril. Arthur Tate dreamed big, planning to greatly enlarge the facility, but without a steady stream of capital to back up his ideas. To accomplish his aim, he borrowed $125,000 from a loan shark, not realizing the syndicate was handling the financing. When he failed to repay the advance at the end of 30 days, the mob had a legal right to acquire the Motor Haven. But Arthur had an ace up his sleeve.

Turning to his affluent, overbearing Aunt Cornelia Simmons (Doris Dalton), he and Jo were able to stave off the bloodthirsty hooligans once more, albeit just in the nick of time. Aunt Cornelia liked Henderson well enough to move there permanently. Yet she, like Irene Barron before her, took an instant dislike to Jo and seized every opportunity to destroy Arthur and Jo's marriage. In the meantime, Jo's mom died, and her dad, Frank Gardner (first Harry Holcombe, then Eric Dressler), and recently widowed sister, Eunice (Marion Brash), also moved to Henderson. The town's magnetic ability to steadily draw so many new citizens must have seemed somewhat misplaced to astute viewers, especially when one considered that the place really didn't have all that much going for it.

Jo and Arthur's marriage was good some of the time, but it consistently tested Jo's valor. Arthur often leaned heavily on the bottle. Eunice found him to be an especially charming man, nonetheless. His paralysis by then cured, Arthur succumbed to her seductive advances, giving in to the sins of the flesh. A guilt-ridden Eunice confessed their infidelity to Jo (which some who've been there would advise against). Disgraced by his lapse, Arthur accepted an offer from Aunt Cornelia that sent him on an extended business venture to Puerto Rico.

Afterward, Cornelia wed an exciting man much younger than she, Rex Twining (Lawrence Hugo). All the same, before the ink dried on their marriage license an utterly unprincipled Eunice had Rex in bed with *her*! When Aunt Cornelia was found murdered, suspicion fell on Rex and Eunice, who were tried for the heinous crime and found guilty. The real perpetrator was Cornelia's housekeeper, Harriet Baxter (Vicki Vola), who was nailed for it in 1960, after Rex and Eunice spent a while cooling their heels in the slammer. Released, the couple wed and took off to handle the old lady's (Cornelia's) business interests in Puerto Rico. Arthur had returned by then from that tropical locale and made amends with Jo, so that his little family was again intact and under one roof.

Jo was to remain a pivotal figure in the drama throughout its 35-year run, but particularly did the storyline revolve around her during its first two decades. Even when she wasn't the focal character, others would approach her for counsel, reassurance and a shoulder to lean on. Following Duncan Eric's death, for instance, the emphasis shifted for a while to Jo's daughter Patti and to Janet Bergman.

In her teenage years (in soap opera, real time meant very little; a child could age from five to 18 in the span of no more than six or eight years!), Patti pursued destructive affairs with two married men, one of which led to pregnancy and a miscarriage. At one point she, too, like her stepfather before her, landed in a wheelchair, the victim of paralysis after an automobile accident. Her real father (Keith Barron) had died in yet another car wreck. The more things changed, the more they stayed the same.

As the 1950s ended, Janet — who had also aged rapidly — wed Jo's orphaned 17-year-old cousin Bud Gardner (Tony Ray, Anthony Cannon, George Maharis) and had a son. Bud was later presumed dead in yet another accident, and in the early 1960s Janet tied the knot with Dr. Dan Walton, with whom she had three kids. As was typical in the serial (and in soap opera in general), Bud resurfaced. He soon died under mysterious circumstances, however, and this time Stu Bergman was accused. It took Jo to clear his name. (In reality, Bud's death was accidental, which Jo proved.) Actress Mary Stuart observed in her book, "In those days it was a standing rule that every two years we had a trial, and if you keep score, you will see that, in every instance, it [the accused] was an innocent victim." Nothing was different here than anywhere else in serialdom!

From the 1960s on, following Arthur's fatal heart attack, Jo engaged in many romantic pursuits. Somehow she had the uncanny ability to pick men destined for unwholesome ends. Her next long-term suitor, Sam Reynolds, with whom she played a cat-and-mouse game for years (yet never took to the altar), also vanished from sight, then turned up as she was about to walk down the aisle with Dr. Tony Vincente! The latter had restored her eyesight following yet another car accident. She soon lost her sight a second time from emotional stress. (Recall that the more things changed, the more they stayed the same.) In due course, Sam was shot dead by two hippies, causing Jo's sight to return, and the wedding with Tony soon followed. Thugs later beat Tony to death. Jo subsequently married Martin Tourneur, the only one she divorced. She couldn't abide his gambling, drinking and infidelities.

Mary Stuart sang a lullaby to Patti on the very first episode of *Search for Tomorrow* as the child waited anxiously for her daddy. Singing was a diversion that was utilized only infrequently on soap operas until vocals came into vogue in the 1970s. From then on Stuart often sang her own compositions, accompanying herself on the guitar. It let her integrate music, a personal love since childhood, with acting, her occupation. She achieved some notoriety in the field, too, by producing a couple of recordings (with Percy Faith in 1956 and Michel Legrand in 1973), becoming a popular commodity with the college crowd as she performed on nationwide concert tours while also penning new compositions. In the 1970s ex–Beatle George Harrison remarked that Mary Stuart was "one of the best songwriters on the scene today."

As hinted previously, things were not always rosy behind the scenes at *Search for Tomorrow*. The bottom fell out, as far as Stuart was concerned, when — after five years of becoming accustomed to a congenial "family" of cast, crew and supervisors — several key individuals were suddenly replaced. This happens in any maturing enterprise, of course, and it shattered a kind of protected space that Stuart and company had enjoyed since their start. They understood one another so well that they could anticipate what each other would do even before they acted, she and others maintained.

With the changes, Stuart soon found herself in the position of defending the integrity of the character she portrayed on a recurring basis, arguing passionately that "Jo simply wouldn't do thus and so" or "She wouldn't say it like that." For a very long time she had emotionally identified with Joanne Barron Tate, so much so that she believed she knew precisely how the heroine would react under given circumstances. "I have never met an actor who was more concerned about a show's success than Mary Stuart," Larry Haines (playing Stu Bergman for 35 years) told an interviewer in recent years. She didn't appreciate the perspectives of newcomers who tampered with a styling that had been set far back in the drama's history. The new arrivals, she realized, couldn't fully comprehend her stance, as they hadn't had her years of exposure to the character.

In the middle of the 1950s the Biow Company — the advertising agency that had employed Roy Winsor, who created *Search for Tomorrow* and hired Mary Stuart — went out of business. By the fall of 1957 the serial was transitioned to Leo Burnett, a Chicago-based agency that was unaccustomed to producing live dramatic programs. "They surveyed our autonomous little operation and decided immediately that things had to change," Stuart recounted in her book. "The problem — or one of many — was that they didn't know quite what to do." The most serious crisis the Burnett brass noticed was that director Charles Irving was often on the West Coast and not in New York. His wife Holly had been hired for a role in *Blondie*, a 1957 NBC-TV sitcom produced in California. Irving was commuting every week (12 hours one way in a pre–jet age plane), and was on the *Search* set only on Tuesdays and Wednesdays, saddling the cast and crew with heavier-than-usual burdens while simultaneously placing a great amount of trust in them. (When *Search* began, Irving, a traditional workaholic, was devoting time to 60 radio shows weekly as an actor, announcer or director, while also producing the Sammy Kaye TV show. "He was the busiest man on Madison Avenue and about to run himself to death," Stuart recounted.)

In the meantime, writer Irving Vendig had left the show to create a new half-hour serial for CBS-TV, *The Edge of Night*, which was to debut in the spring of 1956. In the interim, longtime radio serial scribe Charles Gussman was turning out scripts that might have been lacking some quality that the viewers had come to expect. Bill Craig, the cast's liaison with Procter & Gamble and an understanding friend who often went to bat for the show and its players, had also departed, taking a post with the William Morris agency. Putting it mildly, Leo Burnett felt that things were in a shambles.

To fix it, Irving was fired and a new team was dispatched to "rescue" the program. Arriving all in the same week were Frank Dodge, the new producer; Dan Levin, the new director; and Frank and Doris Hursley, the new writers. Dodge joined Burnett in the early 1950s as commercial coordinator for the various Arthur Godfrey broadcast series. Years later he would be canned, long after he and Stuart developed a great respect for one another. Levin had some experience in working earlier daytime serials, including *The Guiding Light*. He was moved from there, according to Stuart, as a result of ongoing run-ins with the show's actors. The Hursleys were also veterans of early video serials, previously having worked in California. Doug Kramer, the new Procter & Gamble representative, had actually hired Levin and the Hursleys. It was Kramer, incidentally, who fired Charles Irving, the cast and crew's stable comrade since Day One.

And who do you suppose recommended all three of these replacements (Levin and the Hursleys) to Kramer? None other than Irna Phillips, a woman who quite some time before intimated to Mary Stuart that her show and *The Guiding Light* should be combined into a single half-hour series. Was she leading Procter & Gamble in that direction?

The Hursleys had many changes in mind for the show. "Jo has always been too good," a giddy Doris Hursley opined in an early conversation with Mary Stuart. There would be some radical adjustments in the protagonist's outlook. The leading lady, meanwhile, was having misgivings as the wordsmith hinted at what was to come. Stuart didn't know then that when the Hursleys signed their contract they had it written in that they were to receive top billing in the show's credits, even above Stuart. During the years they were responsible for scripting *Search for Tomorrow*, Stuart's name was included in a crawl listing of recurring cast members rather than standing out in larger typeface at the start of the recognitions. "I had no recourse," Stuart wrote in *Both of Me*. "It had never been in my contract that I had star billing. It wasn't necessary, it had always simply been understood."

One critic observed: "From the outset, they [the new writers] seemed to have it in for the character of Jo, and for Stuart herself.... If the Hursleys had had their way, the character of Jo would have been killed off or at least written out of town shortly after they first arrived. Procter & Gamble, who recognized Stuart's popularity, refused to let them do away with her.... The ratings fell, as they would throughout the show's history whenever Jo was taken out of the spotlight." Five years down the line the Hursleys moved on to *General Hospital*, which premiered April 1, 1963, on ABC. It was apparently a good match for them.

Stuart clashed regularly with new director Dan Levin. He gave relentless and sometimes confusing hand signals to the actors (they hadn't been accustomed to that while on camera), and disallowed almost every change they requested in the dialogue (which they usually had been given permission to alter in the past). Stuart, often representing the rest of the cast, sparred vocally, perhaps belligerently at times, with the new director. They weren't on common ground and both knew it. But Procter & Gamble was smart enough to recognize that the show's fans adored Stuart and that anything short of civil disobedience could be tolerated.

In the late 1950s she was summoned to a somber meeting of a handful of stern-faced P&G and Burnett bureaucrats who took her to the woodshed. She was accused of trying to embarrass a new actress on the program, a feminine physician, "because you know she is there to replace you." The possibility of being replaced had never occurred to Mary Stuart, and she had no vendetta against the young woman, she assured her detractors. Their impression was totally mistaken, she insisted.

As Stuart recounted, accompanying her to the exchange was her attorney, who subsequently asked: "Just tell me right now, do you want to fire her? Is that why we're here?" There was a very long pause. Doug Kramer, the new liaison linking P&G and the show, replied, "No, we don't want to go that far." Producer Frank Dodge explained, "We just want to go on record that we won't have that kind of behavior on the set." Milt Slater, of Leo Burnett, added, "We expect professional attitudes from everyone."

Stuart and her lawyer proceeded from that meeting to a bar where she burst into tears. There would be a number of similar confrontations in the years ahead. But a brave and unwavering Stuart would hold her ground when she believed she was right. Wouldn't Joanne Barron Tate have done precisely the same?

Stuart, incidentally, was nominated as Best/Outstanding Actress in a Daytime Series three times—1974, 1976 and 1977—before being honored with a Trustees Award for Distinguished Service to Daytime Television in 1984.

There were several diverse but valuable innovations in the serial as it meandered along on its long journey.

On Wednesday, November 17, 1954, for a single episode, the program made its color debut. As technology and equipment improved, *Search* continued to experiment in the color arena, becoming one of the soaps intensely involved in CBS's color transmission development. In April 1967 the show permanently transitioned from black-and-white to colorcasts.

On Monday, September 9, 1968, some 17 years after it all began, two more defining changes occurred: *Search for Tomorrow* went from a live to a "live tape" production, while it also became the last daytime serial to swell to a half-hour, picking up the extra 15 minutes *The Guiding Light* had long ago vacated, now running from 12:30 to 1 p.m. (The cast's workday expanded from 8 a.m. to 12:45 p.m., with a new quitting time of 2 p.m. to accommodate the "live tape" half-hour schedule.) The show persisted there through June 5, 1981; at that point it occupied the 2:30–3 p.m. slot from June 8, 1981, to March 26, 1982. The shift in time resulted when the ratings dropped significantly, from a 26 to a 22 share. CBS intended to keep the feature running at that hour, programming *The Young and the Restless*, which was doing much better, at 12:30.

Procter & Gamble wasn't satisfied, however, and asked CBS to switch the two shows. When the chain wouldn't budge, P&G moved *Search for Tomorrow* to NBC, which was then experiencing a devastating slump. That transition came at a steep price, however: whereas *Search* held a respectable 7.1 rating at CBS, the serial debuted with a mere 3.6 at NBC, an overnight loss of three million viewing homes! Furthermore, NBC, one scholar affirmed, "seemed clearly uninterested in promoting the show." The program felt justified in generating its own publicity when a videotape of an unaired installment was stolen. Rather than re-shoot the half-hour, the serial went on live on August 4, 1983, the first live daytime drama episode shown on NBC since 1966. That day narrator Don Pardo startled viewers when he introduced it in the same whimsical style he employed at the beginning of the *Saturday Night Live* series that he also announced. This time, however, he cried, "Live, from New York, it's *Search for Tomorrow*!"

Meanwhile, countless shifts in acting, writing and production continued in an effort to reverse the downhill spiral of the numbers game. Only briefly, when ex–*Search* actor Gary Tomlin returned to pen a few scripts, did the bloodletting subside. Tomlin wrote a compelling scenario in which a deranged fellow—convinced that Jo was his deceased mom—kidnapped her. Nearly a half-million new viewers tuned in during that sequence. But once the denouement was reached the ratings again hit the skids. Jo faded once more, downgraded to weekly appearances thereafter. "The decline of the present version of the program," creator Roy Winsor assessed a couple of years before it left the air, as noted in *The Soap Opera Encyclopedia*, "can be traced to its loss of theme and the loss of the integrity of

Joanne Barron." A pundit allowed, "The secret *to Search for Tomorrow's* future ... was in its past."

Over the years, Jo was married to four spouses, widowed thrice, blinded twice, confined to a wheelchair, tried for murder and held at gunpoint a dozen times. And all of that transpired during the serial's heyday, when she appeared in virtually every episode.

There was a memorable September 1986 installment in which clips of shows from the 1950s to the 1980s were run during a 35th anniversary exclusive. But it was not enough. The storylines and the actors weren't consistently attracting and holding substantial numbers of viewers. With the drama languishing squarely at the bottom of the rankings heap, an execution date was set for Friday, December 26, 1986. The rating for that last week was only 3.3. Shortly after receiving the news of the show's impending departure, an ever-sanguine Stuart told a reporter, "Let's be happy for the 35 years."

Celebrating the marriage of Jo's daughter Patti and the most recent man of her dreams on their final day, the cast gathered for a final farewell. Their optimism matched the program's title. At the end, in a poignant moment out on the porch beneath a starlit sky, Stu Bergman, Jo's longtime soul mate, inquired, "What is it, Jo? What are you searching for?" Gazing into the nighttime heavens, she responded, "Tomorrow, and I can't wait!" The scene ended, and Mary Stuart reappeared in a separate setting to bid her multitude of fans farewell, thanking them personally for their years of loyalty to the drama. Then the screen went dark and it was gone forever.

Quite a few celebrated thespians appeared in the cast of *Search for Tomorrow*. Some of the soap's eminent alumni include Kevin Bacon, Robby Benson, Jill Clayburgh, James Coco, Robert De Niro, Olympia Dukakis, Sandy Duncan, Morgan Fairchild, Anita Gillette, Lee Grant, June Havoc, Joel Higgins, Dustin Hoffman, Ken Kercheval, Kevin Kline, Don Knotts, Hal Linden, George Maharis, Robert Mandan, Andrea McArdle, Ross Martin, Michael Nouri, Robert Reed, Wayne Rogers, Susan Sarandon, Roy Scheider and Trish Van Devere.

What became of the principals of *Search for Tomorrow* in the years afterward?

Originator Roy Winsor was linked with some of the more promising daytime shows in television. He created CBS's *Love of Life* (1951–80) and *The Secret Storm* (1954–74), perennial favorites of millions. He formed Roy Winsor Productions in 1955 as the Biow Company dispersed, taking on commercial responsibilities for several major television properties. Winsor created the short-lived CBS anthology serial *Hotel Cosmopolitan* in 1957 and attempted another open-ended daytime yarn for NBC, *Ben Jerrod*, in 1963, which also failed. After his company folded in 1969, the creative ex-honcho became a freelance consultant for a diverse array of CBS and Procter & Gamble enterprises. He wasn't done yet by any means.

In 1974 Winsor accepted the head writing post for the NBC daytime serial *Somerset*, reshaping it from a crime-mystery stance instituted by predecessor scribe Henry Slesar (earlier of *The Edge of Night*) to a more conventional posture of familial and relationship encounters. About the same time, Winsor was coaching students in serial writing at The New School for Social Research while authoring a trio of detective novels: *The Corpse That Walked*, which collected an Edgar Award from the Mystery Writers of America in 1974; and *Three Motives for Murder* and *Always Lock Your Bedroom* (Fawcett, 1976). He was the initial story consultant for the debuting daytime serial of the Christian Broadcasting Network, *Another Life*, in 1981. Winsor died on May 31, 1987, at Pelham Manor, New York. He was 75.

Charles Irving (nee Irving Zipperman), meanwhile, a veteran radio actor-announcer-director (*Bobby Benson and the B-Bar-B Riders, The Breakfast Club, The Fat Man, Here's Morgan, The Milton Berle Show, This Is Nora Drake, Young Doctor Malone,* and many more) and Winsor's handpicked director for the debuting *Search for Tomorrow,* quickly gained the respect and admiration of the cast and crew. He was fired in 1957 after a new advertising agency took over. He moved to the West Coast to be with his wife Holly, an actress who had a part in a short-lived run of TV's *Blondie.*

Irving found work there, too; he won a role in the 1957 Warner Brothers film *A Face in the Crowd,* the first and most important in a string of a half-dozen movies he made by 1968. He directed or acted in TV series like *Bewitched* and *The Andy Griffith Show.* For a year he played Admiral Vincent Beckett on the NBC-TV hour-long drama *The Wackiest Ship in the Army* (1965–66). Born in Minnesota on July 30, 1912, Charles Irving died in Minneapolis on February 15, 1981.

The lives of wordsmiths Agnes Eckhardt Nixon and Irving Vendig will be explored in successive chapters.

Larry Haines, who played Stu Bergman for 35 years, lives in Florida in retirement. His credits beyond this serial have been previously enumerated.

Mary Stuart published her autobiography, *Both of Me* (Doubleday, 1980), a tell-all account of her personal and professional encounters. She married Wolfgang Neumann, her third husband, shortly before the show was cancelled in December 1986. After *Search* ended, she didn't totally vanish from television screens. Stuart returned in 1988 as a presiding judge in a murder trial on ABC's *One Life to Live.* And in 1996 she recreated the part of Meta Bauer, a major figure who hadn't been seen in a quarter-of-a-century, on CBS's *Guiding Light.* Stuart died of cancer in New York City on February 28, 2002. The versatile, gifted, enduring actress who played early daytime television's most celebrated heroine was 75.

9

Love of Life

"Hello everyone. Don Hancock speaking. Welcome to *Love of Life*."

Hancock fronts a Liederkranz black velour drape to dispense his missive. The pronouncement is dispatched live and cold (nothing before it), unadorned by melodic flourish. Another histrionic quarter-hour exploring the lives of two sisters — one benevolent, one malevolent — ensues. After a 30-second cowcatcher commercial for one of American Home Products healthcare or household goods (Aerowax, Heet liniment, Kolynos toothpaste, Kriptin antihistamine, Wizard Wick deodorizer, et al.), often purveyed by Hancock himself, there's a 30-second billboard, backed by Chet Kingsbury's identifying theme (performed by organist John Gart), as announcer Charles Mountain introduces the tale's premise in a pithy snippet: "*Love of Life*, the exciting story of Vanessa Dale and her courageous struggle for human dignity." After a 60-second commercial for Anacin pain reliever, Black Flag insect repellent, Chef Boy-Ar-Dee Italian foods, Easy-Off oven cleaner or Primatene Cold Mist remedy (with Hancock demonstrating the commodity, or possibly a filmed sequence), the organ resounds and the day's installment ensues.

That's how it was in 1953. Can you envision a similar start for a contemporary daytime drama? Hardly. But from the beginning, and for more than two decades on most midcentury soap operas, an announcer's voice, an epigraph, an organ, and commercial pitches before any action commenced were typically the order of the day. Larry Auerbach, *Love of Life*'s director for all of its 28-plus years (a matchless feat among hands-on operatives), insisted that the ads be grouped at the start and close of the serial's quarter-hour during those early years, leaving its middle for uninterrupted narrative action. This differentiated it from several peer dramas that handled the matter by inserting midpoint commercials. Washboard weepers were still popular on radio, and much of what viewers saw on their little black-and-white TV screens was merely a modified version of what they had heard for a long while on their radios. Vestiges of the carryover would be evident for some time.

Love of Life was creator Roy Winsor's second most resilient serial for daytime television. (A critic referred to it as his "second ideal-woman soap opera.") While he experimented with the form as early as the spring of 1950 when he fashioned *Hawkins Falls* for NBC, Winsor honed his ability and perfected it in a trilogy of dramas that arrived a short time thereafter: *Search for Tomorrow, Love of Life* and *The Secret Storm*. His justification for wearing the mantle of "Father of the Television Serial" is documented in the early pages of Chapter Eight. *Love of Life*, meanwhile, arrived unpretentiously, hard on the heels of the inspired intellect's breakthrough yarn, *Search for Tomorrow*, which quickly set a pace for all the successful stories to surface across the following decade. *Search* premiered on September 3, 1951, and *Love* opened September 24, 1951, only three weeks behind it. Both serials were landmark CBS features that incontrovertibly marked the chain as the foremost developer of illustrated soap opera.

Love of Life's production schedule in the early days of TV was relatively painless and simple. Actors rehearsed at Liederkranz Hall from 8 to 9 a.m. daily. Subsequently, they were in makeup by 10 a.m. and blocked scenes on the set until 11 a.m. By 11:30 they completed dress rehearsal and broke for lunch. The quarter-hour live performance went on the air at 12:15 p.m. "It wasn't your whole life," Hildy Parks, a 1950s actress, remembered.[1] The compact timetable allowed the show's thespians to audition elsewhere and accept roles in other radio, television, stage and summer stock productions.

Integrating a one-dimensional thesis that integrity overshadowed iniquity — which quickly became the driving force of *Search for Tomorrow* — *Love of Life* reaffirmed the sanctity of the lone heroine, a remnant that both *Search* and *Love* adapted from their radio ancestors. The early heavy-handed epigraph proffering Van's "courageous struggle for human dignity" underscored that point. Despite the comparisons, in due time it became clear that *Love* was far more urbane than its antecedents in either medium. While never becoming blatant about it, the narrative established sexuality as a customary aspect of life by embracing storylines focusing on adultery, pregnancy out of wedlock, rape, divorce, infertility and impotence.

Compare that with the estimate of a later wordsmith who penned the serial in 1968 and remonstrated about the complexities in stumbling onto crises that the figures in the serial "had not already discovered themselves."[2] Should that unidentified scribe have chosen another occupation for himself, maybe? There didn't appear to be a scarcity of uncharted spheres that daytime dramas could (and eventually would) enter. In practice, the landscape was expanding in soap opera fare, and *Love of Life* was on the cutting edge, blazing trails and proceeding where no serial had gone before it. In stark contrast to resistant radio heroines, whose unsullied pursuits of affection continued unconsummated, a virginal Vanessa ultimately tied the knot.

"Even *Love of Life*'s initial good-versus-evil theme was not as simplistic as it sounded," one source pointed out. "Stories remained focused on home and heart, but the never-ending standoff between Vanessa and her immoral sister Margaret also reflected the deeper societal anxieties of the cold-war world in which the moral threat of Communism appeared equally unrelenting. *Love of Life* reassured viewers with its continual reaffirmation of the quiet rewards of a life lived according to core American values."[3]

Thus, contended another authority, "*Love of Life* ... remained fairly consistent in its resolve to be an 'old-fashioned soap,' where good was good and bad was bad, and characters were delineated more in black and white than in shades of gray."[4] Yet another noted: "Though bad people suffer, they also bleed. It is pointed out that mothers love their bad daughters as fiercely as their good, and that young adults can and should forgive their parents' failings."[5]

Love of Life was, in every sense, a morality play. The differences in the two siblings, Vanessa (Van) and Margaret (Meg) Dale, were striking. The pair could be considered rivals only in the sense that their quests for meaningful ideals could be characterized so differently. The pundits depicted Van (initially played by Peggy McCay, later by Bonnie Bartlett and still later by Audrey Peters) as "chaste," "flawless," "longsuffering," "noble," "faithful" and "considerate"; while Meg (Jean McBride) was invariably portrayed as "amoral," "hedonistic," "promiscuous," "conniving," "opportunistic" and "selfish." Meg, the black sheep in an otherwise decent family, was "everything despicable a soap character could be," one scholar allowed, "a gold digger [who] ... cheated on her husband ... neglected her son ... consorted with criminals."[6] Another painted her abysmally, too, observing that she "flaunted her indiscretions, marrying for money, ... engaging in one affair after another with men of questionable character."[7]

While the serial may have seemed on the surface (at the narrative's start, at least) to be an allegory about *two* women, there was only *one* protagonist here. The righteous ultimately prevailed over the unrighteous, and the viewer habitually championed the just causes that Van represented. An observer distinguished the Dale siblings thusly:

> Vanessa was the pure sister always searching to do the right thing.... Margaret, or "Meg," was the villainous sister who ... preferred the easy road to riches to the harder road to dignity.... Van's hard-earned reward was the self-respect ... Meg never earned.[8]

The play's early plotting seemed analogous to the film noir movies that were trendy in the late 1940s and early 1950s. An unprincipled Meg's attraction to dangerous males allowed her to become the archetypical gun moll, while it often fell to Vanessa to portray the part of her sister's overlooked conscience. Until Meg was written out of the drama seven years after it began (for a 16-year hiatus, in fact), the plot focused almost entirely on the variations between the sibs. Those bold distinctions set the tone for what transpired during the epoch, coloring a great deal of the action, as well as how the other figures rubbed against the principal players.

One of the traits of the serial then was its utter portability. Not only was it the first long-playing daytime soap opera in Videoland to pinpoint a specific state, along with the locale in which it took place, it was also transitory. Will and Sarah Dale (Edwin Jerome and Jane Rose) raised their daughters in the fictional farming hamlet of Barrowsville in upstate New York. Most of the exploits shifted to New York City before long, however, where both daughters moved. They were back in Barrowsville after a while until returning to New York City. And before the 1950s were history the scene shifted again, this time to the collegiate mecca of Rosehill, a little burg in close proximity to Barrowsville. With the exception of some occasional business in Gotham, the action for the remainder of the narrative's air life was centered in Rosehill.

Following high school graduation, Van enrolled in a local art school, but Meg disappointed her parents by informing them that she wouldn't seek any further training. In place of that she pursued every affluent bachelor within a fair radius who could support and would accept her happy-go-lucky lifestyle. It was the ill-fated luck of prosperous capitalist Charles Harper (first portrayed by Paul Potter, then by John Graham) that Meg accepted his proposal of marriage. In time, four other equally disillusioned males were to follow in his footsteps. That quintet could truthfully testify that they suffered appallingly at the hands of an iniquitous Meg during their matrimonial days with her.

The original union with Harper produced a son, Ben (nicknamed Beanie), a lad who was all but abandoned by his mom. (Dennis Parnell and then Tommy White brought the youngster to life during that era.) Meg openly indulged her own whims, preferring to entertain a plethora of sordid gentlemen than dote on her only son. As a wife and mother, she was a shameful role model. Fortunately for Beanie, a compassionate Aunt Van stood nearby, ready and anxious to come to his aid when summoned. Van went to incredible lengths to fill the voids in her nephew's life without being accusatory toward a blithe Meg. In the viewers' minds, Aunt Van's empathy placed her on a pedestal that she would probably never abandon. The show's subsequent wordsmiths didn't permit her to fall from that lofty perch, either.

At Meg's insistence, Charles moved his family to New York City. In 1953, back in Barrowsville, catastrophe befell the Dales when the patriarch, Will, died. Sarah, his widow, was left to battle a lingering illness. Though she appeared to be on the point of death several times across the drama's long life, she was still kicking (and by then remarried) as the serial drew its final breath 27 years later. In the meantime, the peerless Aunt (Saint) Van pulled double duty, shifting between her mom's physical needs in Barrowsville and Beanie's emotional challenges in New York. She found an apartment in the metropolis and shared it with Ellie Crown (Hildy Parks, Mary K. Wells, Bethel Leslie). To underwrite her living expenses, Van was hired as an artist by an advertising agency that produced TV programs.

In the intervening time —

Troubled by the continuing problems heaped upon her young nephew Beanie Harper (played by Dennis Parnell) by his mom and her sibling, Vanessa Dale (Peggy McCay) took the time in *Love of Life* to imbue the lad with lasting values. She filled a void created by Meg, who couldn't be pinned down with the responsibility of raising a son. Yet Meg rebuked her sister when the boy showed more interest in his kindhearted aunt than her. Van was the one who invariably lent an ear to the youth's innermost concerns.

during the serial's first few weeks on the air — an underworld figure, flashy mobster Miles Pardee (Joe Allen Jr.), made overtures to Meg that she accepted with elation. Her rush to welcome his advances helped the audience form immediate and lasting impressions about her moral turpitude and the lifestyle that she had selected for herself. Her "escapades continually shocked and titillated viewers," affirmed one authority. Pardee, it turned out, was a key player in an outfit dealing in contraband, running the setup out of his palatial Long Island digs. On one occasion an inebriated Meg was visiting there while an obviously apprehensive Pardee awaited delivery of illegal imports. That night an assailant or assailants unknown executed Pardee, and an intoxicated Meg Harper was charged with the crime.

It took the combined efforts of attorney Evans Baker (Ronald Long), investigative FBI officer Paul Raven (Richard Coogan) and Meg's sibling, Vanessa Dale, to get Meg off the hook, proving her innocence just before she was sent to prison. As it turned out, a spiteful accomplice in Pardee's smuggling ring had done away with the flamboyant gangster. This would not be the last time somebody in Meg and Van's inner circle was indicted for murder (and sometimes justifiably so). But that was down the road a spell.

In the meantime, accepting the fact that Meg was blatantly bad to the bone, the show's producers and scribes saw no reason to have her display penitence for the shame and strife she had heaped on her parents and sibling. Doing so would have diminished the personality that had been so clearly etched for her thus far. Charles Harper, on the other hand, decided he had had a bellyful of Meg's antics and promptly divorced her, leaving a tidy settlement for his ex before departing for Europe. Upon reflection, leaving behind his son seemed, to him, a very small price to pay for distant separation from Meg.

Van had a brush with crooked dealings, too, after she and Meg accepted posts with a New York travel agency. Under Meg's influence, a colleague, Warren Nash (Grant Richards), tried to abscond with $15,000 of the firm's money. While Nash was thwarted, his liaison with Meg confirmed her pattern of favoring shady characters. She was to travel that course for the remainder of her serial days.

In the interim, Van had also been pursuing matters of the heart. She easily won the affections of the FBI detective who had been instrumental in sparing Meg from confinement. Ultimately Van decided to leave Gotham and return to Barrowsville, where Paul Raven was opening a law practice with Collie Jordan (Carl Betz). In September 1954 — having reached three real-time years on the air as a virgin — Van wed Paul. On the surface, at least, it appeared to be a union made in heaven. But in soap opera, things are seldom what they seem. Stay tuned.

The newlyweds' happiness was soon dashed when they learned that Van would never be able to bear children. To overcome their disappointment, the duo adopted an ill-tempered six-year-old deaf mute named Carol (Tirell Barbery). Lo and behold, not only did Van come to find that Paul had been wedded previously (a fact he simply overlooked when sharing the details of his past), he also insisted that he did not realize that Carol was his own progeny! That little bombshell was let out of the bag when the child's mother, a mentally deficient Judith Lodge (Virginia Robinson), arrived in Barrowsville. She actively challenged Paul and Van for permanent custody of the little girl — his own child, whom he had just adopted! (Only in soap opera.)

It has been noted already that Meg never learned much of anything from her missteps, which she appeared happy to repeat. She seemed hell-bent on keeping her family in the midst of dilemmas that she initiated by continually introducing unscrupulous gents into the family's midst. The next in line in her progression (digression?) of sleazeballs was Matt Slocum (Burt French). When he passed off the scene she took up with gambler Hal Craig (Steven Gethers), a gangster on the run. With him, not just Meg but all of the community's denizens were in peril. He purchased a nightclub in Barrowsville as a cover for his illegal operations. Van, meanwhile, had become an investigative journalist with the local daily; in doing so, she became the conscience of an entire town, as opposed to focusing purely on her own sibling. A series of exposés she penned on Hal's questionable business interests placed her at cross-purposes with both Hal and Meg, and even threatened her safety a few times.

Nevertheless, her articles put the spotlight squarely where it should have been, and

Hal was arrested, tried, convicted and sentenced for his dirty dealings. He suddenly became talkative and admitted killing his twin brother years before, too, an incident witnessed by little Carol, who became a deaf mute as a result. Following Hal's unexpected confession, Carol began to speak again. A short time later she and her grandmother (Judith Lodge's mother) left town together and weren't heard from again. Her daddy, Paul Raven, appeared content with that arrangement and never saw or heard from his flesh-and-blood-offspring-turned-adopted-daughter afterward! Did that strike anybody as even the tiniest bit odd? (Out of sight, out of mind?)

At about the same time, Sarah Dale's home burned to the ground, and the body of Judith Lodge was discovered inside it. And who was arrested and tried for her murder? None other than Van, of course! (It tended to run in the family.) Judith was bludgeoned to death with a cane bearing Vanessa's fingerprint. By then, most viewers—who were probably accustomed to witnessing more than one daytime serial with some regularity—surely realized that the accused on these intriguing dramas was never the guilty party. And particularly was this true in the case of a peerless heroine!

It was finally revealed that Paul Raven's sibling Ben, who carried a grudge against Judith, had done her in. Ben Raven (David Lewis) was the first member of the family to be sent up the river for such a heinous act, but he would not be the last. Before the murder, incidentally, Ben did everything in his power to undermine his brother's relationship with Van, just as his victim had done before he ended her life. A no-account scallywag, that one!

Not to be forgotten, Meg was by then back in action with con artist Jack Andrews (Donald Symington). Throwing caution aside, she returned to New York City and got hitched again, to hubby number two. Andrews' inclusion in the storyline set in motion a succession of events that were to culminate in the departure of a few major figures from the plot. A skeptical Paul Raven took it upon himself to fly to Mexico to ascertain whether a land development scheme Jack was proffering was really on the level. But Paul's plane crashed, and he was believed to have perished. "The plotline had created a great basis for character growth," one critic observed. "Vanessa could understandably have blamed Meg for Paul's death and cut her off, while Meg could have been allowed to feel some real guilt over her role in Paul's death. But neither happened. The writers were content to stick with the black-and-white extremes as they were originally set up."[9]

As it turned out, Jack had married Meg for the sole purpose of getting his grubby paws on the funds that wealthy Charles Harper, her first spouse, and her late father, Will Dale, had left her. Upon gaining access to the dough, he split—taking it with him and leaving in his wake a penniless and pregnant Meg. ("When you lie with fleas, you get fleas," an old adage attests.)

Not to be outdone, Meg soon set her sights on yet another man-to-manipulate. This time she seduced barrister Tom Craythorne (Lauren Gilbert), whom she wed in 1958 upon divorcing Jack, her sole intent being to involve Tom in a paternity suit. Jack made a brief reappearance and attempted to extort $25,000 from Tom. But before completing the deal, some of Jack's underworld comrades absconded with his dough and silenced him permanently. Now, with the lid blown off her deceptive ploy, Meg took Beanie and abandoned the scene. Neither would be heard from for more than a decade-and-a-half. When they did return, Beanie (then called Ben) would be a grown man who had taken to heart the disillusionment about life that his mother instilled in him in the intervening years. But that's a later chapter. As mother and son departed, all of the heartaches and conflict Meg had created through her unbridled behavior ended. Van would just have to meet some others with low ideals to help her rise to new challenges.

The narrative took a decidedly different turn following Meg's exodus. A more complex family labyrinth replaced the simplicity of the sibling discord. *Love of Life* also experienced some cosmetic modifications at about the same time. Chief among them — occurring on April 14, 1958 — was that the show became the first of many quarter-hour daytime dramas to expand its presence into a half-hour feature. Later it was reduced to a 25-minute serial — the first so modified — so that the network could provide viewers with a five-minute midday newscast. That format was retained from October 1, 1962, to September 5, 1969, and again from March 26, 1973, to April 20, 1979.

With Meg gone, the pendulum swung back toward Van, who resided in New York City. She applied for a job as the hostess of a television series, substituting for an alcoholic actress, Tammy Forrest (Scottie McGregor, Ann Loring). After Van was chosen as Tammy's permanent replacement, the mythical show's married producer, Noel Penn (Gene Peterson), fell in love with Van and asked her to marry him. But an honorable Van gallantly returned him to his wife. To handle it any other way would have tarnished the flawless image that the writers had created for her. Van's possibilities for romance didn't evaporate with that rebuff, however. A new suitor, Bruce Sterling (Ron Tomme), was soon in the chase. But it had only been a short while since Vanessa's husband, Paul, was reported killed in an airplane disaster, you will recall.

A widower, Bruce was a teacher at a boys' prep school, Winfield Academy, in nearby Rosehill, New York, in upstate territory. He was the father of two teenagers, Barbara (Nina Reader) and Alan (Jim Bayer), living with their grandparents. As Bruce didn't appear in the storyline until January 1959, and the lovebirds' courtship reached the altar in April that year, their relationship developed like greased lightning. Longtime viewers silently wondered how Vanessa pushed aside her grief so effortlessly after losing Paul, then missing only a few months. She did so nonetheless, and the newlyweds settled in Rosehill. One daytime scholar characterized the plot as "vaguely reminiscent of Hitchcock's *Rebecca*" following their nuptials.

Actress Peggy McCay left the part of Vanessa Dale Raven in 1955 to try her luck in Hollywood. Bonnie Bartlett replaced her as the heroine. By 1959 Bartlett and the show's producers were engaged in a dispute over compensation and could not reach an amicable conclusion. In what must have been a very strange turn of events to the loyal fans, one day Bruce Sterling was putting last minute touches on his wedding with Van, played by Bonnie Bartlett; in the succeeding episode — their big day — the ceremony saw him and an entirely *new* Van exchanging vows — Audrey Peters having stepped in as his bride! (An aside: Did Bonnie Bartlett possibly think to herself, "Always a bridesmaid — never a bride"?) Imagine the surprise to anybody familiar with the show. Peters was to be there for the next 21 years, until the soap opera finally left the air. Her first day began poorly, by the way, when she appeared at the wrong studio! Ron Tomme, playing Bruce, was also to be there until the final day.

A soap reviewer, penning some commentary during the early 1970s, conjectured how onscreen soap opera relationships might affect the actors off-screen, citing Audrey Peters and Ron Tomme as examples:

> The examples of TV soap marriages that carry over into real life seem endless. These offscreen relationships are just like the onscreen marriages or love affairs except that they are devoid of the mystery — and the headache — of sex. Ron Tomme is probably around his soap-opera wife, Audrey Peters (they play Van and Bruce Sterling on *Love of Life*), more than his own girlfriends. In magazine interviews they talk incessantly about each other, about each other's

good qualities. Audrey Peters' son, Jay, called Ron Tomme "Uncle Ron" for many years. Both Audrey and Ron are divorced from their past mates and swear that their unpleasant connubial experiences have left them without any desire for remarriage. Again, one can speculate: Has the onscreen and offscreen "marriage" so satisfied these two, giving them the stability of a relationship they unconsciously need, that they may now scoff at real marriage?[10]

Such suggestions gave serial addicts something to ponder in their quest to ascertain all that they could about the figures behind their favorite characters. Ron Tomme, incidentally, lived three days short of a quarter-century after *Love of Life*'s cancellation on February 1, 1980, passing into eternity on January 29, 2005. And Audrey Peters obviously had a change of heart about remarriage, as we shall see later.

Parenthetically, in April 1967 the serial shifted from black-and-white to color. CBS acquired ownership in 1969 — it was the property of American Home Products until then — and the web immediately began a concerted effort to attract a growing audience of younger viewers, a matter to be explored in greater depth momentarily.

Meanwhile, marriage for Bruce and Van was like a minefield. The couple contended with interfering in-laws, boatloads of envy and Bruce's unfaithfulness — more than once. Leaving academia behind, he took an executive post at the Carlson Paper Company and soon bedded his secretary, Ginny Crandall (Barbara Barrie), in a convoluted plot that nearly cost him his marriage. When Van discovered his infidelity, she left him for a while, moving in with his son Alan. Soon Vanessa was embroiled in a sexless affair that in no way tarnished her shining halo. Maggie Porter (Joan Copeland), who had a terminal illness, attempted to persuade Van to consider marrying her spouse, Link (Gene Pellegrini), following her death, as she tried to protect him from choosing a mate without Van's admirable qualities. "The plotline was one more seal of endorsement for Vanessa — she was the type of woman a dying wife would choose as her replacement," noted a critic. While Van and Bruce ultimately reunited, a few years later he pursued an extramarital affair with the scheming Dr. Jennifer Stark. It was more than Van could abide, and she divorced him, to the chagrin of many of the show's viewers.

"The divorce of flawless heroine Vanessa in this period, and the outrage it caused, reflected both the changing mores of much of American society and the traditional values still held by *Love of Life*'s core audience," explained one source. "The ratings, ... among the weakest in CBS's blockbuster lineup, began to fall precipitously."[11]

This milieu allowed for the most startling revelation in the drama's history. It involved an attorney named Matt Corby who moved to Rosehill in 1970. Soon afterward, he successfully defended a young couple, Bill and Tess Krakauer Prentiss, on trial for the murder of Tess' ex-husband, John Randolph. (Portraying Bill and Tess were Gene Bua and Toni Bull Bua, two actors who met on the show, fell in love and married in real life. Their story thread was one of *Love of Life*'s most popular during the late 1960s and early 1970s.) Unknown to *anybody*, including *himself*, was the fact that barrister Matt Corby was actually Paul Raven (by then played by Robert Burr). He suffered amnesia in his years out of the storyline and had extensive plastic surgery following his plane crash in 1958. Van didn't recognize him, but as they continued to interact, one day Paul's memory abruptly returned. When this came to light, Van was prepared to remarry him, even though she was able to forgive Bruce's indiscretions.

While the writers wanted Vanessa to leave Bruce for Paul, they were afraid that the audience would rebel unless Vanessa had a good reason to do so. Bruce was tossed into another extramarital affair, which pushed Vanessa out the door and into Paul's arms. Despite Vanessa's justifiable motivation for leaving Bruce, the split didn't sit too well with the viewers, who wanted Vanessa back together with him. Again the writers contrived the proper motivation for Vanessa to leave her husband. Fans may have wanted to see Vanessa go back to Bruce, but they refused to see her integrity compromised by the decision. The revelation that Paul had murdered the wife he married during his Matt Corby years, and his subsequent death during a prison riot, not only justified the end of his marriage to Vanessa, it also wiped out the threat of him coming between Vanessa and Bruce in the future.[12]

Paul Raven followed a pattern set by his brother Ben before him, who was fingered as a murderer and sentenced to prison in the 1950s. Paul also had a daughter by the woman he married and murdered. By 1972, when he was beaten to death during the riot behind bars, Van had patched things up with Bruce and remarried him. Bruce remained true to her the rest of the way and eventually became publisher of *The Rosehill Herald*, proving that more than one member of the clan could be a journalist. (Van had earlier been an investigative reporter on the *Barrowsville Dispatch*, exposing the exploits of Meg's playboy gambler beau, Hal Craig.) Although things would never be smooth for Van and Bruce, at that juncture they had already encountered their biggest impediments to a satisfying relationship.

While those issues were being resolved, the producers transformed *Love of Life* into a sexier, faster-paced, youth-oriented daytime drama. An epidemic of drug abuse among teenagers was an early theme. Campus unrest, experimental sex, alcohol and romantic triangles among the young were introduced.

The producers also attempted to simultaneously pacify older viewers, especially those who had followed the tale since the 1950s, largely by dredging up the past. In 1974 Meg (Mary Susan "Tudi" Wiggins) returned to the storyline, accompanied by two adult children, Ben (Christopher Reeve) and Caroline (Cal) Aleata (Deborah Courtney). Ben Harper was in many ways a carbon copy of his mom, employing deception to gain a half-million dollars from her by wedding a certain girl — temporarily ignoring the girl he was secretly married to already. He paid for his bigamy in the pokey. The Dale women, it seemed, were on a first-name basis with the county jailers, thanks to several relatives who were frequent residents.

While the show's ratings — which had been languishing near the bottom of serialdom's roster for some time — dramatically improved during that period, the boost in numbers didn't last. In an effort to juice up the yarn, the producers instituted several revisions in cast and writing. Nothing worked. A reviewer opined: "Jean Holloway, who had worked in soap opera's infancy, became headwriter, and the bottom fell out. Holloway wrote the show as if it were a radio serial, and her ludicrous Bambi Brewster story — a dumb hooker-with-a-heart-of-gold who traveled across the country to discover that her nutty minister father had abused her as a child (Somerset Maugham gone hogwild) — became the laughingstock of the industry."[13]

Adding to its woes, in 1979 CBS transferred *Love of Life* from its customary midday timeslot — where it aired for nearly 28 years — to a late afternoon period at 4 o'clock. That cost the serial a third of its viewers. Many local stations were already using that hour to run repeats of previously aired features and weren't interested in the tale of Van and Bruce Sterling, and Meg Dale Harper Andrews Craythorne Aleata Hart and her five-spouse legacy. The murdering son of her final hubby, by the way, Rosehill's illusory mayor Jeff Hart, conveniently disposed of that partner. It was a continuation of the pattern established two decades earlier, as the rapscallions Meg wed inevitably met with bad ends.

To the dismay of viewers, the word went out on January 5, 1980, that the series was being removed from the ether in less than a month. Instead of using the few weeks it was given to tie up the loose ends of complex plots—a course normally followed by soap operas in similar circumstances—the producers decided to allow what had already been written to play out. The show ended with multiple cliffhangers left hanging; and the decades-old philosophical divisions between Meg and Van were never adequately put to rest.

The thinking among the powers that be was that perhaps another network or TV syndicator would pick up the drama and continue it. After all, ABC had supplied a last-minute reprieve for *The Edge of Night* when CBS banished it in 1975. And in 1982 NBC was to come to the rescue of *Search for Tomorrow* when CBS abandoned it. So why not *Love of Life*?

Despite those laudable hopes, a continuation never happened, and longtime fans felt cheated as the tale rudely left the ether February 1, 1980, at the conclusion of its 7,316th installment. It was a betrayal of the fans' trust. The narrative never returned and never satisfied their quest for answers to a number of unresolved issues. It was a shabby way to treat millions of faithful followers who had bought into the yarn, paid their dues and expected a finish with sufficiently decent closure. Needless to say, it wasn't one of TV's most glorious series exits.

Quite a few celebrated thespians appeared in the cast of *Love of Life*, either before or after becoming luminaries in disparate media. Some of the soap's more eminent alumni include Robert Alda, Martin Balsam, Warren Beatty, Bonnie Bedelia, Zina Bethune, Carl Betz, Dana Delany, Ja'net DuBois, Damon Evans, Peter Falk, Paul Michael Glaser, Anne Jackson, Raul Julia, Tony LoBianco, Nancy Marchand, Marsha Mason, Christopher Reeve, Roy Scheider, Beatrice Straight and Jessica Walter.

What became of the principals of *Love of Life* in the years afterward?

Peggy McCay, the first to play Vanessa Dale Raven Sterling, left the show in 1955 to pursue her professional career on the West Coast. She earned acting credits in several subsequent television series. In 1959–60 McCay was part of a recurring troupe on the CBS daytime anthology serial *For Better or Worse*. She was a regular in the 1962 ABC sitcom *Room for One More*. She played in still more serials: *The Young Marrieds* (1964–66, ABC); *General Hospital* (1966–70, ABC); *Days of Our Lives* (since 1983, NBC). Some of McCay's most pervasive accomplishments were in celluloid. Between 1958 and 2005 she appeared in 13 full-length B-grade motion pictures, beginning with *From the Desk of Margaret Tyding* and persisting through *The Irish Vampire Goes West*. She played in another 22 made-for-TV movies from 1971 to 2001. Among them: *Eleanor and Franklin* (1976), *Eleanor and Franklin — The White House Years* (1977), *Bud and Lou* (1978), *Amityville — The Evil Escapes* (1989) and *James Dean* (2001). Born November 3, 1930, in New York City, McCay was just 20 when she won the lead on *Love of Life*. Before that she was fêted for her skills as a playwright while a student at Barnard College of Columbia University, from which she graduated.

Bonnie Bartlett, McCay's successor as Vanessa, was born June 20, 1929, at Wisconsin Rapids, Wisconsin. Raised in Moline, she attended Northwestern University, where she met actor William Daniels (*Knight Rider, Nancy Walker, The Rebels*). They wed in 1951 and raised a family together. Both Daniels and Bartlett snagged prominent ongoing roles in the NBC primetime drama *St. Elsewhere* (1982–88). She also signed for parts in NBC's *Little House on the Prairie* (1976–77) and the ABC sitcom *Room for Two* (1992–93). Yet it was in cinematic productions and movies for the home screens in which she excelled. Bartlett appeared in 31 made-for-TV movies between 1967 and 2004, including *The Meanest Man in the West* (1967), *The Legend of Lizzie Borden* (1975), *A Long Way Home* (1981), *Dempsey*

(1983), *The Big One — The Great Los Angeles Earthquake* (1990), *A Perry Mason Mystery — The Case of the Grimacing Governor* (1994), *Sleeping with the Devil* (1997) and *It Must Be Love* (2004), plus a trio of TV miniseries—*Ike* (1979), *Celebrity* (1984) and *North and South II* (1986). On the big screen she was cast in another 16 films between 1976 and 1999, among them: *The Last Tycoon* (1976), *Seed of Innocence* (1980), *Shiloh* (1996) and *Shiloh 2 — Shiloh Season* (1999).

Despite earlier protestations to the contrary, Audrey Peters said "I do" again after her first marriage failed. She gained a pair of teenage stepchildren to go with her own son when she wed public relations specialist Johnny Friedkin. Peters appeared as Sarah Shayne in CBS-TV's *The Guiding Light* (1987–91) after her lengthy run as Vanessa on *Love of Life* (1959–80). Her only motion picture role occurred in *Middle of the Night* (1959).

Jean McBride, who portrayed Meg during *Love of Life*'s early era (1951–58), had appeared in high school theater and summer stock productions in and around her hometown of Wilmington, Delaware. At 18 she enrolled in modeling school in New York City. A short time later she gained a bit part in a movie, *Port of New York* (1949). In July 1959, not long after her release from the daytime serial's cast, McBride wed New York state Supreme Court justice Saul S. Streit. With her marriage, her professional career in television and film ended.

Richard Coogan, who was Paul Raven from 1951 to 1958, was born in April 1914 at Madison, New Jersey. (Coogan was 40 when he "married" Peggy McCay, the original Van Dale, then 23, on *Love of Life* in 1954.) He arrived on TV as the star of Dumont's juvenile series *Captain Video and His Video Rangers* (1949–55). Coogan later turned up in the NBC western series *The Californians* (1957–58) and on the CBS daytime serial *The Clear Horizon* (1962). Married to singer Gay Adams, he appeared in many stage productions and in a quartet of B-grade motion pictures: *Girl on the Run* (1953), *Three Hours to Kill* (1954), *The Revolt of Mamie Stover* (1956) and *Vice Raid* (1960).

In a contemporary synopsis of the once popular daytime serial, journalists of a leading entertainment glossy succinctly summarized *Love of Life* like this:

> This New York–based melodrama mined the theater for a tale of two sisters, one good, one wicked, but both top-notch fun. The sibs battled one another, lovers and lying children, including one (played by a future Superman) whose bigamy led to a daytime first involving a swear word that fittingly described the scoundrel's illegitimate child.[14]

It wasn't a lot. But it epitomized the "fun" that those early days of live television brought audiences, and intimated where the serial helped steer a genre later on. Had it not attempted to be all things to all people — including those of multiple age groups—*Love of Life* might have persisted a few more years.

By the end of the 1970s, nevertheless, with the immense popularity of *General Hospital* accentuating daytime's demographic shift, the elder narrative wasn't satisfying much of anybody. It tried to pacify seasoned viewers by reprising the good versus evil theme, reintroducing Meg. Potential new viewers were lured by dazzling doses of young romance coupled with lavish, big-budget sets, furnishings and wardrobes. (A reviewer cited a $30,000 Jaguar kept in the cellar of the CBS studios and a "shameless round bed" belonging to a "smoldering beauty" during the show's latter years.) In the end, neither target group was truly happy.

Perhaps it would have been better to allow one serial to appeal exclusively to the faithful older daytime watchers rather than trying to remake everything in the image of the latest flash in the pan (e.g., *The Young and the Restless* and others of its ilk that so pervasively touted youth and glamour). Television executives then and now swiftly leap onto a winning bandwagon, it so often seems, putting all their eggs in a single basket at the expense of other workable concepts, even when it begets saturation. Think recent reality shows in primetime, and four or five weekly episodes of *Who Wants to Be a Millionaire?* only a few years ago. In the early months of 2005, NBC-TV programmed 12 hours of *Law & Order* in primetime in a single week, followed by nine hours of the same series the next week, according to *USA Today*. Did someone say *overkill?*

There simply was no room for a serial designed primarily for a mature demographic sector. Pity. Meg and Van remained "top-notch fun" to those whose buying power once put them squarely at the center of advertisers' radar screens. Regrettably, after age 54, their kind inescapably "expired." Surely there's a lesson there for the legions of Baby Boomers anticipating and entering their own senior years. Will the media and pitchmen continue to ignore the buying power of such awesome hordes?

10

The Guiding Light

One wag launched her treatise appraising this daytime serial with a conviction that is difficult to refute: "*The Guiding Light* isn't just a soap opera, it's American history."[1] When you stop and think about it, that opinion has a ring of authenticity. *The Guiding Light* is the lengthiest fictional account in broadcasting's existence. Several sources label it "the longest narrative ever told," pointing to its humble origins in radio on January 25, 1937. While the aural incarnation did not persist uninterrupted — alas, the weekday quarter-hour tale was off the air for 12 weeks at the close of 1941 and the start of 1942, and for six months the program was silent during late 1946 and early 1947 — nevertheless, it earned an enduring reputation among dramatic properties on the air that hasn't ever been equaled. In fact, no other narrative has even come close to approaching its enviable longevity.

As of this writing, the end of the serial's seventh decade on the ether is rapidly approaching. While there can never be any guarantees about how long a soap opera will persist — and *The Guiding Light*, like its counterparts, could be canceled at any time should the ratings fall or at the whim of the network brass — the fact that it has aired for so long suggests the drama-by-installment is doing *something* right and could continue for years to come.

The video manifestation of the popular radio serial commenced on June 30, 1952. For four years, through June 29, 1956, when the audio version left the air forever, the dual renderings coexisted side by side — never as a simulcast, mind you, but pursuing the same storyline every day, Monday through Friday, yet airing at different hours. To accomplish that feat, after the first few months of performing both renditions live, the cast taped the radio version a day in advance of those broadcasts. This was done at the CBS Radio studios on East 52nd Street in New York, after which the actors rehearsed for TV until 4 p.m. (On radio, *The Guiding Light* aired at 1:45 p.m.) The tapings followed the current day's live 12:45 p.m. performance on TV, beamed from Liederkranz Hall. (Liederkranz was situated about five blocks from CBS, offering the cast an incentive for a leisurely stroll on sunny afternoons after completing the day's telecast.) The next morning the entourage reassembled at Liederkranz to again practice and block for the TV cameras the show they had recorded for radio the prior afternoon. "I was sad when the radio show stopped," reported actress Charita Bauer. "It was the end of an era. And besides, we were going to lose that extra forty dollars a show!"

The differences in the two versions — television and radio — could easily be distinguished with a cursory glance at a script during the four years the show ran in dual mediums. The libretto for a typical chapter separated the double forms in the instructions appearing herewith in italics.

The Guiding Light
Monday, March 5, 1956

TELOP: (*The Guiding Light*)
ORGAN: *theme*
ANNOUNCER: And now *The Guiding Light* created by Irna Phillips.
ORGAN: *out*

. . . .

FOR RADIO:
SOUND: *steeple clock chiming twelve, fade into background.*
ANNOUNCER: (*over the chimes*) Twelve o'clock. Midnight. Most of the people of the city of Los Angeles are asleep — most of the homes blanketed in darkness. But here and there the lights of living rooms and bedrooms are burning as the early morning edition of a newspaper is read. The account of an eleven-year-old boy named Michael Bauer — missing since early this morning. On the front page of the paper, beneath the headlines, is a charcoal sketch of the young boy's face — the alert, rather sad eyes — the sensitive, unsmiling mouth....
MUSIC: *up for a few notes and out.*
SOUND: *take the last of the chimes in distance.*

. . . .

For TV take a shot of a church steeple silhouetted against the night sky. We hear the clock chiming twelve. Dissolve from steeple to the Bauer living room. Bill is standing at the window. Papa is seated, staring into space. Bert is seated on the couch, her head in her hand.
BILL: Midnight.
PAPA: Ya.
BILL: (*looks at him*) You must be tired, Papa.
PAPA: Nein, but —(*for TV motions toward Bertha*) (*for radio:* Bertha).
BILL: (*for radio:* Yeah) (*for TV Bill walks over to her, puts his hand on her shoulder*) Bert? ... Honey?
BERT: (*looks up*) Yes?
BILL: You're exhausted.
BERT: No, I'm not.

The serial's moniker was shortened to *Guiding Light* in 1977 to "modernize" its image, adding to a transformation that witnessed a new emphasis on youth, glitz and glamour in most of the peer dramas. For continuity purposes, nevertheless, because it was known as *The Guiding Light* for 40 years (including the early TV version), the definite article is included in most references to the serial in the text.

Despite the protestations of some historiographers to the contrary, who still insist that "*The Guiding Light* is the only serial to have made a successful transition from radio to television," there were a handful of dramas that the reader has met previously in this volume which carried over with substantial ease. While none did so with *Light*'s durability, no less than four besides *Light* continued daily on the small screen for four or more years: *The Brighter Day, Modern Romances, Valiant Lady* and *Young Doctor Malone.* That isn't such a shabby showing when compared with the other 85–90 percent airing during that era. To state categorically that *Light* was the *only* drama to shift successfully from radio to TV is incorrect. *The Brighter Day*, for instance, was still running nearly nine years after it began when the network finally pulled its plug.

That said, let us be quick to give *Light* its just due. "This is a soap opera that celebrates the American ideal," a reviewer enthused. "If you work hard, save your money, and stick close to family and home, you'll not only be happier for it, but good fortune will come your way."[2] Family relationships are at the root of virtually every successful daytime narrative. *The Guiding Light* has consistently shifted between some of the brightest and darkest extremes of the human condition, yet family has remained foremost in its focus.

The program was conceived in the mind of the granddame of daytime drama, Irna Phillips—the creator, author and inspiration who influenced almost a score of radio and television serials. (To peruse her background and achievements, see Chapter Six.) Surprisingly, by 1946 Phillips found herself in a legal quagmire over the origins of *The Guiding Light*. One of her former writers, Emmons Carlson, claimed he had helped spawn the popular serial nearly a decade earlier. Phillips dismissed his allegations as falsehoods, claiming Carlson only penned a few of the drama's early scripts, thereby painting him as a mere opportunist. She glibly labeled Carlson "a lying bastard," then went against the advice of counsel and refused to settle with him outside the hall of justice. That cost her. Carlson sufficiently satisfied the court that he had contributed more than a few scripts to *The Guiding Light*, and was awarded $250,000 for his efforts.

Having learned years before by unwelcome experience (upon losing a court case to Chicago's WGN over possession of material she created) to acquire and maintain ownership rights to everything she wrote, a seldom-rattled Phillips had done just that in the years since. Even so, the loss to Carlson was another debilitating setback for the celebrated author, and—in what appeared to be an attempt to maintain solvency—she sold a trilogy of her soap operas to Procter & Gamble for $175,000. The package included *The Guiding Light*, which brought her $50,000; *Road of Life*, for another $50,000; and *The Right to Happiness*, a 1939 spin-off of *The Guiding Light*, which fetched $75,000. Since this transaction occurred not long after she lost her second infamous court case, it certainly gave the impression that the sale might have been a consequence of that verdict.

The shift in ownership didn't remove Phillips' pervasive influence from at least one of those serials, however. On the contrary, the upfront billboard for *The Guiding Light* (on radio, and later during the early TV era) allowed an announcer to continue introducing each day's installment with "*The Guiding Light*, created by Irna Phillips." The name identification was surely gratifying to her, and was worth a great deal, to say nothing of the $200-per-episode P&G paid her for churning out those daily scripts in the final years of the radio-only incarnation. It was, by the way, one of only two serials that she was still writing in the late 1940s and early 1950s, the other being *The Brighter Day*. She paid nameless hacks to flesh out most of those scripts, also.

Chicago was Mecca for soap opera production in the genre's earliest days. By 1946, however, the actual staging of most of the daytime dramas, controlled largely by the advertising agencies, had shifted from Chicago to New York. Gotham was nearer many agency and network headquarters, and was perceived by some industry insiders as possessing a larger pool of readily available talent. Because an active broadcasting center was also simultaneously developing on the West Coast, however, a decision was made to transfer "The General Mills Hour" serials to Hollywood.

"The General Mills Hour" had surfaced during the 1943–44 NBC radio season when three of Irna Phillips' dramas—*The Guiding Light*, *Today's Children* and *Woman in White*—were aired back-to-back beginning at 2 p.m., along with a Frank and Anne Hummert–produced narrative, *The Light of the World*, which rounded out the hour, with all four series being sponsored by General Mills Inc. Phillips was given free reign to permit the characters from any of her three dramas in that timeslot to cross over the boundaries of the adjacent washboard weepers; they might show up in the storylines of those other tales at any given moment. It was a fascinating experiment that other creatives would later attempt to replicate (even Irna herself would try it), but would never find the same success as with the original. A common narrator for the trilogy under Phillips' supervision provided an umbrella or coordinated effect for the series.

In 1946 the trio of serials was to be sent to Hollywood just as Phillips found herself in court, embroiled in the suit brought by ex-scribe for *The Guiding Light* Emmons Carlson. General Mills, in no way desiring to tarnish its image, promptly withdrew its sponsorship of *The Guiding Light*, and the show went off the air on November 29, 1946. Meanwhile, two other serials, plus a new one Phillips introduced to replace *The Guiding Light* called *Masquerade*, shipped out to Hollywood. The California relocation wasn't practical, however (as this trial run revealed), and in 1949 production was finally sent to New York.

In the meantime, *The Guiding Light* returned to the airwaves over CBS Radio on June 2, 1947, after Procter & Gamble purchased it from Phillips. The narrative would never be permanently discontinued after that date, at least until the contemporary epoch.

Now for the drama's backstory: there was 15 years of it on radio, and when TV came along, little of it was offered for those who were unfamiliar with the aural interpretation.

At its inception *The Guiding Light* swirled around the Reverend Dr. John Ruthledge, a kindly cleric of a nonsectarian congregation in the small town of Five Points, California. Nearly a decade later the story transitioned to Selby Flats, a suburb of Los Angeles. Representing the spiritual strength of suburbia, Ruthledge's mission was to demonstrate how to live a good life through understanding and patience.[3] The pastor of the Little Church of Five Points became a champion of life's enriching qualities and the humanitarian ideals of the American way. "No matter how difficult your problems may be," said he, "others have been faced with the same obstacles, and with faith and determination and courage have managed to overcome them."

Some of his sermons, which were popular features of the show during its early days, were collected in a book purchased by more than 250,000 readers. It was one of many examples of popular mailhook premiums offered to listeners of daytime soap operas, where — for a dime and a label or a box top from the sponsor's product — some trinket would be put into the hands of fans as a constant reminder of their favorite series (as well as the commodity advertised).

The show's title could very well have referred to Ruthledge himself, as he became the community's "guiding light." A widower whose daughter moved with him to Five Points, Ruthledge offered helpful advice while displaying an attitude of caring and selflessness.

These formative years revolved around a succession of ministers, including Doctors Ruthledge, Gaylord, Matthews, Andrews and — by the early 1950s — Reverend Marsh. When the actor portraying Ruthledge was called up by the armed services in 1944, the character of Ruthledge departed with him. Phillips sent him overseas as a chaplain in the armed forces, replacing him with Dr. Richard Gaylord. Although Ruthledge returned to Five Points two years later, by then his influence had greatly diminished. Never again did he carry the weight that had burdened him during his pre-war days. When the actor (Arthur Peterson) playing the part refused to relocate following the decision to change the broadcast location from Chicago to Los Angeles, Phillips removed the character entirely.

Several devices insured continuity between the character of the current clergyman and the principles of the "guiding light." During the 1940s the program opened with a prayer or homily delivered by the pastor. Annually, and sometimes more often, the current clerical character delivered a sermon for the duration of the daily installment. On Good Friday during its final decade on radio, the resident minister preached "The Seven Last Words" sermon. On March 30, 1956, during the simulcast era (the last time the sermon was aired), Reverend Marsh delivered it in the fictional storyline by way of a national radio broadcast. This allowed some of the soap's characters then living in New York to hear it from their vantage point.

In the early days, in addition to Dr. Ruthledge, the cast included his daughter Mary and an orphaned boy, Ned Holden. The minister had adopted Ned when the child was eight; Ned would grow up to become Mary's husband. There was also Rose Kransky, Mary's best friend, a Jewish girl whose father, Abe, was a local merchant. Rose was Irna Phillips' alter ego, by the way—born of Jewish parents but refusing to define herself by orthodox convention. Phillips transferred Rose Kransky to *The Right to Happiness* in late 1939, the soap opera that she developed from *The Guiding Light*. It was the first true spinoff of a daytime serial. (While Rose was the focus there for a while, the story eventually shifted its attention to Carolyn Allen, who became the leading lady, spending the remainder of her waking hours in unnerving distress. Carolyn Allen Walker Kramer Nelson MacDonald, "the most married heroine in radio," was one of serialdom's most longsuffering, beleaguered women on the air before she ultimately discovered her "right to happiness" in 1960 and departed the airwaves.)

More characters were introduced into *The Guiding Light* for a limited time, and then faded from the plot. There was Rose's employer, Charles Cunningham, whose marriage ended in a scandalous divorce as the result of his liaison with Rose. A mystical character referred to as "Mr. Nobody from Nowhere" brought intrigue to the story. He lived in the same apartment building as the Kranskys. And Ned's biological mother briefly became the focus, too. She killed her husband, Paul, and reached the threshold of the electric chair before a governor's pardon spared her life.

With the serial's loftier ideals greatly diminished by the time it got to TV, about the only overt carryover beyond the characters themselves was the organ. In the early radio storyline the parson's daughter played that magnificent console instrument. For years it supplied bridges and background notes on the tube version, too, just as it did on virtually every other daytime drama.

The organ virtuoso (in real life, Bernice Yanocek) labored over the keyboard for a thunderous rendition of Anselm Goetzl's "Aphrodite" near the opening of every chapter. "There would be more organ music connected with each episode than even a band of angels could endure," sighed one critic. Another discounted her sharp intrusions into an otherwise reflective performance: "No program in heaven or earth could match *The Guiding Light* in ominous chords, stings and cadences." For the radio broadcast of January 10, 1950, for instance, the organ's erratic exclamations jarred fans 23 times during a quarter-hour episode. Such unexpected and disarming outbursts interrupted every installment in those days, quite likely keeping some of its listeners on edge.

In the late 1940s, over a decade after the program debuted, *The Guiding Light*'s focus shifted from the Ruthledges to the Bauers, who lived in Selby Flats, California, but who would soon relocate to Springfield, a city somewhere in the Midwest. The Bauers were a first-generation German-American brood with Old World ideals battling for a better life in the United States. Ultimately earning a backstage epithet that celebrated their resilience to adversity, "Bauer Power" came to characterize them as an American tribe that was "making it," long-shot odds notwithstanding.

Despite their numerous tragedies and personal dilemmas, the Bauers supplied the adhesive that bound audiences to the show for decades. In fact, after an absence of 22 years from the storyline, in 1996 the character of Meta Bauer — a throwback to that long-faded clan, and by then an elderly woman herself — reentered the plot. The actress selected to play her was a veteran of TV soap opera: Mary Stuart, who had portrayed the invincible Joanne Gardner Barron Tate Vincente Tourneur, the oft-wedded heroine of *Search for Tomorrow*, for 35 years (1951–86). She would represent an era from decades before, and do justice to it while reprising the memorable figure.

The Bauers included Bill and his wife, Bertha; Bill's widowed father, who was affectionately known as Papa Bauer (the pater familias, "kind and loving and not a butinsky," according to an observer), and who lived with his son and daughter-in-law; and Bill's sisters, Meta and Trudy, and their mates and offspring.

A seemingly irrepressible Meta, who tested the limits of acceptable propriety, conceived a child, Chuckie, out of wedlock in the waning radio days. By the late 1940s Chuckie was adopted by Ray and Charlotte Brandon. Meta then decided to reclaim him. That devastating turn of events exacted a heavy toll on the Brandons. Straining their marriage beyond repair, it pushed Charlotte into the waiting arms of theatrical agent Sid Harper, whose affections toward her had been well documented previously.

Meanwhile, Chuckie expressed his preference for Aunt Trudy over his mother, Meta. And Meta professed a romantic interest in Trudy's current heartthrob, Ross Boling, a promising young physician. Ted White, Chuckie's caddish biological dad, at last persuaded Meta to marry him so that Chuckie could have a home with both natural parents. The result was a loveless liaison. But Trudy was ecstatic over the turn of events, seeing it as her chance to win Ross' affection. Ross had other plans, however; he announced that he was in love with Meta.

A short time later Chuckie was injured in a boxing match accident that resulted from his father's ideas about raising a child. Ted was determined to break the control that Meta wielded over their son. He saw the boy's interest in painting as something only sissies did, and he tried to emphasize the youth's masculine developmental needs. But the child responded with neither the desire nor the personality for such strenuous activity. Once Meta threatened her husband: "You're talking to a woman who'd rather see you dead before she can trust a small boy into your care. I'd kill you first, Ted. I'd kill you! I'd kill you!" To longtime listeners, it should have been a premonition of what lay ahead.

Sometime after the accident, Meta returned home from one of many visits to her son's hospital bedside. At about three o'clock in the morning, unable to sleep, she confided to Trudy:

> Ted White!.... I didn't think I was capable of hating him any more than I have.... What's he done to me? To Chuckie? To my family? He's tried to destroy us!.... All of us.... Bill — just an innocent bystander.... Trudy, someday ... someday Ted White is going to meet up with something that'll destroy him! Yes, really destroy him!

The two siblings spent the entire 15-minute episode obsessing over the current issues affecting the Bauer family. The fact that only two people appeared in the cast was not unusual for a Phillips drama. Hers were unlike other broadcast serials in which several characters gathered on any given day in a rather complex (and sometimes disjointed) maze of scenes. Instead, slower action, combined with fewer people in a single chapter, were trademarks of the wordsmith's work. *The Guiding Light* frequently presented installments that featured dialogue between two, and seldom more than three, characters.

The action involving Chuckie reached a climax in 1950 when — instead of healing from his injuries— he died unexpectedly. Meta was overcome with grief and blamed Ted for Chuckie's death. Strained beyond endurance by the unforeseen turn of events, she lost control. In a rage she picked up a gun and shot Ted to death. But a jury acquitted her of the crime, deciding that she was temporarily insane.

Meta was soon off on a new tangent, chasing Joe Roberts, a newspaper reporter who helped her gain her freedom during the trial. Joe's children by a previous marriage resented Meta so deeply that they posed an obstacle to any serious intentions she had. Despite their threats, the couple married anyway. Within months they were on the brink of divorce as a result of ongoing family disputes involving the children. At about the same time, the marriage of Meta's brother, Bill, and his wife, Bertha (who would more often be called Bert, particularly as television came along), began to unravel as a result of Bill's unfaithfulness and alcoholism.

That brought the story to the video era.

In making the decision to air a televised version of its popular radio serial, sponsor Procter & Gamble recognized the possibility that it would lose millions of loyal radio fans. To avoid that, P&G offered the concurrent episodes on both mediums for four years.

Within 18 months *The Guiding Light*'s TV audience increased to 3.5 million viewers, while only 2.6 million were following the show on radio. At the inception of the televised series in the summer of 1952, at least four million fans were tuning in the program on their radios. There could be no mistake which way mass audiences were heading as TV became both accessible and affordable to millions of potential new audience members. In 1956 the decision was made to discontinue the radio series and focus exclusively on the visual manifestation.

The early television era was characterized by numerous casting changes. No fewer than 14 roles were recast by the close of the 1950s, just seven full years into the televised drama, averaging two acting changes annually. Over the serial's long haul some parts were recast multiple times. The role of Hope Bauer went to seven thespians, while there were six individuals who played Mike Bauer and Robin Lang Holden. By the mid–1990s, five different actors had portrayed the same character in three instances, while seven characters featured as many as four different thespians.

Irna Phillips reserved the right to personally oversee the casting of all new characters in the tele-version. This kept her traveling on a frequent basis between her Chicago digs and the casting offices in New York. She kept a tight rein on every aspect of the show, intent that no extreme alterations were allowed in the drama's theme or storyline. *The Brighter Day*, another of her radio creations that went to TV, was modified tremendously in Videoland, beginning with an almost entirely new cast. One observer noted that, as a consequence, "she seemed purposefully to abandon [*The Brighter Day*] after it went to television." That wouldn't happen with future projects, however.

A reviewer's impression of *The Guiding Light* on television prompted this assessment:

> As in other traditional soaps, the hospital is a major setting, pregnancy and paternity are real dilemmas, and sudden death is common as a means of solving story problems. There is little real evil — just temporary lapses and much trouble between parents and children. There is perhaps lots of Momism here than on most soaps. Fathers like Mike Bauer and Ed Bauer have important emotional roles. (Don't ask about their biological roles.)[4]

Pointing back to the early days, there was still a minister on call for the first couple of years the series was on television. The Rev. Dr. Paul Keeler (first played by Ed Begley, then by Melville Ruick) dispensed advice between 1952 and 1954. But when that cleric left town the crowd became a typically churchless society with few ties to its former self. As one scholar put it: "The 'guiding light' theme no longer had religious implications, but was reinterpreted to mean the support that a close family brings to romantic and domestic crisis."

Not long after *The Guiding Light* arrived on television, Bertha (Bert) Bauer became the central figure of the enduring drama. It was a role she would occupy until the actress playing her (whose name, coincidentally, was Charita Bauer) became too ill to continue and died. With her passing in early 1985, the Bauers—for the first time during the television years—would no longer be the serial's most prominent family. Before that change, Charita Bauer was allowed more than three decades to develop the drama's pivotal character.

Originally, at the tale's TV inception, she was viewed as an overbearing, dictatorial, self-centered wife. The alcohol abuse and repeated betrayals exhibited by her spouse Bill (Lyle Sudrow, Ed Bryce, Eugene Smith) might have provoked anybody. Yet it seemed at times that a catty, naughty Bert was the instigator of her own troubles, for she pushed Bill relentlessly, unmercifully carping that they weren't living well enough. Once she bought herself a mink stole, while on another occasion she put money down on a house without her spouse's knowledge. A reviewer quipped:

> Bert began as a compulsive butter; that is, she would butt into everyone's business. Even her patient father-in-law, Papa Bauer, would throw up his hands and say something like, "Ach, libeling, give it a rest."
> But Bert's life was not an easy one, thanks largely to Bill's behavior. They fought often; taunted each other with promises to get a divorce; and seemed determined to inflict as much pain as possible on one another — each believing the other one deserved it more.[5]

Over the years Bert gradually softened into a warm, compassionate matriarch who demonstrated an abiding respect for the Bauer clan despite her years of personal tragedy and heartache. Her egocentricity dissipated and she turned into a kind, considerate woman. One source credited her "philosophical attitude toward life and strict adherence to the Golden Rule" as invaluable aids in maintaining a powerful arsenal of support for her brood. Indeed, one wag suitably dubbed her "the pillar of family strength."

When her husband was declared dead after his plane went down in 1969, Bert became the family's absolute unifier, even as the rest coalesced around her. It was a matriarchal role that she would carry for the rest of her days. Bill Bauer, incidentally, wasn't *really* dead — he paid return visits to the storyline in 1977 and 1983. (The leading man on *Love of Life* did the same thing a dozen years after *his* perceived "fatal" plane crash. In radio serials, amnesia was catching; in television, a handful of amnesiacs *temporarily* perished when their planes went down!)

Bill and Bert were the parents of two sons, Michael (Glenn Walken, Michael Allen) and Edward (Pat Collins), whose shenanigans infused the plots with shocking diversions in the 1960s and 1970s.[6] The young men followed in their daddy's footsteps: Mike, an attorney, became a womanizer; Ed, a physician, became an alcoholic. A woman with lesser resolve than their mother probably couldn't have handled it.

Meanwhile, Meta (Jone Allison, Ellen Demming), who had been a belligerent, free-spirited, dominating force in the radio serial, put aside her hell-raising lifestyle on TV, where she reformed. Her wanton ways were transferred instead to Kathy Roberts (Susan Douglas), her out-of-control teenage stepdaughter, with whom she kept a strained connection. Kathy's marriage to Dr. Richard (Dick) Grant (James Lipton, who would later become one of *The Guiding Light*'s head writers) was a prominent story thread in the 1950s. Their union came to an ignoble end when Kathy confessed that her first spouse, the late Bob Lang (never seen on camera), was the father of her young daughter Robin (Zina Bethune, Judy Robinson). The Grants got an annulment, and Dick Grant's life continued to unravel.

Janet Johnson, R.N. (Ruth Warrick, Lois Wheeler) threw herself at him, although he was in no way attracted to her. Yet when Dr. Jim Kelly (Paul Potter) began pursuing Dick's ex, Kathy, Dick turned green with envy (with maybe a tinge of career resentment added to the mix). Eventually Dick would wed artist Marie Wallace (Joyce Holden, Lynne Rogers), whom he met in New York while on a sabbatical. When they found they couldn't have children, the couple adopted Philip Collins (Carson Woods), and by the early 1960s they all left town, never to return.

Meta had married Joe Roberts (Herb Nelson) on radio. Recall that he assisted in having the murder charges against her dismissed via a plea of temporary insanity after she killed her spouse, Ted White. Joe Roberts died of cancer in 1955. Although she was devastated, she soon began seeing a business associate of her brother-in-law, Mark Holden (Whitfield Connor). Not surprisingly, stepdaughter Kathy vied for Mark's affections, too, and eventually became his wife.

Three years later Irna Phillips decided she had had enough of Kathy Roberts Lang Grant Holden, and caused her to die in an unusually disturbing manner. (Actually, Susan Douglas, the actress playing Kathy, became pregnant, and Phillips realized she wouldn't be available for some crucial scenes that she had in mind for Kathy and Mark.) Kathy was confined to a wheelchair following an automobile mishap. When a group of bicyclists came along, they shoved her out of their way and into oncoming traffic where she was hit. She died from the injuries sustained.

Afterward, CBS was inundated by hostile communications from a myriad of unhappy fans. Unfazed, Phillips responded to the detractors with a form letter: "We would be most unrealistic if we failed to recognize that as there is birth there is also death. You have only to look around you, read your daily papers, to realize that we cannot, any of us, live with life alone. There are times when we must face the loss of a loved one." But one pundit, aware of how Ms. Phillips' mind worked, conjectured: "Although Phillips concluded her letter with the hope that fans would continue to watch *The Guiding Light*, one cannot help but wonder if she might not have been consciously sabotaging *Guiding Light* so that her favorite child, *As the World Turns*, which ranked just behind *Guiding Light* in popularity, might not take over as number one — which it did."[7]

Not long after that, Mark Holden remarried. His bride was his housekeeper, Ruth Jannings (Irja Jensen, Louise Platt, Virginia Dwyer). Meta found contentment as the wife of Dr. Bruce Banning (Les Damon). And in the late 1950s and early 1960s Kathy's own highly strung daughter, Robin, took center stage. In some convoluted plotting, two men pursued Robin — Ruth Jannings' son, Karl (Richard Morse), and Bill and Bert Bauer's eldest son, Mike. In 1960, after Mike accidentally killed Karl, Robin wed Mike. But Bert was not pleased and had the marriage annulled. The story meandered along in a similar vein during the 1960s, with Robin twice marrying men of questionable repute.

And if you're wondering what happened to Trudy (Helen Wagner, Lisa Howard), the third Bauer sibling, she had little to do during the television years except to acknowledge the foibles in the others' lives. She moved to New York City in 1952, although she made a return visit to Springfield in 1957–58. After that, she was never heard from again.

In 1959 Agnes Nixon succeeded Irna Phillips as head writer of *The Guiding Light*. Phillips then concentrated her efforts on her baby, *As the World Turns*, then two years of age.[8] Nixon was a Phillips protégé, having worked with her on radio serials. Nixon also scripted the first quarter of a non–Phillips property, *Search for Tomorrow*, in 1951, and would be responsible for several more successful ventures (see Chapter 12). Her major contributions to *Light* were to jazz up the plots and figures, and introduce some social issues. She would have Bert Bauer battle uterine cancer in 1961. (Her life was spared — the message being that early detection via a pap smear often brings long-term benefits, a message that may have saved many lives among the show's viewers.) In that instance Nixon purposely crafted Bert Bauer into "a woman other women could look at and think, 'there, but for the grace of God, go I.'"

Later in that same decade Nixon added the first prominent African-American player to a daytime serial, Martha Frazier (Cicely Tyson, Ruby Dee). *The Guiding Light*, like some of its contemporary soap operas, frequently found itself on the cutting edge of television.

Charita Bauer, who played Bert Bauer for 35 years, was once the object of a backstage gag during the serial's early TV years.

> The show was on the air at 12:48 — live — and Charita was having a scene with Theo Goetz. Walter Gorman, who had replaced Ted Corday, was directing then. Suddenly his voice came over the loudspeaker: "More voice, Charita!" Charita, stunned that the director was mistaking air for dress, didn't bat an eyelid but kept on doing the scene with Theo. "Come on, Charita, you can do better than that!" came the director's voice again, for millions across the land to hear. Finally, Charita looked into the camera and said in a soft voice, "Walter, are you putting me on?" After the scene was over, Charita stormed furiously into the control booth, only to confront the hysterical laughter of Walter Gorman and his henchmen. She breathed a sigh of relief when she discovered it was all a big joke. They were not on air at all, the show had been preempted.[9]

As noted in Chapter Six, Irna Phillips may be credited with another idea that was to profoundly influence the soap operas that are aired today. By then fully comprehending that televised serials were the wave of the future, in 1954 she launched a new crusade. Appealing to Procter & Gamble, she made a plaintive pitch to extend the show from a quarter-hour to a half-hour.

P&G was stunned. The firm was quite dubious that American homemakers would be willing to lay aside their chores for as long as 30 minutes to watch the unfolding saga of *any* soap opera. Could a drama really be *that* engaging? Phillips insisted that it could. For two years she fought indefatigably to change P&G's collective mind. She even went so far as to produce a couple of pilot episodes of a half-hour show, paid for out of her own pocket. In the end the determined creative won the battle — as she most often did — without outright winning the war. That too would come down the road apiece.

While P&G officials wouldn't agree then to let her tamper with the format of *The Guiding Light*, they gave her the green light to create a new 30-minute serial. Then, at virtually the eleventh hour, P&G decided to launch a second 30-minute soap opera on the same day. CBS premiered both live half-hour weekday dramas on April 2, 1956: *As the World Turns* at 1:30 p.m., created by Irna Phillips; *The Edge of Night* at 4:30 p.m., created by Irving Vendig. Another dozen years would elapse before *The Guiding Light* reached the half-hour zenith that Phillips had fought for so hard — on September 9, 1968. Nine years after that, on November 7, 1977, its airtime increased to an hour. That was yet another Phillips innovation, but one that arrived too late for her — she died nearly four years earlier.

The Guiding Light began airing in color on March 13, 1967. By then the serial had moved to videotape and was no longer aired live.

Charita Bauer, one of the most universally loved actresses in serialdom, made the transition effortlessly from radio to television daytime drama. One pundit dubbed her "a national treasure, a 'guiding light' for generations of Americans." Bauer gained a huge following as matriarch Bertha (Bert) Miller Bauer from 1950 to 1956 on CBS Radio, and from 1952 to 1984 on CBS-TV. In 1983 she received a Lifetime Achievement Award for her passionate efforts in befriending a dying man in the storyline. Four years earlier the National Mother's Day Committee honored her with its Outstanding Mother Award for heading two families, her own and the make-believe one, both of which included a son named Michael. (Michael Crawford, born in 1946, was her real-life son.)

In the late 1970s Bauer offered some provocative insights on how soap opera had changed over the years.

> When we first went on TV we thought that it was going to be wonderful, that we would have the freedom of not being tied to the microphone all the time and be able to invest the action with new life. But that hope was quickly scotched. The potential of these shows has never been touched — and I mean all of them, not just ours. I don't mean to be putting the soaps down. I think some wonderful things have come out. But think of the opportunity of a drama that goes on and on. What could have become a minor art form was nipped in the bud in the beginning. It's an essentially commercial medium. I don't mean that because it's commercial it couldn't be creative. I don't believe those two things are mutually exclusive. But it all got formularized early on. It became a set piece and the forest was lost sight of for the trees....
>
> My two grown sons, Ed and Michael.... They have a good relationship as brothers except for the time that one ended up marrying the other's ex-wife. They wouldn't have had a storyline like that in the old days; a story like that breaks down family ties. Now they don't really care about the idea of the family anymore. That used to be the main theme of the show, but now it's gone.[10]

As a young girl Charita Bauer, a Newark native, was a photographer's model. In 1932, at age nine, she made her professional acting debut on Broadway in Christopher Morley's *Thunder on the Left*. While attending the Professional Children's School, she continued appearing in Broadway productions, notably for two years as Little Mary in Claire Booth Luce's feminine comedy *The Women*. She also won roles in *Good Morning Corporal, Life of Reilly, Madame Capet* and *Your Loving Son*. During the 1930s she entered radio in the *Let's Pretend* ensemble.

Bauer ultimately became a soap opera ingénue, acquiring recurring parts in radio's *David Harum, Front Page Farrell, Lora Lawton, Orphans of Divorce, Our Gal Sunday, The Right to Happiness, Rose of My Dreams, Second Husband, Stella Dallas* and *Young Widder Brown*. She earned more radio credits for her guest shots or ongoing roles on *The FBI in Peace and War, Johnny Presents, Maudie's Diary* and *Mr. Keen, Tracer of Lost Persons*. From 1941 to 1953 she was a cast regular in *The Aldrich Family* radio sitcom, and from 1949 to 1950 in a tele-version of the same feature. On May 24, 1983, she appeared in a made-for-TV movie, *The Cradle Will Fall*, alongside many other members of *The Guiding Light* troupe. The screenplay was based on the epic serial's storyline.

Later in 1983 Bauer began experiencing major health troubles. Part of a leg was amputated that autumn due to an untreatable circulatory problem. Following her recuperation, she returned to *The Guiding Light* in an emotional sequence in spring 1984 that centered on Bert's acceptance of an artificial limb. Gail Kobe, the show's producer at the time, recalled what happened in Mary Ann Copeland's *Soap Opera History*:

It was a difficult decision all the way around. We told her she could work. We would certainly provide her with work and make every effort to make it comfortable for her on the set. I suggested the prosthesis story to her because I knew she had something to contribute and I wanted her to know she was needed on the show.... [A] scene in which Bert dropped a cup and couldn't bend over to pick up the pieces really got to me. It was clear Bert did not burst into tears out of self-pity but sheer frustration. It was a story of courage.

Bauer, still in poor health, performed for the final time on *The Guiding Light* on December 10, 1984. She died on February 28, 1985. A year later the show celebrated the lives of Bert Bauer and Charita Bauer when Bert died off-camera. A service and a photographic mosaic depicted her valued gifts across a 35-year span. Jerry verDorn, then playing the character of Ross Marler, was tapped to verbalize the collective expressions of the cast: "The continuing story *Guiding Light* is dedicated to the memory of Charita Bauer, whose portrayal of Bert Bauer has illuminated our lives for over 35 years. The spirit of Charita Bauer, her strength and her courage, her grand good humor, her passion for life, and her humanity have touched us all. She has graced our lives at *Guiding Light* and will be with us always."

Not long before her demise, Charita Bauer recalled the show's early days for Annie Gilbert's *All My Afternoons*: "Back then we smoked on television. Even though my character was a wife and mother and basically a good character, she was allowed to smoke. Now no one smokes. Since the Surgeon General's report on the dangers of smoking, the Procter & Gamble shows don't allow people to smoke." She, too, had given up her old habit some years before her death.

Not surprisingly, Charita Bauer wasn't the only actor to die during the long run of *The Guiding Light*. Another of the drama's most beloved characters, Papa Bauer, passed away when the longtime thespian playing him, Theo Goetz, died in late 1972. No serious thought was given to replacing him in the lineup; he was simply considered irreplaceable.

A native of France who had migrated to Austria, Goetz fled his homeland as war clouds loomed over the horizon. He was a successful stage actor there, yet left all his earthly possessions behind to journey to America. Unable to speak English, he was sans friends, family or a place to go, with only a couple of bucks in his pocket. The refugee eventually situated himself in a one-room walk-up on New York's Upper West Side, existing on coffee and doughnuts for lunch, and a sandwich for supper. Goetz adopted the nearby movie theater as his English instructor. After making some headway with the new dialect, he began calling on New York casting offices. "I think that at that moment God must have seen my condition and decided that he was going to start his special plan," the thespian declared later. Goetz scored big when he was tapped for the role of a physician on the long-running CBS Radio serial *Young Doctor Malone*.

In 1949 he appeared for a tryout before Irna Phillips for a new part she had in mind of a German immigrant father on CBS Radio's *The Guiding Light*. In Robert LaGuardia's *The Wonderful World of TV Soap Operas*, he remembered: "After I did the audition for Papa Bauer, I saw Irna Phillips applauding me when I looked toward the booth behind a glass partition. 'You will hear from us,' she said. But I didn't hear another word for two months. Then I got a call from some secretary who said, 'You have to make a record for our client, Procter & Gamble.... What? You mean no one called to tell you that you got the part as Papa Bauer?' I didn't know then that I had gotten a lifetime job," he thoughtfully mused.

Goetz and Papa shared more than a stage persona. Goetz was often heard to remark, "God wanted me to play Papa Bauer," and most people believe he basically played himself, affirming the value of the same tenaciousness that had helped him survive in America. He preached love, tolerance, and kindness, and when Papa celebrated his sixty-fifth birthday in the story, over 39,000 letters of congratulations arrived for him at the studio. Goetz, a modest and unassuming man, was quite moved when he saw the piles of mail.[11]

Bruce Cox, then in charge of daytime programming at Compton Advertising (theoretically marking him as Theophile Goetz's superior), recalled how the aging actor routinely called every three weeks at the agency's address at Madison and Fifty-Ninth Streets merely to say "hello." He made the long journey to Compton from the CBS studios at 221 West Twenty-Sixth Street. "He was an Old World gentleman and he was showing us European politeness," Cox reflected. "He'd stick his head in every door with a greeting, and then proceed to tell me all these beautiful stories about the old days on radio. Oh, I loved them! And how he shattered my illusions! When I was a boy I listened to the radio soaps and thought the actors worked so hard, and here he was telling me that they just came in and read their scripts and left. I could have listened to him talk for days at a time."

Upon Goetz' death at age 78, Cox read the eulogy for his friend, held on January 2, 1973:

Theophile Antonius Menu was born in Marseilles, France, on December 14, 1894 — seventy-eight years ago. Seventy-eight years of living — and over half a century working as an artist. That's quite an accomplishment. His mother wanted him to be a banker. The theater was an uncertain way of life. Fortunately for us, he didn't follow her advice, and for more than fifty years Theo Goetz worked successfully, honorably, and happily at his chosen craft.

He was a major figure with the Vienna State Theater, touring all of Europe — playing leading roles in the great classical and contemporary drama. In 1938, this first career — and half a lifetime — came to a halt when, as president of the Austrian Actors' Union, he was forced by Nazism to escape from his homeland with so many thousands of others to the United States of America. Theo made this country his own, and in his own way loved it fiercely and possessively. In mid-life he learned and mastered a new language; he married an American painter, built a fine new reputation, and enchanted audiences for another thirty years: Broadway, the famous radio programs of the forties — and then, in 1949, he made Papa Bauer and *The Guiding Light* his very artistic own.

Just two weeks ago, on his seventy-eighth birthday, Procter & Gamble sent him a telegram which moved him to tears. I would like to read their message, because it expresses so well what we all feel about Theo:

"A very happy birthday, Theo, on this your seventy-eighth. Few actors ever achieve what you achieve with your characterization of Papa — or play their roles with greater dedication. Thank you — for your artistry, your talent, and the endearing humanity you have brought to *The Guiding Light* for so many years."

When Papa Bauer's passing was later observed onscreen, actor Mart Hulswit, then playing Dr. Ed Bauer, Papa's grandson, delivered the eulogy: "When he was young, he loved his native land. But soon some terrible things began to happen there. And so he found his way to this country. And a passionate love for this, his adopted country, began to grow in him. He made it *his* country, its history — *his* history. He would never let us call him a wise man. He would only say that — if you live a long time — you live through so much that you begin to have an understanding of human events."

For two years, 1956–58, *The Guiding Light* held first place in the ratings among all daytime soap operas on television. The drama captured a handful of Emmies for its contributions to the daytime television landscape. It was voted the Outstanding Daytime Drama Series in the 1981–82 season, and was a joint recipient for that award (with *As the World Turns*) in 1988–89.

   The Guiding Light also drew some pretty famous fans over its years on television, including Barry Bonds, Bette Davis and Roy Rogers.

   Quite a few celebrated thespians appeared in the cast of *The Guiding Light*, including Kevin Bacon, Zina Bethune, Phillip Bosco, Ruby Dee, Sandy Dennis, Barnard Hughes, James Earl Jones, Meg Mundy, Carrie Nye, Chris Sarandon, Don Scardino, John Wesley Shipp, Cicely Tyson, Christopher Walken, Michael Wilding Jr., Billy Dee Williams and JoBeth Williams.

   Some of the talent in *The Guiding Light* cast plied their acting skills on other contemporary daytime dramas. They included:

Anne Burr —*City Hospital* (1951–52), *The Greatest Gift* (1954–55), *As the World Turns* (1956–59).

Joseph Campanella —*Days of Our Lives* (1987–88, 1990–92).

Les Damon —*Search for Tomorrow* (1953), *The Seeking Heart* (1954), *As the World Turns* (1956–57), *Kitty Foyle* (1958).

Virginia Dwyer — *The Road of Life* (1954–55), *The Secret Storm* (1955–56), *Young Doctor Malone* (1958–59), *As the World Turns* (1962), *Another World* (1964–75).

Teri Keane —*The Edge of Night* (1964–75), *One Life to Live* (1976–77), *Loving* (1983–84).

Christopher Marcantel —*Another World* (1981–82), *Loving* (1983–85, 1995).

Ethel Remey —*As the World Turns* (1963–77).

Melville Ruick —*City Hospital* (1951–52).

Gillian Spencer —*The Edge of Night* (1962–63), *One Life to Live* (1968–70), *As the World Turns* (1972–75), *All My Children* (1980–87, 1989, 1990, 1995).

Helen Wagner —*The World of Mr. Sweeney* (1954–55), *As the World Turns* (1956–present).

Ruth Warrick —*As the World Turns* (1956–60, 1963), *True Story* (1960), *All My Children* (1970–present).

Victoria Wyndham —*Another World* (1972, 1995).

11

The Secret Storm

The working handle for this serial — and, indeed, the projected title for the series — was *The Storm Within*. But the public was never aware of it, at least not then. When the drama reached the airwaves on February 1, 1954, American Home Products (AHP) had already signed to underwrite it on behalf of several of its healthcare goods. One of those drugs was Bi-So-Dol analgesic stomach distress reliever. AHP plainly wasn't about to allow the show's moniker to provoke so much as the semblance of a titter among the viewers by obliquely hinting at a link between its respected commodity and the sobriquet of the narrative it sponsored. No imagery of upset stomachs, thank you! Consequently, the permanent appellation was switched to *The Secret Storm* before the show hit the ether. It was intended to be a poetic metaphor reflecting the emotional turmoil that each of the main characters was to suffer.

The yarn was another of CBS's most treasured daytime dramas in a parade of seemingly unstoppable fan favorites during the 1950s. One reviewer termed this one "the complete soap opera," certifying it as "the first television soap to be produced with the same production values provided for prime-time shows."[1] It began with the ebullient fervor that accompanied most contemporary soap operas on its network, and persisted for the next two decades as one of the most gripping dramas of the air.

Its 1974 departure prompted a storm of protest (no pun intended) from its addicted fans, the likes of which hadn't been seen in daytime TV history in a very long while, and possibly never.[2] "A storm of indignation erupted, perhaps the largest outpouring of protest caused by a soap opera's cancellation," one historian corroborated. "Angry letters and petitions flooded CBS, switchboards lit up, and letters began appearing in local newspapers all over the country."[3]

Even the critics lamented its passing. "The network did a terrible disservice to long-time, faithful viewers when it canceled *The Secret Storm*," wrote Robert LaGuardia. "Although the show was no longer faithful to its original theme or its original story of the Ames family, the network still had a duty to viewers to reinstate those story qualities that had enabled this popular soap to last for more than twenty years, instead of just giving up. The cancellation of *The Secret Storm* was the *most tragic blow ever to hit daytime television* [italics mine]. The network's later bungling of this fine serial became a tragedy for millions of daytime soap lovers."[4]

From its very inception the narrative was declared an instant success — "exactly what daytime TV audiences were waiting for: complex drama, passion, good characterizations, the story of a big family. Unlike many serials that had soapy-sounding working titles, *The Secret Storm* lived up to the promise of its title. Under Roy Winsor's expert packaging, the serial really did offer viewers a unique 'secret storm' of desperate inner conflicts and hidden desires— all outwardly manifest in the continuing melodrama of the family of Peter Ames.

"And this was melodrama! On Winsor's program there were more shocking deaths, sudden bouts with insanity, illnesses, and embattled love affairs than on any other daytime drama."[5]

Incidentally, this was the very same Roy Winsor who had flung two other brilliant dramas onto daytime television's horizon less than a year-and-a-half before: *Search for Tomorrow* and *Love of Life*. He was to quickly discover that he had created yet another winning entry with his latest attempt. (A comprehensive prologue to Winsor is included in Chapter Eight.) Roy Winsor "exhibited genius," LaGuardia enthused. "Six years after the show started, few daytime devotees dared spend a weekday without peeking in to find out what new tragedies and entanglements were befalling the long-suffering and fascinating Ames family."[6]

> Perhaps no daytime drama demonstrated Roy Winsor's belief that good soap opera was simply a matter of delineating a solid theme and adhering to it than his third creation, *The Secret Storm*.[7] Retaining the simple thematic format of his first two television serials (*Search for Tomorrow* and *Love of Life*), but adding the familial structure that had proved so successful on *Guiding Light*, Winsor devised the story of a family, the Ameses, who were so devastated by tragedy that each of its members retreated into his or her own secret world of despair. Even the father, who possessed the stoic dignity of characters like Jo (*Search for Tomorrow*) and Van (*Love of Life*), succumbed to his overwhelming grief. Raw and immediate in a way never seen on daytime television before, the show became an instant success. Its psychological theme of inner conflict and hidden desire was as resonant with audiences as the domestic, romantic, and moral themes of Winsor's earlier soaps. Only when the show abandoned that original concept, and the Ames family with it, did *Secret Storm* lose its audience. For fifteen years, however, under the guidance of Winsor and director Gloria Monty, a theater veteran new to television and the serial format, it was one of the most compelling and progressive shows on daytime television.[8]

To launch his newest longsuffering epic, Roy Winsor threw out the conventional thesis that often called for abrupt widowhood at a drama's start, a happenstance that distinguished several other highly successful daytime serials in two broadcast mediums. An unexpected squeal of tires at the debut of this tale launched an awful string of circumstances that would unfold over the next 15 years. Instead of misfortune befalling the patriarch early in the show's run, as happened elsewhere, his opposite number felt the brunt of a vehicle mishap. Lying in critical condition, Ellen Ames was rushed to the hospital in their little burg of Woodbridge, New York. There, two days later, with her supportive clan gathered about her, the family matriarch passed from this life.

Ellen Ames' immediate family included her spouse, Peter (Peter Hobbs), 18-year-old daughter Susan (Jean Mowry, Rachel Taylor, Norma Moore, Mary Foskett), 16-year-old son Jerry (Dick Trask, Robert Morse, Warren Berlinger, Ken Gerard, Wayne Tippit) and nine-year-old daughter Amy (Jada Rowland, Beverly Lunsford). Each was left to process the tragedy in his or her own way.

Introducing the program with a swift and shattering climax was certainly novel, and daytime spectators were taken by surprise. It also proved useful. "The opening episodes were shocking to many viewers not yet used to the immediacy of television, and the gambit proved an effective hook, capturing a large early audience and building a loyal following from that base," one author explained. The yarn's dark tone that was set in motion on the first day, coupled with the realism and sensationalism of the sequence, was riveting. It offered a premonition of what viewers of this show might anticipate in the days and years ahead.

It further proffered a drama in which there was no obvious heroine, an astonishing departure from most other triumphant daytime serials. "Winsor had taken quite a chance killing off Ellen Ames," one scholar observed. "*Search for Tomorrow* had become the immediate success it did because the housewives who accounted for the vast majority of the soap audience at that time could identify with her. The same could be said of *Guiding Light*'s Bert Bauer. Breaking far afield from that tradition, *The Secret Storm* was asking women to tune in to a show without a central mother figure."[9] It left the industry critics pondering: Just how well will this play in Peoria?

While mercantile emporium manager Peter Ames worked tenaciously to hold his besieged brood together and set an example for coping with their pain, it became more than a man who was usually perceived as a rock of Gibraltar could handle. So devastating was the blow that he slipped into bouts of depression, which resulted in a reliance on the bottle to assuage his grief. For his livelihood, Peter operated Tyrell's Department Store for his father-in-law, Judge J. T. Tyrell (Russell Hicks), and his wife, Grace (Marjorie Gateson).

Meanwhile, Susan, the eldest child, attempted to fill the void in her home by assuming many of her late mother's responsibilities. While her pursuits were often credible and well intended, she sometimes performed her tasks in a manner that proved overbearing and therefore distasteful to the others. In time, when it appeared that her father might have a chance for future happiness with a new mate, Susan intervened, determined that he would remain a widower forever.

Then there was Jerry. He deliberately went after the driver who was responsible for his mom's death and attempted to kill him. Jerry didn't accomplish his mission, but for a while he did land in a reformatory institution as a consequence of his actions.

And finally there was little Amy. She was nearly lost in the shuffle. While the others grieved openly in their way, she internalized. She needed her mother perhaps more than her siblings, and she felt very lonely and abandoned.

The Ames tribe expanded when, shortly after Ellen's death, Pauline Tyrell (Haila Stoddard), the late woman's seditious sister, started to intrude into their lives. A quarter-of-a-century earlier she had dated her future brother-in-law, prior to the time Peter Ames began seriously seeing Ellen. Ellen and Peter had eloped, and Pauline had never quite forgiven them. Actually, it was obvious to everyone that Pauline still harbored amorous feelings for the man that got away. Perhaps she could correct the "oversight" on his part by becoming the new Mrs. Ames. For a period of time, Peter was unable to properly process Pauline's designs on him, as he was going through the early stages of a mental breakdown.

Aunt Pauline precipitated a rather intricate romantic triangle that, according to one source, "bordered on the incestuous." Peter fell head over heels for — would you believe? — the family housekeeper, Jane Edwards (Marylyn Monk, Barbara Joyce, Virginia Dwyer). But a conniving Pauline, apparently determined that if she couldn't have him, nobody would, set about obliterating their pangs of passion. (Susan Ames was secretly cheering her aunt from the sidelines, by the way.) Pauline's machinations resulted in the discovery that

Pauline Tyrell (Haila Stoddard) harbored more than just familial concern for a distraught Peter Ames (Peter Hobbs) after the accidental death of her sister, Ames' wife, in *The Secret Storm.* It was her intent to marry the man who got away, and she used her wily charms to try to make him fall for her while he was especially vulnerable. As the shock of his loss set in, Peter turned to alcohol to soothe his troubled soul. While they wouldn't wed, Pauline remained a major complication in his life.

Jane's husband, long presumed dead, was actually marooned on an island and had been there for years. (By then the return-from-the-dead gambit had become a well-worn cliché, one that wouldn't disappear any time soon.) Meanwhile, in 1955 Pauline summoned Bruce Edwards (Biff McGuire, Ed Bryce) to Woodbridge, putting whatever quixotic plans Peter and Jane had had on ice.

Within a short time Pauline had cozied up to several nefarious types, the kind that do their talking with their guns. (Pauline is comparable to Meg Harper in *Love of Life*.) By 1956 the underworld figures crossed paths with Bruce Edwards, and he died in a blaze of glory during a gangland slaying. A short while afterward, ex-domestic Jane Edwards checked out of Woodbridge, never to return.

On another front, Peter Ames—the hero—wasn't fiddling while Rome burned. In 1958 the lovesick man turned his affections toward a new intended, Amy's schoolteacher, the striking Myra Lake (Joan Hotchkis, June Graham), who reciprocated his feelings. Susan and Pauline again pulled out all the stops to prevent any potential union. It was too little too late that time, however—the duo married in mid–1959, despite the obstacles placed in their path. But in winning this battle, Peter and Myra lost the war. Members of both families mounted strong opposition to their relationship, even after the fact, apparently removing any chances those two might have had for long-term fulfillment. Consequently, they divorced. It was not a pretty picture, nor a cause for genuine rejoicing from anybody.

A few years later Peter found happiness with his third wife, the voluptuous Valerie Hill, who married him in the mid–1960s. But their joy was short-lived too. In 1968, while on a business trip, he suffered a fatal heart attack. His death, in fact, triggered numerous revisions in the storyline's direction and sealed the show's fate.

Meanwhile, seemingly following in her aunt's footsteps, Susan Ames ran after golf pro Alan Dunbar (James Vickery), who possessed some shady connections of his own. When the pair fell in love, Alan cleaned up his act, dropped his mob friends, and turned into a respectable citizen, wedding Susan. He pursued investment banking as a source of livelihood for a while, and ditched Susan for a fling with an heiress. After Susan gave birth to Alan's son, whom she named Peter, she fought off the advances of newspaper reporter Joe Sullivan, yet had an illicit affair with Jeff Nichols before she and Alan reunited. It was emblematic soap opera saga.

Alan left investing to join *The Woodbridge Herald* as a reporter, presumably taking a hefty reduction in salary. (It was a real stretch to think that a golf pro with underworld thugs as pals, who reformed and traded those lucrative outlets for a career in finances, might suddenly become an effective investigative journalist, having had no training or experience in the field. But then, this wasn't for real, and nobody watching had time to cogitate over stuff like that anyway.) Alan acquired another diversion in the form of newspaper staffer Ann Wicker, who melted into his waiting arms. (Parenthetically, the actors playing Alan and Ann — James Vickery and Diana Muldaur — were also clinching one another offstage. In the mid–1960s the duo departed the cast, married and took off for the West Coast.)

Afterward, Alan was believed to be a prisoner of war in Vietnam; Susan remarried; Alan returned (naturally); the mafia finished him off; Susan was accused — then cleared — of his murder (naturally); and she and new spouse Frank Carver were banished to Never-Neverland by the writers.

Not a lot was heard from Jerry, Susan's younger brother, for the rest of the 1950s after he completed his stint in reform school. He gained a couple of wives in the next decade, however. The first was soon murdered, and it appeared he'd take the rap for it. (It was like a family duty.) But, of course, he was exonerated. He married again and also left Woodbridge, effectively exiled from the show except for one brief return visit.

And what became of Amy? Possibly more than any other child in daytime drama, she "grew up" before the viewers' eyes, just like in real time.[10] Jada Rowland, who portrayed her longer than anybody else, was 10 as the show began. In the 1960s, more than any other Ames, she became an enduring and key character. Exhaustion and an ambition to become a writer prompted Rowland to leave the show in 1971. She returned to her role a couple of years later. Not only did Amy experience several love affairs, a trio of marriages and have a child out of wedlock, she also outlasted every one of the original principals. By the end of the 1960s, in fact, she was the only Ames still in the storyline. She persisted until the show left the air 20 years after it began.

If anybody is keeping score, the family patriarch (Peter) and the youngest child (Amy) married three times each, while the other children (Susan and Jerry) both wed twice. One companion for a lifetime just didn't cut it with the Ameses. As a matter of practical reality, however, all of them had one or more lovers on the side, sometimes between nuptials and sometimes otherwise. Of their collective 10 mates, three died violently (one the victim of a car cash, the others murdered and their surviving spouses suspected in each case), and three more unions ended in divorce. None of it came to very neat ends as the show drew to a close (and it surely was not the family-oriented drama that it had been at its start): Peter had died, leaving a widow; Susan and Jerry were presumably still with their current spouses but residing far from their Woodbridge roots; and Amy was still with a paraplegic husband, who stood up from his wheelchair on the final show and literally fell into her arms. The family "togetherness" just wasn't the same.

There were numerous actor turnovers in this narrative, just like in some other serials. Over the drama's long run it took four actors to play the leading role of Peter Ames, who was written out a half-dozen years before the series ended. Seven thespians portrayed Susan; seven played Jerry; with three as Amy. The part of Paul Britton, one of Amy's husbands, was cast six times within a six-year span, while numerous other parts featured at least three different actors or actresses. To state the obvious, it was a very transient mix.

If *The Secret Storm* seemed appealing to CBS audiences who had been watching the network earlier in the day, it certainly should have been. Not only was it created and produced by the same man (Roy Winsor) who invented and supervised *Love of Life*, it had the "feel" and "look" of that midday quarter-hour drama.

In addition to the familiar-sounding organ and the high profile cards with the cast principals' names printed on them, it was also backed by the same sponsor, American Home Products, and its long line of healthcare and household goods. And who better to deliver those commercials in person than the same guy pitching them earlier in the day, Don Hancock? And the announcer?—*Love of Life*'s Charles Mountain! And, at their inception, *Love of Life* and *The Secret Storm* both originated in Studio 54 at Liederkranz Hall! One would rehearse and block camera angles in the morning while the other did so in the afternoon. Yes, it *did* seem like there was something rather familiar going on there.

In late October 1968 a fascinating anecdote connected with the longsuffering drama generated plenty of talk and is worth telling. Christina Crawford, 24-year-old daughter of legendary movie actress Joan Crawford, who was 64 at the time, was appearing in the role of Joan Borman Kane on *The Secret Storm*. To protect her from the possibility of losing her role to another actress while a tumor was removed from Christina's fallopian tubes, her infamous mom offered to step in during her absence. Never mind that 40-year difference in their ages. In spite of this, CBS jumped at the chance, certain that they could generate a lot of favorable publicity by having an Academy Award winner on the set for a brief tenure.[11] With the show facing heavy serialized competition on other networks at its same hour (ABC's *General Hospital* and NBC's *Another World*), the senior Ms. Crawford just might prompt boatloads of prospective new fans to steal a glance, CBS reasoned.

An on-camera announcer gleefully proclaimed the casting switch before each quarter-hour segment of the program. And to accommodate the feted luminary's calendar, the producers taped all of her scenes in one weekend and subsequently aired them over a four-day period. Imagine everybody's surprise (and absolute horror)—and particularly that of an on-looking Christina Crawford, then confined to a hospital recovery room — as the aging ingénue appeared before the cameras totally smashed! Christina recorded the embarrassing account of that episode in her autobiography, *Mommie Dearest* (Morrow, 1978).

Bob Thomas, Joan Crawford's biographer, confirmed it, labeling her vodka imbibing on the set "prodigious." Her booze arrived disguised in soft drink containers. The same incident was later ballyhooed in a Faye Dunaway film. One critic disclosed: "Those who remember her [Joan Crawford's] performance retain the image of a graying woman hanging on to an illusion — stiff, scared, vulnerable."[12] For her services, Joan Crawford was paid $585 by CBS, which she gave to her hairdresser. According to *Mommie Dearest*, Joan's presentation ultimately cost Christiana the role she was attempting to salvage anyway. "The audience ... could not readjust to her after having seen her mother play the part."[13] Her character departed the storyline not long afterward.

Meanwhile ... "For fifteen long years, viewers stayed tuned in large numbers as the Ames family struggled to move beyond their original tragedy — with little success," a historiography confirmed.[14] While Peter's marriage to Valerie brought the family some stability and relief from their stormy emotions that at times reached the depths of despair, "as the children grew older their problems only worsened." Amy, a young adult by then, "remained haunted by the loss of her mother." The insecurities they all felt were manifest in a myriad of ways. Longtime viewers could appreciate the fact that none of them fully recovered from Ellen Ames' death. It seemed obvious that they likely never would.

In 1968 a year-long conflict arose backstage over who would control the writers on the show. It involved the network and the show's packager (Roy Winsor Productions, which acquired the mantle left by the departing Milton H. Biow agency after Biow ceased operations in 1955). Said Winsor: "I had been working on a fixed budget from American Home Products to do *The Secret Storm* and *Love of Life*. I got their money, and they got their show, and for a long time both shows were very popular. I always worked on sound principles of theme and story, the same principles that dictate great novels, and they worked for my shows. Then, when the ratings competition got heavy, CBS kept pressuring me for fancier sets, better trimmings, and with the money spent there we had to lower our acting budget and the story suffered."[15]

Out of the discord emerged a serial that could hardly be recognized by audiences who earlier found it so beguiling. The plotting and the number of viewers started to slip badly, the latter clearly linked to the former. "Ratings began to sink faster than the *Titanic*," reported one source. The downward spiral was one from which the show never successfully rallied.

American Home Products (Aerowax, Anacin, Bi-So-Dol, Black Flag, Chef-Boy-Ar-Dee, Easy-Off, Heet, Kriptin, Sani-Flush, Wizard Wick, et al.), which owned *The Secret Storm* and *Love of Life* since their inceptions, sold both serials directly to CBS in 1969. Having little experience in actually producing a televised soap opera, CBS imported a raft of new personnel to run the two features, including producers, directors, actors and writers. Winsor contended that his "principles of good story and theme were thrown out the window." *The Secret Storm*'s focus suddenly turned away from the Ames entourage, a centerpiece that had persisted for 15 years and had made the serial a compelling drama for millions. "By 1970 the show was a mess, and CBS execs, unskilled as soap producers, didn't know what to do," a media critic noted.[16] Actress Jada Rowland, the longtime Amy Ames and the last of a dying breed, confirmed: "By this time new viewers didn't even know who the Ames family were."[17] Another author offered: "Successful serials, such as *As the World Turns*, simply do not get rid of major longstanding characters so cavalierly."[18]

> The greatest tragedy to befall the Ames family during the decade was the 1969 departure of Winsor and [director Gloria] Monty following CBS's acquisition of *The Secret Storm* from its sponsor American Home Products. New writers killed off Peter and wrote out Jerry, Susan, and Valerie, obliterating the show's continuity and theme. Provocative story lines about a priest

renouncing his vows for love and then being drawn back to the church, or Amy's artificial insemination by a doctor who was in love with her, did nothing to appease the audience's devotion to the Ames family. It was their story the audience wanted to see and their disappearance from the show that ultimately sealed its fate.[19]

Within a few months everything was overhauled and the serial became a crime drama similar to *The Edge of Night* that immediately followed it on CBS. *Edge* was only marginally behind *As the World Turns*, then in first place in the daytime ratings. The new emphasis improved *The Secret Storm*'s numbers, but only briefly. A fickle crowd of onlookers soon looked the other way. Nothing CBS tried, in fact, bolstered the figures for a sustained period.

In the final weeks of 1973, CBS announced that it was canceling *The Secret Storm*, then languishing in the cellar of the daytime ratings. A pundit blamed the network for the soap's unfortunate — yet highly predictable — end: "CBS ... had mismanaged the show for five years."[20]

What finally made CBS concede its failure? Said an inside CBS source, "It was a matter of pride. CBS didn't like being third in the ratings. So, rather than struggle to improve the quality ... it just canceled...."[21]

As sequences were tidied up at a quickened pace, audience indignation over the news encouraged American Home Products— which regained control of the show— to seek a new outlet for the serial that still maintained legions of loyal fans. When ABC and NBC balked at those overtures, however, the firm put together an arrangement to syndicate its durable video series. Although the pact was successfully negotiated with 140 TV outlets, it all fell apart before it could be set into cement. As a result, the show left the air permanently on February 8, 1974. It had run for 20 years and one week.

A daytime TV historian offered what could have been a eulogy:[22]

> It's a shame that epigraphs aren't still being used before the beginning of each episode [of TV soap operas] as a way of conveying the theme. If they were, some shows that have gone astray, losing both their original themes *and* their ratings, might not have been so willing to change horses midstream. With an epigraph, *The Secret Storm* ... might not be just another memory, but as popular today as it was in the early sixties, when it was still dealing with the anguish and strife of the Ames family.

Before or after becoming luminaries in disparate media, quite a few celebrated thespians joined the cast of *The Secret Storm*. Some of the soap's eminent alumni were Christina Crawford, Joan Crawford, Ken Kercheval, Diane Ladd, Audrey Landers, Diana Muldaur, Patricia Neal, Jane Rose, Gary Sandy and Roy Scheider.

What became of the principals of *The Secret Storm*?

Peter Hobbs, who played Peter Ames during the show's first eight years, was born in France about 1918 while his dad was a practicing physician during World War I. His father, incidentally, contracted influenza shortly after delivering Peter and died there. The infant and his mother returned to New York City where Peter grew up and attended Columbia University. In 1938 he joined a summer stock company and was soon touring in bit parts. He subsequently understudied for Marlon Brando in theatrical productions. Hobbs appeared in a bit part in the NBC daytime serial *Bright Promise* between the years 1969 and 1972. He showed up in the ABC sitcom *9 to 5* (1982), which ran for another year in syndication (1982–83). Between 1945 and 1988 Hobbs acquired 22 Hollywood movie roles, including features like *The Andromeda Strain* (1971), *The Star Spangled Girl* (1971) and *Any Which Way You Can* (1980). He was in 20 made-for-TV movies between 1970 and 1988, plus a trio of TV miniseries: *Ike* (1979), *Beulah Land* (1980) and *Nutcracker* (1987).

Jean Mowry, the first in a long line of actresses to appear as Susan Ames, was born January 14, 1928, at Madison, Wisconsin, where she graduated from the University of Wisconsin at an unbelievable 19! The following year she launched an acting career in Chicago theater, which projected her into *The Secret Storm* at 23. No further acting credits were documented for her in television or film.

Rachel Taylor, the successive Susan Ames, was born at South Bend, Indiana, in 1927. While she, too, maintained a blank vita sheet following her TV stint, she married celebrated actor Jason Robards Jr. in 1959. They divorced in 1961, and he wed actress Lauren Bacall that year.

Norma Moore, the next Susan Ames, was born February 20, 1937, at Chambersburg, Pennsylvania. She was cast in a small recurring role in the ABC-TV frontier series *Texas John Slaughter* (1958–61). Between 1957 and 1990 she acquired parts in a half-dozen Hollywood B-movies, and between 1984 and 1991 she appeared in another five made-for-TV movies.

Jada Rowland, the longtime Amy Ames, was the most active soap opera thespian among the original cast. She subsequently appeared in *As the World Turns* (1967–68), *The Doctors* (1976–82) and *The Hamptons* (1983). Born February 23, 1943, in New York City, she was only 10 when *The Secret Storm* premiered. With a painter-illustrator grandfather and artist-writer parents, Rowland began sketching and scribbling early. She drew outlines of other actors on the backs of her scripts, in fact. After three decades of Broadway and television acting, she quit to become a professional artist and scribe. She still draws, paints and writes today. She has been published in periodicals like *Soap Opera Digest* and *Soap Opera Weekly*. Her landscapes, figure and genre scenes have been in juried exhibitions hosted by the Allied Artists of America, American Watercolor Society, Houston Watercolor Society and other recognized fine art clusters.

12

As the World Turns

It was (and may still be) the epitome of daytime serials.

It set the pace for every other new drama when it became the first to air in a half-hour format, casting aside tradition by eschewing the quarter-hour design that had ruled for a quarter century. While another narrative, *The Edge of Night*, arrived three hours later on inaugural day, April 2, 1956, *As the World Turns* eclipsed it by those three hours.

It was the first bona fide family epic specifically shaped for a daytime video audience.

It may have won more awards than any other soap opera in the genre's history, particularly during its earliest decades.

It made CBS the daytime broadcasting titan of its day, extending the chain's unequivocal authority over two decades.

Its enormous popularity threatened the rights to happiness of more daytime serial heroines than any other program.

It was invariably the favorite saga of its creator, the granddame of daytime drama, Irna Phillips. Until she died, she considered it her baby.

It persists to this day. Only one other drama, *The Guiding Light*, can match its track record for endurance, and that might be because it started first. In spring 2006, *As the World Turns* reached the half-century mark. Beyond those two, nothing else comes even close in longevity.

For all its many achievements, *As the World Turns* continues as the most respected serial on daytime television. It is the gauge by which every one of its contemporaries is quantified. Its legions of followers are loyal to a fault, for decades having idolized the denizens that populate the fictitious city of Oakdale, Illinois.

At first, viewers did not respond to the new half-hour serial, but ratings picked up in its second year, eventually reaching the top spot in the daytime Nielsen ratings by the fall of 1958. In 1959, the show started a streak of weekly ratings wins that would not be interrupted for over twelve years. In the year-to-date ratings, *As the World Turns* was the most watched daytime drama from 1958 until 1978, with ten million viewers tuning in each day. At its height, the show was spoofed on *The Carol Burnett Show*, in a skit called *As the Stomach Turns*.[1]

Not only was it the most parodied of the lot, it has also been the most emulated. "A thoroughbred amid a field of barking mutts," one critic labeled it.

Welcome to the Summit of Serialdom!

As the World Turns is the result of a persistence that Irna Phillips maintained with officials at Procter & Gamble for a long, long while. Emboldened by the combined video triumphs of *The Brighter Day* and *The Guiding Light*, she shared her conviction that expanding the latter narrative — her most durable drama, originating on radio in 1937 — would lure new viewers and ultimately benefit everybody. Not only did she offer figures showing that a half-hour series could be produced less expensively than two quarter-hour features, she was absolutely positive that an audience eagerly awaited the visual upgrade and would be willing to commit to it. She fantasized aloud about how much more could be accomplished in a longer format with fewer words, while relying on nuances of facial expression and other physical cues to communicate meaning. She visualized idle conversations between two actors as they lingered over cups of coffee instead of cramming so much critical detail into about 10 minutes of actual playing time.

But Procter & Gamble stood its ground. In no way was it to be easily persuaded that homemakers with long lists of duties to perform could or would take a half-hour from their impending chores to sit down and watch a soap opera. While P&G liked the idea of saving money, the issue of that unproven audience's existence was a major sticking point.

For two years a passionate Irna Phillips lobbied the P&G team. For two years it responded with "No thanks." Ultimately, possibly realizing she typically got what she wanted and obviously wasn't going away, P&G gave in — to a point. While the firm wouldn't agree to let her tamper with the 15-minute format of the highly successful series she desired to expand, *The Guiding Light*, in the end she received permission to create a new drama especially for daytime audiences that would allow her to incorporate all of the ideas she was hoping to try. As one historian chronicled, "P&G remained unexcited about *As the World Turns* and only gave in to Phillips when they realized that this irascible woman was not going to abandon her pet project."[2]

It was like manna from heaven to Phillips — she virtually had a blank check for a half-hour to do with as she wished. She set about writing an outline, complete with backstory and plot projections. And she wrestled something else of great importance out of P&G: she got it to agree that — no matter how low the ratings on the new show dipped — it would not be canceled for at least a full year. That would allow it time, she insisted, to sufficiently build an audience that would form a base for its future.[3]

In the meantime, a number of people at Benton and Bowles, the advertising agency handling the account for P&G, became sanguine over the prospects of a half-hour serial. Somebody there proposed doing a second narrative, one to debut the same day as Irna Phillips' show, but with a mystery motif. Almost at the eleventh hour, P&G OK'd the brainchild. It hoped to successfully negotiate for the rights to air radio's "defender of human rights — champion of all those who seek justice," *Perry Mason*. When that didn't fly, it commissioned the veteran radio (*Perry Mason*) and television (*Search for Tomorrow*) wordsmith Irving Vendig — one of the most talented scribes in both mediums — to invent a new soap, one with a dark theme mixed with melodrama and seasoned with a pinch of humor. *The Edge of Night* was the result. It, too, was to win high marks on the ratings charts for years.

Irna's new show wasn't just an expanded 15-minute serial, however; it offered a novel approach to a 26-year-old blueprint, a totally visual slant to a heretofore aurally focused medium. A genre observer commented on the innovative half-hour model:

> It was an approach perfectly suited to television. There were long conversations, more close-ups, flawed "good" characters, and ambiguous dialogue that had viewers guessing what was happening under the surface, and why. The cameras caught the subtleties, ironies, and domestic wit. What are now considered soap opera clichés — people chatting over continuous cups of coffee,

pregnant pauses, long close-ups precipitating fade-out — were strikingly original. As more dramatic ambiguities were developed, audiences felt their loyalties divided and challenged. By the end of its first year, with [*As the World Turns'*] Phillips and Agnes Nixon writing and Ted Corday handling the directing and production chores, the live show was a certified hit.[4]

In creating her epic narrative, one source noted that Irna Phillips "threw out the rules of the radio serial" and "reconceived the genre for the visual medium." Few realized that, in so doing she had "revolutionized the dynamics of serial storytelling."[5] Time slowed to a near halt. Cameras peered at length into the faces of actors that she and Ted Corday had chosen with assiduous care. Corday picked the leading man (actor Don MacLaughlin), while Phillips selected the leading lady (actress Helen Wagner). Slowly, ever so slowly, increasing numbers of viewers were drawn to the program, awestruck by its pragmatic capabilities.

"Never before had a soap probed its characters ... so thoroughly," a serials chronicle recounted. "There weren't even flawless heroines.... The situations were real and as slowly observed as in life.... [It was] the most adult drama yet televised in the afternoon."[6]

From the soap's inception, the populace of Oakdale was comprised of longtime dwellers with lots of kin, plus outsiders who were drifting through, often as the result of a hurt or disappointment elsewhere. *As the World Turns* still can be readily distinguished as a clan-oriented saga. One wag pontificated: "In Oakdale, acceptance of life seems to require the renunciation of all fun other than family fun. Single people are a temporary misfortune."[7]

The drama's original focus was on two broods, the middle-class Hugheses and the aristocratic yet troubled Lowells. Their connections stemmed from matters of love and livelihood. In 1956 the serial was touted as "the day-to-day story of the affections that bind and conflicts that threaten two closely related families in an American community." All of Phillips' dramas boasted at least one nuclear unit at their core. This one had two. And nearly every subsequent soap opera emulated this same basic formula, although none exploited its potential as fully as has *As the World Turns*. Phillips maintained that her viewers preferred that, and she habitually tried to give them what they wanted.

"Every day," wrote Annie Gilbert in *All My Afternoons*, "viewers get a dose of old American values. Right below the surface of the stories are the messages of any minister's Sunday sermons." The appeal of those "messages" was strong, luring and maintaining significant numbers of onlookers.

Two years after the narrative's premier, Phillips compared the story to the very first serial she ever penned way back in the autumn of 1930 for a Chicago radio station: "*Painted Dreams* of the 1930s and *As the World Turns* of the 1950s are alike in many respects.... Life is more complex, but the emotions are the same ... the frustrations and the dreams are the same."[8]

Assessing the serial's early years, a reviewer characterized it similarly: "*As the World Turns* is primarily a calm and endearing portrayal of ordinary middle-class life, or what middle-class life once was in America. As the arch-typical Irna Phillips creation, drama and action are almost superfluous; it's people — their foibles, interests, habits, and worries — that make the world turn."[9]

Irna Phillips could hardly have put it any better.

As the World Turns, put simply, could be seen as "a reassuring visit with old friends."

Chris Hughes (Don MacLaughlin), the patriarch of *ATWT*'s foremost family, was in law partnership with Jim Lowell (Les Damon), whose father, Judge James Lowell (William Johnstone), a widower, founded the firm. Chris and his wife Nancy (Helen Wagner) were

On the fifteenth anniversary of *As the World Turns* in 1971, four celebrated members of the august serial's cast, still in their same roles, were pictured in this CBS-TV publicity photo, left to right: Santos Ortega (Grandpa Hughes), Don MacLaughlin (Chris Hughes), Helen Wagner (Nancy Hughes) and William Johnstone (Judge James T. Lowell). Johnstone remained with the show until 1979 and died in 1996; Ortega stayed until his death in 1976; MacLaughlin remained until his death in 1986; and Wagner is still with the series as of 2005.

parents of four: Donald (Hal Studer, Richard Holland), Penny (Rosemary Prinz), Bob (Bobby Alford, Ronnie Welch) and Susan (who died earlier when struck by lightning while swimming). Living with the Hugheses was Chris' dad, Grandpa Hughes (William Lee, Santos Ortega). Chris' free-spirited sibling, Edith (Ruth Warrick), who lived nearby, was also heavily involved during the serial's first quadrennial. Jim Lowell was in a loveless marriage to Claire Lowell (Anne Burr), and they had a daughter, Ellen (Wendy Drew). They lived under Judge Lowell's (his father's) roof.

"Nancy and Chris's marriage is the example of what is possible if two people love each other with the proper respect and forgiveness," said one observer. "The young folks, by contrast, are all too impatient, unwilling to put in the hard work it takes to make marriages succeed, and are destined to wreak havoc on themselves and their children."

The theme of the show is difficult to succinctly summarize for it is most concerned with the thrill that comes from relating to and understanding other people. As one serials historian delineated: "Nancy's joy in relating to others during ... family occasions is really what *As the World Turns* is all about — and why the closeup camera is so important in making the theme come alive."[10]

Another incisive appraisal of the drama described it thus:

> *As the World Turns* is concerned with the reactions of people to inevitable suffering. It is concerned with the penalties for caring deeply, and the penalties for letting go. It is also concerned with change, the sometimes painful sloughing off of one's past. About the only reward in sight is family support. The characters get by because someone (usually Nancy Hughes) believes in their future. Half the time she's wrong.[11]

One of Phillips' innovations was to include a sort of Greek chorus in her narratives. The key purpose of figures like Nancy Hughes was to react to the predicaments resulting from the actions and decisions of Oakdale's more vibrant characters. The custom added to the show's widespread acceptance and was quickly adopted by other soap opera pacesetters.

Creator-writer Irna Phillips possessed a free hand in most instances that allowed her to control virtually every aspect of the show's production. (You can read more of her intimidating and hard-boiled tactics in Chapter Six.) When something displeased her, somebody knew it quickly. As already mentioned, *As the World Turns* was her pride and joy, and she ran it like a mother lioness shepherding her cub.

On the third day on the air, for example, Phillips fired actor William Lee (in the part of Grandpa Hughes), replacing him with radio serial veteran Santos Ortega. That turned out to be a prudent move but might have been tough on Lee. Ortega was to be a critical part of the show's makeup for two decades, until he died in the spring of 1976.

Not long after that firing, Phillips pulled the rug from under actor Hal Studer, another radio drama carryover, claiming he was "too short" to portray the character of Donald Hughes. Richard Holland was substituted for Studer.

And at the end of the show's first 13 weeks on the air, Helen Wagner — heroine Nancy Hughes — was abruptly terminated over a contract dispute. Wagner went directly into a stage play. However, once Phillips thought her decision over more carefully, she realized she had acted in haste. She summoned Wagner, asking her to return. But Wagner couldn't do so at once due to her stage obligation. "Irna loved being at my mercy," Wagner recalled years later. "She wanted me back on the show all the more."

The premier show began with a classic "good morning" exchange between Chris and Nancy, typical of scads of similar playful interactions across the decades. "Characters on

As the World Turns did little more some days than sit around drinking coffee and talking about the everyday problems of life," a reviewer lamented. "There are more kitchen sets here than elsewhere [in televised soap opera]," observed another. "It is said that entire cakes and salads have been prepared in the course of a kitchen scene."

> For the first several months, the show went nowhere. No one had become pregnant (maybe); no one died; no one killed anyone; no one came down with an exotic disease; no one gave away (maybe) or kidnapped a new-born infant. Audiences tuned in, and tuned out. But by the second year, word got around that this was a series to watch![12]

At the drama's start, Chris and Nancy's eldest child, Don, 18, who would eventually follow in his dad's footsteps and become an attorney, was head over heels in love with Janice Turner (Joyce Van Patten). But Nancy took a personal interest in the romantic lives of all her offspring. In no way would she approve of Janice as a potential daughter-in-law, and certainly not at age 18!

With some persistence she influenced the girl to look elsewhere for husband material instead of confining her sights to her son. That occurred in 1957, and Nancy thought that that was the end of it. Five years later, however, a widowed Janice returned to Oakdale with a bratty daughter in tow. That time Janice and Don made good on their long-forfeited desires, despite Nancy's strong protests. After their wedding the couple and the little girl moved to Texas. Following Janice's unexpected death a few years later, Don got mixed up romantically with several women, but didn't remarry until the 1970s.

During the drama's first few months on the ether, Jim Lowell pursued an extramarital affair with Edith Hughes, Chris' sister. One critic pinpointed Edith as the drama's "pivotal character" during the early run. A conservative Procter & Gamble hesitantly proceeded with the storyline, moving cautiously. When Irna Phillips acknowledged that she planned to have Jim and Claire Lowell divorce, P&G reluctantly accepted it. But when those same officials learned that Edith and Jim were to marry, the firm put its collective foot down. To allow that, said the soapmaker with the deep pockets, would be to condone infidelity and reward the philanderers for breaking up a home. That just wouldn't do. Having maintained an oft-documented affair with a married man earlier in her own life, Phillips had hoped to include a happy ending to the scenario. But to her consternation, P&G answered with an unqualified "no" to any projected nuptials.

In 1957 the blithe couple was instead punished for their illicit behavior. While on a Florida pleasure spree, awaiting a divorce from Claire, Jim Lowell got what some viewers must have taken as episodic justice: he was killed in a boating accident. But other fans were peeved by that bit of realism and unequivicably told the network so. Phillips, who by then was becoming accustomed to issuing veiled "apologies" via public form letters mailed to her shows' critics, replied to this latter group in God-like metaphors: "As the world turns, we know the bleakness of winter, the promise of spring, the fullness of summer, and the harvest of autumn ... the cycle of life is complete.... What is true of the world, nature, is also true of man. He too has his cycle."

Let us digress for a moment to reiterate some of the personality quirks that Irna Phillips exhibited. To overlook them in connection with her ultimate creation would be to miss some powerful motivations that influenced her decisions. In his little book *The Wonderful World of TV Soap Operas* (Ballantine, 1974, and several successive editions), author Robert LaGuardia may have probed those hang-ups as thoroughly as any documented source.

"Behind the scenes of the show that exalted the vast joys of love and small-town peace," he elucidated, "Irna created what could only be described as a reign of terror. For instance, compared with her daily calls to New York [to the studio following *ATWT* telecasts in which she routinely reprimanded the cast], her personal calls to the homes of actors were as bomb-bursts to mere firecrackers." LaGuardia continued: "From Irna's point of view, the least deviation from her idea of Oakdale — whether it was something as minor as a change of wording that an actor made in her original dialogue — was an assault on the reality of Oakdale. While she managed in the 'unreal' world to cause others great pain, Irna would, in her 'real' world of Oakdale, insist on all the virtues of family love and peace."[13] It seems she was clearly operating in two widely distinct arenas.

Delineating many more examples of the great author's eccentricities, including a revelation of the scorching that P&G officials, show producers and actors took when they crossed her, LaGuardia explained: "Much as Irna cared about her viewers, she bade good-bye to her link with them when she was irate."[14] She performed radical surgery on the drama that she loved the most, taking it in extreme directions that were foreign to common sense while leaving everybody connected with the show wholly bewildered by her actions. It was a peculiar way to do business. For all of her extraordinary and unparalleled creativity, she demonstrated an innate ability to confound those around her by some of her stunts, making life extremely difficult for everybody on an ongoing (not just occasional) basis. LaGuardia's introspective is worthy of examination by anyone who is seriously attracted to the backstage environment that transpired across nearly two decades of America's foremost daytime soap opera.

For his part, actor Don MacLaughlin, who played Chris Hughes, let Irna know in no uncertain terms what he thought of her petrifying strategy. "Irna was talented and neurotic. The content of her scenes was brilliant, but her dialogue was terrible. Many actors, including myself, would change her lines.... In the first year of the show she told me flatly she didn't want me rewriting her lines, and I just told her: 'Irna, I'll say what you've written and I'll follow the content of your script. But if you want me to say your lines word for word, you'd better get yourself another actor.'" She hastily retreated, and he — unlike most others — lasted for three decades!

Meanwhile in the storyline, following the imbroglio that resulted in her estranged husband's death, Edith Hughes found temporary work as an office technician for Dr. Doug Cassen (Nat Polen). Soon enough Doug fell for and married Claire Lowell, the very dame that Edith's late lover had jilted to make whoopee with her! Talk about a fine state of (literal) affairs! Nonplussed by this turn of events, Edith found herself a doting physician, too; in 1959 she married Dr. George Frye (George Petrie). The couple left town in 1960, and — with only a brief return visit three years later — Edith Hughes Frye were never heard from again.

In the meantime, Penny Hughes — the eldest daughter, who was also Ellen Lowell's best friend — had long revered her Aunt Edith. Edith and Jim's affair was a particularly crushing blow to the impressionable young Penny, then an older teen. After her role model disillusioned her, in 1957 Penny eloped with defiant troublemaker Jeff Baker (Mark Rydell) and married him. One source alleged that it was "daytime's first major youth romance," even "creating soap opera's first stars, Rosemary Prinz and Mark Rydell." A second informant dubbed the pair "daytime's first supercouple." Years later still another serial scholar confirmed Prinz as "possibly the most popular of all daytime serial performers." It was pretty heady stuff.

Chris and Nancy forced Jeff and Penny to annul their union. Nancy had previously expressed a hope that Penny might pick Tom Pope — often referred to but never seen — as her life's mate. That simply didn't happen. Jeff and Penny continued in love and, having gained some perceived depth and maturity in the interim, remarried on Christmas Eve 1959, that time with parental consent. Not long afterward, a succession of misfortunes came Penny's way: she had a miscarriage and learned that she couldn't conceive again; while Jeff became an alcoholic and a murder suspect, and broke with his genetic family shortly before dying in a vehicular accident on a rain-slick road (a convenient method of disposing of serial heroes who needed it).

Actually actor Mark Rydell, who played Jeff, wouldn't sign a contract extension with *As the World Turns*, preferring to try his hand at film directing instead. Thus he was written out. The fans registered irate protests over his departure, no matter what the circumstances. The number of heated complaints was unprecedented, in fact. *TV Guide* termed it "the automobile accident that shook the nation." Not long ago, the periodical hyped the incident in a video presentation of a conjectural "100 Most Memorable Moments in TV History." On a positive note, Jeff's death left Penny with many storyline options for her future.

In passing, a soap opera historiographer offered some astute insights about how events occurred in the wider form and in Phillips serials in particular:

> As slow as events might seem to move in an Irna Phillips serial, strange accelerations could occur chronologically. Selected individuals could age in miraculous fashion. Jeff Baker, a teenager ... was a successful man in his thirties just six years later. Married a second time to Penny, Jeff became one of the more popular male characters of afternoon television.... Other boys of *As the World Turns* shot forward in age in startling manner to fill the romantic-male gap left by Baker's death. Through a biological miracle these youths were explaining the facts of life to their offsprings at a time they themselves should only have been emerging from puberty.[15]

All of that notwithstanding, would you believe that Penny's second spouse also died in an automobile accident? A smirking critic mused: "Didn't someone warn these men about turning up a bad penny?" Divorce concluded marriage number three. Presumably, she was to find lasting happiness with suitor number four, a European racing car driver, after she moved from Oakdale to England. (Just what was it about this woman and husbands and automobiles anyway?) From then on, Penny returned to the storyline only sporadically, her last visit occurring in 1993. Contemporary viewers joining the show in the modern epoch would hardly recognize her illustrious legacy, or indeed most of her family if they were reintroduced today without some detailed explanation about who they were. But, by golly, nothing lasts forever.

Bob Hughes' first serious romantic fling didn't begin until 1960, a time period beyond the parameters of this text. Yet it would be unthinkable not to acknowledge the girl who got him into her bed. Irna Phillips intended that the farm lass from Rockford, Illinois, Lisa Miller (Eileen Fulton), would be in the plotline for a mere summer romance, nothing more. But viewers liked her character (not to mention her wildly passionate actions), so much so that Irna decided to keep her and enlarge her role.

Lisa became pregnant, eloped with Bob, and wound up living with him under the Hughes' roof. Their frolicking produced a boy some time later. Some of the captivating details of Lisa's life and the outrageous actress who played her (who, incidentally, began her own life as a Methodist minister's daughter) are recorded in Fulton's revealing chronicle *As My World Still Turns: The Uncensored Memoirs of America's Soap Opera Queen* (Birch Lane, 1995). The viewers would eventually herald Lisa Miller Hughes Eldridge Shea Colman

McColl Mitchell as "television's most famous and longest-running villainess." (In real life she had only *half* that many husbands!)

Parenthetically, in the mid–1960s Lisa divorced Bob, left their son with the Hugheses and took off for Chicago in search of new amorous (and amoral) conquests. It was all part of a master plan by the mistress of melodrama, Irna Phillips. Lisa resurfaced in a CBS primetime soap opera titled *Our Private World* that was also penned by Phillips, the first daytime serial to be spun off into a nighttime extension. There were occasional references to figures and events in *As the World Turns*, just as on the afternoon source series the philandering Lisa was spoken of in inquiring but usually hushed tones.

While *Our Private World*'s leading character was inordinately popular with the ladies— "the vamp they loved to hate"[16]— the rest of the potential viewers in this family-oriented time slot didn't connect with the new series. Its short life persisted from May 5 to September 10, 1965. With Lisa's show now cancelled, she resurfaced a short time later in Oakdale, practically as if nothing had ever happened.

Despite all of the conservative talk about this show (e.g., "family values" in modern dictum), *As the World Turns* can take credit for breaking down conventional stereotypes. In another major sequence during its first few years, *ATWT* according to one source, became the first serial in which a major figure bore an illegitimate child. It occurred in 1958 when Ellen Lowell, Jim and Claire's daughter, conceived a child by Dr. Tim Cole (William Redfield), then gave him up for adoption. Years later she would reclaim the child, but that's another story. Tim and his wife Louise (Mary K. Wells) split up over his betrayal, and, subsequently discovering that he had a terminal illness, Ellen married him. When he died not long afterward, she left town for a while. But she was to return and remain active in the storyline, appearing as recently as 1995, nearly four decades after she was introduced.

After 14 years Irna Phillips resigned as head writer of *As the World Turns* in 1970, terminating her contract with Procter & Gamble for "health reasons." Not long after that she was hired as a story consultant for *A World Apart*, an ABC soap created by Irna's adopted daughter, Katherine L. Phillips. Following in her mother's footsteps, Katherine had gained some credentials by toiling as a head writer on *As the World Turns*. In reality, *A World Apart* was simply the story of Irna's own life; its heroine was a serial writer and adoptive parent. The serial aired for 15 months before the network withdrew it.

In 1972, when *As the World Turns* suffered an unaccustomed and significant decline it its ratings, dipping into single digits for the first time in 14 seasons, P&G prevailed on its legendary dramatist to return to "her show" as its head writer. In retrospect, it might have been the only time a decision by both parties, P&G and Irna Phillips, proved to be an utter miscalculation. The effect of their mistake was decidedly ruinous.

"Irna had always been difficult and often destructive, but rarely in a way that would actually have hurt her most famous creation. But the Irna who was now once again head writer of *As the World Turns* seemed to be operating as if demonically possessed," insisted one student of Phillipsiana.[17]

She was absolutely horrified at what she discovered when she picked up the reins again. Two brothers were actively pursuing the same woman for a seamy rendezvous. Still more revolting to Phillips was the fact that one of those men was the father of two daughters, one by his wife and a second by the woman he was chasing. The dramatist was appalled. In her opinion the show had proceeded a long way in a flawed direction following Jim Lowell's then-ancient dalliance with Edith Hughes. One could ponder: if she was so shocked by it, who was it that pointed her narrative down that road in the first place?

There was little time to waste, however. Phillips set about instituting sweeping story-line changes. The three points of this romantic triangle, along with their sullied reputations, would pay for their moral turpitude. Thus, she did what she always did when she was angry — she began killing off popular characters. The woman and one of the men were removed almost instantly. The other man, father of two, was banished to England for his sins. Even his wife, who had remarried, was dealt with harshly; her new spouse was impotent and their union was quickly annulled. Yet, as one critic revealed, "These melodramatic twists not only failed to win back the audience but alienated viewers even more."

Given her initial outrage, what Phillips did next seemed totally incongruous. She brought a new character into the plot, an exceedingly attractive Kim Reynolds, an ex-professional vocalist. Kim was the sibling of then-pregnant Jennifer Hughes, wife of Bob Hughes. That didn't seem to matter, however, as Kim was soon coming on to Bob Hughes — or was it the other way around? No matter, to the disbelief of millions of onlookers, the physician bedded Kim, leaving her also expecting his child! It wasn't Bob's first indiscretion, and it surely wasn't to be his last. Over the years he exhibited a pattern of promiscuity before, during and after multiple marriages. Longtime viewers must have felt he was trying to prove something. But what? Nevertheless, it was the first time he had impregnated two ladies at the same time.

Following the episode between Kim and Bob, Irna Phillips opened up to Mary Ann Copeland and revealed some self-perceptions in the process:

> Everyone asks me how I got the idea for Kim Reynolds on the show, because she certainly is an unusual character. She's really me — at a much younger age. She's fiercely independent, as I was, and she won't settle for second best. She looks in the mirror and refers to herself as 'the lady in the mirror.' Well, that was her other self, which no one knew about: the true me, the person I always hid from the world. She's having a child out of wedlock, which will be only hers. I adopted two children — Kathy and Tommy — without having a husband. We're both the same. And she's going to have that child to prove that a woman can do it alone.

Whatever prompted Phillips' sudden change of heart by creating the Kim-Bob tryst, she was totally unprepared for the reaction of the show's fan base to her latest indignity. Cheating on one's wife — and with the wife's own sister, yet, not to mention impregnating two women simultaneously — was simply too much for the show's legions of reactionaries. CBS received thousands of irate denunciations, and in the summer of 1973 the ratings plummeted swiftly and sharply.[18]

The next step, obviously, was unanticipated. Procter & Gamble had had enough of the iron-willed creative genius accustomed to doing her own thing in her own way; in an instant they permanently severed her ties with the show she had given birth to and loved and nurtured like a mother hen for so many years. When the dust settled after that awful separation, she telephoned Joe Willmore, *ATWT*'s producer, to inquire if "there would be any point in my talking to Procter & Gamble again." He responded: "I don't think so, Irna." Subsequently, on the evening of December 22, 1973, six months after her firing, having just set aside writing an unfinished memoir, Irna Phillips died peacefully in her sleep.

As the World Turns moved from black-and-white to color in the mid–1960s, with the final non-colorcast airing February 17, 1967. The show was still being produced live every day through November 1975, together with *The Edge of Night*, the other half-hour drama that debuted on *ATWT*'s premier day in 1956. The dramatic pair were the only CBS shows that hadn't yet gone to "live tape," continuing to afford them an immediacy — and thus a distinctive branding others didn't share — in a virtual sea of prerecorded programming, a wistful throwback to TV's earliest days.

ATWT increased from a half-hour's duration to a full hour starting December 1, 1975, the first daytime serial on its network to swell to 60 minutes. To provide the extra 30 minutes, CBS dumped *The Edge of Night*. *Edge* transitioned seamlessly to ABC at that juncture and continued for another nine years. (See Chapter 13.) NBC executives were shocked to learn that their full-hour *Days of Our Lives*— one of the peacock chain's strongest daytime shows, counter-programmed against *As the World Turns*—lost two million viewers to *ATWT* after the latter serial emerged as a one-hour edition!

"Irna Phillips' special genius for understanding what women wanted in a daytime serial gave the show its initial impact," an authority stated.[19]

Reference was made to *Our Private World* previously, the unsuccessful primetime spinoff Phillips created for CBS in 1965 that adopted one of the major figures from *As the World Turns* as its leading lady. Phillips had invoked a similar concept the year before when NBC prevailed on her to create a daytime serial for *their* network, hoping some of the magic of the dramatist's CBS victories would work at NBC. She endowed that web with *Another World*, which obliquely resembled its older CBS sibling *As the World Turns*. (Note the not coincidental similarity in titles, for example.)

In *Another World*, Phillips took the well-heeled Lowells and the less well-off Hugheses as models, and applied their contrasting environments to a couple of branches of the Matthews tribe — one prosperous and one not, comparatively speaking. In both cases, mind you, the less affluent contingent was consistently the happier group. Nevertheless, things didn't quite work out the way the legendary author visualized them in planning a connection between the dual dramas. More than one explanation has been proffered about what went wrong.

Phillips' scheme was to situate *Another World*'s Bay City, home of the Matthews clan, in close proximity to *ATWT*'s Oakdale. That would permit the chief denizens of that burg, the Hugheses, to visit with their new "neighbors," the Matthewses, and vice-versa, crossing over to each other's turf (i.e., dramas). Phillips would, in effect, reprise and refine a pattern that had so fruitfully prevailed for her on radio two decades before (under the umbrella designated "The General Mills Hour"). Figures on a trio of adjacent audio serials turned up in the plotlines of all three dramas. But now, the sole underwriter of both video features had issues with the modified concept.

There arose a concern within P&G's cloistered confines that somehow — as the proposed new characters arrived — longtime *ATWT* viewers might be overwhelmed, fairly bewildered to find them in the middle of unaccustomed storylines. This was definitely a cause for concern. Yet a second anxiety evolved out of pure rivalry: CBS didn't like the idea of giving a debuting NBC series even a little fleeting support, whether perceptual or actual; nor did NBC wish to encourage its viewers to tune in a nemesis (yea, an intimidating behemoth) on the opposite chain. Therefore, the ongoing device for characters journeying between serials proposed by the daytime doyenne simply collapsed before it ever reached the cameras.[20] The chasm between Oakdale and Bay City apparently was just too great.

Although most of the credit for the creation and introduction of *As the World Turns* has deservedly gone to Irna Phillips, without the sizeable help of two more skilled artisans— Ted Corday and Agnes Eckhardt Nixon — the celebrated drama might never have attained the early phenomenal plateau that it did. Upon that base of support emerged an opportunity for the show to capture first place in daytime programming and to maintain its lead for many years. From its earliest days the program was held in the hands of two people — author Irna Phillips and executive director Ted Corday. She managed from Chicago and he managed on the set in New York.

A strict and humorless disciplinarian, Ted handled his actors with an invisible whip.... He expected every actor to show up at rehearsals knowing every word of dialogue and in a somberly professional mood. You waited for Ted in the rehearsal hall as if waiting for the Second Coming....

Yet everyone respected Ted Corday. Unlike the majority of directors of daytime serials, who have little time during their hectic days to give actors detailed instructions on matters of interpretation, Ted always did find the time. He had an uncommon understanding of every personality in Oakdale. He put himself in complete command of the unusual pacing that he and Irna had worked out well before the premiere, the delicate interrelationships that his three cameras would catch in startling closeups, the defiance of normal dramatic time.[21]

Ted Corday left *As the World Turns* in the mid–1960s to create his own daytime serial, *Days of Our Lives,* carried on NBC. In doing so he drew upon the substantial input of his friends and associates, Irna Phillips and one Allan Chase. But on that occasion he had the upper hand, developing the serial under the banner of Corday Productions. When he died in 1966 his wife Betty became that show's executive producer.

Meanwhile, back in the Windy City ...

Daily at 1:30 her [Irna's] secretaries and assistant writers would lapse into silence while she watched the ... day's episode. One or two minutes after the live broadcast, an assistant of Ted's at the New York studio ... received a call from Irna. A typical ... call ... was fraught with tension, frosted over with a bit of polite sickly sweet goo ... before going into her ten or twenty criticisms of what had gone wrong. When speaking to anyone besides Ted Corday, whom she respected, she used an interesting ... technique.... She would speak softer and softer, until the listener was nearly mesmerized. It was her way of controlling the conversation.[22]

Among the less-unnerved decision-makers, a running joke to Irna was: "Irna, please don't lower your voice to me!" Once she replied, "Oh, you figured it out." Not many, however, had the chutzpah to joke with her candidly once her cleverly paced Midwestern modulation launched into its monotonous tedium on the other end of the line.

Agnes Eckhardt Nixon had been writing for Irna Phillips well before she arrived on *As the World Turns.* The Chicago native, born December 10, 1927, was raised in Nashville, Tennessee, and graduated from Chicago's Northwestern University in 1948. During her undergraduate days, according to *Time,* she "yearned to write drama" as an apprentice to the undisputed "queen of soap opera." In that epoch she churned out dialogue for several of Phillips' "traditional formula" radio soaps. By mid-century and afterward she penned scripts for notable television properties like *Cameo Theatre, Hallmark Hall of Fame, Philco Playhouse, Robert Montgomery Presents, Somerset Maugham Theatre* and *Studio One.*

She married auto manufacturing executive Robert Henry Adolphus Nixon on April 6, 1951, and they had four children. In the fall of 1951 Agnes Nixon contributed the first quarter's dialogue for CBS's debuting serial *Search for Tomorrow,* created by Roy Winsor. Consequently, she had worked not only for the *mother* of daytime serials but also the *father.* Nixon assisted Phillips and Ted Corday in the launch of *As the World Turns* in 1956 and was the new show's head writer from 1957 to 1959. She transferred from it to *The Guiding Light,* a show she had written for radio, and remained its head writer to 1965. At that juncture Nixon became head writer of *Another World.*

In 1968 she left soap packager Procter & Gamble to become an independent developer. She put her own serial on the air that year, ABC's *One Life to Live.* Two years later she followed it with another winning entry for the same network, *All My Children.* With the help of Douglas Marland, she created *Loving* in 1983. It lasted almost 14 years. As it left the air, with the help of James H. Brown and Barbara Esensten, Nixon put a fourth original creation on the air, *The City*. It lasted two years.

An aside: The influence of the originating craftswoman, Irna Phillips, continues today through the works of several protégés (scriptwriters) and their successors. They include the soap operas *The Guiding Light* and *As the World Turns* (Phillips), *Days of Our Lives* (Ted and Betty Corday), *One Life to Live* and *All My Children* (Nixon), and *The Young and the Restless* and *The Bold and the Beautiful* (Bill and Lee Phillip Bell). As of spring 2005, only two of the nine daily continuing dramatic features currently aired on American TV — *General Hospital* and *Passions*— do not directly or indirectly reflect the inspiration of Irna Phillips.

As the World Turns reportedly holds the record among daytime serials for the most actors to have kept their recurring roles for a decade or longer. One pundit allowed that the serial "made phenomenal stars out of all of its long-time actors, simply because it was a phenomenal show." It also can be noted that a substantial segment of those early actors were signed directly from the aural medium. "In so many ways, radio created *As the World Turns*," the reviewer confirmed.

Quite a few celebrated thespians appeared in the cast of *As the World Turns*, including Jason Biggs, Jordana Brewster, Margaret Colin, Courtney Cox, Dana Delany, Lindsay Frost, Lauryn Hill, James Earl Jones, Swoozie Kurtz, Kristanna Loken, Kathy McNeil, Julianne Moore, Michael Nader, Parker Posey, Meg Ryan, Mark Rydell, Martin Sheen, John Wesley Shipp, Richard Thomas, Marisa Tomei and Joyce Van Patten. The show has also hosted a number of guest celebs, among them Tony Bennett, Phyllis Diller, Betsy von Furstenberg, Zsa Zsa Gabor, Robert Horton, Jermaine Jackson and Robert Vaughn.

In its second season on the air, *As the World Turns* catapulted to second place in the daytime drama ratings. In its third season, 1958–59, it became the leader of the pack, occupying that coveted spot for 20 consecutive seasons, until the youth-oriented *All My Children* overtook it in 1978–79. *General Hospital* captured first place a year later and retained it for eight years until *The Young and the Restless* won it in 1987–88, holding the reins for several successive seasons. When ABC's and NBC's youth-oriented soaps began to knock *As the World Turns* from its accustomed perch as the perennial champion in 1978, the plots of *ATWT* were refocused on younger members of the core families. Gradually, the serial's ratings began to move upward.

While it was in first place, *As the World Turns*' numbers were unprecedented and unequaled during most of those years. Audience share frequently exceeded half of all viewers watching TV when the show was on, climbing as high as 57 percent during the 1963–64 season. For more than half of those 20 years the home audience regularly topped 40 percent of all TV viewers. Few, if any, other daytime series could boast such lofty figures, then or now.

Douglas Marland, head writer in the 1980s and early 1990s, infused the narrative with some of its most stimulating post–Phillips storylines. Again and again he mined the enduring drama's rich history for fresh material, especially rewarding longtime viewers with emotionally satisfying restorations of past relationships and startling new discoveries of long-buried secrets. About 1980 the Hugheses had become second-class citizens when they had always been paramount before. Their displacement was a direct consequence of the new emphasis on youthful characters.

Nancy and Chris were relegated to infrequent appearances. For about three years they disappeared altogether. Helen Wagner, who played Nancy, quit the show in 1981, confirming that the older characters had virtually vanished. Most of the Lowells, Oakdale's other leading family when the story began a quarter-of-a-century earlier, were gone. One source acknowledged: "They ceased to be important when the theme of social differences between rich families [the Lowells] and middle-class ones [the Hugheses] lost its appeal for Irna."[23]

One of the first things new author Marland did in taking over the reins was to pluck the Hugheses from mothballs and restore them to their familiar place in the three-decades-old drama. There they continued giving their children and grandchildren assistance. Don MacLaughlin, who had portrayed Chris since the serial's inception, died in 1986 and was not replaced. Meanwhile, Helen Wagner, who returned after a three-year absence, persists to this day in her role of Nancy, and could reach her gold anniversary (50 years) in 2006 — a milestone that no other actor in the history of soap opera has reached.

Marland also infused the resurgence of this strong original familial backdrop with topical subjects, some of which would have been taboo (if they were even relevant) decades earlier — abortion, AIDS, alcoholism among teens, bulimia, euthanasia, homosexuality, incest, interracial relationships and more. With each one he called for love, forgiveness and understanding in healing the wounds and overcoming the differences in attitudes.

According to one assessor: "While second in longevity to *Guiding Light*, *As the World Turns* has retained a better sense of history, due in no small part to the continued presence of original cast-member Nancy Hughes. As Doug Marland proved from the mid '80s into the early '90s, the show's history is one of its strongest assets, and by no means an impediment to progressive storytelling."[24]

Helen Wagner was born September 3, 1918, in Lubbock, Texas. She graduated from Monmouth College in Illinois with degrees in dramatics and music, an institution that awarded her the honorary Doctor of Human Letters degree in 1988. Following her formal education she moved to New York City to continue piano and voice training, gaining experience in church choirs there. Her Broadway credits include the Sigmund Romberg–Oscar Hammerstein musical *Sunny River*, the Richard Rodgers-Oscar Hammerstein musical *Oklahoma!*, *The Bad Seed*, *My Name Is Acquilon* (with Jean Pierre Aumont and Lilli Palmer) and *Love of Four Colonels* (with Rex Harrison and Lilli Palmer). Wagner toured as Blanche in *A Streetcar Named Desire* (with Lee Marvin); was Eleanor in *The Lion in Winter* during regional theater appearances in Illinois; and portrayed all of the women's roles in *Lovers and Other Strangers*. She performed in many off–Broadway and summer stock productions, at hospital benefits and on several Gilbert & Sullivan operetta tours.

Wagner's TV debut came in the form of a queen in a fairy tale that General Electric produced on its experimental station in Schenectady, New York. She appeared in numerous dramatic television roles on series like *Philco Television Playhouse*, *Studio One*, *Suspense* and more. Wagner was a principal in the cast of NBC's *The World of Mr. Sweeney* (1953–55) when Irna Phillips "discovered" her and chose her for the part of Nancy Hughes. She married Broadway producer Robert Willey.

Don MacLaughlin, who was Chris Hughes in *As the World Turns*, was born November 24, 1906, at Webster, Iowa. An English and speech major at the University of Iowa, he both taught and coached before leaving educational institutions at 26 to audition for acting roles in New York City. He soon had all the work he could handle, including parts in a couple of Broadway plays, *Fifth Column* and *South Pacific*. He also acquired roles in many long-running radio features, several of those as leads: *Buck Private and His Girl*, *Chaplain Jim U.S.A.*, *David Harding — Counterspy*, *Lora Lawton*, *Road of Life* (both radio and TV versions), *The Romance of Helen Trent*, *The Story of Mary Marlin*, *Young Widder Brown* and

You're in the Army Now. MacLaughlin died on May 28, 1986, at Goshen, Connecticut, having been in *As the World Turns* for three decades.

Santos Ortega, who appeared in the role of Grandpa Hughes, was born in New York City in June 1899. He got his show business start at 17 by singing at his hometown's Hippodrome Theatre. By 1930 he launched both stage and radio careers. He became one of the busiest actors across the latter medium's golden age. Due to his versatility in voice inflections, Ortega was quickly in demand for guest shots, support roles and leads in a variety of features, particularly crime dramas but also recurring roles in a great many soap operas.

His credits included no fewer than 55 aural series: *The Adventures of Ellery Queen, The Adventures of Nero Wolfe, The Affairs of Peter Salem, The Amazing Mr. Smith, Arch Oboler's Plays, Barrie Craig — Confidential Investigator, Big Sister, Blackstone Plantation, Bright Horizon, Broadway Matinee, Bulldog Drummond, By Kathleen Norris, Casey — Crime Photographer, The CBS Radio Mystery Theater, Charlie Chan, City Hospital, Criminal Casebook, Crooked Square, Dimension X, Don Ameche's Real Life Stories, The Ethel Merman Show, The Ford Theater, Gangbusters, Green Valley U.S.A., Hannibal Cobb, Joyce Jordan, M.D., The Light of the World, The Man I Married, Mr. and Mrs. North, Myrt and Marge, The Mysterious Traveler, Mystery Theater, The Newlyweds, The O'Neills, Our Gal Sunday, Perry Mason, Portia Faces Life, Quick as a Flash, The Radio Hall of Fame, The Robert Burns Panatela Show, Roger Kilgore — Public Defender, Romance, The Scorpion, The Shadow, Special Investigator, Stroke of Fate, The Third Man, This Day Is Ours, This Is Your FBI, Treasury Agent, Valiant Lady, Who Dun It?, Words at War, X-Minus One* and *Yours Truly — Johnny Dollar*. Ortega died April 10, 1976, in Fort Lauderdale, Florida. He wasn't replaced in the cast of *As the World Turns*.

Rosemary Prinz, who played Penny Hughes and was considered by pundits as "possibly the most popular of all daytime serial performers," was born January 4, 1931, on Long Island, New York. After attending high school in Forest Hills, New York, Prinz married actor/stage manager Michael Thoma in 1952. She landed a part in NBC's early soap opera *First Love* (1954–55). Her TV career was set when she became Penny in *ATWT*, turning up sporadically over successive decades (1956–68, 1985, 1986–87, 1993). Between those gigs she appeared in briefer roles on a trio of daytime serials: *All My Children* (1970), *How to Survive a Marriage* (1974) and *Ryan's Hope* (1988–89).

A critic wrote: "On the TV screen she was known as the impeccable Penny, nearly worshipped by the audience for her virtuousness, her even-temperedness, and above all her ability to face constant hardship with a kind of simple nobility. Off the TV screen ... Rosemary Prinz was playing out her own stormy, real-life soap opera. In the latter she was not the lovable, simple Penny, but the complicated, explosive, often-temperamental Rosemary.

"While Penny carried on a five-year romance with Jeff Baker, culminating in their marriage and then the tragedy of his sudden death, Rosemary was undergoing intensive psychoanalysis, suffering a nervous breakdown, and divorcing....

"The producers also knew how important Rosemary was to the continued ratings success of the show. During her stay on *As the World Turns* she was able to bargain for enough time off to do at least fifty stock plays — each time, Penny would be sent off on a little trip — and to raise her final salary to an unheard-of $750 a day, probably more money than any other daytime actor was receiving."[25] (Her guarantee for *How to Survive a Marriage* in 1974 was for three shows a week and compensation in excess of $1,000 per appearance, far beyond almost any soap opera actor's most carefully crafted contract.)

When Prinz originally quit the show in 1968, she told the press she "might consider going back only if her father were in a Nazi concentration camp and only her reappearance as Penny would get him out." She returned briefly three times, however; yet not before 17 years had elapsed in the interim.

Penny's best friend on *ATWT*, Ellen Lowell, was played in the early days by Wendy (nee Belinda) Drew, born May 8, 1929, in Brooklyn, New York. Moving to California in 1943, Drew apprenticed at the Pasadena Playhouse. She was a regular in the short-lived 1953 Dumont half-hour primetime drama *Jimmy Hughes, Rookie Cop*. She acquired some dramatic roles on radio, most notably as the heroine of NBC's *Young Widder Brown* during that popular serial's waning days (1954–56). Leaving *ATWT* in 1960 for marriage and to raise a family, Drew never revisited broadcasting.

William S. (Bill) Johnstone, who appeared in *ATWT* as Judge James T. Lowell from 1956 to 1979, was a New Yorker by birth, circa 1908. He died in November 1996. Johnstone's parts in radio were multifaceted, including soap opera character roles and parts in other dramatic and comedic series: *The Amazing Mrs. Danberry, The Bill Goodwin Show, The Casebook of Gregory Hood, The Cavalcade of America, Crime Classics, Five Star Jones, Irene Rich Dramas, Joyce Jordan, M.D., Les Miserables, The Lineup, The Lux Radio Theater, The March of Time, Maudie's Diary, Mrs. Wiggs of the Cabbage Patch, The Mysterious Traveler, Nick Carter—Master Detective, Nightbeat, Portia Faces Life, Pursuit, The Shadow, The Story of Bess Johnson, T-Man, Valiant Lady* and *Wilderness Road*.

13

The Edge of Night

When 50 percent of a soap opera's audience is male, and an ample segment of the remaining half is schoolchildren, something is happening entirely outside any predictable norm. But with an emphasis on mayhem rather than melodrama, *The Edge of Night*, which fused both concepts into an appealing hybrid, was ostensibly daytime's longest-running eccentricity. It also translated into intense viewer loyalty, while boasting celebs like Tallulah Bankhead, Joan Crawford, Bette Davis, Cole Porter, Eleanor Roosevelt and celebrated novelist P. G. Wodehouse among its faithful addicts. Unlike other daytime serials that gathered their loyalists slowly, *The Edge of Night* was an instant hit. In its first few months on the ether the serial picked up nine million followers who could hardly miss an episode, swiftly catapulting it into fourth place among a myriad of daytime dramas. *Time* dubbed it "the greatest hypnotic to appear since the video tube nudged the U.S. housewife away from radio's *Stella Dallas*."

Strategically positioned in CBS's final afternoon slot at 4:30 p.m. Eastern Time, its arrival at dusk reflected both its eloquent title (literally, the edge of night) and its portentous display of maniacal and mysterious properties. Emerging after its daytime peer dramas — yet before the evening agenda began — it provided a thematic transition between the housewives' domain and the primetime whodunit mysteries. While it was the first dark drama of daytime TV, it wouldn't be the last. *The Edge of Night* was unequivocally the most successful of all those that entered that arena, however. As a result, it solidified storylines involving criminal activity, becoming a pacesetter for similar divergencies among mainstream serials that were largely devoted to passion, melodrama and domesticity.

Before continuing, let us briefly examine how *The Edge of Night* came into being. Since 1943 Procter & Gamble had underwritten a suspenseful serialized *Perry Mason* cat-and-mouse program weekday afternoons over CBS Radio. In the early 1950s the soapmaker began to consider backing a mystery-slanted drama for daytime TV, too. P&G made overtures to Erle Stanley Gardner — he was the author of the *Mason* novels, and creative consultant for the film and radio adaptations. The firm hoped Gardner would permit it to shift his "defender of human rights ... champion of all those who seek justice" to the tube. But alas, it was not to be; Gardner was hung up on picturing his famous mythical character in serialized form and wanted no part of it.[1]

Unable to let go of its desire for a sleuthing daytime hero on the small screen, however, Procter & Gamble in 1955 — just as *Perry Mason* was about to exit the aural airwaves forever — engaged that series' brilliantly innovative craftsman, Irving Vendig, to design a new serial with a similar protagonist. The result was *The Edge of Night*, which premiered on April 2, 1956, over CBS, the second half-hour daytime soap opera ever telecast. The first was *As the World Turns*, launched three hours earlier on the same day.[2] (See Chapter 12.) Considerable apprehension existed on P&G's part about whether there would be a ready-made audience for even one 30-minute serial. Irna Phillips lobbied the corporate brass hard — for two years, in fact — before selling them on the innovative notion. Once they agreed to let her proceed with a half-hour *As the World Turns*, they added *The Edge of Night* to the mix. "At least, they reasoned, they would still have *Edge of Night* ... if the other new show ... turned sour," a critic noted.

To add impetus to its new offering, P&G hired the debonair, ruggedly handsome actor John Larkin — who had been Mason on radio during the previous eight years — as its leading man, the so-called hero of the vibrant new series. Larkin's in-charge, action-oriented demeanor demonstrated all of the qualities that radio listeners found to their liking in the famous mythical character he portrayed on the air. Media historians have subsequently compared *Perry Mason* and *The Edge of Night* favorably on numerous occasions. "It was almost a carbon copy," said one.

The Edge of Night projected an outdated and unrecognizable photographic composition of Cincinnati as it flickered onto television screens across the land every afternoon. Not coincidentally, Cincinnati is the hometown of Procter & Gamble, the show's sponsor. But the yarn itself was set in the mythical Midwestern burg of Monticello, which might have been nondescript had it not been for the fact that it seemingly possessed the highest corruption and mortality rates in the United States. "Hell is a city much like Monticello," *Time* revealed. Why the underworld focused on Monticello's denizens was never explained; the result, however, made for a lively outcome.

By investing in the characters of this annual play in 260 acts, the show's fans became accustomed to the fact that many of those figures would be gone within a few months or a few years at most — primarily due to accidents or assassins. One wag branded it "a drama of ordinary people in trying circumstances ... [that] stressed the resiliency and resource of work-a-day civilians under the threat of collective loss or even death," noting further: "Although seldom granted a moment of safety, the righteous citizenry unfailingly overcame the sinister forces that polluted their community."[3] Few residents merely moved out of town as a means of leaving the plot, as on most other daytime dramas. Even some of the audience's favorites would perish at strategic spots in the storyline. Unnerving encounters and dire developments kept a vast throng of viewers coming back for more.

The appeal of the serial to a substantial contingent of men and adolescents could be credited largely to the mixture of gunfights and mystery it proffered. Those infusions of jarring thrills in *The Edge of Night* favorably resembled the action serials that cinema palaces programmed on Saturday afternoons — as opposed to the traditional soap opera fare that wives and mothers habitually watched. The serial format was perfect for the whodunit storylines, and the audience found the cops-and-robbers stuff refreshing.

To make the gunfights even more dazzling, Don Wallace, the show's inaugural director, carried his cameras to the roof of the CBS studios to air those exploits live. While most soaps of that era merely *talked* about physical actions that encompassed accidents, fires and murders, *The Edge of Night* actually *showed* them as they occurred. It was something new in daytime television. A single year's episodes, for example, included three homicides, two attempted murders, a lengthy courtroom case (there was at least one sensational jury trial every year) and sundry added felonies and misdemeanors of lesser sorts. An aside: the fans were so loyal to this show that—during the frequent courtroom scenes—many buffs volunteered as unpaid human props to sit in the jury boxes so they could witness the action of their favorite soap up close!

Despite the foreboding plotlines, the leading characters found time for romance just as in other serials, yet without the prolific infidelity, incest and immorality witnessed elsewhere. Such amorous aberrations were, for the most part, irrelevant on *Edge*. Nor did the drama campaign on behalf of social issues as did some of its peers. All the while, it provided something that was usually missing from most contemporary narratives: *Edge* presented levity as ordinary behavior, even introducing it into suspenseful situations. The serial's light-hearted moments gave it a lift that made the storylines even more natural and believable, without forcing the humor. Indu-

Romantic diversions were hard to come by in *The Edge of Night*. Unlike most of its contemporary daytime dramas, this one majored in murder and mayhem. Still, on rare occasions, there were brief respites when the central characters, Sara Lane and Mike Karr—who wed near the end of the drama's first year—managed to steal a few private moments. Teal Ames and John Larkin played the leads, although both of those thespians abandoned their roles after five years to seek acting challenges on the West Coast.

bitably, the elements of great love affairs, thrills, off-the-wall characters, labyrinthine plotting and irreverent wit joined together to furnish an unparalleled production.

A *TV Guide* appraisal in the early epoch cited *The Edge of Night* as daytime's *best* soap opera. "The serial is loaded with action, suspense and emotion...," claimed critic Marya Mannes, "logically worked out, cleverly contrived and written with some sophistication. It is refreshing to find the sentiment occasionally leavened with humor, and some indication that the American female exists outside the kitchen."

At its inception, *Edge* focused on Monticello's assistant district attorney, Mike Karr

(John Larkin), and his soon-to-be bride, Sara Lane (Teal Ames), the proprietress of a flower shop. Sara offered some (not surprising) comparisons to Della Street for the fans of radio's *Perry Mason*. That counselor had long carried on a platonic relationship with his long-serving, confidential secretary. Ms. Lane, however, was much more amorously inclined towards *her* opposite than Ms. Street was to *hers*, and Mike Karr reciprocated. And the audience fell madly in love with both of them.

Nevertheless, *The Edge of Night*'s protagonist was a virile *male*, distancing the serial still further from its counterparts laden with damsels in distress and happy homemaking heroines. Karr was a champion against every form of crime, particularly that of the organized variety. In his professional capacity he proved to be the Mob's worst nightmare.

While he would later become a crusading attorney who fought the bands of baddies that were attempting to overthrow Monticello, at the beginning of the story he was thrust into the precarious and less-desirable posture of investigating his fiancée's own family. As it turned out, she was the clan's white sheep. Others, including a brother, Jack (Don Hastings), and an uncle, Harry (Lauren Gilbert), were involved in gangster-related ventures, prompting the persevering Mike to probe deeply into their day-to-day lives. The Mob's pastimes included drug dealing, robbery, hijacking, blackmailing, kidnapping, murder and a myriad of other offenses.

Shortly before Christmas 1956, after just eight months on the air, Mike Karr — who was supposed to get married then — took a bullet from a cold-blooded killer he had been tracking, Larry White (the actor wasn't identified). Larry died in a shoot-out with the police. Meanwhile, as the calendar year ended, Mike hovered perilously close to death. (By then the show's audience had swelled to the aforementioned nine million adherents.)

If the viewers had had any idea what their favorite new soap did to likable figures, as well as to gangsters, they might have been unable to swallow their Christmas pie, let alone do much celebrating as the new year arrived. But during the short time the show had been airing, they hadn't encountered any *real* familiarity with the outcomes of master tactician Irving Vendig. Of course, Vendig had plotted *Perry Mason* on CBS Radio for a dozen years, and was concurrently adding chicanery aplenty to his dossier for the storyline of CBS-TV's *Search for Tomorrow*. He was to reach his zenith with *The Edge of Night*, underscoring just why Procter & Gamble picked him to construct its chilling new drama. The fact is he wouldn't dispose of Mike Karr on that occasion, or ever; indeed, Vendig and a handful of successor scribes were dissuaded from pursuing such a painful course by an unpredicted circumstance that transpired just a few years into the run.

Mike and Sara did marry, in early 1957. A couple of years later they became parents of a beautiful little girl whom they named Laurie Ann Karr (initially played by John Larkin's own daughter, Victoria). With the aid of a half-dozen thespians, she was to reach maturity, disappear and reappear across the decades, and be summoned for a final reprise shortly before the serial left the air in 1984. No such hope could be extended for her mother, however. The audience had followed Sara and Mike's love story from the start and were fervently drawn to them as a couple deeply in love. On February 17, 1961, nearly five years into the run, an aging postwar Buick hit Sara as she pushed her two-year-old daughter from its path, the hulking monster's chrome-plated grille coming to rest menacingly over its comatose, pure and wholesome victim. Five days later, on February 22, as she lay unresponsive in a hospital bed, Sara's injuries proved fatal. A journalist reflected pensively: "Over her corpse, her husband Mike, a cop turned attorney, writhed in a manner to make Orson Welles' *Macbeth* or [Sir Laurence] Olivier's *Heathcliff* seem studies in understatement."[4]

In the meantime, absolutely nobody connected with the show had adequately prepared for the deluge of enraged responses that the network received from the fans. One estimate put the irate telephone calls, incensed telegrams and hate mail at 9,000 inflamed protests. The show even received 260 telegrams while it was still on the air! One distraught letter writer chastised the sponsors with a tinge of biting sarcasm, stating: "I had baked a Pet-Ritz cherry pie, but could hardly eat it following that terrible episode." Another remonstrated: "Shakespeare himself did not create a more convincing cast of praiseworthy personalities. What perversion of common decency prompted anyone to shatter such a team?" And those were mild compared to most of the hostile communications.

So sudden, so vehement and so voluminous were the responses that CBS had to hire additional telephone operators and mailroom personnel to process the missives following that incident. Worse, the show's ratings took an immediate nosedive, plummeting from 9.5 to 8.2 in a single season. It was a gross miscalculation, and the producers and Procter & Gamble learned a great deal in the aftermath: don't throw away a strong character that the audience adores and expect to recover from those actions overnight — invariably there will be repercussions and reprisals, and none of it will be pretty. (Parenthetically, what it all demonstrated, of course, was that even an atypical serial like *The Edge of Night* generated a strong emotional attachment between its viewers and its continuing characters.)

Teal Ames, the actress playing Sara Karr, wanted out of the show's lineup in order to pursue other opportunities, specifically in Hollywood, the theater and to reportedly go on a speaking circuit touting organic vegetables. To reassure the audience that she was indeed alive and well, the producers brought her back during the height of the eruption to speak directly to the fans and tell them why she left. She appeared with John Larkin on February 23, 1961, and both were smiling into the camera.

A few months later, when Larkin decided that he, too, had had enough of the routine and preferred to try his luck at acting on the West Coast, the producers hardly debated over whether to replace him or not. They knew already that they could hardly recover from killing him off also, so on October 10, 1961, they sent him to the state capital to organize a crime commission. He was absent for a good while. When he returned to Monticello in 1962, presto! — Larkin was long gone and in his stead actor Laurence Hugo appeared as Mike Karr.[5]

A couple of postscripts to John Larkin's reign as the original Mike Karr seems in order, particularly in light of the jesting that prevailed on this series (despite the deadly nature of its plots). A serials cataloguer recalled an incident that surprised everybody in those days of live television.

> If John Larkin were alive today he'd still be embarrassed about the scene in which he, as Mike Karr on *The Edge of Night*, came through a door and yelled at the cameras: "Hello, all you folks out there in TV land," and then started cutting up and dancing around. He wondered why none of the other actors were laughing along with him. When the commercial break came, he found out that he had mistaken the live broadcast for the dress rehearsal and that ten million or so people had watched the whole charade. John was destroyed.[6]

On yet another occasion, Larkin found himself hindered by an inflexible door that wouldn't open. Due on camera, he grappled with it gamely, then gave up and raced around backstage to another door — to suddenly come bursting onto the set out of a closet with a Clark Kent–like coolness! Only in live TV.

We return you now to our story.

When we last left Mike Karr at the close of 1956, he was lingering between life and death, his and Sara Lane's planned Christmas nuptials on hold indefinitely as she hovered by his side. Slowly the assistant DA rallied from his life-threatening injuries. By the end of January 1957 he told her he wanted to marry her soon. The wedding took place at last the following month. Thereafter, Sara frequently found herself interjected into the middle of Mike's exploits in the affairs of the syndicate, most often against his wishes and good judgment. They argued often. All of it made for a lively, spellbinding adventure, keeping viewers coming back for more.

In the episode of December 12, 1957, Mike told Sara that he intended to quit as Monticello's assistant district attorney and pursue private law practice. He made it clear, however, that he wasn't giving up hounding the hooligans that he had prosecuted while working for the city — that he would continue to pursue big game from the mob scene with a vengeance. Before leaving his post, Mike was framed by a shady district attorney and had to expose his mentor for nefarious activities.

Subsequently, Winston Grimsley (Walter Greaza) — an upstanding citizen of Monticello, who became Mike's friend and lifelong confidante, and remained with the show until the actor playing him died in 1973 — married Sara's mother, Mattie Lane (Betty Garde, Peggy Allenby). Winston prevailed on Mike to uncover the dastardly dealings of an underworld bully. Afterward, Mike briefly accepted the Monticello DA's post before returning to private law practice. The latter occasion marked a watershed in his career; forevermore he would be a crusading attorney as opposed to a public official. By 1959 Mike was working alongside another comrade, Monticello police chief Bill Marceau (Mandel Kramer). Together that pair forged an imposing duo intent on cleaning up corruption in America's most despicable metropolis. They would be a formidable team for two full decades, in fact.

Nonetheless, *The Edge of Night* continued to dispense with thespians at a fast clip via plotlines involving mischief and murder. A large contingent of evildoers received their just desserts, including the DA's cunning blackmailing mistress-secretary, Sybil Gordon (Doris Belack); sadistic serial strangler Big Frankie Dubeck (Michael Conrad), who was equipped with enormously imposing hands for his work; and many more ruffians. With each new storyline a corps of secondary characters was introduced. Most would be gone in less than two years as their plotlines played out. "The offbeat nature of the drama required constant turnover of actors who were able to make an impression quickly," a reviewer confirmed. "Over the years the show employed many of the finest actors of the American stage."

As an aside, only a handful of core figures prevailed over the long haul, including Mike and his second wife Nancy Pollack Karr, whom he married on April 23, 1963; his new law partner Adam Drake and *his* love interest Nicole Travis, who ran a fashion boutique; and Bill and Martha Marceau.[7] Nicole, whose father had ties to the syndicate (and didn't almost everybody in Monticello have a family link there?), originally set her sights on happily wedded Mike. That kind of thing didn't fly on this serial, the reader will recall, and she soon turned her focus to Adam. That pairing resulted in sensational exposure for the actors playing the couple, Donald May and Maeve McGuire, who dominated the fanzine polls for many issues. Bill Marceau, meanwhile, a widower with a troubled teenage daughter, married his secretary, Martha Spears, in the mid–1960s.

The Edge of Night continued to boast incredible ratings until 1972, more than 16 years into the run. That year the show's owner, Procter & Gamble, took a calculated risk (and lost), insisting that CBS move the program from its long-held late-afternoon timeslot to an early afternoon appearance on the weekday schedule. P&G ordered the shift so that all of its serials could be grouped into an adjacent block of soaps. Thus, on September 4, 1972, the drama transitioned to 2 p.m.—hardly the favorable "edge of night" proffered in its title—and immediately lost huge parcels of its established territory.

Overnight the drama's ratings plunged southward, dropping from its traditionally accustomed ranking of fourth place (and occasionally second) among all daytime serials to the 10th spot after 1972. *Edge* would never climb any higher than the 10th position in 13 seasons to follow, and would consistently languish perilously close to the bottom of the stack every single year from then on. What happened? The men who worked the early shifts that had comprised so much of the narrative's loyal audience vanished overnight. So did the youngsters and teenagers that bounded home from school to catch the captivating thrills. Two o'clock was simply too early for both groups (even worse—one o'clock in the Central time zone!) and the ratings dip was the result.

It was a gross misstep, so devastating to the show's long-term viability that various attempts to counteract the effect of that decision failed to recapture the prestige and lofty numbers the feature had enjoyed for so long. While probably no single cause could be cited for a serial's demise, there appears to be little doubt that the transition to the earlier times- lot contributed heavily to *Edge*'s downhill spiral, with only occasional glimpses of past glory enjoyed thereafter.

With the show still floundering three years later, reduced from a 32 share of the day- time TV audience in 1972 to a 24 share in 1975 (a 25 percent loss), CBS announced the program's cancellation to follow the telecast of November 28, 1975.[8] But ABC-TV execu- tives took a hard look at the opening *Edge* might present to a chain that was dead last among a trio of national hookups. A show with a diminished but supremely loyal fan base, plus the potential of luring lost admirers, proffered an extraordinary opportunity. Reasoning thus, ABC stepped up to the plate and agreed to air the crime-topper, rescuing it from its imminent, gloomy fate. The show was to become the only sponsor-owned soap on ABC, all others being produced by the network itself. Without missing a beat, therefore, after the drama departed CBS on Friday afternoon, it reappeared the next Monday afternoon on ABC. Its new permanent timeslot there, 4 p.m., had been purposely selected to recapture the old guard. It also should be noted that *The Edge of Night* was the first video daytime serial to transfer from one network to another, a pattern that *Search for Tomorrow* was to pursue only a half-dozen years down the road.

While *Edge*'s numbers gradually perked up, suddenly there was a new obstacle in the mix that nobody had counted on, threatening the newly inked pact big-time. In many parts of the country ABC outlets were programming syndicated and locally-produced features at 4 o'clock instead of taking the network feed. In those markets *The Edge of Night* was some- times screened in the morning hours a day following its afternoon transmission from New York. Even worse, less than half of the web's affiliates carried the show at all, denying acces- sibility to it for 38 percent of the nation's households. This significantly weakened the intended quick fix. There was an ongoing drag on the numbers because so many stations didn't run the show or didn't do so when its potentially larger audience was available. Once again, the drama simply never recovered from the fatal 1972 decision that dislodged it from the safety of its late-afternoon CBS cocoon.

Let us digress momentarily to explore the matter of the transition from "live" to "live tape" status as it impacted *The Edge of Night*. By the autumn of 1975 both *Edge* and its twin narrative, *As the World Turns*, were still being aired live every weekday afternoon. Both had followed that pattern since their inception nearly two decades earlier, in the spring of 1956. They were, in fact, the only two soaps not yet on tape. *Edge*'s executive producer,

Erwin Nicholson, fought tape every time the subject surfaced. He was convinced the use of tape would have a negative effect, diminishing energy and spontaneity. Nicholson allowed:

> We have 80 people working here — actors, technicians, stagehands and production people. When we're on video tape, there's not exactly a lackadaisical approach, but there is a feeling that, well, if we don't get on the air at 3:30, we can always delay it to 3:32 or 3:34. But if they see that second hand rushing around to 3:30, and they know that some 200 stations are waiting for this show live, everything starts working. Without sounding sadistic about it, I think it shakes people up. And the result is a much better show.
>
> Actors who like going live sometimes compare it to the stage, where the same cardiac psychology prevails. But serials are even more harrowing in a way, since the scripts change every day, and an actor faces a withering succession of deadlines.[9]

Even during those days of live broadcasts, however, *Edge* prerecorded its episodes in five instances:

1. New York law prohibited children under the age of three from appearing on live television. Whenever small children were needed, *Edge* prerecorded those scenes and dropped them into the live broadcast.

2. To maintain story continuity, *Edge* allowed some actors to pre-tape scenes when vacations and other necessary absences could not be scheduled around the live show.

3. Due to logistical problems, remote segments and particularly difficult stunts (such as fires and car crashes) were sometimes pre-taped.

4. The most frequent reason for prerecording occurred when *Edge* was preempted for news coverage and other special events. Cast calls were issued roughly two weeks before performance dates, and union rules required that actors be paid for all scheduled performances, regardless whether the actor actually appeared. For that reason, whenever *Edge* was pre-empted, the show videotaped the scheduled episode on the day of the pre-emption and continued taping one day in advance until all scheduled cast calls were depleted. This prevented *Edge* from being forced to pay actors double salaries.

5. To accommodate the transition from CBS to ABC, *Edge* ceased live telecasts in October 1975. For weeks prior to the last show on CBS, *Edge* pre-taped seven or eight shows per week to have at least two full weeks' worth of episodes ready for the debut on ABC. *Edge* taped its last episode at CBS on Friday, November 14, 1975. For the next two weeks, the show ceased production while sets and equipment were moved to the show's new Screen Gems studio.[10]

A final word about taping: unlike some of its contemporaries, *Edge* usually taped its scenes sequentially, following the precise order of the script.

In the midst of the show's decline, the producers of *The Edge of Night* seemed predisposed to continue shooting themselves in the foot — by dispensing with the services of the well-liked figure of Adam Drake, played by actor Donald May, who had only recently been voted Favorite Hero by subscribers to *Soap Opera Digest*. It wasn't a prudent move for the show to throw away such a popular character at that unstable juncture.[11]

To try to win back some of those missing viewers, on opening day at ABC the 30-minute serial was given an hour-and-a-half's exposure that offered some high-impact moments, including a shooting on the steps of the Hall of Justice. It wouldn't be the only time the show attempted an unusual diversion. In November 1968 actor Donald May, in the part of barrister Adam Drake, flawlessly delivered 42 pages of monologue while summarizing a case before a jury. During that unusual half-hour, Drake was the only individual to speak. Keep in mind that it was performed live, an absolutely astonishing feat! During the ABC epoch, on November 11, 1976, only Forrest Compton (as Mike Karr) and Ann Flood (as Nancy Karr) appeared onscreen during the half-hour. She was packing her things to separate from him, disillusioned by her spouse's intense passion for crimefighting. It was a poignant 30 minutes.[12]

Veteran mystery wordsmith Henry Slesar penned all three of those impressive installments. Slesar inherited the head scripting assignment for *The Edge of Night* from the successors of Irving Vendig, who had long departed the drama to pursue other writing challenges. A scribe for TV's *Alfred Hitchcock Presents, Batman* and *The Twilight Zone*, as well as a magazine contributor, the author of over 500 short stories and mystery books (*The Bridge of Lions, Clean Crimes and Neat Murders, The Gray Flannel Shroud*), Slesar proved the most resilient and one of the most innovative dialoguers among a handful who took the top writing job for *Edge*. He even won an Emmy for his work. Slesar's tenure, beginning in March 1968, the year after the show moved from black-and-white to colorcasts, persisted for 15 years, until May 1983, a few months before the show departed. He imbued bizarre plots with suspenseful action that kept audiences sitting on the edge of their chairs, intricately inserting riveting intrigue into melodramatic moments. There was something for everybody, in fact; Slesar knew the show's heritage and built upon its storyline traditions.

Upon leaving *Edge*, Slesar became head writer at NBC's Procter & Gamble — sponsored *Somerset* (*Another World* — *Somerset* at its 1970 debut, another spinoff), where he had been moonlighting for a spell. They ordered him to turn that serial into a crime fest, much as he had been doing at CBS. Murders, rapes and a myriad of other reprehensible behaviors invaded the township of Somerset just like the residents were accustomed to in Monticello.[13]

Now languishing in the soap opera ratings basement (at 23rd of all 26 network daytime programs), *The Edge of Night* was considered a lost cause by ABC. In November 1984 the chain announced it was dropping the show at the end of the calendar year. It said it would return the half-hour at 4 p.m. to its affiliates to fill with other programming. By then *Edge*'s rating was nearly nonexistent (2.6), with an eight percent share of the audience despite a lead-in of daytime's most popular series, also on ABC, *General Hospital* (9.1 rating, 28 percent share). After 7,420 performances, the promising venture envisioned nearly 29 years earlier by Irving Vendig and Procter & Gamble had reached its end.

Nevertheless, hoping that a syndicator might take pity and pick the show up for subsequent distribution to local stations, P&G ordered that some storylines be left unresolved so the tale could be continued. A total of 1,798 episodes could be syndicated, beginning in February 1978 through the end of the run. There was no second rescue, however. The fans that remained through the finale on December 28, 1984, could take little solace beyond the fact that they had enjoyed the ride for as long as it lasted.

But never say die.

Not long after the series was cancelled, the president of The Edge of Night International Fan Club, Frances Nonenmacher, speaking for 1,768 patrons, pronounced: "We're going out with our heads held high. This will be the daytime drama that people won't forget." It appeared as if there was more to her pronouncement than just hollow words. On August 5, 1985, and for a few years afterward, the USA cable network reprised episodes of the series nightly after midnight. Installments that were originally produced in June 1980 and beyond were repeated. If more of the chapters had been on videotape instead of having been aired live, there would have been still greater opportunity to run more episodes a second time. Previously, in 1976 ABC intended to air same-day rebroadcasts of *The Edge of Night* on its late night schedule. But when an actor couldn't come to terms regarding residual compensation, that deal collapsed.

During its earliest years (before 1960) the show was populated by radio actors looking for work. In addition to leading men types John Larkin and Mandel Kramer — who often worked together in audio— there was Peggy Allenby, Eric Dressler, Betty Garde, Lauren Gilbert, Walter Greaza, Ian Martin, George Petrie and Helen Shields, all inexhaustible players behind a microphone.

Quite a few celebrated thespians appeared in *The Edge of Night* over the years. Employing victims and villains for only a year or two before killing them off or sending them away put the show in the enviable position of hiring sizeable numbers of talented actors across its nearly three decades. Some of the soap's eminent alumni include Amanda Blake, Frank Campanella, Kate Capshaw, Dixie Carter, Dick Cavett, Gary Coleman, Margaret Colin, John Cullum, Ruby Dee, Dana Elcar, Constance Ford, Scott Glenn, Frank Gorshin, David Groh, Larry Hagman, Don Hastings, Celeste Holm, Kim Hunter, Lori Loughlin, Robert Mandan, Bette Midler, Barry Newman, Tony Roberts, Eva Marie Saint, Martin Sheen, Holland Taylor and John Travolta.

What became of the principals of *The Edge of Night* in the years afterward?

The man who initially penned the program for Procter & Gamble, Irving Vendig, was denied a chance to actually witness the show he wrote. He lived in Sarasota, Florida, when *The Edge of Night* began. At that time Sarasota had no CBS-TV outlet; thus Vendig missed the daily installments he wrote that most of the rest of the country had access to. He was born on October 11, 1902, and died in Sarasota on January 7, 1995. In between, Vendig became one of the most esteemed and prolific wordsmiths in serialized broadcast narratives. He cut his teeth in Chicago dialoguing the early syndicated radio drama *Judy and Jane* for segments spanning a decade (1932–42). In the same epoch he was also penning *Helpmate, Houseboat Hannah* and *The O'Neills* for network audiences.

Daytime radio listeners began to recognize Vendig's name as he was introduced each weekday afternoon as the craftsman of the inspired *Perry Mason* (1943–55). The show was to become a template for *The Edge of Night*. At the same time, the scribe was also writing another promising serial, CBS-TV's *Search for Tomorrow*, during its first quadrennial on the air (1951–55), plus the romantic soap *Three Steps to Heaven* (1953–54) on NBC. *Perry Mason* and *Search for Tomorrow* offered Vendig opportunities to audition many of the crime concepts that were to become staples of his most imaginative creation, *The Edge of Night*. After he left the latter in the 1960s, Vendig focused his keyboard efforts on a pair of NBC daytime properties, the dark-themed melodrama *Paradise Bay* (1965–66) and the crime serial *Hidden Faces*, which lasted only six months (1968–69) opposite CBS's *As the World Turns*. In *Hidden Faces*, an embattled criminal attorney was the protagonist (shades of *Edge!*). A collection of the prolific author's contributions to daytime serials is catalogued at Boston University.

John Larkin, the original Mike Karr, left the show in late 1961 to try out for parts on the West Coast. He died of a heart attack in Hollywood only a short time afterward, on January 29, 1965, while playing the lead in an ABC primetime dramatic series. Born in Oakland, California, in late 1926, Larkin graduated from the University of Missouri and entered radio in Kansas City. He served with the U.S. Army during the Second World War, resuming his broadcast career in Chicago and New York City. Larkin married daytime serial actress Teri Keane on June 10, 1950 (radio's Chi Chi Conrad in *Life Can Be Beautiful* and heroine of *The Second Mrs. Burton*, later in *The Edge of Night* as Martha Marceau), and they had a daughter in 1951.

In addition to the sleuthing attorney in *Perry Mason*— a part Larkin played from March 31, 1947, until the aural feature ended on December 30, 1955 — his radio roles were numerous, including leads, guest shots or character figures in more than two dozen series: *The Adventures of Dick Tracy, Backstage Wife, The Brighter Day, Buck Rogers in the Twenty-Fifth Century, Candid Microphone, The Chicago Theater of the Air, Dimension X, Ever Since Eve, The Ford Theater, Gentleman Adventurer, Helpmate, High Adventure, Houseboat Hannah, John Steele— Adventurer, Kay Fairchild— Stepmother, Lone Journey, Ma Perkins, Mark Trail, Mr. Mercury, Mr. Moto, Portia Faces Life, Radio City Playhouse, The Right to Happiness, Road of Life, The Romance of Helen Trent, Special Agent, A Tree Grows in Brooklyn, Under Arrest* and *X-Minus One*. On television he also appeared in the recurring casts of *The Road of Life* (1954–55), *Saints and Sinners* (1962–63) and *Twelve O' Clock High* (1964–65). After moving to California, Larkin showed up in a trio of motion pictures: *Seven Days in May* (1964), *The Satan Bug* and *Those Calloways* (the last two released after his death in 1965).

Teal Ames, Larkin's opposite, who portrayed Sara Lane Karr, left the show following her "death" in the automobile accident that netted so much fan fury in February 1961. Her announced intent was to try her luck in Hollywood. Ames was born at Binghamton, New York, on December 7, 1930 — she prepared for an acting career by studying drama at Missouri's Stevens College and earning a degree from Syracuse University in New York in 1953. Yet her career as a thespian beyond *The Edge of Night* was minimal. She appeared in a play on CBS-TV's *Studio One* on October 11, 1954, and in an episode on the same web's *Nash Bridges* on April 10, 1998. She also had a brief stint on ABC's *General Hospital* and was in TV commercials. During most of the years since *Edge*, however, Ames has lived in northern California where she married, had three children and several grandchildren, and opened a private practice as a marriage, family and child therapist.

From the show's early years two gentlemen with the surname Kramer — each with a long history as a recognizable broadcasting voice — were associated with *The Edge of Night* for durable runs. Mandel Kramer appeared as Monticello's chief of police Bill Marceau for two decades, from 1959 to 1979; while Harry Kramer was the show's most enduring announcer, stretching from 1958 to 1972. No familial connection is known to exist between the two Kramers.

Mandel Kramer, the son of Russian immigrants, was born at Cleveland, Ohio, on March 12, 1916. He died at Westchester, New York, on January 29, 1989. Between those years the nasal-tongued thespian was one of the busiest actors in broadcast drama, devoting a professional career primarily to radio— with the exception of that long stretch on *Edge* and one previous appointment (beginning in 1957 Kramer turned up weekday afternoons as the court bailiff on the CBS serialized anthology centering on the Hall of Justice, *The Verdict Is Yours*).

Kramer's aural credits are staggering. Like Larkin, he played leads, recurring roles and in company casts on more than two-dozen ongoing series: *The Adventures of Dick Tracy, The Adventures of Ellery Queen, The Adventures of Superman, Backstage Wife, Call the Police, Casey— Crime Photographer, The CBS Radio Mystery Theater, The Chase, David Harding— Counterspy, Dimension X, Exploring Tomorrow, The Falcon, Famous Jury Trials, Gangbusters, It's a Crime Mr. Collins, The Joe Dimaggio Show, The Light of the World, Mr. and Mrs. North,*

Perry Mason (Kramer was police lieutenant Tragg while Larkin was playing Mason), *Police-woman, Quick as a Flash, The Shadow, Stella Dallas, Terry and the Pirates, This Is Your FBI, True Detective Mysteries, Words at War, X-Minus One* and *Yours Truly—Johnny Dollar*. Following his TV escapades, Kramer appeared in one movie, *Fighting Back* (1982). There was a touch of irony in the film title, for the production was the capstone to an illustrious but fading career.

Media historiographers have, regrettably, missed much of the primary data concerning Harry Kramer. He, too, had a protracted history in radio. *This* Kramer's earliest documented engagement was in 1937 over New York's WNEW as a news analyst for *New York Lighting Electric Stores News*. In 1939 he ushered in Alfredo Antonini's orchestra over MBS and bade listeners farewell at the end of their concerts. (Antonini would later become an important staff conductor for CBS.) Kramer introduced a couple of early CBS-TV daytime features, the fleetingly innocuous game show *Winner Take All* in 1951 and *The Mel Torme Show* in 1951–52. From May 1, 1952, through its final broadcast on September 26, 1955, Kramer narrated the weekly CBS Radio dramatic thriller *Mr. Keen, Tracer of Lost Persons*, broadcasting's most durable detective series. He was the interlocutor for *Mike and Buff's Mail Bag*, a weekday 1954 CBS quarter-hour of lighthearted banter featuring Mike Wallace and his wife Buff Cobb.

Kramer's memorable voice was soon addressing millions of Americans every weekday evening as he delivered this familiar missive to TV viewers: "Direct from our CBS newsroom in New York ... this is ... *The CBS Evening News* ... with Walter Cronkite." At that juncture, he'd add whatever was appropriate for that night's agenda: "*and* ... Hughes Rudd in Dallas ... Morley Safer in Amsterdam ... Eric Sevareid at the United Nations ... Winston Burdett in Rome ... Dan Rather at the White House ... Harry Reasoner at the Pentagon ... and Bob Schieffer in London." From the 1950s, and for many years following, he introduced one of the nation's most watched programs, and his voice became recognized by Americans everywhere.

Two hours earlier, of course, he invited another audience to follow the exploits of an afternoon crime tale. In ominous tones, delivered immediately after 10 stinging piano chords that could enthrall an audience all by themselves, Kramer proclaimed: "*Theeeeee Edggggeeee of Night!*" At that juncture the opening act inaugurated a half-hour of suspenseful action that was intermittently punctuated by Kramer's interjections at appropriate intervals over the organ theme or background melody.

Never seen but heard daily, Kramer's cutaways reminded the fans who was making it possible and informed them what they could anticipate next across the half-hour gamut: "This portion of *The Edge of Night* is brought to you by Kellogg's," he'd sometimes say after the opening act. "The best to you each morning ... with Kellogg's Frosted Flakes" (or some similar plug). At other spots he'd announce: "We return you now to our story," a throwback to radio serials; "The first half of *The Edge of Night* has been brought to you by Tide ... nothing else washes clothes cleaner than Tide, yet is so mild" (it was *never* the product that he said was bringing that portion to you earlier, even when Procter & Gamble bought the whole show!); "The second half of *The Edge of Night* is brought to you by Pampers, for drier, happier babies"; "We'll return to our story in a moment" (another aural throwback before a commercial); and conclude with the show's credits, possibly a verbal public service announcement, and then finally, "This is Harry Kramer inviting you to join us every weekday afternoon for "*Theeeeee Edggggeeee of Night!*" And he continued welcoming the viewers to the dark drama as late as 1972, when he retired and was given a royal send-off by the cast and crew.

The show's signature theme, "The Edge of Night," composed by Paul Taubman, persisted from its 1956 debut through mid–1976, a healthy run for daytime serial music. Taubman was the show's musician — he played the theme live on an organ as well as all of its background music. Including piano and celeste, the theme aired from a tape recording beginning in 1973 as Taubman continued to offer the show's accompanying music live.[14]

And of course, Kramer's missives and the distinctive tune arrived packaged with a foreboding visual of Cincinnati with darkness falling diagonally over one-half of the screen and the show's familiar moniker emblazoned across the city. It was a chilling inception and it worked neatly to set the stage for the menacing yarn to follow.

Thank goodness early daytime TV had a place for a serial like that! The fans would have been cheated big-time without a daily dose of those dastardly deeds. The school kids became addicted to it. And the many men among its steadfast fanatics might never have been exposed to a soap opera in the traditional sense if it hadn't been in place. *The Edge of Night* offered a winning formula for every segment of its diversified audience. In what it attempted to do, the drama had no equal; it was a perfect thesis presented at the right moment, luring millions of Americans into its tangled labyrinth just before twilight every day.

Epilogue:
The Land of Beginning Again

In the decades since the 1950s there have been many efforts to dislodge the daytime serial from its accustomed privileged perch. Common sense has prevailed despite those attempts. "Efforts to change the face of daytime have gone largely unrewarded," ABC-TV executive Edwin Vane observed in 1977.[1] While intermittently some game shows have generated higher ratings than soap opera, and are less costly to produce, more viewers in the soaps' traditionally targeted demographic cluster are consistently drawn to narratives than any other daytime programming model. If you're unconvinced, check your local listings.

Writing in 1985, one serials scholar affirmed: "The soap opera's longevity and remarkable resilience derive from its ability to serve the same economic function today that it first served nearly a half-century ago: it provides access to a huge audience of heavy consumers (women eighteen to forty-nine years of age) in a cost-effective manner. Networks have from time to time experimented with other programming forms, but no functional replacement for the soap opera has yet been discovered."[2]

And what is available today reaches back to those truly humble beginnings when producers, directors, actors, writers, designers, musicians, stagehands, technicians, costumers, soundmen, cameramen, engineers, advertisers and networks fumbled in the dark, hoping to make their concerted efforts pay off eventually. Sometimes it did; more often, it didn't — not immediately, at least. Their experiences, nevertheless, resulted in series that finally took root and persevered, and ultimately became downright enthralling entertainment.

Watching a televised daytime serial is, in a sense, like residing in the land of beginning again. A media historiographer submitted fittingly: "Comic strips and soap operas were created to *vanish*. Each episode gives way to the next, repeatedly renewing an experience that eternally changes and eternally remains the same."[3]

In *Pickwick Papers*, Charles Dickens illustrated the matchless qualities of the serial as he wistfully allowed, "We shall keep perpetually going on beginning again, regularly." We're still doing it in the 21st century, just as we were at the middle of the 20th. The daytime serial as an art form appears likely to be with us for a while. So drag up a chair and sit a spell. You're in the land of beginning again.

Appendix A:
Daytime Serials Chronology

These Are My Children	1949	NBC
A Woman to Remember	1949	Dumont
The First Hundred Years	1950–52	CBS
Miss Susan (aka *Martinsville, U.S.A.*)	1951	NBC
Hawkins Falls	1951–55	NBC
The Egg and I	1951–52	CBS
Search for Tomorrow	1951–86	CBS, NBC
Love of Life	1951–80	CBS
Fairmeadows, U.S.A. (aka *The House in the Garden*)	1951–53	NBC
The Guiding Light (aka *Guiding Light*)	1952–present	CBS
The Bennetts	1953–54	NBC
Three Steps to Heaven	1953–54	NBC
Follow Your Heart	1953–54	NBC
Valiant Lady	1953–57	CBS
The World of Mr. Sweeney	1953–55	NBC
The Brighter Day	1954–62	CBS
Woman with a Past	1954	CBS
The Secret Storm	1954–74	CBS
One Man's Family	1954–55	NBC
Portia Faces Life (aka *The Inner Flame*)	1954–55	CBS
A Time to Live	1954	NBC
The Seeking Heart	1954	CBS
Golden Windows	1954–55	NBC
First Love	1954–55	NBC
Concerning Miss Marlowe	1954–55	NBC
The Greatest Gift	1954–55	NBC
Modern Romances	1954–58	NBC
The Road of Life (aka *Road of Life*)	1954–55	CBS
Way of the World	1955	NBC
A Date with Life	1955–56	NBC
As the World Turns	1956–present	CBS
The Edge of Night	1956–84	CBS, ABC
Hotel Cosmopolitan	1957–58	CBS
The Verdict Is Yours	1957–62	CBS
Kitty Foyle	1958	NBC
Today Is Ours	1958	NBC

From These Roots	1958–61	NBC
Young Doctor Malone	1958–63	NBC
For Better or Worse	1959–60	CBS
The House on High Street	1959–60	NBC

Appendix B:
Daytime Serials Superlatives

10 Most Durable Daytime Serials Debuting Before 1960

1. *The Guiding Light*, CBS, 1952–present — 54 years (June 2006)*
2. *As the World Turns*, CBS, 1956–present — 50 years (and counting)
3. *Search for Tomorrow*, CBS/NBC, 1951–86 — 35 years, 4 months
4. *The Edge of Night*, CBS/ABC, 1956–84 — 28 years, 9 months
5. *Love of Life*, CBS, 1951–80 — 28 years, 4 months
6. *The Secret Storm*, CBS, 1954–74 — 20 years
7. *The Brighter Day*, CBS, 1954–62 — 8 years, 9 months†
8. *The Verdict Is Yours*, CBS, 1957–62 — 5 years, 1 month
9–10. *Hawkins Falls*, NBC, 1951–55 (daytime)— 4 years, 3 months
   Young Doctor Malone, NBC, 1958–63 — 4 years, 3 months

*Preceded by approximately 14 additional years on radio
†Preceded by more than 5 additional years on radio
Figures for contemporary serials as of 2006

10 Least Durable Daytime Serials Debuting Before 1960

1. *These Are My Children*, NBC, 1949 — 4 weeks
2. *A Woman to Remember*, Dumont, 1949 — 10 weeks (daytime plus 11 weeks nighttime)
3. *The House on High Street*, NBC, 1959–60 — 19 weeks
4. *Woman with a Past*, CBS, 1954 — 22 weeks
5–6. *Follow Your Heart*, NBC, 1953–54 — 23 weeks
   The Seeking Heart, CBS, 1954 — 23 weeks
7. *Kitty Foyle*, NBC, 1958 — 24 weeks
8. *Today Is Ours*, NBC, 1958 — 25 weeks
9–10. *The Bennetts*, NBC, 1953–54 — 26 weeks
   A Time to Live, NBC, 1954 — 26 weeks

20 of the 40 daytime serials debuting before 1960 did not survive past their first birthday

10 Most Durable Actors in Roles Debuting Before 1960

1. Larry Haines (Stu Bergman, *Search for Tomorrow*), 1951–86 — 35 years
2. Don MacLaughlin* (Chris Hughes, *As the World Turns*), 1956–86 — 30 years
3. William Johnstone (Judge James Lowell, *As the World Turns*), 1956–79 — 23 years
4. Ron Tomme (Bruce Sterling, *Love of Life*), 1959–80 — 21 years
5–7. Theo Goetz* (Papa Bauer, *The Guiding Light*), 1952–72 — 20 years†

Mandel Kramer (Bill Marceau, *The Edge of Night*), 1959–79 — 20 years
Santos Ortega* (Grandpa Hughes, *As the World Turns*), 1956–76 — 20 years
8. Walter Greaza* (Winston Grimsley, *The Edge of Night*), 1956–73 —17 years
9. Terry O'Sullivan (Arthur Tate, *Search for Tomorrow*), 1952–55, 1956–68 —15 years
10. Bernard Grant (Dr. Paul Fletcher, *The Guiding Light*), 1956–70 —14 years

*Died while still playing the role
†Also spent about three preceding years in the same role on radio
Average tenure for these most durable actors: 21.5 years

10 Most Durable Actresses in Roles Debuting Before 1960

1. Helen Wagner (Nancy Hughes, *As the World Turns*), 1956–81, 1984–present — 47 years (April 2006)
2. Mary Stuart (Joanne Gardner Barron Tate Vincente Tourneur, *Search for Tomorrow*), 1951–86 — 35 years
3. Charita Bauer* (Bert Bauer, *The Guiding Light*), 1952–84 — 32 years†
4–5. Ellen Demming (Meta Bauer Roberts, *The Guiding Light*), 1953–74 — 21 years
Audrey Peters (Vanessa Dale Raven Sterling, *Love of Life*), 1959–80 — 21 years
6. Melba Rae* (Marge Bergman, *Search for Tomorrow*), 1951–71 — 20 years
7–8. Jada Rowland (Amy Ames, *The Secret Storm*), 1954–58, 1960–71, 1973–74 —16 years
Haila Stoddard (Pauline Rysdale Tyrell, *The Secret Storm*), 1954–70 —16 years
9. Marjorie Gateson (Grace Tyrell, *The Secret Storm*), 1954–69 —15 years
10. Ann Loring (Tammy Forrest, *Love of Life*), 1956–70 —14 years

*Died while still playing the role
†Also spent two preceding years in the same role on radio
Average tenure for these most durable actresses: 23.7 years

4 Most Durable Announcers Debuting Before 1960

1. Dwight Weist (*Search for Tomorrow*), 1951–82 — 31 years
2. Dan McCullough (*As the World Turns*), 1956–82 — 26 years
3–4. Harry Kramer (*The Edge of Night*), 1958–72 —14 years
Ken Roberts (*The Secret Storm*), 1960–74 —14 years

Most Prolific Sponsors of Daytime Serials Debuting Before 1960

Procter & Gamble —17 serials
Alberto-Culver — 5 serials
Lever Brothers— 4 serials
American Home Products, Borden, Sterling Drugs— 3 serials each
Andrew Jergens, Colgate-Palmolive-Peet, General Mills, Miles Laboratories— 2 serials each

Sustaining (unsponsored)— 8 serials

Appendix C:
Daytime Serials Directory

*This appendix provides a précis of all network televised daytime serials airing in America that premiered during the seasons between 1946 and 1960. In addition to the commentary in the text (found in the indicated chapters under "**Annotations**")— which is often more descriptive than the summaries presented here — the alphabetical program directory offers artist lists and other pertinent data that is as inclusive as can be authenticated. Every precaution has been taken to assure precision, even though it can never be guaranteed. When multiple sources are unmistakably in error or do not agree with one another, information has been corrected or omitted, intensifying the reliability of the notations that are included. Care has been taken to furnish the most comprehensive interpretation yet published on the early epoch of the televised daytime serial. While this material has been proofread repeatedly, if obvious mistakes persist, the reader's indulgence is asked.*

As the World Turns

April 2, 1956–present

Black & White, Color (effective February 20, 1967)— **Live, Videotape** (effective December 1, 1975)

Origination: Studio 61 (Monroe Studios), New York City, 1956; Studio 63 (Dumont Studios), New York City, late 1950s

Annotations: Chapters 6, 12

Theme Songs: "Theme for As the World Turns" (Charles Paul), in D-major on organ and piano, principal opening/closing through October 30, 1981

Opening Billboard: Almost exclusively from April 2, 1956, to February 17, 1967, the program launched with a black and white globe whirling slowly in outer space. The sphere was initially set to the right of center. As the camera drew closer, it transferred to the screen's middle. The show's title, fashioned in a dual-line Lydian font in white letters, appeared abruptly across Earth's horizon. An announcer affirmed: "And now, live—for the next 30 minutes—*As the World Turns.*" As the years progressed, many subsequent alterations of this original image occurred, including many glitzy main title splashes, symptomatic of a classy, sophisticated presentation.

Sponsors: Procter & Gamble, Best Foods, Carnation, others

Agencies: Benton and Bowles, Compton Advertising (both P&G), others undocumented

Broadcast Schedule:
April 2, 1956–November 28, 1975   M–F   1:30–2:00 p.m.   CBS
December 1, 1975–February 1, 1980   M–F   1:30–2:30 p.m.   CBS
February 4, 1980–June 5, 1981   M–F   2:00–3:00 p.m.   CBS
June 8, 1981–March 20, 1987   M–F   1:30–2:30 p.m.   CBS

March 23, 1987–present   M–F   2:00–3:00 p.m.   CBS
Creator: Irna Phillips
Executive Producers: Ted Corday, Joe Willmore, Joe Rothenberger, Fred Bartholemew, Mary-Ellis Bunim, Robert Calhoun, more (specific years undocumented)
Producers: Charles Fisher, Allen Potter, Lyle B. Hill, Mary Harris, Robert Driscoll, Arthur Richards, Susan Bedsow Horgan, Robert Rigamonti, Michael Laibson, Brenda Greenberg, Bonnie Bogard, Christine Banas, Ken Fitts, Lisa Wilson, more (specific years undocumented)
Directors: Ted Corday, Bill Howell, Walter Gorman, James MacAllen, Cort Steen, Leonard Valenta, Paul Lammers, Robert Myhrum, Allen Fristoe, Heather H. Hill, Bruce Barry, Richard Dunlap, Robert Schwarz, Peter Brickerhoff, Maria Wagner, Bruce Minnix, Richard Pepperman, Joel Arnowitz, Michael Kerner, Jill Mitwell, more (specific years undocumented)
Head Writers: Irna Phillips with Agnes Nixon, Irna Phillips with William J. Bell, Irna Phillips (solo), Joe Kane and Winifred Wolfe, Katherine L. Phillips, Warren Swanson, Elizabeth Tillman and John Boruff, Irna Phillips with David Lesan, Robert Soderberg and Edith Sommer, Ralph Ellis and Eugenie Hunt, Douglas Marland, Bridget and Jerome Dobson, Paul Roberts, K. C. Collier and Tom King, Bridget and Jerome Dobson (second time), Caroline Franz and John Saffron, John Saffron (solo), Tom King and Millee Taggart, Cynthia Benjamin and Susan Bedsow Horgan, Douglas Marland (again), more (specific years undocumented)
Organists-Pianists: Charles Paul (1956–73), Lee Erwin and Billy Nalle (substitutes)
Announcer: Dan McCullough (1956–82)
Cast: *Chris Hughes* Don MacLaughlin; *Nancy Hughes* Helen Wagner; *Jim Lowell Jr.* Les Damon; *Judge James T. Lowell* William (Bill) Johnstone; *Donald Hughes* Hal Studer (1956), Richard Holland (1956–62); *Penny Hughes Baker Wade McGuire Cunningham* Rosemary Prinz; *Bob Hughes* Bobby Alford (1956–58), Ronnie Welch (1958–60); *Grandpa Hughes* William Lee (1956), Santos Ortega (1956–76); *Edith Hughes Frye* Ruth Warrick; *Claire Lowell Cassen* Anne Burr; *Ellen Lowell Stewart* Wendy Drew; *Janice Turner Hughes* Joyce Van Patten; *Dr. Doug Cassen* Nat Polen; *Dr. George Frye* George Petrie; *Jeff Baker* Mark Rydell; *Dr. Tim Cole* William Redfield; *Louise Cole* Mary K. Wells; *Mrs. Turner* Leona Powers. Note: *Only actors signed prior to 1960 are named due to this project's emphasis on golden age serials*
Plot: An early CBS press release revealed: "*As the World Turns* concerns itself with the day-to-day problems of a moderately successful lawyer, his wife, their three children, and associates of the family." That was the Hughes brood, and those associates— who stuck closer than a brother, intermingling both love and livelihood —were the flourishing Lowells (flourishing as in "privileged circumstances," not sizable number). In the first few months on the ether, Jim Lowell Jr. dallied with Edith Hughes, sibling of the middle-income clan's hero. It was all to the consternation of Lowell's wife, father, daughter and the remainder of the Hugheses, who were shaken by the insensitive display. Lowell's wife Claire filed for divorce, but before that became official, her estranged spouse died in an accident. Over the next decade the storyline's chief focus was the offspring of the dual clans. The plotting featured numerous screw-ups that the kids brought into their lives through sexual improprieties and ill-fated marriages. The latter often ended in sudden death, but divorce took care of quite a few mates. Meanwhile, backstage, compelling imbroglios occupied the thoughts of many as series creator Irna Phillips ruled with an iron hand, controlling virtually every important decision affecting "her" show. She got away with it for years, being respected but despised by cast and management. When the show's owner could tolerate it no longer, it separated her from the serial she loved more dearly than any of nearly a score she had influenced over her lifetime. As her own melodrama played out, it proved a sad ending to an illustrious career.

The Bennetts

July 6, 1953–January 8, 1954
Black & White — Live
Origination: WMAQ–TV, Chicago
Annotations: Chapter 4
Sponsor: Sustaining
Broadcast Schedule:
July 6, 1953–January 8, 1954   M–F   11:15–11:30 a.m.   NBC

Executive Producer: Ted Sisson
Producer: Ben Park
Directors: John Hinsey, Lynwood King
Writer: Bill Barrett
Announcer: Dick Noble
Cast: *Wayne Bennett* Don Gibson; *Nancy Bennett* Paula Houston, Eloise Kummer (later episodes); *Blaney Cobb* Jack Lester; *Meg Cobb* Beverly Younger; *Speedy Winters* Viola Berwick; *George Konosis* Sam Siegel; *Alma Wells* Kay Westfall. *Also in the cast:* Jerry Harvey

Plot: The denizens of the little burg of Kingsport found in barrister Wayne Bennett and his wife Nancy a couple to whom they could bring their troubles and gain empathetic responses, prudent advice and professional help. Their neighbors, Blaney and Meg Cobb, needed all of it when charlatans operating an adoption scam ripped them off. One of Wayne's own chums did the same when Wayne represented him in court, then frustrated the attorney once again by tossing aside his recently-wedded spouse for a new mate. Encountering these issues was about all the show had time to do.

The Brighter Day

January 4, 1954–September 28, 1962
Black and White — Live
Origination: Studio 42 (Grand Central Terminal Studios), New York City, 1954–61; Studio 43 (CBS Television City), Los Angeles, 1961–62
Annotations: Chapter 7
Aural Antecedent: 1948–49, NBC Radio; 1949–56, CBS Radio
Theme Songs: "Thunder" (Richard W. Leibert), "Morning" (Richard W. Leibert), "Prism" (Roy Eaton), "Brighter Day" (Roy Eaton)
Opening Billboard: To the right of a church spire the title emerged in a fusion of calligraphy (for the initials "B" in *Brighter* and "D" in *Day*) and Times Roman lettering. At one juncture in the program's history, iron gates swung open as the title appeared. Earlier, a needlepoint picture of a house was the focus. The same epigraph heard on the radio series applied: "Our years are as the falling leaves. We live, we love, we dream, and then we go. But somehow we keep hoping — don't we? — that our dreams come true on that brighter day!"
Sponsor: Procter & Gamble (Cheer, Lilt, Ivory, et al.)
Agencies: Young & Rubicam, Compton Advertising
Broadcast Schedule:
January 4, 1954–May 14, 1954   M–F   1:00–1:15 p.m.   CBS
July 5, 1954–June 15, 1962   M–F   4:00–4:15 p.m.   CBS
June 18, 1962–September 28, 1962   M–F   11:30–11:55 a.m.   CBS
Creator: Irna Phillips
Producers: Bob Steele (New York), Leonard Blair (Los Angeles)
Director: Hal Cooper (Los Angeles)
Writers: Irna Phillips, John Haggart, Sam Hall, Eileen and Robert Mason Pollock, Hendrik Vollaerts (Los Angeles)
Organists: Dick Leibert (1950s), Arlo Hults (c1960–61), Kip Walton (Los Angeles)
Announcers: Jimmy Blaine, Ron Rawson (commercials), John Harlan (Los Angeles)
Cast: *Rev. Richard Dennis* William Smith (1954), Blair Davies (1954–62); *Aunt Emily Potter* Mona Bruns; *Grayling Dennis* Hal Holbrook (1954–59), James Noble (1959–60), Forrest Compton (1961–62); *Althea Dennis* Brooke Byron (1954–55), Jane Heller (1956), Maggie O'Neill (1960), Anne Meacham (1960–61); *Patsy Dennis Hamilton* Lois Nettleton (1954–57), June Dayton (1961–62); *Barbara (Babby) Dennis* Mary Linn Beller (1954–59), Nancy Malone (1959–60); *Dr. Randy Hamilton* Larry Ward; *Sandra Talbot Dennis* Diane Gentner (1956), Gloria Hoye (1957–59), Mary K. Wells (1960–61), Nancy Rennick (1961–62); *Rev. Max Canfield* Herb Nelson; *Lydia Harrick Canfield* Murial Williams; *Donald Harrick* Walter Brooke; *Lenore Bradley* Lori March; *Robert Ralston* Mark Daniels; *Ellen Williams Dennis* Patty Duke (1958–59), Lanna Saunders (1960–61); *Steven Markley* Peter Donat; *Tom Bradley* Robert Webber; *Crystal Carpenter* Vivian Dorsett; *Peter Niro* Joe Sirola; *Eliot Clark* Lawrence Weber (1959), Ernest Graves (1960); *Bud Clark* Charles Taylor; *Diane Clark* Lin Pierson; *Lois Williams, R.N.* Marian Winters; *Adolph McClure* Frank Thomas; *Dr. Charles Fuller* Dean Harens; *Chris Hamilton*

Mike Barton; *Uncle Walter Dennis* Paul Langton; *Toby Ballard* Don Penny; *Judith Potter* Bennye Gatteys; *Maggie Quincy* Patsy Garrett; *Dean Wilbur* Perry Ivins; *Mort Barrows* Benny Rubin. *Also in the cast:* Rex Ingram, Jack Lemmon, Judy Lewis, Santos Ortega, William Windom. Note: *As the serial ended early in the 1960s, and considerable reference is made in the body text to its transition to the West Coast, the complete cast is included*

   Plot: For two years this daytime serial persisted over radio and television, pursuing the same storyline with small modifications for visual interpretation. Its aural form dated to 1948. Rev. Richard Dennis, a widowed parson, and his brood of five children lived under a microscope in the little hamlet of New Hope, Pennsylvania, and later in the academic arena of Columbus. All their dirty laundry was hung out to dry before the townsfolk and parishioners, some of whose tongues wagged incessantly. Reinforcing the notion that every mortal is born with feet of clay, some of Dennis' offspring seemed to provide as much heartache as joy as their selfish, at times rebellious natures pursued interests in contrast to the principles held by the holy man of God. A surrogate mother, a relative, came to live with them to help fill the maternal void in their lives. Papa Dennis didn't have an easy go of it, but neither did his offspring. The perplexing dilemmas in which they were mired offered an absorbing family drama until many alterations in plotting, characters, locale and timing led to the show's collapse.

Concerning Miss Marlowe

   July 5, 1954–July 1, 1955
   Black & White — Live
   Origination: Studio A (106th Street Studios), New York City
   Annotations: Chapter 4
   Sponsor: Procter & Gamble
   Agency: Benton and Bowles
   Broadcast Schedule:
   July 5, 1954–July 1, 1955   M–F   3:45–4:00 p.m.   NBC
   Producer: Tom McDermont
   Director: Larry White
   Writers: John Pickard and Frank Provo
   Announcer: Hugh James
   Cast: *Margo (Maggie) Marlowe* Louise Allbritton (1954–55), Helen Shields (1955); *Kit Christy* Chris White; *Ralph* David Buka; *Jim Gavin* Efrem Zimbalist Jr.; *Barbara Gavin* Sarah Burton; *Belle Mere Gavin* Kathleen Comegys; *Bojalian* Ross Martin; *Mike Donovan* Byron Sanders; *Dot Clayton* Helen Shields; *Harriet the Hat* Jane Seymour; *Bill Cooke* John Raby; *Augusta Gorme* Meggie Leubecker; *Cindy Clayton* Patricia Bosworth; *Harry Clayton* John Gibson; *Tommy Clayton* Eddie Brien; *Hugh Fraser* Lauren Gilbert; *Katie Patrick* Vera Rivers; *Linda Cabot* Sarah Burton; *Ronald Blake* Bert Thorn

   Plot: An aging theater actress decided to hang it up and marry again but learned the tragic news that her beau was dead. The grieving Maggie Marlow returned to the stage and a bomb of a play in which she was routinely upstaged by an up-and-coming younger actress, Kit Christy. Meanwhile, viewers learned that Maggie and a young daughter were separated some 14 years earlier in France. Did it come as any surprise that the girl then jeopardizing her future was her very own offspring? After all, it was only make believe. With youthful abandon, Kit thought she was putting her career on the fast track by carousing with the director. Perhaps not to be outdone, a rejuvenated Maggie fell for Jim Gavin, a married attorney. When his wife was murdered, suspicion fell on him. Mike Donovan, the suitor nobody knew she had, confessed to the foul deed and the serial abruptly ended.

A Date with Life

   October 10, 1955–June 29, 1956
   Black & White — Live
   Origination: Studio 3B (30 Rockefeller Plaza), New York City
   Annotations: Chapter 4
   Theme Song: original composition (John Gart)

Packager: Hollis Productions
Sponsor: Borden
Agency: Young & Rubicam
Broadcast Schedule:
October 10, 1955–June 29, 1956   M–F   4:00–4:15 p.m.   NBC
Director: Frederick Carr
Writer: Jesse Sandler
Organist: John Gart
Hosts: Logan Field (as Jim Bradley, in 1955); Mark Roberts (as Tom Bradley, in 1956). *Also in the company:* Barbara Britton, Stephen Chase, June Dayton, Ann Dere, Anthony Eisley, Peter Fernandez, Susan Halloran, Dean Harens, Don Hastings, Phyllis Hill, Georgann Johnson, Stanja Lowe, Jack MacGregor, Joe Maross, Barbara O'Neal, Neva Patterson, Gordon Peters, William Redfield, Marion Russell, Pat Sully, Dolores Sutton, Lois Wilson, others
Plot: The imaginary burg of Bay City was home to Jim Bradley, newspaper editor, and his brother, Tom, who swapped narrating duties for a series of yarns, each tale of at least a week's duration and most lasting for about five weeks. Occasionally characters in one story appeared in a succeeding one. Some of the actors were little more than recognizable faces borrowed from other soap operas. The series was one of a small handful of anthologies NBC aired in the mid–1950s in an attempt to lure viewers away from traditional closed-end dramas at CBS. With the exception of *Modern Romances*, which achieved moderate success using that form, the returns were fairly dismal.

The Edge of Night

April 2, 1956–December 28, 1984
Black & White, Color (effective 1967)— **Live, Videotape** (effective October 1975)
Origination: Studio 61 (Monroe Studios), New York City, 1956; Studio 64 (Dumont Studios), New York City, late 1950s–1961
Aural Antecedent: Conceived in the tradition of *Perry Mason* and bearing a strong resemblance to the serialized "defender of human rights ... champion of all those who seek justice" from 1943–55, CBS Radio
Annotations: Chapters 7, 13
Theme Song: "The Edge of Night" (Paul Taubman) (1956–76)
Opening/Closing Billboard: A foreboding visual of Cincinnati, home of Procter & Gamble, with darkness falling diagonally over one-half of the screen and the show's familiar moniker emblazoned across the city, reflecting the approaching nightfall. Ten riveting chords struck on a piano precedes the announcer's ominous pronouncement, *"Theeeeee Edggggeeee of Night!"*
Sponsors: Procter & Gamble, W. K. Kellogg Company, French's
Agency: Benton and Bowles
Broadcast Schedule:
April 2, 1956–June 28, 1963   M–F   4:30–5:00 p.m.   CBS
July 1, 1963–September 1, 1972   M–F   3:30–4:00 p.m.   CBS
September 4, 1972–November 28, 1975   M–F   2:30–3:00 p.m.   CBS
December 1, 1975–December 28, 1984   M–F   4:00–4:30 p.m.   ABC
Creator: Irving Vendig
Executive Producers: Lawrence White, Don Wallace, Erwin Nicholson (complete run — years undocumented)
Producers: Werner Michel, Charles Pollacheck, Charles Fisher, Erwin Nicholson, Rich Edelstein, Robert Driscoll, Jacqueline Haber (complete run)
Directors: Don Wallace, Fred Bartholomew, Allen Fristoe, Leonard Valenta, John Sedwick, Andrew D. Weyman, Richard Pepperman, Joanne GoodhartFreddie Bartholomew and John Wallace (complete run)
Head Writers: Irving Vendig, Lou Scofield, James Lipton, Henry Slesar, Lee Sheldon (complete run)
Organist: Paul Taubman (1956–spring 1976)
Announcers: Bob Dixon (1956), Herbert Duncan (1956–58), Harry Kramer (1958–72)
Cast: *Mike Karr* John Larkin; *Sara Lane Karr* Teal Ames; *Winston Grimsley* Walter Greaza; *Mat-*

tie Lane Grimsley Betty Garde (1956), Peggy Allenby (1956–66); *Bill Marceau* Mandel Kramer; *Sybil Gordon* Doris Belack; *Big Frankie Dubeck* Michael Conrad; *Jack Lane* Don Hastings; *Uncle Harry Lane* Lauren Gilbert; *Cora Lane* Sara Burton; *Louise Grimsley Capice* Lisa Howard; *Phil Capice* Robert Webber (1956–57), Earl Hammond (1957); *Willie Bryan* Ed Holmes; *Martin Spode* Eric Dressler (1956); Henderson Forsythe (circa 1957); *Hester Spode* Helen Shields; *Grace O'Keefe* Maxine Stuart; *Charlie Brooks* Ian Martin; *Walt Johnson* Mark Rydell; *Rose La Tour* Henrietta Moore; *Betty Jean Battle Lane* Mary Moore; *Gail Armstrong* Millette Alexander; *Dr. Hugh Campbell* Wesley Addy; *Peter Dalton* George Petrie; *Dick Appleman* Michael Strong; *Mary Appleman* Joan Copeland; *Marilyn* Mary Alice Moore. Note: *Only actors signed prior to 1960 are named due to this volume's emphasis on golden age serials*

Plot: Lieutenant Mike Karr shifted his occupation between being a cop, an assistant district attorney, a lawyer, district attorney and again a lawyer. Whatever his capacity, he excelled at his avocation—to catch the most despicable desperadoes and underworld types that had infiltrated his Midwestern community of Monticello. He would not rest until the last one was put away. Assisting him three years into the run was police chief Bill Marceau; together they made a formidable team from which any hoodlum would have recoiled. Their actions were set in a storyline focusing on cops and robbers, a surprising departure from the typical daytime dramatic fare milady was exposed to. In airing this tale of the macabre intermingled with melodramatic moments, the sponsors gave viewers something new. This particularly appealed to men and youngsters of school age who loved whodunits and lots of gunplay. On the side, Mike Karr, the play's protagonist, had a girlfriend, Sara Lane, whom he married in due time. But first he took a bullet from one of those gangland marauders. It was all in a day's work, and it kept a spellbound audience hanging on every word and irreverent exploit.

The Egg and I

September 3, 1951–August 1, 1952
Black & White—Live
Origination: Studio 57 (Peace Theater), New York City
Annotations: Chapter 3
Opening Billboard: A hand turned several illustrations bearing droll images of hens and roosters clucking, crowing and gossiping. The show's title was stenciled in block letters on a single sketch of four eggs, one word per egg. All the while a folk tune reverberated in the background, reminiscent of rustic life.
Sponsor: Procter & Gamble (Tuesdays and Thursdays starting February 26, 1952, through June for Ivory Flakes)
Agency: Compton Advertising
Broadcast Schedule:
September 3, 1951–August 1, 1952   M–F   12:00–12:15 p.m.   CBS
Producer: Montgomery Ford
Directors: Jack Gage, Judson Whiting
Writers: Robert Soderberg, Manya Starr, Joe Bates Smith, Sam Locke
Announcer: Allyn Edwards
Cast: *Betty MacDonald* Pat Kirkland (1951–52), Betty Lynn (after March 7, 1952); *Bob MacDonald* John Craven; *Ma Kettle* Doris Rich; *Pa Kettle* Frank Twedell; *Jed Simmons* Grady Sutton; *Lisa Schumacher* Ingeborg Theek; *Paula French* Karen Hale; *Mother* Nancy Carroll
Plot: Betty MacDonald wrote a book about her experiences in moving from a metropolis to a Washington chicken farm that became a best seller in 1945. The tale was turned into a box office smash at theaters nationwide in 1947. CBS bought the rights to the story and implemented it as a daily quarter-hour soap opera. Loaded with humor, it was a departure from the normal melodramatic narratives dominating the skyline. CBS predicted it would be a hit, too, capitalizing on the popularity of the earlier variations, plus a series of comedic films about the MacDonalds' hilarious neighboring farmers, Ma and Pa Kettle. Instead, the soap opera never found an audience, departing the airwaves in less than a year, and providing CBS with its first failure in televised daytime drama.

Fairmeadows, U.S.A./The House in the Garden

November 4, 1951–53*
Black & White — Live
Origination: Studio 3B (30 Rockefeller Plaza), New York City
Annotations: Chapter 4
Sponsor: Johns-Manville (Sunday)
Agency: J. Walter Thompson
Broadcast Schedule:
November 4, 1951–April 27, 1952   Sunday   3:00–3:30 p.m.   NBC
September 8, 1952–53*   M–F   4:30–4:45 p.m.   NBC
Producer: Tony Stanford
Directors: Alan Neuman, Alan Rhone
Writer: Agnes Ridgeway
Cast: *John Olcott* Howard St. John (Sunday), Lauren Gilbert (M–F); *Alice Olcott* Ruth Matteson; *Mary Olcott* Hazel Dawn Jr. (Sunday), Monica Lovett (M–F); *Jim Olcott* Tom Taylor; *Evie Olcott* Mimi Strongin; *Reverend* (name unidentified) James Vickery (M–F)
   Plot: In the only network soap opera telecast on Sunday, John Olcott — who suffered a career reversal after a colleague faltered — returned from the city with his family to their hometown of Fairmeadows, U.S.A., where John began operating the town's general store. Their relationships with the locals and each other were paramount to the developing story. A young cleric added to the daily portrayal merited older daughter Mary's infatuation.

*When the serial was resumed on weekdays it appeared as the third quarter-hour of *The Kate Smith Show* and was tagged *The House in the Garden*. The narrative vanished before Smith's seasonal run ended on June 5, 1953.

The First Hundred Years

December 4, 1950–June 27, 1952
Black & White — Live with videotape exteriors
Origination: Studio 56 (Liederkranz Hall), New York City
Annotations: Chapter 3
Aural Antecedent: The premise was loosely drawn from an ABC Radio Thursday night half-hour comedy in the summer of 1949 that possessed a similar theme revolving around the trials and tribulations of a young married couple. Sam Edwards and Barbara Eiler starred; the support cast included Bea Benaderet, Joseph Kearns, Myra Marsh and Earle Ross
   Theme Song: "The First Hundred Years" (Clark Warren)
   Sponsor: Procter & Gamble (Tide)
   Agency: Benton and Bowles
   Broadcast Schedule:
December 4, 1950–June 27, 1952   M–F   2:30–2:45 p.m.   CBS
   Producers: Hoyt Allen, Gloria Monty, Murray Bolen
   Director: Everett Gammon
   Writer: Jean Holloway
   Organist: Clarke Morgan
   Announcers: Cy Harrice, Casey Allen
   Cast: *Chris Thayer* Jimmy Lydon; *Connie Martin Thayer* Olive Stacey (to January 1952), Anne Sargent (thereafter); *Mr. Thayer* Dan Tobin; *Mrs. Thayer* Valerie Cossart; *Mr. Martin* Robert Armstrong; *Mrs. Martin* Nana Bryant; *Margy Martin* Nancy Malone. *Also in the cast:* Charles Baxter, Mary Linn Beller, Larry Haines, Nat Polen
   Plot: A couple's first years of marriage got off to a rollicking start in a dilapidated old mansion given them by the bride's father. The at-times-hilarious antics resulting from dealing with the realities of life, plus the meddlesome interventions into their private affairs from five relatives representing both sides of the family, provided a lilting storyline that proved atypical of the breed. The lighthearted approach could be amusing, even though it wasn't enough to attract a sustained following.

First Love

July 5, 1954–December 30, 1955
Black & White — Live
Origination: WPTZ–TV, Philadelphia, July 5–August 27, 1954; Studio B (106th Street Studios), New York City, August 30, 1954–December 30, 1955
Annotations: Chapter 4
Theme Song: "All My Life" (George Milliades and Johnny Brandon)
Sponsor: Sustaining (at start), Andrew Jergens (Jergens lotion, Woodbury soap)
Broadcast Schedule:
July 5, 1954–August 27, 1954   M–F   3:30–3:45 p.m.   NBC
August 30, 1954–December 30, 1955   M–F   4:15–4:30 p.m.   NBC
Creator-Producer: Adrian Samish
Directors: Joe Behar (Philadelphia), John Goetz, Ed Kogan (New York)
Writer: Manya Starr
Announcer: Wayne Howell
Cast: *Zach James* Val Dufour (through April 8, 1955), Tod Andrews (starting April 11, 1955); *Laurie James* Patricia Barry; *Paul Kennedy* Melvin Ruick; *Doris Kennedy* Peggy Allenby; *Chris* Frankie Thomas; *Amy* Rosemary Prinz; *Wallace Grant* Henry Stanton; *Priscilla (Petey) Cummings* Rita Fredericks; *David* Bob Courtleigh (early 1955), Dean Harens (starting May 1955); *Tony Morgan* Peter Cookson; *Bruce McKee* Jay Barney; *Jenny* Barbara Myers; *Matthew James* Paul McGrath; *Jack Doyle* Court Benson; *Judge Kennedy* Howard Smith; *Mike Kennedy* John Dutra; *Ruth Taylor* Scotty MacGregor; *Sam Morrison* Hal Currier; *Quentin Andrews* Frederic Downs; *Leona* Nancy Pollock; *Phil Gordon* Joe Warren; *Peggy Gordon* Henrietta Moore
Plot: Zach James worked in a jet airplane plant. Due to lingering troubling images from his service in the Second World War, he threw himself into his work. His young wife Laurie rolled with the punches until she learned her spouse was cheating on her with Priscilla (Petey) Cummings. The couple separated; Laurie took a job in another town and was seeing a young attorney there. He would be instrumental in helping her later prove that her husband didn't kill Petey, who was murdered, even though there was strong evidence to the contrary. She and Zach reunited and she took a job in a ladies' garment emporium. Zach broke the news to Laurie and their good friend Amy that Amy's husband Chris had been killed in a plane crash. After Zach's dad, Matthew James, took a job at the same plant as his son, a lunatic entered their workplace and killed Matthew, possibly releasing some pent-up emotions Zach had carried for years since becoming convinced he was unwanted as a child.

Follow Your Heart

August 3, 1953–January 8, 1954
Black & White — Live
Origination: Studio A (106th Street Studios), New York City
Annotations: Chapters 4, 7
Aural Antecedent: Original storyline and characters "borrowed" from the author's successful *When a Girl Marries*, based on scripts aired 14 years earlier, from 1939 to 1941, CBS Radio; 1941–51, NBC Radio; 1951–57, ABC Radio
Sponsor: Sustaining
Broadcast Schedule:
August 3, 1953–January 8, 1954   M–F   11:45 a.m.–12:00 Noon   NBC
Creator-Writer: Elaine Sterne Carrington
Producer: Adrian Samish
Director: Norman Morgan
Announcer: Don Pardo
Cast: *Julie Fielding* Sallie Brophy; *Mrs. Fielding* Nancy Sheridan; *Peter Davis* Grant Williams; *Samuel Tilden Fielding* John Seymour; *Jocelyn Fielding* Laura Weber; *Harry Phillips* Howard Erskine; *Sharon Richard* Maxine Stuart; *Mrs. MacDonald* Anne Seymour
Plot: In what appeared to be two dramas in one, the story began with an engagement that was abruptly broken off by the heroine, Julie Fielding, so she could pursue a new love in her life, Peter

Davis, to the vexation of her socialite mom. When viewers rejected that theme, however — one the author lifted from the outline of her radio serial *When a Girl Marries* 14 years earlier — the premise changed dramatically. Peter's work as an FBI crusader took center stage, complete with all the accouterments that could be anticipated (desperadoes, blackmail, deception, drugs, seduction, kidnapping, et al.). The viewers en masse, however, would have little of it, and another serial bit the dust in just five months, 15 days short of Julie and Peter's planned nuptials. It was not a smooth exodus.

For Better or Worse

June 29, 1959–June 24, 1960
Black & White — Videotape
Origination: Studio 41 (CBS Television City), Los Angeles
Annotations: Chapter 7
Packager: John Guedel Productions
Sponsor: Lever Brothers
Agency: SSC & B
Broadcast Schedule:
June 29, 1959–June 24, 1960   M–F   2:00–2:30 p.m.   CBS
Producer-Director: Hal Cooper
Music: Kip Walton
Host-Announcer: Jim Bannon
Commentator: Dr. James A. Peterson
Also in the company: Barry Cahill, Dyan Cannon, Ronald Foster, Peggy McCay, William Redfield, Marge Redmond, June Walker

Plot: This was an anthology of three-week-long romantic tales that posed interesting dilemmas for a psychologist and a narrator to discuss before presenting each new chapter. The show was one of the first in daytime to be videotaped and produced in Hollywood. It didn't fare well, however, losing lots of the audience delivered by *As the World Turns* immediately preceding its airing.

From These Roots

June 30, 1958–December 29, 1961
Black & White — Live
Origination: Studio 3A (30 Rockefeller Plaza), New York City
Annotations: Chapter 4
Sponsors: Procter & Gamble, Alberto-Culver
Agencies: Benton and Bowles (P&G), Geoffrey Wade Advertising (Alberto-Culver)
Broadcast Schedule:
June 30, 1958–December 29, 1961   M–F   3:30–4:00 p.m.   NBC
Creators-Writers: John Pickard and Frank Provo
Producers: Paul Lammers, Don Wallace
Directors: Don Wallace, Paul Lammers, Leonard Valenta, Joseph Behar
Announcer: Mel Brandt
Cast: *Liz Fraser Allen* Ann Flood, Susan Brown (temporarily, 1959); *Ben Fraser Sr.* Grant Code (1958), Rod Hendrickson (1958–61), Joseph Macauley (1961); *Emily Fraser Benson Teton* Helen Shields; *Jim Benson* Henderson Forsythe; *Frank Teton* George Smith; *Ben Fraser Jr.* Frank Marth; *Rose Corelli Fraser* Julia Bovasso (1958–60), Tresa Hughes (1960–61); *Bruce Crawford* Byron Sanders; *Dr. Buck Weaver* Len Wayland; *David Allen* Robert Mandan; *Enid Chambers Allen* Mary Alice Moore; *Lynn Franklin* Barbara Berjer; *Tom Jennings* Craig Huebing; *Lyddy Benson* Sarah Hardy; *Tim Benson* John Stewart; *Dan Fraser* Dan White; *Kass* Vera Allen; *Maggie Barker Weaver* Billie Lou Watt; *Lance* David Daniels; *Luisa Corelli* Dolores Sutton; *Artie Corelli* Frank Campanella; *Jimmy Hull* John Colenback; *Gloria Saxon* Millette Alexander; *Hilda Furman* Charlotte Rae; *Richard* Richard Thomas; *Laura Tompkins* Audra Lindley; *Fred Barnes* Tom Shirley; *George Weimer* Donald Madden; *Jack Lander* Joseph Mascolo; *Jamie* Alan Howard; *Nate Tompkins* Ward Costello; *Peggy Tompkins Benson* Mae

Munro (1958–59), Ursula Stevens (1959), Ellen Madison (1959–61); *Stanley Kreiser* Leon Janney; *Mildred Barnes* Sarah Burton; *Dr. McAndrew* Charles Egleston; *Peggy Tomkins* Mae Munroe; *Robin* Gary Morgan. *Note:* As the serial ended early in the 1960s, the complete cast is included here.

Plot: The most successful soap operas were those that were family-oriented, focusing on one clan and the complications resulting when its members tested the waters against the norms set by the body. *From These Roots* followed that pattern, revolving around the Frasers of Stratfield in New England. Patriarch Ben Sr. was the town's newspaper publisher. After he suffered a heart attack, his only unmarried offspring, Liz, a fiction author, returned from the nation's capitol to assume the paper's reins. Son Ben Jr. ran the faltering family farm; he did well despite several interventions, and was elected town mayor in due course. The eldest daughter of Ben Sr., Emily, divorced her philandering husband Jim and then wed the district attorney. Jim was later bumped off. By the show's end, the Frasers controlled the mayoral and D. A. offices of their little community, as well as the newspaper. Most tribes didn't do as well. Liz had several serious admirers and eventually picked an inconsistent playwright, David Allen, for a life partner. He had married and divorced less than 12 months before their vows. Liz ultimately forgave him after he fooled around with Lynn Franklin, an actress who imbibed heavily, and the couple seemed relatively content as the story came to an end.

Golden Windows

July 5, 1954–April 8, 1955
Black & White — Live
Origination: Studio B (101 West 67th Street), New York City
Sponsor: Procter & Gamble (Cheer, on an alternating schedule of Monday/Wednesday/Friday one week and Tuesday/Thursday the next)
Agency: Young & Rubicam
Annotations: Chapter 4
Broadcast Schedule:
July 5, 1954–April 8, 1955   M–F   3:15–3:30 p.m.   NBC
Producers: Mary Harris, Thomas Riley
Director: Dan Levin
Writers: John M. Young and Corlis Wilbur
Cast: *Juliet Goodwin* Leila Martin; *Charles Goodwin* Eric Dressler; *John Brandon* Grant Sullivan; *Joseph Kindler* Frank Hammerton; *Tom Anderson* Herbert Patterson; *Carl Grant* Joe De Santis; *Ann Summers* Sonny Adams; *Ruth Brandon* Harriet MacGibbon; *Dr. Paul Anderson* Philip Pine; *Otto* Martin Kosleck; *Ellen Stockwell* Millicent Brower; *Streicher* E. A. Krumschmidt; *Hazel* Barbara Cook; *Jane Talbert* Vicki Cummings; *Larry* Dean Harens; *Miss Bigelow* Ethel Remey; *Lieutenant Thomas* Ralph Camargo

Plot: Ditching both fiancée and foster father in her native Maine, impulsive Juliet Goodwin tore off to Gotham to seek her fortune as a singer. There she encountered new men to help her forget the one she left behind. She helped one, Tom Anderson, get out of trouble with the law. Then he took a hike, evidently not looking back either. Meanwhile, her ex wasted little time getting hitched at home. Juliet next fell for a doctor, improving her circumstances. She sang on the air occasionally, too, a custom that wouldn't become standard in soap opera until another two decades. Before her story folded, she was abducted by a pair of reprehensible criminals and eventually released, just in time to go on living "happily ever after." But don't bet the rent.

The Greatest Gift

August 30, 1954–July 1, 1955
Black & White — Live
Origination: WPTZ–TV, Philadelphia
Annotations: Chapter 4
Sponsor: Sustaining
Broadcast Schedule:
August 30, 1954–April 1, 1955   M–F   3:00–3:15 p.m.   NBC

April 4, 1955–July 1, 1955   M–F   3:30–3:45 p.m.   NBC
Creator: Adrian Samish
Producer: Al Morrison
Directors: Joseph Behar, Ben Squires (substitute from Nov. 29–Dec. 10, 1954)
Writer: James P. Cavanaugh
Cast: *Dr. Eve Allen* Anne Burr; *Dr. Phil Stone* Philip Foster; *Fran Allen* Janet Ward; *Ned Blackman* Ward Costello (early), Gene Peterson (late); *Harold (Hal) Matthews* Martin Balsam (early), Will Hare (late); *Betty Matthews* Athena Lorde; *Jim Hanson* Jack Klugman; *Lee Connor* Marian Russell; *Harriet* Anne Meara; *Sam Blake* Josef Drake; *Peter Blake* Henry Barnard; *Mrs. Blake* Helen Warren

Plot: In this medical drama, Dr. Eve Allen returned from Korea to assume her late uncle's medical practice in Ridgeton amid a doubting local clientele. They hadn't encountered a woman doctor before, and — as for that — neither had most daytime television viewers until then. Eve conducted herself in an erratic fashion, delving into the personal trials of her patients and others while dallying on the side with another physician, Phil Stone, in an oft-turbulent liaison. The drama, seemingly unfocused for a long spell, dwelled on the baby black market as it wound toward its inevitable conclusion, hardly making a noticeable impression.

The Guiding Light

June 30, 1952–present
Black & White, Color — Live, Videotape
Origination: Studio 56 (Liederkranz Hall), New York City, early 1950s; Studio 41 (Grand Central Terminal Studios), New York City, late 1950s
Annotations: Chapters 6, 7, 10
Aural Antecedent: 1937–46 (but not continuous), NBC Radio; 1947–56, CBS Radio
Theme Song: "Aphrodite" (Goetzl), 1952–56; "Romance" from *Violin Concerto No. 2 in D Minor* (Wieniawski), 1956–March 10, 1967
Opening Billboard: While the camera focused on a sketch of a lighthouse, the announcer introduced initial installments with "The new Duz brings you *The Guiding Light*." That depiction was altered by 1953 to the sun's rays bursting through a cloudy sky, the title materializing in three lines of white block Futura Bold italic type in all caps. A couple of years later the image reverted to the lighthouse at night, positioned in the extreme right-hand corner of the screen and set along a coastline, a triple-line Futura Bold italicized moniker to the left. The most enduring logo of the period, from about 1956 through March 10, 1967, featured the tri-line appellation in bold Clarendon type overlaid on a horizontal spotlight beam shining from the northeast to the southwest.
Sponsor: Procter & Gamble (Duz, Ivory, Crisco)
Agency: Compton Advertising
Broadcast Schedule:
June 30, 1952–December 26, 1952   M–F   2:30–2:45 p.m.   CBS
December 29, 1952–September 6, 1968   M–F   12:45–1:00 p.m.   CBS
September 9, 1968–September 1, 1972   M–F   2:30–3:00 p.m.   CBS
September 4, 1972–November 28, 1975   M–F   2:00–2:30 p.m.   CBS
December 1, 1975–November 4, 1977   M–F   2:30–3:00 p.m.   CBS
November 7, 1977–February 1, 1980   M–F   2:30–3:30 p.m.   CBS
February 4, 1980–present   M–F   3:00–4:00 p.m.   CBS
Creator: Irna Phillips
Executive Producers: Lucy Ferri Rittenberg, Allen Potter, Gail Kobe, Joe Willmore, more (specific years undocumented)
Producers: David Lesan, Richard Dunn, Peter Andrews, Harry Eggart, Charlotte Savitz, Leslie Kwartin, Joe Willmore, Robert Calhoun, John P. Whitesell II, Robert D. Kochman, Kathlyn Chambers, more
Directors: Ted Corday, Walter Gorman, Jack Wood, Leonard Valenta, Nick Havinga, John Ritvack, Jeff Bleckner, Peter Miner, John Sedwick, Allen Fristoe, Harry Eggart, Lynwood King, John Pasquin, Michael Gliona, Bruce Barry, Jill Mitwell, John P. Whitesell II, Irene M. Pace, Dan Smith, Matthew Diamond, Scott McKinsey, M. J. McDonnell, Joe Ann Rivituso, Jo Anne Sedwick, more

Head Writers: Irna Phillips, Agnes Nixon (1950s)
Organists: Rosa Rio (1950s), William Meeder (1950s)
Announcers: Clayton (Bud) Collyer (1950s), Hal Simms
Cast: *Rev. Dr. Paul Keeler* Ed Begley (1952), Melville Ruick (1952–54); *Bertha (Bert) Miller Bauer* Charita Bauer; *Bill Bauer* Lyle Sudrow (1952–59), Ed Bryce (1959–63, 1965–69, 1977–78, 1983); *Michael (Mike) Bauer* Glenn Walken (1954–56), Michael Allen (1959–62); *Edward Bauer* Pat Collins; *Meta Bauer White Roberts Banning* Jone Allison (1952), Ellen Demming (1953–74); *Kathy Roberts Lang Grant Holden* Susan Douglas; *Dr. Richard (Dick) Grant* James Lipton; *Robin Lang Holden Bauer* Zina Bethune (1956–58), Judy Robinson (1959–60); *Janet Johnson* Ruth Warrick (1953–54), Lois Wheeler (1954–58); *Dr. Jim Kelly* Paul Potter; *Marie Wallace Kelly* Joyce Holden (1954), Lynne Rogers (1955–62); *Philip Collins Kelly* Carson Woods; *Joe Roberts* Herb Nelson; *Mark Holden* Whitfield Connor; *Ruth Jannings Holden* Irja Jensen (1958), Louise Platt (1958–59), Virginia Dwyer (1959–60); *Dr. Bruce Banning* Les Damon; *Karl Jannings* Richard Morse; *Trudy Bauer* Helen Wagner (1952), Lisa Howard (1957–58); *Papa Bauer* Theodore Goetz; *Joey Roberts* Tarry Green (1952–53), Richard Holland (1953); *Sid Harper* Philip Sterling; *Gloria LaRue Harper* Anne Burr; *Laura Grant* Katherine Anderson (1953), Alice Yourman (1953–62); *Lila Taylor* Nancy Wickwire (1954–55), Teri Keane (1957); *Dr. Paul Fletcher* Michael Kane (1956), Bernard Grant (1956–70); *Anne Benedict Fletcher* Joan Gray; *Alice Holden* Sandy Dennis (1956), Diane Gentner (1956–58), Lin Pierson (1958–60); *Elsie Miller Franklin* Ethel Remey; *Helene Benedict* Kay Campbell; *Henry Benedict* John Gibson; *Joe Turino* Joseph Campanella; *Alex Bowden* Ernest Graves; *Amy Sinclair* Joanne Linville. *Note: Only actors signed prior to 1960 are named here due to this volume's emphasis on golden age serials.*
Plot: At its inception, when the soap opera was still running on radio and pursuing the same script but aired at a separate hour, a CBS press release described it as "the poignant story of the problems confronting Meta Roberts and her husband, Joe." The serial, said a publicist, "develops human problems from cause to solution and has covered many facts in the lives of the residents of the underprivileged community of Selby Flats." But not for long. Early on the drama and its denizens left the village outside Los Angeles to relocate in the municipality of Springfield in an unidentified Midwestern state. The Bauer family was at the apex of the story from its TV start and would remain so for more than three decades. But Meta and Joe didn't occupy center stage for very long. He died and she found fulfillment with another mate. Meta's brother Bill, and, more importantly, his wife Bertha (Bert) and their two offspring, dominated the yarn for most of the 1950s, 1960s and 1970s. Plots were characterized by interpersonal strife, alcoholism, infidelities, self-centeredness, divorce, annulments, physical maladies, violent accidental deaths and an occasional murder — the stuff of which lasting serials were composed. There was also a sensible Papa Bauer, the head of the clan, who had a moderating effect on its members. Adored by all, he witnessed a strong-willed Bert, given to narcissism at the drama's video launch, gradually melt into a compassionate, warm-hearted family matriarch, having fully acquired the elderly man's genuine love for all humanity.

Hawkins Falls

June 17, 1950–July 1, 1955
Black & White — Live with videotape exteriors
Origination: WNBQ-TV, Chicago
Annotations: Chapter 3
Theme Song: "Skip to My Lou"
Sponsor: Lever Brothers (Surf)
Agency: N. W. Ayer
Broadcast Schedule:
June 17, 1950–August 19, 1950   Sat   8:00–9:00 p.m.   NBC
August 24, 1950–October 12, 1950   Thur   8:30–9:00 p.m.   NBC
April 2, 1951–July 3, 1953   M–F   5:00–5:15 p.m.   NBC
July 6, 1953–January 8, 1954   M–F   11–11:15 a.m.   NBC
January 11, 1954–July 2, 1954   M–F   12:15–12:30 p.m.   NBC
July 5, 1954–July 1, 1955   M–F   4:00–4:15 p.m.   NBC
Creator: Roy Winsor and Doug Johnson
Producer: Ben Park

Director: Frank Pacelli
Writers: Doug Johnson, Bill Barrett
Announcer: Hugh Downs
Cast: *Clate Weathers* (in primetime) Frank Dane; *Judge* Phil Lord; *Laif Flaigle* Win Stracke; *Mrs. Belinda Catherwood* Hope Summers; *Knap Drewer* Frank Dane; *Roy Bettert* Bruce Dane; *Lona Drewer Corey* Bernadine Flynn; *Dr. Floyd Corey* Michael Golda (1952–53), Maurice Copeland (c1953–55); *Toby Winfield* Tom Poston; *Millie Flagle* Ros Twohey; *Sheriff Boylan* Doug Chandler; *Mitch Fredericks* Jim Bannon; *Dr. Glen Bowdon* Lee Henry; *Calvin Sperry* Art Van Harvey; *Elmira Cleebe* Elmira Roessler; *Spec Bassett* Russ Reed; *Betty Sawtel* Helen Bernie. *Also in the cast:* Barbara Berjer, Jackie Berkey, Jean Christian, Richard Clary, Peter Donat, Marie Engstrand-Brady, Sam Gray, Bill Griskey, Will Hussing, Carlton KaDell, Arthur Peterson, Ron Tomme, Emmet Vogan, Beverly Younger
Plot: Originally a weekly nighttime comedy-drama set in the hayseed community of Hawkins Falls, the homespun yarn was reprised six months after it originally left the air. In its comeback it appeared as a daytime serial. Surprisingly, the show not only survived beyond historical NBC–TV soap opera traditions but also thrived, continuing in that format for four more years and establishing a precedent for the web. The storyline revolved around typical characters in rural Americana and the day-to-day events in those figures' lives. To hold viewer interest, murder, illicit relationships, estrangement and divorce were introduced. Principals included Knap Drewer, Lona Drewer Corey, Belinda Catherwood, Dr. Floyd Corey and Laif Flagle. There were many others who were summoned sporadically to stir the action.

Hotel Cosmopolitan

August 19, 1957–April 11, 1958
Black & White — Live
Origination: Studio 58 (Town Theater), New York City
Annotations: Chapter 7
Theme Song: "A Portrait in Rhythm" (John Gart)
Packager: Roy Winsor Productions
Sponsor: Swift & Company (partial), Sustaining, American Home Products (Anacin, Bi-So-Dol, Dristan, Freezone, Heet, Infrarub, Kolynos, Kriptin, Neet, Preparation H, Primatene, Sleep-Eze, et al.)
Broadcast Schedule:
August 19, 1957–April 11, 1958   M–F   12:00–12:15 p.m.   CBS
Producer: Ernest Ricca
Director: John Desmond
Organist: Charles Paul
Cast: Donald Woods (host-narrator); Henderson Forsythe (house detective). *Also in the company:* Walter Brooke, John Holmes, James Pritchett, Tom Shirley, Dinna Smith
Plot: Can the guests of a hotel provide enough incentive for TV watchers to drop what they are doing to view the exploits every day at lunchtime? CBS bet that they could. When *Valiant Lady* folded after nearly four years, the web rolled out this series of mythical tales about a New York inn's clientele and their supposedly fascinating lives. Donald Woods narrated and Henderson Forsythe was a house detective, while the customers came and went. Ultimately not enough viewers were mesmerized by the omnibus approach, however, and the show left the air less than eight months after its debut.

The House on High Street

September 28, 1959–February 5, 1960
Black & White — Videotape
Origination: Studio A (67th Street Studios), New York City
Annotations: Chapter 4
Sponsors: Sterling Drugs, Procter & Gamble, Alberto-Culver, Chesebrough-Ponds
Agencies: Dancer-Fitzgerald-Sample (Sterling, P&G), Wade Advertising (Alberto-Culver), J. Walter Thompson (Chesebrough-Ponds)

Broadcast Schedule:
September 28, 1959–February 5, 1960   M–F   4:00–4:30 p.m.   NBC
Executive Producer: Roger Gimbel
Producer: John Haggart
Directors: Elliot Silverstein, Lela Swift
Writers: William Kendall Clarke, James Elward
Announcer: Roger Bowman
Cast: Philip Abbott (as John Collier); Judge James Gehrig (as himself, a former domestic relations court justice); Dr. Harris B. Peck (as himself, a former court psychiatrist). *Also in the company:* Alan Alda, Martin Balsam, Patricia Bosworth, William Cottrell, Irene Dailey, Leora Dana, Shaun Dooley, Clay Hall, Frances Heflin, Lynn Loring, Donald Madden, Enid Markey, Anne Meacham, Kay Medford, Sylvia Miles, Jan Miner, Dorothy Rice, Frances Sternhagen, others

Plot: In one of the first daytime serials to be videotaped, the series offered three- to five-part dramas about divorce and juvenile delinquency that were purportedly drawn from actual case histories. Caseworker John Collier provided continuity, along with a couple of experts who offered their respected opinions.

Kitty Foyle

January 13, 1958–June 27, 1958
Black & White — Live
Origination: Studio 8G (30 Rockefeller Plaza), New York City
Production Company: Henry Jaffee Enterprises, Inc.
Annotations: Chapters 4, 7
Aural Antecedent: 1941–44, CBS Radio
Theme Song: "Kitty" (Carl Sigman)
Sponsors: Sustaining, Multiple Participation
Broadcast Schedule:
January 13, 1958–June 27, 1958   M–F   2:30–3:00 p.m.   NBC
Executive Producer: Charles Irving
Directors: Hal Cooper, Al Beaumont
Writers: Carlton E. Morse, Sarett Rudley (assistant)
Organist: William Meeder
Announcer: Bill Wendell
Cast: *Kitty Foyle* Kathleen Murray; *Flip Martin* Conrad Fowkes; *Pop Foyle* Ralph Dunn; *Ed Foyle* Bob Hastings; *Mack Foyle* Larry Robinson; *Sophie Foyle* Kay Medford (early), Teri Keane (late); *Wyn Strafford* William Redfield; *Nick Amsted* Lee Bergere; *Stacylea Balla* Marie Worsham; *Molly Scharf* Judy Lewis; *Olivia Strafford* Valerie Cossart; *Rosemont (Rosie) Rittenhouse* Les Damon; *Mr. Strafford* Staats Cotsworth; *Myrtle* Mae Barnes; *Della* Arlene Golonka; *Cora* Jeanne Barr; *Mr. Balla* Casey Allen; *Dorothy Sayers* Julienne Marie; *Kennett* Jan Marlin; *Mac Hoyle* Larry Robinson; *Danny Foyle* Ralph Bell; *Kitty Foyle* (as a youngster) Patty Duke; *Molly Scharf* (as a youngster) Judy Sanford; *Oscar* Martin Newman; *Lola* Ann Carroll; *Delphine DeTaille* Lisa Ferraday; *Carolyn Foyle* Marian Winters. *Also in the cast:* Ginger McManus, Rosetta LeMoire, Karl Weber

Plot: Based on earlier novel, film and radio incarnations, *Kitty Foyle* offered a convoluted plot that swirled about an Irish lass who hailed from the sticks. The tale constantly revealed her inability to establish a rewarding relationship with a prosperous snob. Not only was her love life in peril, she had siblings whose elevators didn't seem to go all the way to the top, and who kept making bad decisions. In the midst of the turmoil was her adoring father, who was on the sick list. While the Philadelphia-set story may have begun with a worthy premise (matching waif and wastrel), in the end it left something to be desired. The technique of keeping the heroine out of sight for the first month could have doomed it beyond repair — the critics weren't kind. More than one blamed poor literary quality. It was obvious the viewers didn't care much about Kitty or what happened to her, and as a result her show didn't make it as a TV commodity, evaporating within six months.

Love of Life

September 24, 1951–February 1, 1980
Black & White, Color (from April 1967) — **Live, Videotape**
Origination: Studio 54 (Liederkranz Hall), New York City, early 1950s; Studio 56 (Liederkranz Hall), New York City, late 1950s
Annotations: Chapter 9
Theme Song: "Love of Life" (Chet Kingsbury), September 24, 1951–spring 1967
Opening Billboard: In the early years announcer Don Hancock, who also delivered most of the serial's live commercials (which were abundant), daily stood before a camera offering this cold proclamation (meaning that nothing preceded it): "Hello everyone. Don Hancock speaking. Welcome to *Love of Life*." The scene shifted to the title icon as an organ hastily — possibly urgently — belted out the identifying theme in C-Major key. Ornamented in expansive, gracefully distinctive calligraphy, the appellation emerged as a descending triple line banner superimposed over the stylish fountain adorning the exterior of New York City's Plaza Hotel. After a cowcatcher commercial, the visual reappeared as announcer Charles Mountain opined: "*Love of Life*, the exciting story of Vanessa Dale and her courageous struggle for human dignity." During that brief interlude, accompanied by the organ theme, partial cast credits were shown in a white Lydian bold font in all caps on an indented dark gray screen. A longer commercial followed before the day's installment commenced in earnest. In 1958 the opening visuals were twice altered. Initially a time-lapse shot of a flower opening surfaced as the announcer imparted: "To live each day for whatever life may bring — this is *Love of Life*." The image was quickly displaced by a twinkling nocturnal sky, possibly synonymous with the inception of the half-hour episodes in April 1958.
Sponsors: American Home Products, Procter & Gamble
Agencies: Ted Bates & Company (AHP), Tathan-Laird (P&G)
Production Companies: Milton H. Biow Company (1951–55), Roy Winsor Productions (1955–69)
Broadcast Schedule:
September 24, 1951–April 11, 1958	M–F	12:15–12:30 p.m.	CBS
April 14, 1958–September 28, 1962	M–F	12:00–12:30 p.m.	CBS
October 1, 1962–September 5, 1969	M–F	12:00–12:25 p.m.	CBS
September 8, 1969–March 23, 1973	M–F	11:30–12:00 a.m.	CBS
March 26, 1973–April 20, 1979	M–F	11:30–11:55 a.m.	CBS
April 23, 1979–February 1, 1980	M–F	4:00–4:30 p.m.	CBS

Creator: Roy Winsor
Executive Producers: Roy Winsor, Al Morrison, Bertram Berman, Darryl Hickman (complete run — specific years undocumented)
Producers: Charles Schenck, Richard Dunn, Ernest Ricca, John Green, Robert Driscoll, Joseph Hardy, Tony Converse, Freyda Rothstein, Tom Donovan, Jean Arley, Cathy Abbi (complete run)
Directors: Larry Auerbach (executive from start to finish), Burt Brinckerhoff, Art Wolff, Jerry Evans, Gordon Rigsby, Robert Myhrum, Dino Narizzano, Heather H. Hill, Lynwood King, Robert Nigro, Robert Scinto, John Pasquin (complete run)
Head Writers: John D. Hess, Harry Junkin, Dom Errlinger, John Pickard and Frank Provo, Lillian and Martin Andrews, Loring Mandel, Robert Soderberg, Robert J. Shaw, Roy Winsor, Eileen and Robert Mason Pollock, Ray Goldstone, Paul Roberts and Don Wallace, Esther and Richard Shapiro, Claire Labine and Paul Avila Mayer, Margaret DePriest, Paul and Margaret Schneider, Gabrielle Upton, Jean Holloway, Ann Marcus (complete run)
Organist: John Gart
Announcers: Charles Mountain (1950s), Don Hancock (commercials, 1950s), Herbert Duncan (late 1950s–early 1960s)
Cast: *Vanessa Dale Raven Sterling* Peggy McCay (1951–55), Bonnie Bartlett (1955–59), Audrey Peters (1959–80); *Meg Dale Harper Andrews Craythorne Aleata Hart* Jean McBride; *Will Dale* Edwin Jerome; *Sarah Dale* Jane Rose; *Charles Harper* Paul Potter (1951–53), John Graham (1953); *Ben (Beanie) Harper* Dennis Parnell (1951–57), Tommy White (1957–58); *Ellie Crown* Hildy Parks (1951–55), Mary K. Wells (1955–56), Bethel Leslie (1956); *Miles Pardee* Joe Allen Jr.; *Evans Baker* Ronald Long; *Paul Raven* Richard Coogan (1951–58), Robert Burr (1970–72, aka Matt Corby); *Warren Nash* Grant Richards; *Collie Jordan* Carl Betz; *Carol Raven* Tirell Barbery; *Judith Lodge Raven*

Virginia Robinson; *Matt Slocum* Burt French; *Hal Craig* Steven Gethers; *Ben Raven* David Lewis; *Jack Andrews* Donald Symington; *Tom Craythorne* Lauren Gilbert; *Tammy Forrest* Scottie McGregor (1956), Ann Loring (1956–70); *Noel Penn* Gene Peterson; *Bruce Sterling* Ron Tomme; *Barbara Sterling* Nina Reader; *Alan Sterling* Jim Bayer; *Ginny Crandall* Barbara Barrie; *Maggie Porter* Joan Copeland; *Link Porter* Gene Pellegrini; *Mrs. Rivers* Marie Kenney; *Marty* Earl Montgomery; *Vivian Carlson* Eleanor Wilson (1959), Helene Dumas (1959–71); *Henry Carlson* Tom Shirley; *Dr. Tony Vento* Ron Jackson; *Cindy Craythorne* Kimetha Laurie; *Rick Latimer* Paul Savior; *Alex Crown* Russell Thorson; *Jill Crown* Natalie Priest; *Althea Raven* Joanna Roos. *Also in the cast:* Dennis Parnell. Note: *Only actors signed prior to 1960 are listed due to this volume's emphasis on golden age serials.*

Plot: A pair of siblings exhibiting contradictory moral stances were at the apex of the storyline as the serial began, and remained so during much of its initial seven and final half-dozen years on the air. A compassionate Vanessa Dale respected family and friends, while her sister Meg pursued personal pleasure at the expense of others. Their enduring conflict, consistently an undercurrent in the plotting even when not on the front burner, contributed many tension-filled sequences. The story was filled with multiple marriages (of both women); mystery and mayhem provoked by the unscrupulous men (often with underworld connections) whom Meg introduced as lovers and spouses; frequent murder trials (often with the principals as the accused); ongoing dilemmas involving various offspring; and ethical lapses in endless permutations. The serial was at the forefront of the sexual revolution and all of its implications. Upon departing the air, the drama left many plots unresolved as producers anticipated that another network would rush to the show's aid and pick it up for continuation elsewhere. It didn't happen and the audience was left dangling—an unsatisfying scheme for saying good-bye.

Miss Susan/Martinsville, U.S.A.

March 12, 1951–December 28, 1951
Black & White—Live
Origination: WPTZ–TV, Philadelphia
Annotations: Chapter 3
Theme Song: "Ballet of the Flowers" (C. Fischer)
Sponsor: Colgate-Palmolive-Peet (Ajax, Fab)
Agency: William Estey
Broadcast Schedule:
March 12, 1951–December 28, 1951   M–F   3:00–3:15 p.m.   NBC
Producer: Ted Ashley
Director: Kenneth Buckridge
Writers: William Kendall Clarke, Helen Walpole, Norman Lessing, Alice Marcus
Announcer: Earl Gill
Cast: *Susan Martin* Susan Peters; *Laura* Helen Ray; *Bill Carter* Mark Roberts; *Mrs. Peck* Kathryn Grill; *Roger Nystrom* Robert McQueeney; *Daisy* Natalie Priest; *Sam Martin* Don Hanmer; *Chris Martin* Ralph Robertson; *Mrs. Benson* Florence Dunlap; *Joan Benson* Gerry Lock; *Judge Brown* Robert Pike; *Gus* Bill Brower; *Sergeant Stengle* Frank Sutton; *Mr. Croft* Joseph Foley; *Andrea Blake* Elaine Ellis; *Bruce Langdon* Robert Courtleigh; *Duke Andrews* Arnie Freeman (early), Ken Bukreder (late); *Ruth* Lucy Vries; *Miles* Ted Newton. *Also in the cast:* Jon Lormer, Betsy Palmer

Plot: Susan Martin was a lady attorney confined to a wheelchair. Susan Peters, a real paraplegic and ex–movie actress, played the heroine. As the drama began, Susan (Martin) had decided to leave the big city and return to her family mansion in Martinsville, Ohio. For many of her decisions her physical impediment influenced the outcome, and her health issues were an ongoing part of the dialogue. She was in love with Bill Carter, who frequently boasted of his plans for a large family. Bill, however, hadn't yet learned that Susan could never produce children. The tale didn't last long enough for the pair to wed. When a public outcry erupted over the perceived exploitation of Susan Peter's real-life misfortune, the title was quickly altered to *Martinsville, U.S.A.*, and attempts were made to focus the yarn on other characters. In real life, Susan Peters was not doing well physically, and critics weren't kind to the series either. The sponsor decided it could more profitably offer viewers a game show instead. Susan Peters died shortly after the show's cancellation.

Modern Romances

October 4, 1954–September 19, 1958
Black & White — Live
Origination: Studio 8G (30 Rockefeller Plaza), New York City (premier); Century Theater, New York City (later)
Annotations: Chapters 4, 7
Aural Antecedents: 1936–37, NBC Blue Radio; 1949–51, ABC Radio; 1953, NBC Radio; 1953–55 ABC Radio
Sponsors: Multiple Participation (Alberto-Culver, Brillo, Colgate-Palmolive-Peet, Corn Products, Dixie Cup, Kraft, Miles Laboratories, Sterling Drugs)
Broadcast Schedule:
October 4, 1954–December 30, 1955   M–F   4:45–5:00 p.m.   NBC
January 2, 1956–June 29, 1956   M–F   4:15–4:30 p.m.   NBC
July 2, 1956–September 19, 1958   M–F   4:45–5:00 p.m.   NBC
Director: H. Wesley Kenney
Writer: Harry W. Junkin
Hosts: Martha Scott (October 4, 1954–November 29, 1957); Mel Brandt (December 2, 1957–March 28, 1958); Weekly celebrity guests (March 31, 1958–September 19, 1958). *Also in the company:* Millette Alexander, Augusta Dabney, Ann Flood, Marjorie Gateson, Don Hastings, Phyllis Hill, Georgann Johnson, Robert Mandan, Meg Mundy, William Prince, Paul Stevens, Lawrence Weber, Mary K. Wells

Plot: A collection of confessional tales narrated by Martha Scott, Mel Brandt and eventually a weekly guest pop idol, the fiction presented in five-part installments was loosely based on stories published in *Modern Romances* magazine. At its debut the program was still airing on ABC Radio (through February 25, 1955). The television reception was a cause for some rejoicing at NBC; no daytime dramatic vehicle had worked as successfully for the web since the debut of *Hawkins Falls* in 1951. *Modern Romances* enticed NBC to subsequently pursue other anthologies for its sunlight schedule.

One Man's Family

November 4, 1949–April 1, 1955
Black & White — Live
Origination: Studio 3 (NBC Television), Burbank
Annotations: Chapters 4, 7
Aural Antecedent: Original storyline and characters "borrowed" from the audio version nearly two decades earlier, from 1932 tri-station West Coast radio hookup; 1932–33, NBC Radio West Coast stations; 1933–59, NBC Radio
Sponsor: U. S. Army, Sustaining (e.g., public service announcements for forest fire prevention featuring Smoky the Bear)
Agency: Lord & Taylor
Broadcast Schedule:
November 4, 1949–January 1950   Friday   8:00–8:30 p.m.   NBC
January 1950–May 1950   Thursday   8:30–9:00 p.m.   NBC
July 1950–June 21, 1952 (off summer 1951)   Saturday   7:30–8:00 p.m.   NBC
March 1, 1954–July 2, 1954   M–F   10:30–10:45 a.m.   NBC
July 5, 1954–August 27, 1954   M–F   3:00–3:15 p.m.   NBC
August 30, 1954–April 1, 1955   M–F   3:30–3:45 p.m.   NBC
Creator: Carlton E. Morse
Producers: Richard Clemmer, Gino Conte
Director: Jack Smight
Writer: Carlton E. Morse
Organist: Paul Watson
Announcer: Don Stanley
Cast (daytime version only): *Henry Barbour* Theodore von Eltz; *Fanny Barbour* Mary Adams; *Hazel Barbour* Linda Leighton; *Jack Barbour* Martin Dean; *Clifford Barbour* James Lee; *Paul Barbour*

Russell Thorson; *Claudia Barbour* Anne Whitfield; *Johnny Roberts* Jack Edwards; *Johnny MacPherson* Glen Vernon; *Joe Yarborough* Roy Engel; *Beth Holly* Lois Hall; *Bill Herbert* Les Tremayne; *Dr. Fred Thompson* Emerson Treacy

Plot: Two attempts to create a television series based on an award-winning radio show that lasted 27 years ended in failure both times. More than one critic laid much of the blame at the producers' initial insistence that the show revert back to radio's starting storyline, which occurred in 1932; but the subsequent effort to transfer the tale to the present fared no better. It didn't attract enough viewers with either try. *One Man's Family* was one of radio's warmest, most compelling and beloved family dramas across the decades. It concerned a conformist patriarch, Henry Barbour, and his mellowed wife, Fanny, and their "bewildering offspring"—a generally unconventional clan of five children who were often at odds with their father's conservative lifestyle. Barbour was a prosperous banker. The family dwelled in upper-middle-class digs in the Sea Cliff section of San Francisco overlooking the Golden Gate Bridge. The romantic pursuits of the Barbour brood, as well as the continuing conflicts between generations, took center stage during the 13-month reprisal in daytime serialization. The same premise hadn't worked satisfactorily as a primetime half-hour a few years before. Millions of fans still tuned in the altogether separate storyline (22 years beyond the one debuting on TV in 1954) every night on their radios but apparently didn't want to see what might have transpired with the Barbours in the early 1930s—*again.*

Portia Faces Life/The Inner Flame

April 5, 1954–July 1, 1955
Black & White — Live
Origination: Studio 53 (Liederkranz Hall), New York City
Annotations: Chapter 7
Aural Antecedent: 1940–41, CBS Radio; 1941–44, NBC Radio; 1944, CBS Radio; 1944–51, NBC Radio
Sponsor: General Foods (Post Grape-Nuts Flakes, Postum, Swans Down, et al.)
Agency: Young & Rubicam
Broadcast Schedule:
April 5, 1954–July 1, 1955   M–F   1:00–1:15 p.m.   CBS
Creator: Mona Kent
Producer: Beverly Smith
Director: Lloyd Gross
Writer: Mona Kent
Guitarist: Tony Mottola
Announcer: Bill Shipley
Cast: *Portia Blake Manning* Frances Reid (1954), Fran Carlon (1954–55); *Walter Manning* Donald Woods (1954), Karl Swenson (1954–55); *Shirley Manning* Renee Jarrett (1954), Ginger McManus (1955); *Dick (Dickie) Blake* Charles Taylor; *Dorie Blake* Jean Gillespie; *Kathy Baker* Elizabeth York; *Bill Baker* Richard Kendrick; *Karl Manning* Patrick O'Neal; *Morgan Elliott* Byron Sanders; *Tony Faraday* Mark Miller; *Phoebe Faraday* Sally Gracie; *Ruth Byfield* Mary Fickett; *Rolland Teneyck (Rollie) Blake* William Redfield

Plot: Newspaper owner Walter Manning wasn't enamored of the fact that his wife, Portia Blake Manning, a barrister, was knocking 'em dead down at the courthouse with her agile legal maneuvering. He complained about it constantly, demanding that she stay home. Fortunately, temptress Dorie Blake was available and anxious to rescue him from his misery; but poor Walter was accused of murder. The series was re-titled *The Inner Flame* in its last weeks on the ether, yet that wasn't enough to recapture a thinning audience. It had been a popular radio play for almost 11 years, but its earlier triumphs simply weren't repeated in Videoland.

The Road of Life

December 13, 1954–July 1, 1955
Black & White — Live

Origination: Studio 42 (Grand Central Terminal Studios), New York City
Annotations: Chapter 7
Aural Antecedent: 1937–42, CBS/NBC Radio (concurrent but aired at separate hours); 1942–45, NBC Radio; 1945–47, CBS/NBC Radio (concurrent/separate); 1947–52, NBC Radio; 1952–54, CBS/NBC Radio (concurrent/separate); 1954–59, CBS Radio
    Sponsor: Procter & Gamble (Ivory)
    Agency: Compton Advertising
    Broadcast Schedule:
    December 13, 1954–July 1, 1955   M–F   1:15–1:30 p.m.   CBS
    Creator: Irna Phillips
    Producer: John Egan
    Director: Walter Gorman
    Writer: Charles J. Gussman
    Organist: Charles Paul
    Announcer: Nelson Case
    Cast: *Dr. Jim Brent* Don MacLaughlin; *Jocelyn McLeod Brent* Virginia Dwyer; *John (Butch) Brent* Bill Lipton; *Francie Brent* Elizabeth Lawrence; *Frank Dana* Chuck Webster (early), John Larkin (late); *Malcolm Overton* Harry Holcombe; *Sybil Overton Fuller* Barbara Becker; *Conrad Overton* Charles Dingle; *Aunt Reggie Ellis* Dorothy Sands; *Lil Monet* Elspeth Eric; *Armand Monet* Michael Kane; *Pearl Snow* Hollis Irving. *Also in the cast:* Michael Kane, Jack Lemmon
    Plot: Dr. Jim Brent, Merrimac surgeon, was "between wives" at this point in the radio serial. The short tele-version reprised the radio scripts that led to his marriage to Jocelyn McLeod Brent, foster daughter of wealthy Malcolm Overton. The Brents and the Overtons had long clashed over everything; there was little love lost between their families, so the union was both peculiar and spectacular. Particularly vexing was spiteful Sybil Overton Fuller, daughter of Conrad Overton, who was head-over-heels in love with Jim Brent and tried to curtail his wedding plans. He didn't return her affections, but that didn't prevent her from aiming her full fury at Jocelyn. Regrettably, the video drama was never the popular serial that it was on radio, where it lasted from 1937 to 1959.

Search for Tomorrow

    September 3, 1951–December 26, 1986
    Black & White, Color (from April 1967)— **Live, Videotape** (from September 9, 1968)
    Origination: Studio 55 (Liederkranz Hall), New York City, 1951–circa 1964; Studio 43 (Broadcast Center), New York City, circa 1964–; NBC, New York City, 1982–86
    Annotations: Chapters 5, 6, 8
    Theme Song: "Search for Tomorrow" (Chet Kingsbury), 1951–75
    Opening/Closing Billboard: In the early years—between every few notes of the dramatic organ arrangement of the theme — an announcer cited a couple of the sponsor's household cleaners, extolling them in brief advertising pitches before informing the fans that those goods "...present *Search for Tomorrow!*" as the theme built to a booming crescendo. While this was taking place, a familiar image (that identified the serial thereafter) was screened. The visual consisted of a time-lapse image of clouds floating through the sky, with the show's moniker set in a three-line white italic font overlaid across the clouds. While on occasion both the typeface and vapors were altered (and color was added in April 1967 as the show transitioned from a black-and-white feature), the modified classic icon persisted through a 35-year run. End credits in the early years flashed on and off the screen as separate cards.
    Sponsor: Procter & Gamble (Joy, Spic and Span, Cheer, Gleem, Pamper, et al.)
    Agency: Milton H. Biow Company (1951–55), Leo Burnett (1955–)
    Broadcast Schedule:
    September 3, 1951–September 6, 1968   M–F   12:30–12:45 p.m.   CBS
    September 9, 1968–June 5, 1981   M–F   12:30–1:00 p.m.   CBS
    June 8, 1981–March 26, 1982   M–F   2:30–3:00 p.m.   CBS
    March 29, 1982–December 26, 1986   M–F   12:30–1:00 p.m.   NBC
    Creator: Roy Winsor
    Executive Producers: Roy Winsor, Woody Klose, Mary-Ellis Bunim, Fred Bartholemew, Joanna

Lee, Ellen Barrett, Erwin Nicholson, John P. Whitesell II, David Lawrence (complete run — specific years undocumented)

Producers: Charles Irving, Myron Golden, Everett Gammon, Frank Dodge, Robert Driscoll, John Edwards, Bernie Solfronski, Mary-Ellis Bunim, Robert Getz, Gail Starkey, Jean Arley, John Valente (complete run)

Directors: Charles Irving, Hal Cooper, Ira Cirker, Dan Levin, John Frankenheimer, Bruce Minnix, Ned Stark, Joseph Stuart, Robert Schwarz, Richard T. McCue, Don Wallace, Paul Lammers, Robert Nigro, Henry Kaplan, Andrew D. Weyman, Richard Dunlap, Robert Rigamonti, Charles Dyer, Jim Kramer, Harry Eggart, Gregory Lehane, Ned Stark (complete run)

Head Writers: Agnes Eckhardt Nixon, Irving Vendig, Charles J. Gussman, Frank and Doris Hursley, Julian Funt and David Lesan, Leonard Kantor and Doris Frankel, Lou Scofield, Robert Soderberg and Edith Summer, Ralph Ellis and Eugenie Hunt, Theodore Apstein, Gabrielle Upton, Ann Marcus, Peggy O'Shea, Irving and Tex Elman, Robert J. Shaw, Henry Slesar, Joyce and John William Corrington, Linda Grover, Harding Lemay, Don Chastain, Ralph Ellis and Eugenie Hunt (second stint), C. David Colson, Gary Tomlin, Jeanne Glynn and Madeline David, Caroline Franz and Jeanne Glynn, Paul Avila Mayer and Stephanie Braxton, Gary Tomlin (second stint), Pamela K. Long and Addie Walsh (complete run)

Organists: Chet Kingsbury (1951), William Meeder (1951–69)

Announcers: Jay Jackson (1951), Dwight Weist (1951–82), Don Hancock (commercials, 1950s), Ron Rawson (commercials, 1950s)

Cast: *Joanne Gardner Barron*, et al. Mary Stuart; *Keith Barron* Johnny Sylvester; *Patti Barron* Lynn Loring (1951–61); *Stu Bergman* Larry Haines; *Marge Bergman* Melba Rae; *Janet Bergman* Ellen Spencer (1951–56), Sandy Robinson (1956–61); *Irene Barron* Bess Johnson; *Victor Barron* Cliff Hall; *Arthur Tate* Terry O'Sullivan (1952–55, 1956–68), Karl Weber (1955–56); *Mortimer Higbee* Ian Martin; *Hazel/Sue* Mary Patton; *Nathan Walsh* David Orrick (1953); George Petrie (1954–58), Frank Overton (1959), Richard Derr (1959), Mark Lenard (1959–60); *Rose Peterson* Lee Grant (1953–54), Nita Talbot (1954–55), Constance Ford (1955–56); *Wilbur Peterson* Don Knotts; *Aunt Cornelia Simmons* Doris Dalton; *Frank Gardner* Harry Holcombe (1957), Eric Dressler (1957–58); *Eunice Gardner* Marion Brash; *Rex Twining* Lawrence Hugo; *Bud Gardner* Tony Ray; *Jim Wilcox* Les Damon; *John Eddy* Earl Hammond; *Allison Simmons* Nina Reader (1958–59), Anne Pearson (1959–65); *Jessie Bergman* Joanna Roos (1958–59), Nydia Westman (1959–60); *Pearl March* Isabel Price (1959), Sylvia Field (1959–60); *Harriet Baxter* Vicki Vola; *Dr. Ned Hilton* Coe Norton; *Louise Barron* Sara Anderson; *Slim Davis* Wayne Rogers; *Hester Walsh* Kay Medford; *Also in the cast:* Ralph Bell, John Gibson, William Redfield. Note: *Only the actors signed prior to 1960 are included here due to this volume's emphasis on golden age serials*

Plot: Joanne Gardner Barron was an amazing woman, possessing an unnatural resiliency found only in daytime serial heroines and a few exceptional women with a bent toward bravery and optimism for the future. She was the first protagonist in daytime TV with staying power (emphasis on power), a throwback to the leading ladies of radio's washboard weepers, yet crafted for a visual context. Across a 35-year "career" she railed against seemingly impossible odds — and came out victorious at every turn. Over that course she lost three husbands (one in an auto accident, one to a heart attack and a third during an assault) and divorced a fourth. She went blind a couple of times, stood trial for murder once, witnessed many of those she loved enduring similar courtroom challenges, was in car wrecks, was shot at a dozen times and provided a shoulder for everybody to lean against on more occasions than anybody could remember. All the while she maintained a coolness that spoke volumes about her ability to cope with life's trying situations. It was the stuff of which heroines were made in 1951, and it — and she — became the model for successive first ladies for years to follow. In addition to the romantic entanglements and domesticity that included raising a young daughter, she encountered and overcame many forms of crime that was routinely interjected into her environment as a gripping diversion to the melodrama.

The Secret Storm

February 1, 1954–February 8, 1974
Black & White, Color — Live, Videotape
Origination: Studio 54 (Liederkranz Hall), New York City, 1954–64

Annotations: Chapter 11

Theme Songs: "Secret Storm Theme" (Chet Kingsbury), 1954; "Secret Storm Opening" (Charles Paul), late 1954–summer 1971

Opening Billboard: At its inception, the show's title in capital Latin Bold typeface (except for the definite article, appearing in cap and lower case) was superimposed upon a gnarled windswept tree. Planted on a small hill, the tree's branches were nearly barren, while a foreboding, threatening sky surrounded it. By the close of the 1950s, the image was replaced by a menacing seashore, waves crashing on sand as an upswept brush stroke script substituted for the early block title typeface. Some variation on that panorama persisted for the remainder of the show's life. A critic described the introductory/departure melody (employed from 1954 to 1971) as "a rather eerie-sounding piece in C-Minor played on organ and piano." In later years a harpsichord replaced those instruments to unique advantage.

Closing Billboard: For a while in the 1960s, the announcer read this ending epigram: "You have been watching *The Secret Storm*, the story of the Ames family and of deep-rooted human emotions, and how these emotions are stirred up into becoming the secret storm. All his life Peter had believed in honesty, kindness and justice, qualities which have brought him into conflict with both members of his family and friends. The children are grown and married now and they often turn to Peter and Valerie for advice. But ultimately, it is the individual who must solve his own problems."

Sponsor: American Home Products

Production Company: Milton H. Biow Company, Roy Winsor Productions, CBS Inc.

Broadcast Schedule:

February 1, 1954–July 15, 1962   M–F   4:15–4:30 p.m.   CBS
July 18, 1962–September 6, 1968   M–F   4:00–4:30 p.m.   CBS
September 9, 1968–September 1, 1972   M–F   3:00–3:30 p.m.   CBS
September 4, 1972–March 23, 1973   M–F   3:30–4:00 p.m.   CBS
March 26, 1973–February 8, 1974   M–F   4:00–4:30 p.m.   CBS

Creator: Roy Winsor

Executive Producers: Roy Winsor (1954–69), Charles Weiss (1969–74)

Producers: Richard Dunn, Ernest Ricca, Tony Converse, Robert Driscoll, Robert Costello, Joseph D. Manetta (complete run)

Directors: Gloria Monty (1954–69), Portman Paget, David Roth, Robert Myhrum, Joe Scanlan (complete run)

Head Writers: William Kendall Clarke, Henry Selinger and Harrison Y. Bingham, Stanley H. Silverman, Lou Scofield, Will Lorin, Max Wylie, Orin Tovrov, Carl Bixby, Jane and Ira Avery, John Hess and Don Ettlinger, Don Ettlinger (solo), Gabrielle Upton, Gerry Day and Bethel Leslie, Robert Cenedella, Frances Rickett and Sheldon Stark, Gabrielle Upton (again) (complete run)

Organists-Pianists-Harpsichordists: Chet Kingsbury, Charles Paul (1954–summer 1969)

Announcers: Charles Mountain (1950s), Don Hancock (commercials, 1950s), Ken Roberts (1960–74)

Cast: *Ellen Ames* Ellen Cobb-Hill; *Peter Ames* Peter Hobbs; *Susan Ames Dunbar Carver* Jean Mowry (1954–56), Rachel Taylor (1956–57), Norma Moore (1958), Mary Foskett (1958–64); *Jerry Ames* Dick Trask (1954), Robert Morse (1954), Warren Berlinger (1954–57), Ken Gerard (1957–59), Wayne Tippit (1959–65); *Amy Ames Rysdale Britton Kincaid* Jada Rowland (1954–58, 1960–67, 1968–71, 1973–74), Beverly Lunsford (1958–60); *Judge J. T. Tyrell* Russell Hicks; *Grace Tyrell* Marjorie Gateson; *Pauline Rysdale Tyrell* Haila Stoddard; *Jane Edwards* Marylyn Monk (1954, 1958), Barbara Joyce (1955), Virginia Dwyer (1955–56); *Bruce Edwards* Biff McGuire (1955), Ed Bryce (1955–56); *Myra Lake Ames* Joan Hotchkis (1958), June Graham (1959–63); *Alan Dunbar* James Vickery; *Ezra Lake* Wendell Phillips (1958), Don McHenry (1959–63); *Joe Sullivan* James Broderick; *Bryan Fuller* Carl King; *Bert Fenway* Whitfield Connor; *Dr. Spence Hadley* Jay Jostyn (1954–56), Ray Poole (1956–59), George Smith (1959–60), Addison Powell (1960–61), Skip Curtis Martin E. Brooks (1955–56). Note: *Only actors signed prior to 1960 are included due to this volume's focus on golden age serials*

Plot: In a shocking start for a serial, the presumed heroine of the drama dies on their third day on the air, leaving a grieving family to deal with the aftermath: Peter Ames, her spouse, and three children — Susan, Jerry and Amy. What seems painfully clear to viewers riveted by the tragic circumstances is that none of the troupe ever completely recover from that life-changing event. While each one deals with it in his or her own way, it still holds sway over the drama 15 years later. Peter's eldest child and a conniving sister-in-law with designs for him thwart his initial attempts at love and remarriage. While he does ultimately wed — twice more — the first union ends in a quick divorce.

The foibles of the offspring and their own many matrimonial experiences provide a riveting study in human behavior, still dominated by their mother's death.

The Seeking Heart

July 5, 1954–December 10, 1954
Black & White — Live
Origination: Studio 42 (Grand Central Terminal Studios), New York City
Annotations: Chapter 7
Sponsor: Procter & Gamble
Agency: Compton Advertising
Broadcast Schedule:
July 5, 1954–December 10, 1954   M–F   1:15–1:30 p.m.   CBS
Producer: Minerva Ellis
Director: James Yarborough
Writer: Welbourn Kelley
Organist: William Meeder
Announcer: Donald Briggs
Cast: *Dr. John Adam* Scott Forbes; *Grace Adam* Dorothy Lovett; *Dr. Robinson McKay* Flora Campbell. *Also in the cast:* Judith Braun, Audrey Christie, Les Damon, Christopher Plummer, Robert Webber
Plot: Some substantive plotting saw Dr. John Adam, medical criminologist, and his assistant Dr. Robinson McKay labor alongside the cops, who utilized their specialized skills for investigations. But more of the time was spent with their hands all over each other, Adam having cast his wife Grace aside and thrown caution to the wind. McKay felt likewise. Low ratings prompted CBS to cut off whatever came next, however; and their rendezvous was halted before anything could be resolved, a fretful ending for anybody who cared. Regrettably, there weren't very many.

These Are My Children

January 31, 1949–February 25, 1949
Black & White — Live
Origination: WMAQ–TV, Chicago
Annotations: Chapters 3, 7
Aural Antecedents: Storyline premises and characters based upon two of the author's earlier audio series: *Painted Dreams*, 1930–33, local radio station in Chicago; 1933–34, CBS Radio; 1935–36, MBS Radio; 1940, NBC Blue Radio; also from *Today's Children*, 1933–36, NBC Blue Radio; 1936–37, NBC Radio; 1943–50, NBC Radio
Broadcast Schedule:
January 31, 1949–February 25, 1949   M–F   5:00–5:15 p.m.   NBC
Creator-Writer: Irna Phillips
Director: Norman Felton
Cast: *Mrs. Henehan* Alma Platts; *John Henehan* George Kluge; *Jean Henehan* Joan Arlt; *Patricia Henehan* Jane Brooksmith; *Penny Henehan* Martha McClain; *Aunt Kitty Henehan* Margaret Heneghan; *Katherine Carter* Eloise Kummer; *Mrs. Berkovitch* Mignon Schreiber
Plot: In a remake of her once popular radio serial *Painted Dreams* (the first of the breed), which was twice reprised on radio under the banner *Today's Children*, Irna Phillips brought her inaugural soap opera to the tube — making it the first continuing serial on daytime TV (although it was gone in the blink of an eye). It concerned an ethnic neighborhood in suburban Chicago, and specifically revolved around a family headed by a matriarch who ruled her clan with well-meant injunctions that had stood the test of time. They rented a room to a boarder to enhance their meager means. Even such a fleeting exposure to the hot lights and cameras as enjoyed by *These Are My Children* was enough to convince Irna Phillips that she should spend the rest of her days concentrating on video. Her final debuting radio serial (*The Brighter Day*) arrived only three months earlier; from then on she would never look back. The smell of the grease paint had her under its spell: *These Are My Children*

was pivotal not only for being the first, but—more importantly—for the profound effect it would have on the future of daytime television. In every sense, it was a watershed event.

Three Steps to Heaven

August 3, 1953–December 31, 1954
Black & White (in Color, March 23, 1954)—Live
Origination: Studio A (106th Street Studios), New York City
Annotations: Chapter 4
Sponsor: Procter & Gamble (partially until February 15, 1954, then full)
Agency: Compton Advertising
Broadcast Schedule:
August 3, 1953–December 25, 1953   M–F   11:30–11:45 a.m.   NBC
March 1, 1954–December 31, 1954   M–F   10:45–11:00 a.m.   NBC
Creator-Writer: Irving Vendig
Producers: Adrian Samish, Caroline Burke
Directors: Gordon Rigsby, Norman Morgan
Announcer: Don Pardo
Cast: *Mary Jane (Poco) Thurmond* Phyllis Hill (1953), Diana Douglas (1954), Kathleen Maguire (from October 1954); *Bill Morgan* Walter Brooke (1953–54), Gene Blakely (1954), Mark Roberts (1954); *Vince Bannister* John Marley; *Barry Thurmond* Roger Sullivan; *Jennifer Alden* Lori March; *Alice Trent* Laurie Ann Vendig; *Jason Cleve* Lauren Gilbert; *Nan Waring* Beth Douglas; *Beth Waring* Madeline Belgard; *Angela* Ginger McManus; *Mrs. Montgomery* Harriet MacGibbon; *Mike* Joe Brown Jr.; *Charlotte Doane* Mona Bruns; *Chip Morrison* Robert Webber; *Alan Anderson* Dort Clark; *Uncle Frank* Frank Twedwell; *Pigeon Malloy* Eata Linden; *Walter Jones* Earl George; *Mrs. Doane* Doris Rich; *Dr. Campbell* Harry Holcombe; *Max Bremner* Mercer McLeod; *Laura* Inge Adams; *Pigeon* Eeta Linden
Plot: Mary Jane (Poco) Thurmond left her native hamlet far behind to pursue a modeling career in New York City. Soon paired with Bill Morgan, an author troubled by his wartime memories, she became his soul mate as the two shared some space in a tumbledown tenement. Poco formed lasting friendships with several people, including an ex-rival for Bill's affections, Jennifer Alden. Meanwhile, on the seamy side, Vince Bannister was but one of the nefarious figures making mischief and engaging in criminal activity in their neighborhood (including threatening Poco). Before the show left the air, Bill and Poco exchanged wedding vows, despite foreboding clouds looming overhead.

A Time to Live

July 5, 1954–December 31, 1954
Black & White—Live
Origination: WMAQ–TV, Chicago
Annotations: Chapter 4
Sponsor: Sustaining
Broadcast Schedule:
July 5, 1954–December 31, 1954   M–F   10:30–10:45 a.m.   NBC
Creator: Adrian Samish
Producer-Director: Alan Beaumont
Writer: William Barrett
Announcers: Norm Barry, Dick Noble
Cast: *Julie Byron* Pat Sully; *Don Riker* Larry Kerr (July), John Himes (from August); *Greta Powers* Zohra Alton (early), Jeanne Jerrems (late); *Justine Powers* John Devoe ; *Lenore Eustice* Barbara Foley; *Chick Buchanan* Len Wayland; *Madge Byron* Viola Berwick; *Rudy Marion* Zachary Charles; *Lieutenant Miles Dow* Dort Clark; *Donna Sims* Muriel Monsel; *Carl Sherman* Jack Lester; *Daphne* Toni Gilman; *Dr. Clay* Dana Elcar; *Lucy Karns* Nell Clark; *Kroger* Carlton KaDell; *Paul Cheney* Tom Neal
Plot: Working alongside Don Riker in a news organization, proofreader Julie Byron sought to

make it as an investigative reporter, a mission she accomplished rather quickly. She was carrying on hot and heavy with Chick Buchanan in her private life, a matter brought to the front burner whenever she and Don weren't covering racketeering, homicides and a myriad of other misdeeds by assorted ruffians. There really wasn't a lot of time to do much of anything in this serial. Chick became the scapegoat for a killing he didn't commit, and had to be cleared of any wrongdoing. After that, he and Julie said, "I do." It happened on the show's last day, and everybody faded quietly into the far reaches of outer serialdom — vanishing as quickly as they had surfaced, never to be heard from again.

Today Is Ours

June 30, 1958–December 26, 1958
Black & White — Live
Origination: Studio 3B (30 Rockefeller Plaza), New York City
Annotations: Chapter 4
Sponsors: Procter & Gamble, Alberto-Culver, H. J. Heinz, Sterling Drugs, Whirlpool Corp.
Agencies: Benton and Bowles (P&G), Geoffrey Wade Advertising (Alberto-Culver), Maxon Inc. (Heinz), Dancer-Fitzgerald-Sample (Sterling), Kenyon and Eckhardt Inc. (Whirlpool)
Broadcast Schedule:
June 30, 1958–December 26, 1958   M–F   3:00–3:30 p.m.   NBC
Creators: Julian Funt and David Lesan
Executive Producer: Richard M. Dunn
Producers: Robert M. Rehbock, Lucy Ferri, John Egan
Director: Walter Gorman
Writer: Julian Funt
Story Editor: David Lesan
Announcer: Wayne Howell
Cast: *Laura Manning* Patricia Benoit; *Nick (Nicky) Manning* Peter Lazar; *Karl Manning* Patrick O'Neal; *Leslie Williams Manning* Joyce Lear; *Glenn Turner* Ernest Graves; *Ellen Wilson* Chase Crosley; *Peter Hall* Tom Carlin; *Adam Holt* John McGovern; *Betty Winters* Nancy Sheridan; *Maxine Wells* Barbara Loden; *Rhoda Spencer* Audrey Christie; *Chester Crowley Sr.* Martin Blaine; *Chester Crowley Jr.* Martin Houston; *Mrs. Wilson* Joanna Roos; *Ted Brown* Nelson Olmsted; *Lester Williams* Barry Thomson
Plot: Looking for the first divorced heroine in TV daytime drama? Look no further. Laura Manning, assistant principal at Central High in Bolton, left her husband, Karl, and took their son Nicky, age 12, with her. At first Karl wasn't very happy with the arrangement, but she told him he didn't have a chance with her. He swiftly married a big city socialite, an event that made Nicky wonder if his father loved him any longer. Meanwhile, mom dealt with constant tribulations at home and work. On the sidelines, she hit it off with a guy she had argued with earlier, Glenn Turner, an architect doing work for the school. Would they wind up together? Nobody knew. The show was canceled before anything definitive developed.

Valiant Lady

October 12, 1953–August 16, 1957
Black & White — Live
Origination: Studio 57 (Peace Theater), New York City
Annotations: Chapter 7
Aural Antecedent: 1938, CBS Radio; 1938–42, NBC Radio; 1942–46, CBS Radio; 1951–52, ABC Radio
Opening/Closing Billboards: A woman was shown walking alone in a public park on a blustery day while the organ belted out the show's familiar theme song.
Sponsor: General Mills (Betty Crocker pie mix, Bisquick, Gold Medal flour, Softasilk cake flour, et al.)
Agency: Dancer-Fitzgerald-Sample

Broadcast Schedule:
October 12, 1953–August 16, 1957   M–F   12:00–12:15 p.m.   CBS
Creator: Allan Chase
Producers: Leonard Blair, Carl Green
Directors: Herb Kenwith, Ted Corday, Ira Cirker
Writers: Martha Alexander, Charles Elwyn
Organist: John Gart
Announcers: Win Elliot, Bob Pfeiffer
Cast: *Helen Emerson* Nancy Coleman (to December 10, 1954), Flora Campbell (from December 13, 1954); *Frank Emerson* Jerome Cowan; *Kim Emerson* Lydia Reed (1953–54), Bonnie Sawyer (1954–57); *Mickey Emerson* James Kirkwood Jr.; *Diane Emerson Soames* Anne Pearson (1953–54), Delores Sutton (1954–55), Sue Randall (1955–56), Leila Martin (1956–57); *Bonnie Withers* Joan Lorring (1954–55), Shirley Egleston (1955); *Hal Soames* Earl Hammond; *Gov. Lawrence Walker* John Graham; *Chris Kendall* Lawrence Weber; *Linda Kendall* Frances Helm; *David Kendall* Johnny Coleman; *Margot Finchley* Katherine Anderson; *Elliott Norris* Terry O'Sullivan; *Joey Gordon* Martin Balsam; *Roberta Wilcox* Betty Oakes. *Also in the cast:* Win Eliot as an occasional extra (and the show's announcer), Margaret Hamilton, Ann Louise
Plot: This at-times tear-jerking drama had the soon-widowed heroine withstanding an avalanche of forces that threatened her little brood, comprised of two daughters and a son. The eldest daughter pursued a divorced male, while the son chased a married female. This only added to the mounting troubles the brave mom faced, including economic woes, loneliness and the sadness felt by her grade school daughter. In time, Helen Emerson assuaged her own grief with a newly divorced man, but his ex interfered and the prospects fell apart. Near the end of the run it appeared she was finally destined for long-term bliss with a sitting governor, whom she married. That resolved most of her earlier dilemmas, leaving little room for a valiant lady designate. Love had apparently conquered all of her uncertainties and predicaments.

The Verdict Is Yours

September 2, 1957–September 28, 1962
Black & White — Live
Origination: Studio 42 (Grand Central Terminal Studios), New York City; Studio 72 (2248 Broadway at 81st Street), New York City; Studio 41 (CBS Television City), Los Angeles
Annotations: Chapter 7
Sponsor: Lever Brothers (Breeze), also Multiple Participation
Broadcast Schedule:
September 2, 1957–October 9, 1961   M–F   3:30–4:00 p.m.   CBS
October 12, 1961–June 15, 1962   M–F   3:30–3:55 p.m.   CBS
June 18, 1962–September 28, 1962   M–F   11:00–11:30 a.m.   CBS
Producer: Eugene Burr
Directors: Byron Paul (New York), Al Rafkin (Los Angeles)
Legal Advisor: Robert Simon
Announcers: Bob Hite (New York), Bern Bennett (Los Angeles)
Cast: Courtroom reporter Jim McKay, Bill Stout, Jake Whittaker; Court bailiff Mandel Kramer. *Also in the company:* Forrest Compton, Ellen McRae (Ellen Burstyn), Audrey Peters, Esther Ralston, more
Plot: While not really a continuing story, each of the courtroom cases extended over nine episodes before arriving at a denouement, and included many of the elements that make soap opera intriguing. Veteran thespians were given brief summaries in advance and instructed to improvise without scripts as they were cross-examined. Authentic barristers appeared as the lawyers, while a revolving company of actors portrayed plaintiffs, defendants and witnesses. Twelve volunteers from the studio audience comprised the jury and had to appear at each day's trial hearing. These fascinating snippets of the human tragedy compelled viewers to tune in for five years.

Way of the World

January 3, 1955–October 7, 1955
Black & White — Live

Origination: Studio 8G (30 Rockefeller Plaza), New York City
Annotations: Chapter 4
Sponsor: Borden
Agency: Young & Rubicam
Broadcast Schedule:
January 3, 1955–July 1, 1955   M–F   10:30–10:45 a.m.   NBC
July 4, 1955–October 7, 1955   M–F   4:00–4:15 p.m.   NBC
Producers: Therese Lewis, Joseph Scibetta
Director: Frederick Carr
Writers: William Kendall Clarke, Harry W. Junkin, Anne Howard Bailey
Host: Gloria Louis (as Linda Porter). *Also in the company:* Louise Allbritton, Anne Burr, Constance Ford, Margaret Hamilton, Margaret Heneghan, Kathleen Maguire, Claudia Morgan, Meg Mundy, Addison Powell, William Prince, Phillip Reed, Ethel Remey, Gena Rowlands, Lilia Skala, Gloria Strook, Thomas Tryon
Plot: This anthology drew its fictional accounts from the slick women's magazines. The tales ranged in duration from one day to roughly two weeks, the audience never certain how long a feature would persist. This proved difficult for fans with limited time who couldn't commit to soap operas with narratives that never reached conclusions. Their ability to become involved sometimes depended on when a fable would end. The show debuted as NBC–TV's first weekday 30-minute dramatic vehicle, but was cut back to a quarter-hour after six months.

A Woman to Remember

February 21, 1949–July 15, 1949
Black & White — Live
Origination: Wanamaker's Department Store Basement Studios, New York City
Annotations: Chapter 3
Sponsor: Sustaining
Broadcast Schedule:
February 21, 1949–April 29, 1949   M–F   3:00–3:15 p.m.   Dumont
May 2, 1949–July 15, 1959   M–F   7:15–7:30 p.m.   Dumont
Creator-Writer: John Haggart
Producer: Jack Rayel
Director: Bob Steele
Cast: *Christine Baker* Patricia Wheel; *Steve Hammond* John Raby; *Bessie Thatcher* Ruth McDevitt; *Charley Anderson* Frankie Thomas; *Carol Winstead* Joan Catlin. *Also in the cast:* Mona Bruns, Frank Thomas Sr.
Plot: Life upon the wicked stage at a radio soap opera formed the basis of this televised yarn. Christine Baker, the heroine, got along famously with most of her cohorts. As could be anticipated, however, there was a troublemaker in the bunch (actress Carol Winstead) who created as much misery as she could for the leading lady. Program director Steve Hammond was engaged to Christine, adding a diversionary and sometimes conflicting dimension to the plot. The story of backstage life was engaging, often better than the mythical soap opera they were all pretending to air.

Woman with a Past

February 1, 1954–July 2, 1954
Black & White — Live
Origination: Studio 42 (Grand Central Terminal Studios), New York City
Annotations: Chapter 7
Sponsor: Sustaining
Broadcast Schedule:
February 1, 1954–July 2, 1954   M–F   4:00–4:15 p.m.   CBS
Creator-Writer: Mona Kent
Organist: Billy Nale

Cast: *Lynn Sherwood* Constance Ford; *Steve Rockwell* Gene Lyons; *Sylvia Rockwell* Mary Sinclair (to May), Geraldine Brooks (from May); *Diane Sherwood* Felice Camargo (early weeks), Barbara Myers (later); *Gwen* Jean Stapleton; *Pegs* Ann Hegira; *Tiffany Buchanan* Linda Laubach. *Also in the cast:* Jay Barney, Maurice Burke, John Conte, Kathleen Comegys, Dennis Harrison, Marta Linden, Geoffrey Lumb, Bram Nossen, John Ridgely, Beverly Roberts, Lila Skala

Plot: Illegitimacy and having an ex-con for one's spouse are two things most women probably don't reveal when they set out to snare a new dreamy conquest, even when the prey is already hitched. Apparel stylist Lynn Sherwood found herself in that very dilemma when she sought to find a little lasting happiness with the man who put up the dough to help her become an enterprising business-woman. His estranged spouse had other ideas, however, and she hampered their tryst. Oddly, she was painted as the villain of the trio. In any case, the viewers poked fun at the whole thing and hastily turned the lackluster company out to pasture. Comparatively speaking, it was one of but a handful of miscalculations CBS made in programming the web's early daytime serials, even though it temporarily colored the chain's trademark eye a solid black.

The World of Mr. Sweeney

October 14, 1953–December 31, 1955
Black & White — Live
Origination: Studio 6B (30 Rockefeller Plaza), New York City; Burbank (effective November 7, 1955)
Annotations: Chapter 4
Theme Song: original composition (Frank Novak)
Sponsor: Sustaining (weekdays)
Broadcast Schedule:
October 14, 1953–June 18, 1954   Wkly   3:00–4:00 p.m.*   NBC
June 30, 1954–August 20, 1954   Tu/W/F   7:30–7:45 p.m.   NBC
October 4, 1954–December 31, 1955   M–F   4:00–4:15 p.m.   NBC
Producer: Sam Schiff
Directors: Alan Neuman, Gary Simpson
Writer: Arthur Stander
Announcer: Don Pardo
Cast: *Cicero P. Sweeney* Charles Ruggles; *Marge Franklin* Helen Wagner; *Kippie Franklin* Glenn Walken; *Liz Thompson* Helen Warnow; *Timmy Thompson* Jimmy Baird; *Sue Thompson* Susan Odin; *Harvey* Harrison Dowd; *Hannah* Nell Harris; *Abigail Milikan* Betty Garde; *Alice Franklin* Mimi Strongin; *Ed* Bob Hastings; *Eva* Lydia Reed; *Henrietta* Janet Fox

Plot: The affable, chatty Cicero P. Sweeney operated the general store in Mapleton. There he dispensed friendly advice to customers while dialoguing with his daughter Marge Franklin and grandson Kippie Franklin — at least until NBC shifted the show to the West Coast and that pair vanished from the scene. Their replacements were more of Sweeney's offspring, daughter Liz Thompson and her kids, Timmy and Sue. But the alteration may have been fatal for a series that didn't have a lot of audience to begin with: even though it was a pleasant reverie, less than two months after the casting changes the show went off the air. In an unusual twist in scheduling, it had begun as a weekly feature on vocalist Kate Smith's daily matinee variety program, then aired three nights a week and finally as a daytime serial.

*A 10-minute sketch floated within *The Kate Smith Show* once a week

Young Doctor Malone

December 29, 1958–March 29, 1963
Black & White, then Color — Live
Origination: Studio 3B (30 Rockefeller Plaza), New York City; Studio C (67th Street Studios), New York City
Annotations: Chapters 4, 7
Aural Antecedents: 1939–40, NBC Blue Radio; 1940–42, CBS Radio; 1942–43, CBS/NBC Radio (concurrent but aired at separate hours); 1943–60, CBS Radio

Sponsors: Procter & Gamble, Armour, National Biscuit, Alberto-Culver, General Mills Inc., H. J. Heinz, Andrew Jergens, Lever Brothers, Mennen, Miles Laboratories Inc., Plough Inc., Purex Corp., Toni, U. S. Borax & Chemical Corp., Borden, Kayser-Roth Hosiery Corp.

Agencies: Compton Advertising (P&G, Alberto-Culver), Foote, Cone and Belding (Armour), McCann-Erickson (National Biscuit, Borax), Dancer-Fitzgerald-Sample (General Mills, P&G, Sterling, Borden), Maxon Inc. (Heinz), Cunningham & Walsh Inc. (Jergens), Batten, Barton, Durstine & Osborn Inc. (Lever), Grey Advertising (Mennen), Wade Advertising (Miles), Lake-Spiro-Shurman Inc. (Plough), Edward H. Weiss & Company (Purex), North Advertising Inc. (Toni), Daniel & Charles (Kayser-Roth)

Broadcast Schedule:
December 29, 1958–September 28, 1962   M–F   3:00–3:30 p.m.   NBC
October 1, 1962–March 29, 1963   M–F   3:30–4:00 p.m.   NBC
Creator (television incarnation): Irna Phillips
Executive Producer: John Egan
Producers: Doris Quinlan, Lucy Ferri, Carol Irwin
Directors: Walter Gorman, James Young, Tom Donovan
Writers: Charles Gussman, Julian Funt, Richard Holland, Ian Martin
Organists: Charles Paul, Billy Nalle
Announcers: Jack Costello, Wayne Howell
Cast: *Dr. Jerry Malone* William Prince; *Tracey Bannister Malone* Virginia Dwyer (1958–59), Augusta Dabney (1959–63); *Jill Malone Renfrew* Kathleen Widdoes (1958–59), Freda Holloway (1959–62), Sarah Hardy (1962–63); *Dr. David Malone* John Connell; *Dorothy Ferris* Liz Gardner (1960), Florence Mitchell (1960); *Eve Dunbar* Loretta Leversee; *Gig Houseman Malone* Diana Hyland; *Lillian Houseman* Elizabeth Watts (early), Ann Shoemaker (circa 1961); *Clare Bannister Steele* Lesley Woods; *Faye Bannister Koda* Lenka Peterson (1959–61), Chase Crosley (1961–63); *Lionel Steele* Martin Blaine; *Emory Bannister* Judson Laire; *Larry Renfrew* Dick Van Patten; *Dr. Stefan Koda* Michael Ingram; *Dr. Matt Steele* Eddie Jones (1961), Franklyn Spodak (1961), Nicolas Coster (1962–63); *Lisha Steele Koda* Zina Bethune (1959–60), Michele Tuttle (1960), Susan Hallaran (1960–61), Patty McCormack (1962); *Dr. Ted Powell* Peter Brandon; *Peter Brooks* Robert Lansing; *Phyllis Brooks* Barbara O'Neill; *Jody Baker* Stephen Bolster; *Deirdre (Dee Dee) Bannister* Elizabeth St. Clair; *Pete Ferris* Luke Halpin; *Harold Cranston* William Post Jr.; *Miss Fisher* Betty Sinclair; *Erica Brandt* Ann Williams; *Lieutenant Flagler* William Smithers; *Natalie* Joan Wetmore; *Clara Kershaw* Joyce Van Patten; *Dr. Eileen Seaton* Emily McLaughlin; *Ernest Cooper* Robert Drivas (1959), Nicholas Pryor (1959); *Fran Merrill* Patricia Bosworth; *Fred McNeill* Hugh Franklin; *Gail Prentiss* Joan Hackett; *Marge Wagner* Teri Keane; *Rick Hampton* Louis Edmonds; *Miss Jones* Mary Fickett; *Dr. Paul Brown* David G. Stewart (1958–59), Edmon Ryan (from 1959); *Christabel Fisher* Betty Sinclair. *Note:* As the serial ended early in the 1960s, the complete cast is listed here.

Plot: Unlike in the radio play (1939–60), in this version Dr. Jerry Malone had an adopted son, Dr. David Malone, who was his dad's protégé and the true *young* doctor Malone. Instead of being situated at obscure Three Oaks Hospital, this tele-version was set in the more urban locale of Denison, Maryland. Jerry was chief of staff at Valley Hospital, and his son was a prominent physician. The show dealt with the foibles of families in medical practice, including malpractice, and lots of deaths and lawsuits. Two of daytime TV's earliest rogues were introduced, Clare and Lionel Steele, who were dedicated to making life hell for everybody, including themselves. Ultimately they paid high prices for their callous treatment of others (soap opera writers loved to make examples of wrongdoers). Clare had first wed Emory Bannister, possibly the richest man in town, and father of Tracey, Jerry Malone's second wife. Jill Malone, the apple of her dad's eye on radio, led a more subdued existence on TV until she wed notorious gambler Larry Renfrew, whose uncle was Lionel Steele. Viewers discovered the apple didn't fall far from the tree in that clan and, following a surgical procedure that didn't work, Larry was confined to a wheelchair for the rest of his life. That wasn't long in coming; he was bumped off rather quickly, leading to a series-ending trial, with Jill as the accused. She wasn't guilty, of course. Her brother faced like charges earlier when Lillian Houseman, mother of his wife Gig, met a similar fate. While these people surely lived skewed existences, they were nonetheless absorbing to entrenched soap opera addicts, who remained fans until the end.

Chapter Notes

Chapter 1

1. Hayward, Jennifer. *Consuming Pleasures: Active Audiences and Serial Fictions from Dickens to Soap Opera*. Lexington, Ky.: The University Press of Kentucky, 1997, p. 3.
2. DeForest, Tim. *Storytelling in the Pulps, Comics, and Radio: How Technology Changed Popular Fiction in America*. Jefferson, N.C.: McFarland, 2004, p. 5.
3. www.candlelightstories.com/arabianpage.asp
4. Groves, Seli. *The Ultimate Soap Opera Guide*. Detroit: Visible Ink, 1995, p. xi.
5. Ibid.
6. DeForest, p. 110.
7. Simon, Ron. "Serial Seduction: Living in Other Worlds." *Worlds Without End: The Art and History of the Soap Opera*. New York: Harry N. Abrams, 1997, p. 12.
8. *www.bibliomania.com/0/0/19/40/; www.literature-web.net/dickens; www.encarta.msn.com/encyclopedia_7615 56924/Dickens_Charles_John_Huffam.html*
9. Johnson, Edgar. *Charles Dickens: His Tragedy and Triumph*. New York: Penguin Books, 1986, p. 196.
10. Groves, p. xi.
11. Lund, Michael. *America's Continuing Story: An Introduction to Serial Fiction 1850–1900*. Detroit: Wayne State University Press, 1993.
12. Simon, p. 13.
13. DeForest, p. 109.
14. Ibid., p. 110.
15. Simon, p. 13.
16. Ibid.
17. Harvey, Robert C. *The Art of the Funnies: An Aesthetic History*. Jackson: University of Mississippi Press, 1994, p. 63.
18. Simon, p. 15; Stedman, Raymond William. *The Serials: Suspense and Drama by Installment*. Norman, Okla.: University of Oklahoma Press, 1971, p. 278.
19. DeForest, p. 147.
20. Lahue, Kalton C. *Continued Next Week: A History of the Moving Picture Serial*. Norman, Okla.: University of Oklahoma Press, 1964.
21. Poindexter, Ray. *Golden Throats and Silver Tongues: The Radio Announcers*. Conway, Ark.: River Road Press, 1978, pp. 36–38; Edmondson, Madeleine, and David Rounds. *The Soaps: Daytime Serials of Radio and TV*. New York: Stein and Day, 1973, pp. 26–27.
22. Chase, Francis, Jr. *Sound and Fury: An Informal History of Broadcasting*. New York: Harper & Brothers, 1942, p. 180.
23. Edmondson and Rounds, p. 27; Sies, Luther F. *Encyclopedia of American Radio, 1920–1960*. Jefferson, N.C.: McFarland, 2000, p. 154; Stedman, p. 226.
24. Groves, p. 2.
25. Sies, pp. 154, 44–45.
26. Chase, p. 181.
27. Barnouw, Erik. *A Tower in Babel: A History of Broadcasting in the United States, Volume I — to 1933*. New York: Oxford University Press, 1966, p. 229.
28. Allen, Robert C. *Speaking of Soap Operas*. Chapel Hill, N.C.: University of North Carolina Press, 1985, p. 104; Groves, p. 2.
29. Stedman, pp. 177, 181.
30. Stedman, p. 181.

Chapter 2

1. Nachman, Gerald. *Raised on Radio: In Quest of The Lone Ranger, Jack Benny, Amos 'n' Andy, The Shadow, Mary Noble, The Great Gildersleeve, Fibber McGee and Molly, Bill Stern, Our Miss Brooks, Henry Aldrich, The Quiz Kids, Mr. First Nighter, Fred Allen, Vic and Sade, The Cisco Kid, Jack Armstrong, Arthur Godfrey, Bob and Ray, The Barbour Family, Henry Morgan, Joe Friday, and Other Lost Heroes from Radio's Heyday*. New York: Pantheon Books, 1998, p. 368.
2. Wolfe, Charles Hull. *Modern Radio Advertising*. New York: Printers' Ink, 1949, p. 298.
3. Batscha, Robert M., "Foreword," in Morton, Robert, ed., *Worlds Without End: The Art and History of the Soap Opera*. New York: Harry N. Abrams, 1997, p. 7.
4. Groves, Seli. *The Ultimate Soap Opera Guide*. Detroit: Visible Ink, 1995, p. 2.
5. Allen, Robert C. *Speaking of Soap Operas*. Chapel Hill, N.C.: University of North Carolina Press, 1985, p. 117.
6. Ibid.
7. Chase, Francis, Jr. *Sound and Fury: An Informal History of Broadcasting*. New York: Harper & Brothers, 1942, p. 187.
8. Wolfe, p. 304.
9. Cox, Jim. *The Great Radio Soap Operas*. Jefferson, N.C.: McFarland, 1999, p. 127.
10. LaGuardia, Robert. *From Ma Perkins to Mary Hartman: The Illustrated History of Soap Operas*. New York: Ballantine, 1977, p. 7.

11. Ibid.

12. Andrews, Robert Hardy. "A Voice in the Room," adapted from *Legend of a Lady: The Story of Rita Martin*. New York: Coward-McCann, 1949, pp. 111–112.

13. Nachman, p. 368.

14. Ibid., p. 370.

15. LaGuardia, Robert. *The Wonderful World of TV Soap Operas*. Rev. Ed. New York: Ballantine, 1980, p. 69.

16. Edmondson, Madeleine, and David Rounds. *The Soaps: Daytime Serials of Radio and TV*. New York: Stein and Day, 1973, p. 17.

17. Ibid., p. 60.

18. Cox, Jim. *The Great Radio Soap Operas*, pp. 3–4; Summers, Harrison B., ed. *A Thirty-Year History of Programs Carried on National Radio Networks in the United States, 1926–1956*. New York: Arno Press and The New York Times, 1971; *www.dg125.com/Gazette/BestOfThe Best/* by decade and year.

Chapter 3

1. www.internetcampus.com/frtv/frtv025.htm

2. Cox, Jim. *The Great Radio Soap Operas*. Jefferson, N.C.: McFarland, 1999, p. 126; LaGuardia, Robert. *The Wonderful World of TV Soap Operas*. Rev. Ed. New York: Ballantine, 1980, p. 84.

3. Edmondson, Madeleine, and David Rounds. *The Soaps: Daytime Serials of Radio and TV*. New York: Stein and Day, 1973, p. 131.

4. Hyatt, Wesley. *The Encyclopedia of Daytime Television: Everything You Ever Wanted to Know About Daytime TV but Didn't Know Where to Look! From American Bandstand, As the World Turns, and Bugs Bunny, to Meet the Press, The Price Is Right, and Wide World of Sports, the Rich History of Daytime Television in All Its Glory!* New York: Billboard Books, 1997, pp. viii–ix.

5. Hyatt states that the NBC station in New York went on the air in 1928. While the government granted a permit for such a station that year, it appears that it was July 1930 before there was any successful transmission (initially a fuzzy image of Felix the Cat). See Smith, Sally Bedell. *In All His Glory: The Life of William S. Paley, the Legendary Tycoon and His Brilliant Circle*. New York: Simon and Schuster, 1990, p. 186.

6. LaGuardia, Robert. *From Ma Perkins to Mary Hartman: The Illustrated History of Soap Operas*. New York: Ballantine, 1977, p. 42.

7. Hyatt, pp. ix, 306.

8. Stedman, Raymond William. *The Serials: Suspense and Drama by Installment*. Norman, Okla.: University of Oklahoma Press, 1971, p. 351.

9. Edmondson and Rounds, p. 130; LaGuardia, Robert, 1980, p. 82; Simon, Ron. "Serial Seduction: Living in Other Worlds," appearing in Morton, Robert, ed. *Worlds Without End: The Art and History of the Soap Opera*. New York: Harry N. Abrams, 1997, p. 20.

10. Daniel P. Lewis, quoted in "A Unique Twist to the Tele Soap Opera Given by Caples' Man Lewis." *The Televiser*, November-December 1946, p. 33.

11. Brooks, Tim, and Earle Marsh. *The Complete Directory to Prime Time Network TV Shows, 1946–Present*. 4th Ed. New York: Ballantine, 1988, p. 255.

12. Schemering, Christopher. *The Soap Opera Encyclopedia*. Rev. Ed. New York: Ballantine, 1988, p. 105.

13. Letter from Irna Phillips to William Ramsey, Sept. 7, 1948.

14. A few researchers conjecture that this serial was launched in 1947. However, overwhelming evidence from numerous respected sources substantiate the 1949 date.

15. Edmondson and Rounds, p. 130.

16. Waggett, Gerard J. *The Soap Opera Encyclopedia*. New York: HarperCollins, 1997, p. 270.

17. Schemering, p. 106.

18. Copeland, Mary Ann. *Soap Opera History*. Lincolnwood, Ill.: Publications International, 1991, p. 266.

19. LaGuardia, 1977, p. 44.

20. Ibid., p. 45.

21. Copeland, p. 271; Hyatt, p. 293.

22. Waggett, 1997, p. 328.

23. Hyatt, p. 208.

24. Cox, Jim. *Frank and Anne Hummert's Radio Factory: The Programs and Personalities of Broadcasting's Most Prolific Producers*. Jefferson, N.C.: McFarland, 2003, p. 42; Edmondson and Rounds, p. 61; Nachman, Gerald. *Raised on Radio: In Quest of The Lone Ranger, Jack Benny, Amos 'n' Andy, The Shadow, Mary Noble, The Great Gildersleeve, Fibber McGee and Molly, Bill Stern, Our Miss Brooks, Henry Aldrich, The Quiz Kids, Mr. First Nighter, Fred Allen, Vic and Sade, The Cisco Kid, Jack Armstrong, Arthur Godfrey, Bob and Ray, The Barbour Family, Henry Morgan, Joe Friday, and Other Lost Heroes from Radio's Heyday*. New York: Pantheon, 1998, p. 371.

25. Waggett, 1997, p. 267.

26. LaGuardia, 1980, p. 98.

27. Edmondson and Rounds, p. 215.

28. www.fiftiesweb.com/variety.htm

29. www.museum.tv/archives/etv/G/htmlG/goldenage /goldenage.htm

Chapter 4

1. Brooks, Tim, and Earle Marsh. *The Complete Directory to Prime Time Network TV Shows, 1946–Present*. 4th Ed. New York: Ballantine, 1988, p. xiii.

2. Ibid., p. xiv.

3. Waggett, Gerard J. *The Soap Opera Encyclopedia*. New York: HarperCollins, 1997, p. 336.

4. Ibid.

5. Stedman, Raymond William. *The Serials: Suspense and Drama by Installment*. Norman: University of Oklahoma Press, 1971, p. 374.

6. Hyatt, Wesley. *The Encyclopedia of Daytime Television: Everything You Ever Wanted to Know About Daytime TV but Didn't Know Where to Look! From American Bandstand, As the World Turns, and Bugs Bunny, to Meet the Press, The Price Is Right, and Wide World of Sports, the Rich History of Daytime Television in All Its Glory!* New York: Billboard, 1997, p. 157.

7. Schemering, p. 107.

8. Editors of *TV Guide*. *TV Guide Guide to TV*. New York: Barnes & Noble Publishing, 2004, p. 154.

9. Hyatt, p. 251.

10. Waggett, 1997, p. 409.

11. While some documentarians credit only Provo as the originator of the television series, others link the pair with the scripting. As the duo jointly penned dialogue and action for multiple broadcast features (e.g., *Concerning Miss Marlowe*, *Love of Life*), it's apparent that both men probably contributed to this drama, too, although it can't be stated with unqualified certainty.

12. Some documentarians have named the town "Strathfield," but multiple NBC press releases spelled it "Stratfield."

13. Schemering, Christopher. *The Soap Opera Encyclopedia*. Rev. Ed. New York: Ballantine, 1988.

14. LaGuardia, Robert. *The Wonderful World of TV Soap Operas*. Rev. Ed. New York: Ballantine, 1980, pp. 84, 87.

15. Waggett, 1997, p. 402.

16. Ibid., p. 288.

17. Stedman, p. 373.

18. LaGuardia, 1980, p. 89.

Chapter 5

1. Soares, Manuela. *The Soap Opera Book*. New York: Harmony, 1978, p. 123.

2. Some sources spell the German word for which this facility is named "Liederkrantz." The confusion lies in the pronunciation. In German, a Z is always preceded by a T sound. As an example, if you telephone the retail emporium F.A.O. Schwarz, they answer with "F.A.O. Schwartz."

3. Smith, Sally Bedell. *In All His Glory: The Life of William S. Paley, The Legendary Tycoon and His Brilliant Circle*. New York: Simon and Schuster, 1990, p. 185.

4. Ibid., p. 186.

5. Lyons, Eugene. *David Sarnoff: A Biography*. New York: Harper & Row, 1966, p. 204.

6. Ibid.

7. Ibid., p. 205.

8. Smith, p. 277.

9. Paley's astonishing talent raids on NBC in 1949 ultimately culminated in boosting CBS–TV. "He may have thought he was building radio," said his biographer, "but his gut — the visceral, even primitive, love for stars and shows that figured in every move he made — was to give his fledgling television network an advantage Sarnoff would never match." Some within the industry believed the CBS mogul was merely shoring up the web's horde of performers to switch them to the rapidly emerging tube. "Paley undertook the talent raids to strengthen radio, not to push into television," his chronicler confirmed. "The raids were designed to establish him, at last, as the undisputed leader — in radio."

10. For a deeper examination of Paley's and Sarnoff's differing stances on television, see *Say Goodnight, Gracie: The Last Years of Network Radio* by this author (McFarland, 2002), pp. 25–29.

11. Stuart, Mary. *Both of Me*. Garden City, N.Y.: Doubleday, 1980, p. 22.

12. Ibid., pp. 16, 21.

13. Stuart, p. 24.

14. Ibid., p. 24.

15. LaGuardia, Robert. *The Wonderful World of TV Soap Operas*. New York: Ballantine, 1980, p. 29.

16. As this is written, only four daytime serials are still videotaped in New York. *Guiding Light* has been performed at CBS's Studio 51 at 222 East Forty-Fourth Street since the mid–1980s. CBS's *As the World Turns* has originated at 1268 East Fourteenth Street in Brooklyn since early 2000. *All My Children* is taped at ABC's Studio 23 at 320 West Sixty-Sixth Street. Airing from ABC's Studio 17 at 56 West Sixty-Sixth Street is *One Life to Live*. Both current NBC dramas (*Days of Our Lives* and *Passions*), and two more CBS serials (*The Young and the Restless* and *The Bold and the Beautiful*), are taped at Los Angeles–area studios.

17. 7. Stuart, Mary. *Both of Me*. Garden City, NY: Doubleday, 1980, p. 22.

18. LaGuardia, 1980, p. 22.

19. Gilbert, Annie. *All My Afternoons: The Heart and Soul of the TV Soap Opera*. New York: A&W Visual Library, 1979, p. 106.

20. Kutler, Jane, and Patricia Kearney. *Super Soaps: The Complete Book of Daytime Drama*. New York: Grosset & Dunlap, 1977, p. 9.

21. Gilbert, p. 130.

22. Ibid., p. 8.

Chapter 6

1. Edmondson, Madeleine, and David Rounds. *The Soaps: Daytime Serials of Radio and TV*. New York: Stein and Day, 1973, p. 46.

2. She penned 520 scripts for this six-day-a-week classic while also acting in multiple roles in the production.

3. By 1947 Phillips had sold three of her radio serials to Procter & Gamble, although she remained as writer for one of that trio. Every day an announcer introduced it as "*The Guiding Light*, created by Irna Phillips." It was a constant reminder to listeners of the program's original inspiration. It had to be gratifying to her to be able to maintain the upfront identification for many years after she no longer owned the series.

4. Schemering, Christopher. *The Soap Opera Encyclopedia: Newly Updated and Expanded Edition*. New York: Ballantine, 1988, p. 281.

5. Siepmann, Charles A. *Radio's Second Chance*. Boston: Little, Brown, 1947, pp. 54–55.

6. Morrison, Hobe. *Variety*, August 18, 1943.

7. Thurber, James. "O Pioneers!" *The New Yorker*, May 15, 1948.

8. On radio's *The Guiding Light*, the console virtuoso (in real life, Bernice Yanocek) labored over the keyboard for a thunderous rendition of Goetzl's "Aphrodite" near the opening of each chapter. One observer recounted her sharp intrusions into an otherwise reflective performance, noting: "No program in heaven or earth could match *The Guiding Light* in ominous chords, stings and cadences." In the broadcast of January 10, 1950, for instance, the organ's erratic exclamations jarred fans 23 times. Such unexpected and disarming outbursts interrupted every episode in those days, possibly keeping some of its listeners on unnerving edge.

9. MacDonald, J. Fred. *Don't Touch That Dial!: Radio Programming in American Life from 1920 to 1960*. Chicago: Nelson-Hall, 1991, p. 251.

10. Ibid., p. 252.

11. Gilbert, Annie. *All My Afternoons: The Heart and Soul of the TV Soap Opera*. New York: A & W Visual Library, 1979, p. 18.

12. http://en.wikipedia.org/wiki/Irna_Phillips

13. Schemering, p. 280.

14. The unique practice of accommodating both radio and video incarnations airing at separate hours, which *The Guiding Light* did for four years, is covered in Chapter 10.

15. Technically, at least one of Phillips' serials was canceled for a while. In 1946 she was involved in a legal dispute with one of her former dialoguers, Emmons Carlson. Carlson successfully proved he had helped Phillips spawn *The Guiding Light* in 1937 and was awarded $250,000. Before their court case was resolved, however — to avoid possibly tarnishing its own reputation — sponsor General Mills withdrew and the show left the air. Procter & Gamble subsequently purchased the drama from Phillips for $50,000 and restored it on the ether six months later. At the same time, P&G also bought two more Phillips serials, *The Road of Life* (for $50,000) and *The Right to Happiness* (for $75,000), the latter a 1939 spinoff with its roots deep in *The Guiding Light*.

16. Gilbert, p. 67.

17. Waggett, Gerard J. *The Soap Opera Encyclopedia*. New York: HarperCollins, 1997, p. 482.

18. Phillips had shared her mom's bedroom for decades before she acquired her own apartment. Her mother inspired *Today's Children*, the second drama, and when the elder Phillips died in 1938 the younger was so grieved

that she removed the series from the air. For many years Irna Phillips resided at 1335 North Astor Street in Chicago.

19. Gilbert, p. 18.

20. LaGuardia, Robert. *The Wonderful World of TV Soap Operas*, rev. ed. New York: Ballantine, 1980, pp. 128–129.

21. Schemering, p. 30.

22. In its second season on the air, *As the World Turns* catapulted over all other daytime dramas to second place in the ratings. In its third season, 1958–59, it became the leader of the pack, occupying that coveted spot for 20 consecutive seasons, until the youth-oriented *All My Children* overtook it in 1978–79. *General Hospital* captured first place a year later and retained it for eight years until *The Young and the Restless* won it in 1987–88, holding the reins for several successive seasons. While it was in first place, *As the World Turns'* numbers were phenomenal for most of those years. For instance, audience share frequently exceeded half of all viewers watching TV when it was on, climbing as high as 57 percent during the 1963–64 season. In more than half of those dual decades, the home audience regularly topped 40 percent of TV viewers, a phenomenon since unequaled on a sustained basis.

23. A Phillips conception she didn't live to see materialize occurred a year following her death. On January 6, 1975, *Another World* was extended to an hour, the first daytime serial to make that move. Others followed and a new trend was set. For 17 months in 1979–80 *Another World* was seen for an hour-and-a-half but without appreciable added benefit, and was reduced to an hour. The fact that these programs were increased to 60 minutes would likely have gratified Phillips.

24. LaGuardia, Robert. *From Ma Perkins to Mary Hartman: The Illustrated History of Soap Operas*. New York: Ballantine, 1977, p. 64.

25. Schemering, p. 30.

26. Cox, Jim. "In Soap City, Not All Dreams Come True." *Nostalgia Digest*, Autumn 2004, pp. 44–45.

27. Schemering, p. 20.

28. Gilbert, p. 106.

29. Morton, Robert, ed. *Worlds Without End: The Art and History of the Soap Opera*. New York: Harry N. Abrams, 1997, p. 16.

30. Stedman, pp. 409, 410, 411.

31. Cantor, Muriel G., and Suzanne Pingree. *The Soap Opera*. Beverly Hills, Calif.: Sage, 1983, p. 44.

32. Edmondson and Rounds, p. 163.

33. Phillips, Irna. "Every Woman's Life Is a Soap Opera," *McCall's*, March 1965.

Chapter 7

1. Halberstam, David. *The Fifties*. New York: Villard, 1993, p. 185.

2. Helen Emerson Walker was not the first soap opera heroine to wed a governor, as she was preceded by Carolyn Allen Walker Kramer Nelson MacDonald of radio's *The Right to Happiness*. Carolyn's third mate, attorney Miles Nelson, was elected chief executive of an undisclosed state.

3. The show left the radio airwaves under a cloud. Some unjust charges were brought against Portia at the end of the run. Instead of being acquitted, Portia was sent to prison following a guilty verdict. It was a ploy the producers set up to prompt NBC to reconsider its cancellation directive and return the soap opera to the air, a frequent reaction when an audience's ire was sufficiently stirred. In Portia's case, either the fans weren't vociferous

enough or NBC developed a cold heart, for the show didn't come back and Portia faced life imprisonment for a crime she didn't commit. Suddenly the title held plenty of irony!

4. The TV serial began with Portia as mother of a daughter, Shirley, in addition to a son, Dickie Blake, the latter from her first marriage. At the inception of the radio serial Dickie was her only offspring, although she gave birth to a girl named Sheila (correct name) later.

5. Portia took over her late husband's legal business when he was killed in an accident on the first day of the radio serial.

6. Hyatt, Wesley. *The Encyclopedia of Daytime Television: Everything You Ever Wanted to Know About Daytime TV but Didn't Know Where to Look! From American Bandstand, As the World Turns, and Bugs Bunny, to Meet the Press, The Price Is Right, and Wide World of Sports, the Rich History of Daytime Television in All Its Glory!* New York: Billboard, 1997, p. 361.

7. Copeland, Mary Ann. *Soap Opera History*. Lincolnwood, Ill.: Mallard Press, 1991, p. 279.

Chapter 8

1. For a provocative discussion of how this radio/TV feature was formulated, see *The Great Radio Audience Participation Shows: Seventeen Programs from the 1940s and 1950s* (McFarland, 2001), by this author, devoting particular attention to pp. 160–172.

2. In an incessant drive to win higher ratings against the competition, the producers of several of the giveaways—among them, *The $64,000 Question, The $64,000 Challenge* and *Twenty-One*—tainted their breed by discussing potential questions and answers with some of the players beforehand. Author Maxene Fabe declared: "Three of the best games ever were also the crookedest." Had a disgruntled *Dotto* contestant in August 1958 not revealed the shenanigans by declaring the show was "fixed," the scandal that destroyed Americans' confidence in what they had been watching might never have leaked. This revelation was but the tip of the iceberg. In an ensuing investigation numerous individuals from several shows were indicted. As other contestants testified that they were coached, deep secrets were unlocked and the species was banished for many years.

3. Biow created a financial windfall for his outfit when he packaged *Take It or Leave It* for the Eversharp Pen and Pencil Company, increasing its sales from $2 million at the show's inception to $28 million within five years. That exposure brought Biow more clients, including Anacin, Lady Esther, Pepsi and Ruppert beer; with annual billings of $50 million, it boosted the agency to the enviable top 10 such firms in the nation.

4. LaGuardia, Robert. *The Wonderful World of TV Soap Operas*, rev. ed. New York: Ballantine, 1980, pp. 239–240.

5. Morton, Robert, ed. *Worlds Without End: The Art and History of the Soap Opera*. New York: Harry N. Abrams, 1997, p. 124.

6. Gilbert, Annie. *All My Afternoons: The Heart and Soul of the TV Soap Opera*. New York: A&W Visual Library, 1979, p. 40.

7. The piano-wire and black velour sets upon which *Search for Tomorrow* and other serial casts acted during CBS–TV's early days at Liederkranz Hall is described in detail in Chapter Five.

8. Simon, Ron. "Serial Seduction: Living in Other Worlds." *Worlds Without End: The Art and History of the Soap Opera*. New York: Harry N. Abrams, 1997, pp. 22, 26.

9. Morton, p. 124.

10. The organ continued on the serial into the 1970s providing the theme as well as important stings, cadences and transitional buffers to highlight action and denote scene changes. William Meeder was the show's longtime organist. A veteran of radio serials, he accompanied *Big Sister*, *The Brighter Day*, *Pepper Young's Family*, *Perry Mason* and *The Right to Happiness*.

11. Stuart, Mary. *Both of Me*. Garden City, N.Y.: Doubleday, 1980, pp. 17, 19.

12. Stedman, Raymond William. *The Serials: Suspense and Drama by Installment*. Norman, Oklahoma: University of Oklahoma Press, 1971, p. 324.

13. Morton, p. 22.

Chapter 9

1. LaGuardia, Robert. *From Ma Perkins to Mary Hartman: The Illustrated History of Soap Operas*. New York: Ballantine, 1977, p. 46.

2. Stedman, Raymond William. *The Serials: Suspense and Drama by Installment*. Norman, Oklahoma: University of Oklahoma Press, 1971, p. 354.

3. Morton, Robert, ed. *Worlds Without End: The Art and History of the Soap Opera*. New York: Harry N. Abrams, 1997, p. 127.

4. Hyatt, Wesley. *The Encyclopedia of Daytime Television: Everything You Ever Wanted to Know About Daytime TV but Didn't Know Where to Look! From American Bandstand, As the World Turns, and Bugs Bunny, to Meet the Press, The Price Is Richt, and Wide World of Sports, the Rich History of Daytime Television in All Its Glory!* New York: Billboard, 1997, p. 268.

5. Soares, Manuela. *The Soap Opera Book*. New York: Harmony, 1978, p. 39.

6. Waggett, Gerard J. *The Soap Opera Encyclopedia*. New York: HarperCollins, 1997, p. 300.

7. Morton, p. 127.

8. LaGuardia, 1977, p. 122.

9. Waggett, p. 302.

10. LaGuardia, Robert. *The Wonderful World of TV Soap Operas*. rev. ed. New York: Ballantine, 1980, p. 226.

11. Morton, p. 127.

12. Waggett, p. 304.

13. Schemering, Christopher. *The Soap Opera Encyclopedia*. New York: Ballantine, 1988, pp. 152–153.

14. Editors of TV Guide. *TV Guide Guide to TV*. New York: Barnes & Noble, 2004, p. 380.

Chapter 10

1. Gilbert, Annie. *All My Afternoons: The Heart and Soul of the TV Soap Opera*. New York: A&W Visual Library, 1979, p. 23.

2. Ibid.

3. Dr. Ruthledge was based upon an actual Protestant minister, Dr. Preston Bradley, whose missives on peace and tolerance some years earlier had inspired Irna Phillips, then a youthful and impressionable aspiring Jewish author.

4. Soares, Manuela. *The Soap Opera Book*. New York: Harmony, 1978, p. 40.

5. Groves, Seli. *The Ultimate Soap Opera Guide*. Detroit: Visible Ink Press, 1995, p. 264.

6. Charita Bauer (who played Bert Bauer) requested that her first son be named Mike, after her own son's name. She was afraid that some day on live television she would slip and call her onscreen son by her real son's moniker instead.

7. Waggett, Gerard J. *The Soap Opera Encyclopedia*. New York: HarperCollins, 1997, p. 139.

8. When Phillips returned to *The Guiding Light* in the 1960s as head writer, she discovered that some of the

power she had formerly been accustomed to had dissipated. Producer Lucy Rittenberg failed to accept collect phone calls from Phillips' home in Chicago. Before leaving the show a second time, Phillips abruptly killed off Kathy Roberts' daughter Robin, as she had done with Kathy before leaving the first time.

9. LaGuardia, Robert. *The Wonderful World of TV Soap Operas*, rev. ed. New York: Ballantine, 1980, p. 53.

10. Gilbert, pp. 28, 37.

11. Gilbert, p. 26.

Chapter 11

1. Groves, Seli. *The Ultimate Soap Opera Guide*. Detroit: Visible Ink Press, 1995, p. 12.

2. *The Secret Storm* was the first to bite the dust of the venerated six serials that debuted in the 1950s which maintained longstanding reputations. All of the others persisted for at least a half-dozen years beyond *Storm*'s existence, while two are still airing: *Love of Life* (cancelled in 1980), *The Edge of Night* (1984), *Search for Tomorrow* (1986), and *The Guiding Light* and *As the World Turns*.

3. Schemering, Christopher. *The Soap Opera Encyclopedia*. New York: Ballantine, 1988, p. 214.

4. LaGuardia, Robert. *The Wonderful World of TV Soap Operas*, rev. ed. New York: Ballantine, 1980, pp. 116–117.

5. Ibid., p. 89–90.

6. Ibid., p. 90.

7. Actually, this was Roy Winsor's *fourth* creation for daytime television. His first, *Hawkins Falls* on NBC, never as successful as his CBS inspirations, preceded the others, airing between 1951 and 1955 in daytime, and still earlier (1950) in primetime. (See Chapter Three.)

8. Morton, Robert, ed. *Worlds Without End: The Art and History of the Soap Opera*. New York: Harry N. Abrams, 1997, p. 131.

9. Waggett, Gerard J. *The Soap Opera Encyclopedia*. New York: HarperCollins, 1997, p. 384.

10. While Lynn Loring (as Patti Barron) did the same on *Search for Tomorrow*, after 10 years—at age 16 in real time—Loring departed and never returned. With brief interruptions, Jada Rowland was with *The Secret Storm* during its full 20-year run.

11. Joan Crawford wouldn't be the first silver screen luminary to appear in daytime serials on TV. Joan Bennett, Gloria DeHaven, Colleen Gray and Ann Sheridan were among several who had been there and done that earlier. Her performance was believed to be a first for *The Secret Storm*, however.

12. Schemering, p. 213.

13. Waggett, 1997, p. 385.

14. Morton, p. 131.

15. LaGuardia, 1980, p. 114.

16. LaGuardia, Robert. *From Ma Perkins to Mary Hartman: The Illustrated History of Soap Operas*. New York: Ballantine, 1977, p. 382.

17. Ibid.

18. LaGuardia, 1980, p. 489.

19. Morton, p. 131.

20. Schemering, p. 214.

21. LaGuardia, 1980, p. 116.

22. Ibid., p. 76.

Chapter 12

1. www.nationmaster.com/encyclopedia/As-the-World-Turns

2. Schemering, Christopher. *The Soap Opera Encyclopedia*. New York: Ballantine, 1988, p. 30.

3. The wordsmith with the normally invincible spirit

hadn't forgotten that a CBS competitor, NBC, had canceled her very first daytime TV effort, *These Are My Children*, just four weeks into it in early 1949. She vowed that wouldn't happen again. It never did.

4. Schemering, p. 30.

5. Simon, Ron. "Serial Seduction: Living in Other Worlds." *Worlds Without End: The Art and History of the Soap Opera.* New York: Harry N. Abrams, 1977, p. 26.

6. LaGuardia, Robert. *From Ma Perkins to Mary Hartman: The Illustrated History of Soap Operas.* New York: Ballantine, 1997, p. 64.

7. Soares, Manuela. *The Soap Opera Book.* New York: Harmony, 1978, p. 31.

8. Stedman , Raymond William. *The Serials: Suspense and Drama by Installment.* Norman, Oklahoma: University of Oklahoma Press, 1971, p. 390.

9. Gilbert, Annie. *All My Afternoons: The Heart and Soul of the TV Soap Opera.* New York: A & W Visual Library, 1979, p. 67.

10. LaGuardia, 1977, pp. 168–169.

11. Soares, p. 31.

12. Groves, Seli. *The Ultimate Soap Opera Guide.* Detroit: Visible Ink Press, 1995, p. 108.

13. LaGuardia, 1980, pp. 132–133.

14. Ibid., p. 135.

15. Stedman, p. 378.

16. So great was actress Eileen Fulton's hate mail that bodyguards were reportedly hired to escort her to and from the studio.

17. LaGuardia, 1980, p. 136.

18. Ironically, Kim and Bob's reunion a decade later proved extremely popular with audiences. Their illegitimate baby, lost to miscarriage as penance for their adulterous affair, was brought back to life. Such are the fortunes of soap opera (and stunted fan memories).

19. LaGuardia, 1977, p. 168.

20. Fleetingly, Irna Phillips "borrowed" the character of Michael Bauer from the cast of *The Guiding Light* to help *Another World* establish a foothold, a most unusual but only temporary move.

21. LaGuardia, 1980, p. 130.

22. Ibid., pp. 130–131.

23. LaGuardia, 1977, p. 168.

24. Waggett, Gerard J. *The Soap Opera Encyclopedia.* New York: HarperCollins, 1997, p. 64.

25. LaGuardia, 1980, pp. 142–50 (includes condensed excerpts).

Chapter 13

1. Erle Stanley Gardner did give permission a short time later for CBS–TV to proceed with a 60-minute complete-episode version, however. That long-running weekly series in primetime, from 1957 to 1966, starred actor Raymond Burr as the champion of justice.

2. In pre-production, *The Edge of Night* was given a working appellation of *The Edge of Darkness*. Originally expected to air at 1:30 p.m., it was switched to 4:30 p.m. before the premier and its moniker altered to better reflect the late afternoon timeslot. Therefore, *As the World Turns* preceded *Edge* by three hours, becoming the first 30-minute daytime drama on the ether.

3. http://lavender.fortunecity.com//casino/403/scholar.html

4. "Edgeville, USA." *Time*, March 17, 1961.

5. The producers learned a valuable lesson about killing off well-liked characters with the abrupt demise of Sara Lane Karr. The lesson stuck for a very long while. Possibly the most important figure to be subsequently disposed of was Adam Drake, Mike Karr's law partner,

whom a syndicate member shot in the back in 1977. Adam died before he could disclose some revelations he had discovered which were essential to a case. For a full decade, Adam had been prominent in crucial investigations. His developing romances with Nicole Travis and — when Nicole was believed dead — Brandy Henderson were among the most popular storylines with viewers of the late 1960s and the 1970s. Other major cast members who were written out included Martha Marceau in 1975, and her husband, Bill, in 1979. After two decades he was replaced as police commissioner by a sexy youngster, Derek Mallory, portrayed by an ex-porn actor, as a wave of youth-oriented storylines and characters swept across every major soap opera of the epoch. Nicole, who was really alive and returned to the storyline after an 18-month absence, was also murdered in 1983, a fitting prelude to the show's own demise shortly thereafter.

6. LaGuardia, Robert. *The Wonderful World of TV Soap Operas*, rev. ed. New York: Ballantine, 1980, p. 210.

7. The actress playing Nancy Pollack Karr, a strikingly attractive, redheaded Ann Flood, became the show's real veteran among its numerous thespians. She arrived on March 24, 1962, and was still in her role on December 28, 1984, when the program left the air nearly 23 years later.

8. With other network dramas already moving to an hour's daily broadcast, CBS was looking for a way to add a half-hour to its most popular serial, *As the World Turns*, still running in a 30-minute format. Killing off the show in last place among all daytime soaps offered an easy out. CBS then assigned *Edge*'s vacated half-hour to its most promising feature.

9. http://lavender.fortunecity.com//casino/403/livelier.html

10. Adapted from http://lavender.fortunecity.com//casino/403/livetape.html

11. Donald May left the show in a dispute over the direction of his character and his leading lady. May wanted Adam paired with Brandy Henderson (played by Dixie Carter), despite the audience's and head writer Henry Slesar's preference for a reunion with Nicole Travis Drake (played by Maeve McGuire), who had returned to the lineup after an 18-month absence.

12. Shortly before the series was withdrawn, Mike and Nancy Karr's marriage leaped into the stratosphere when they traded in their two twin beds for one king-size!

13. About a half-year later, Slesar was dismissed from *Somerset* and replaced by veteran soap inventor Roy Winsor (*Hawkins Falls, Love of Life, Search for Tomorrow, The Secret Storm*). Winsor seemingly returned the show to its roots, although his initial yarn was comprised of villains and diabolical plotting reminiscent of *The Edge of Night*. When his efforts proved futile as ratings tumbled, Winsor, too, was rejected, suggesting *Somerset* had mega-troubles it couldn't fix. The serial was gone by the close of 1976.

14. The Taubman theme song was displaced in June 1976 by a new one penned by Jack Cortner and John Barranco described as both "moody and melancholy," which was offered in two renderings— instrumental and vocal. The latter version normally aired only once a week as the cast credits rolled.

Epilogue

1. *Broadcasting*, November 7, 1977, p. 35.

2. Allen, Robert C. *Speaking of Soap Operas.* Chapel Hill, N.C.: University of North Carolina Press, 1985, p. 127.

3. Hayward, Jennifer. *Consuming Pleasures: Active Audiences and Serial Fictions from Dickens to Soap Opera.* Lexington, Kentucky: The University Press of Kentucky, 1997, p. 135.

Bibliography

Books

Allen, Robert C. *Speaking of Soap Operas.* Chapel Hill, N.C.: University of North Carolina Press, 1985.
Andrews, Robert Hardy. *Legend of a Lady: The Story of Rita Martin.* New York: Coward-McCann, 1949.
Barnouw, Erik. *The Golden Web: A History of Broadcasting in the United States, Vol. II–1933 to 1953.* New York: Oxford University Press, 1968.
_____. *The Image Empire: A History of Broadcasting in the United States, Vol. III — from 1953.* New York: Oxford University Press, 1970.
_____. *A Tower in Babel: A History of Broadcasting in the United States, Vol. I — to 1933.* New York: Oxford University Press, 1966.
Brooks, Tim, and Earle Marsh. *The Complete Directory to Prime Time Network TV Shows 1946–Present,* 4th ed. New York: Ballantine, 1988.
Buxton, Frank, and Bill Owen. *The Big Broadcast 1920–1950,* 2nd ed. Lanham, Md.: Scarecrow, 1997.
Campbell, Robert. *The Golden Years of Broadcasting: A Celebration of the First 50 Years of Radio and TV on NBC.* New York: Scribner's, 1976.
Cantor, Muriel G., and Suzanne Pingree. *The Soap Opera.* Beverly Hills, Calif.: Sage, 1983.
Chase, Francis, Jr. *Sound and Fury: An Informal History of Broadcasting.* New York: Harper & Brothers, 1942.
Copeland, Mary Ann. *Soap Opera History.* Lincolnwood, Ill.: Mallard Press, 1991.
Cox, Jim. *Frank and Anne Hummert's Radio Factory: The Programs and Personalities of Broadcasting's Most Prolific Producers.* Jefferson, N.C.: McFarland, 2003.
_____. *The Great Radio Audience Participation Shows: Seventeen Programs from the 1940s and 1950s.* Jefferson, N.C.: McFarland, 2001.
_____. *The Great Radio Soap Operas.* Jefferson, N.C.: McFarland, 1999.
_____. *Mr. Keen, Tracer of Lost Persons: A Complete History and Episode Log of Radio's Most Durable Detective.* Jefferson, N.C.: McFarland, 2004.
_____. *Radio Crime Fighters: Over 300 Programs from the Golden Age.* Jefferson, N.C.: McFarland, 2002.
_____. *Say Goodnight, Gracie: The Last Years of Network Radio.* Jefferson, N.C.: McFarland, 2002.
DeForest, Tim. *Storytelling in the Pulps, Comics, and Radio: How Technology Changed Popular Fiction in America.* Jefferson, N.C.: McFarland, 2004.
DeLong, Thomas A. *Radio Stars: An Illustrated Biographical Dictionary of 953 Performers, 1920 through 1960.* Jefferson, N.C.: McFarland, 1996.
Duncan, Jacci. *Making Waves: The 50 Greatest Women in Radio and Television, as Selected by American Women in Radio and Television, Inc.* Kansas City: Andrews McMeel, 2001.
Dunning, John. *On the Air: The Encyclopedia of Old-Time Radio.* New York: Oxford University Press, 1998.
_____. *Tune in Yesterday: The Ultimate Encyclopedia of Old-Time Radio 1925–1976.* Englewood Cliffs, N.J.: Prentice-Hall, 1976.
Editors of *TV Guide. TV Guide: Guide to TV.* New York: Barnes & Noble, 2004.
Editors of *TV Guide* Online's CineBooks Database. *TV Guide Film & Video Companion 2004.* New York: Barnes & Noble, 2004.
Edmondson, Madeleine, and David Rounds. *The Soaps: Daytime Serials of Radio and TV.* New York: Stein and Day, 1973.

Fulton, Eileen, Desmond Atholl and Michael Cherkinian. *As My World Still Turns: The Uncensored Memoirs of America's Soap Opera Queen*. New York: Birch Lane Press, 1995.

Fulton, Eileen. *Soap Opera: A Novel*. New York: St. Martin's Press, 1999.

Gilbert, Annie. *All My Afternoons: The Heart and Soul of the TV Soap Opera*. New York: A & W Visual Library, 1979.

Groves, Seli. *The Ultimate Soap Opera Guide*. Detroit: Visible Ink Press, 1995.

Halberstam, David. *The Fifties*. New York: Villard, 1993.

Harvey, Robert C. *The Art of the Funnies: An Aesthetic History*. Jackson: University of Mississippi Press, 1994.

Hayward, Jennifer. *Consuming Pleasures: Active Audiences and Serial Fictions from Dickens to Soap Opera*. Lexington, Ky.: The University Press of Kentucky, 1997.

Hickerson, Jay. *The 2nd, Revised Ultimate History of Network Radio Programming and Guide to All Circulating Shows*. Hamden, Conn.: Presto Print II, 2001.

Hyatt, Wesley. *The Encyclopedia of Daytime Television: Everything You Ever Wanted to Know About Daytime TV but Didn't Know Where to Look! From American Bandstand, As the World Turns, and Bugs Bunny, to Meet the Press, The Price Is Right, and Wide World of Sports, the Rich History of Daytime Television in All Its Glory!* New York: Billboard, 1997.

Johnson, Edgar. *Charles Dickens: His Tragedy and Triumph*. New York: Penguin Books, 1986.

Kutler, Jane, and Patricia Kearney. *Super Soaps: The Complete Book of Daytime Drama*. New York: Grosset & Dunlap, 1977.

LaGuardia, Robert. *From Ma Perkins to Mary Hartman: The Illustrated History of Soap Operas*. New York: Ballantine, 1977.

_____. *The Wonderful World of TV Soap Operas*, rev. ed. New York: Ballantine, 1980.

Lahue, Kalton C. *Continued Next Week: A History of the Moving Picture Serial*. Norman, Okla.: University of Oklahoma Press, 1964.

Lund, Michael. *America's Continuing Story: An Introduction to Serial Fiction 1850–1900*. Detroit: Wayne State University Press, 1993.

Lyons, Eugene. *David Sarnoff: A Biography*. New York: Harper & Row, 1966.

McNeil, Alex. *Total Television: The Comprehensive Guide to Programming from 1948 to the Present*, 4th ed. New York: Penguin, 1996.

Morton, Robert, ed. *Worlds Without End: The Art and History of the Soap Opera*. New York: Harry N. Abrams, 1997.

Nachman, Gerald. *Raised on Radio: In Quest of The Lone Ranger, Jack Benny, Amos 'n' Andy, The Shadow, Mary Noble, The Great Gildersleeve, Fibber McGee and Molly, Bill Stern, Our Miss Brooks, Henry Aldrich, The Quiz Kids, Mr. First Nighter, Fred Allen, Vic and Sade, The Cisco Kid, Jack Armstrong, Arthur Godfrey, Bob and Ray, The Barbour Family, Henry Morgan, Joe Friday, and Other Lost Heroes from Radio's Heyday*. New York: Pantheon, 1998.

Poindexter, Ray. *Golden Throats and Silver Tongues: The Radio Announcers*. Conway, Ark.: River Road Press, 1978.

Robinson, Marc. *Brought to You in Living Color: 75 Years of Great Moments in Television & Radio from NBC*. New York: Wiley, 2002.

Schemering, Christopher. *The Soap Opera Encyclopedia*, rev. ed. New York: Ballantine, 1988.

Shapiro, Mitchell E. *Television Network Daytime and Late-Night Programming, 1959–1989*. Jefferson, N.C.: McFarland, 1990.

Sies, Luther F. *Encyclopedia of American Radio, 1920–1960*. Jefferson, N.C.: McFarland, 2000.

Smith, Sally Bedell. *In All His Glory: The Life of William S. Paley, the Legendary Tycoon and His Brilliant Circle*. New York: Simon and Schuster, 1990.

Soares, Manuela. *The Soap Opera Book*. New York: Harmony, 1978.

Stedman, Raymond William. *The Serials: Suspense and Drama by Installment*. Norman, Okla.: University of Oklahoma Press, 1971.

Sterling, Christopher H., and John M. Kittross. *Stay Tuned: A Concise History of American Broadcasting*, 2nd ed. Belmont, Calif.: Wadsworth, 1990.

Stuart, Mary. *Both of Me*. Garden City, N.Y.: Doubleday, 1980.

Summers, Harrison B., ed. *A Thirty-Year History of Programs Carried on National Radio Networks in the United States, 1926–1956*. New York: Arno Press and The New York Times, 1971.

Swasy, Alecia. *Soap Opera: The Inside Story of Procter & Gamble*. New York: Random House, 1993.

Terrace, Vincent. *Radio Programs, 1924–1984: A Catalog of Over 1800 Shows*. Jefferson, N.C.: McFarland, 1999.

Tylo, Hunter. *Making a Miracle*. New York: Pocket Books, 2000.

Waggett, Gerard J. *The Soap Opera Book of Lists*. New York: HarperCollins, 1996.

_____. *The Soap Opera Encyclopedia*. New York: HarperCollins, 1997.
Waldron, Robert. *The Bold and the Beautiful: A Tenth Anniversary Celebration*. New York: HarperCollins, 1996.
Wolfe, Charles Hull. *Modern Radio Advertising*. New York: Printers' Ink, 1949.

Web Sites

The Arabian Nights: www.candlelightstories.com/arabianpage.asp
As the World Turns: www.nationmaster.com/encyclopedia/As-the-World-Turns
Charles Dickens: www.literature-web.net/dickens
Charles Dickens: www.encarta.msn.com/encyclopedia_761556924/Dickens_Charles _John_Huffam.html
Edge Live vs. Edge Videotaped: http://lavender.fortunecity.com//casino/403/livetape.html
The Edge of Night: http://lavender.fortunecity.com//casino/403/scholar.html
The Golden Age of Television: www.internetcampus.com/frtv/frtv025.htm
Irna Phillips: http://en.wikipedia.org/wiki/Irna_Phillips
Museum of Broadcast Communications: www.museum.tv/archives/etv/G/htmlG/goldenage/goldenage.htm
My Soap is Livelier Than Yours: http://lavender.fortunecity.com//casino/403/livelier.html
The Pickwick Papers: www.bibliomania.com/0/0/19/40/frameset.html

Periodicals

Also consulted were issues of *Advertising Age, Billboard, The Courier-Journal, Life, Los Angeles Times, New York Times, Newsweek, TV-Radio Mirror, Time, TV Guide, USA Today* and additional periodicals, including newspapers, many of which are identified within the text.

Index

Index